1960s GAY PULP FICTION

A volume in the series
*Studies in Print Culture and the History of the Book*

# 1960s GAY PULP FICTION

## *The Misplaced Heritage*

Edited by

Drewey Wayne Gunn

Jaime Harker

University of Massachusetts Press

*Amherst and Boston*

ISBN 978-1-62534-045-0 (paper); 044-3 (hardcover)

Designed by Sally Nichols
Set in Adobe Garamond Pro
Printed and bound by IBT/Hamilton, Inc.

Library of Congress Cataloging-in-Publication Data

1960s Gay Pulp Fiction : the Misplaced Heritage / edited by
Drewey Wayne Gunn, Jaime Harker.
pages cm. — (Studies in Print Culture and the History of the Book)
Includes bibliographical references and index.
ISBN 978-1-62534-045-0 (pbk. : alk. paper) — ISBN 978-1-62534-044-3
(hardcover : alk. paper) 1. Gays' writings, American—History and criticism.
2. Pulp literature, American—History and criticism. 3. American fiction—
20th century—History and criticism. 4. Homosexuality and literature—History—
20th century. 5. Gays in literature. I. Gunn, Drewey Wayne, 1939– editor of
compilation. II. Harker, Jaime, editor of compilation.
PS153.G38A25 2013
810.9′920664—dc23
2013031735

British Library Cataloguing-in-Publication Data
A catalogue record for this book is available from the British Library.

# Contents

# Acknowledgments

Though only two names appear on the title page, the present collection is, of course, the collaborative effort of twelve scholars. In various ways each has aided the others, and has been aided individually by yet other colleagues and friends. We wish collectively to acknowledge these people, with apologies to anyone we may have inadvertently forgotten: Mohamed Abdelrahman, Alex Almador, Doug Armato, Don Bachardy, Kasey D. Baker, Victor J. Banis, Jason Baumann, Delinda Stephens Buie, Lloyd Christison, John W. Crowley, Tyler Curtain, Helena Davies, S. C. Delaney, C. Downs, Martin Duberman, Wayne R. Dynes, Jan Ewing, Richard Fullmer, Pip Gordon, Elisa Guerra, Peter Harvey, Rocky Heck, Scott Herring, Sue Hodson, John Howard, Ivo Kamps, Maree Kelly, Charles Leslie, Glenn Loney, Ruth Machalias, Brenda J. Marston, Elizabeth McClelland, Laura Micham, Scott Morelock, Will Parish, Brooks Peters, Darryl Poulsen, Richard Reitsma, John Sherlock, Erin Smith, Paul D. Stern, Christina Strasburger, John B. Thomas III, Carol Tipton, Ann Weldy, Gill Willis, Tim Wilson, Kelly Wooten, Ian Young, Eli Zal, and Abbey Zink.

We appreciate the staff and their help at the following libraries and archives: Ekstom Library at University of Louisville, Gerber/Hart Library and Archives, Huntington Library, Jernigan Library at Texas A&M University–Kingsville, Kroch Library at Cornell University, Leather Archives and Museum, Mitchell Library of the State Library of New South Wales, New York Public Library, ONE Institute and Archives, San Francisco Public Library

History Center and Gay & Lesbian Center, Shields Library at University of California–Davis and J. D. Williams Library of the University of Mississippi. We would be remiss not to thank all those anonymous readers who preserved their gay pulps, which became the source for the holdings in these public archives and for our individual private collections.

The editors thank the Department of English at the University of Mississippi and the College of Arts and Sciences at Texas A&M University–Kingsville for providing financial support for this project. The twelve of us thank Brian Halley, Mary Bellino, and the staff at University of Massachusetts Press for their care in overseeing the publication of this book.

1960s GAY PULP FICTION

# Introduction

Drewey Wayne Gunn and Jaime Harker

During the last half of the 1960s, American publishers brought out over seven hundred works of fiction written by mostly gay men about gay men and marketed predominantly to a gay readership. Only a tenth of that number had appeared in the first half of the 1960s (see table), and the two previous decades had been similarly barren. Before 1965 publishers generally adopted the guise of advertising their few gay works as exposés aimed at enlightening heterosexual audiences (though they used code words—"shame," "twilight," "strange"—to indicate the content for potential homosexual readers). These new books from the second half of the 1960s were mostly paperback originals. They usually (but not always) measured a uniform 7" by 4¼", and they were printed on cheap stock—hence the name commonly ascribed them, gay pulps. In common with other paperbacks at the time, their come-hither covers promised sex, but with the difference that these had provocatively posed men rather than provocatively posed women. And their blurbs were fairly blatant. Potential readers found them everywhere, even in rural areas, stuffed into metal bookracks at supermarkets, convenience stores, drugstores, five-and-tens, tobacconists, newsstands, bus stations, railway stations, and airline terminals—everywhere save in regular bookstores. It is with these books that the gay literary revolution began in earnest.

Gay Fiction Published in the United States, 1960–1969

| YEAR | HARDBACKS | PAPERBACKS | |
|---|---|---|---|
| | | Reprints | Originals |
| 1960 | 5 | 2 | 1 |
| 1961 | 9 | 3 | 3 |
| 1962 | 5 | 7 | 2 |
| 1963 | 7 | 1 | 3 |
| 1964 | 10 | 9 | 8 |
| 1965 | 15 | 19 | 26 |
| 1966 | 14 | 14 | 53 |
| 1967 | 14 | 13 | 71 |
| 1968 | 9 | 13 | 176 |
| 1969 | 9 | 9 | 250 |

Note: "Gay Fiction" is, of course, a subjective label. Thus someone else may arrive at a slightly different count; still, the general outline remains quite clear.

This literary heritage, however, has become misplaced in at least two senses of the word. If not quite altogether, it largely has been lost, forgotten, disregarded—one might even say discarded. And it has become mislabeled, viewed as subgenre pornography by cultural historians, who seem to assume that the contemporary examples they encountered after Stonewall had to be typical of pulps throughout their history, or viewed solely as a source for campy illustrations from their covers. At the same time, many critics also seem to assume that the 1960s pulps, since they are pre-Stonewall fiction after all, must have continued the postwar strategy of depicting what miserable lives gays lead.[1] None of these assumptions could be further from the truth. But as a consequence of such misunderstandings, the actual contents of this large body of work and its importance to the development of gay literature have gone virtually unexamined.

This loss is unfortunate. Gay pulps from the 1960s offer a cultural portal on the zeitgeist that set the stage for the Stonewall uprising; indeed, some argue that pulp novels contributed to the sense of pride that led to lines being drawn. These novels give a sense of the varied ways gay men, including those who lived outside the cities, perceived themselves during a tumultuous period in American history. Since so many gay pulps are about ordinary people—sometimes behaving heroically against all odds, sometimes just being basically good humans—they may actually have a wider appeal than more mainstream works being published at the same time.

Incorporating the gay pulp phenomenon into the history of gay American literature as a means of gaining a keener understanding of contemporary gay fiction is fully as important as recuperating "lost novels" from the nineteenth and early twentieth centuries. The omission of the gay pulps from gay literary history is all the more surprising given the long acceptance of lesbian pulp fiction into the literary canon. The scholars contributing to the present collection of essays unite in the belief that it is time to look at gay pulps from a similar perspective. To this end, they have taken steps to establish and apply interpretive frameworks for delineating the diverse significations of early gay pulp fiction and to make value judgments about which ones are of particular literary worth. The undertaking has yielded any number of unexpected pleasures.

## THE BIRTH OF GAY PULPS

Changes in a number of quite different paradigms had to converge before the great explosion of gay pulp fiction could come about in the mid-1960s. The experiences of homosexuals serving in World War II led to their greater awareness of their numbers, and writers began to treat homosexual themes more freely in the 1940s and 1950s. During those two decades some 150 titles, of greater (Gore Vidal, *The City and the Pillar*) or lesser (Edgar Box, *Death in the Fifth Position*) interest, made it onto the paperback bookracks as reprints of hardcover editions. At least seventeen, however, were paperback originals, the brainchild of Fawcett Publications beginning in 1950.[2] Some of these, notably Vin Packer's crime novel *Whisper His Sin* (1954) and Ben Travis's story of a gigolo, *The Strange Ones* (1959), are virtually indistinguishable from the mid-1960s gay pulps. Because of the threat of obscenity laws, however, many novelists continued to encode gay and lesbian content. Those who chose to be more open, from Gore Vidal through John Rechy, from Vin Packer through Ann Bannon, often wrote about it in appropriately depressing ways in order to escape the charges of obscenity and immorality. Though the number of novels with happy endings published between 1906 (*Imre*) and 1959 (*Sam*) is greater than is usually thought, it became a literary truism that homosexual men and women were filled with self-hatred and led miserable, unhappy lives that ended in bodily violence or death, often by suicide, unless they converted to heterosexuality.

It was necessary to adopt such subterfuges in a culture that legally defined homosexuals as criminals, morally labeled them as sinners, and psychologically viewed them as suffering from a mental disorder. The very presence of a homosexual in a work of fiction, even without any description of sexual acts, was enough for federal authorities to define it as "obscene."[3] By this standard, in the early 1950s the Greenberg publishing house had been "indicted on a federal charge of sending obscene materials through the mail," Charles Kaiser records. "The offending books were three volumes of gay fiction—*Quatrefoil*, a fine wartime novel by James [Barr] Fugate; *The Divided Path;* and *The Invisible Glass.* Vociferous complaints from the mother of one of their mail-order customers resulted in the indictment. After the charges had dragged on for five years, they were settled for a fine of $3,500—and a promise to keep the three novels out of print."[4] Meanwhile, heterosexual writers were successfully pushing the obscenity envelope: for example, John O'Hara, Grace Metalious with her 1956 *succès de scandale*, *Peyton Place*, and, most notoriously, Vladimir Nabokov with *Lolita* (first published in the United States in 1958).

The first step toward the liberation of homosexual literature was a change in the legal definition of obscenity. Greater literary freedom of expression was finally granted through a series of federal court decisions beginning in 1957 and continuing through the early 1970s. As a result, the mails were opened to sending works depicting homosexuality in a positive light (just as long as the work had some "literary value" and did not appeal solely to "prurient interest"). Meanwhile, heterosexual writers such as Philip Roth (from *Goodbye, Columbus* in 1959 to his own *succès de scandale*, *Portnoy's Complaint*, in 1969), Mary McCarthy (*The Group*, 1963), John Updike (*Couples*, 1968), and Kurt Vonnegut (*Slaughterhouse-Five*, 1969) were including fairly explicit sex scenes in their novels. People were openly reading and discussing the first American publication of *Lady Chatterley's Lover, Naked Lunch, Fanny Hill,* and works by the Marquis de Sade. Allen Ginsberg and Jack Kerouac were moving into respectability. As a result, the time was obviously ripe for a different kind of gay fiction.

Mainstream publishers, however, were slow to catch on. Even though several early gay novels had gone into second and third printings and had done well as paperback reprints, the big houses seemed oblivious to the fact that a large gay reading public existed. Grove Press, which had joined in a number of the groundbreaking legal challenges, was the most adventurous mainstream house. Under the visionary drive of one of its editors, Donald M. Allen, Grove became William Burroughs's and John Rechy's publisher, and it brought out American editions of works by Jean Genet and the Marquis de Sade. Meanwhile, in Washington, DC, Guild Press (which had also been the defendant in an important legal challenge) set out under the leadership of H. Lynn Womack to be a totally gay press. But Womack was always suffering financial and managerial woes, in addition to the legal ones, and could not build a lasting publishing house.[5]

Therefore, it was left up to paperback houses specializing in heterosexual and lesbian-for-straights erotica to seize the market. Though their catalogs contained a few reprints of erotic works published first in hardback, they were mostly made up of original works. These houses also were used to taking risks; thus it was a small step to add a gay line to their lesbian and straight lines. Greenleaf Classics' chief editor, the straight Earl Kemp, in fact, insists that it was gay readers, not entrepreneurial publishers, who were responsible for the origins of gay pulp fiction. He described the large number of articulate letters the press received, unsolicited, from gay readers: "The overt, active gays were frequently very specific with their literary requests. Some sent entire plot outlines, summarizing for us what they would like to read. And many also spelled out what they did *not* want to read any more of—gay stories with obligatorily sordid and extremely bad endings, wherein almost every character somehow becomes crippled, impaired, or otherwise useless to society in general. What they wanted to read about was themselves, engaged in hot, forbidden romances that did not end in tragedy."[6]

Greenleaf, based in San Diego, California, brought out its gay line in

1966 and quickly became the acknowledged leader. It was not alone—and was not even the first. Other presses specializing in straight erotica who early on had gay lines included Publisher's Export Co., also in San Diego; Brandon House, Barclay House, and Cameo Library in North Hollywood; Lancer Books, Midwood Books, and 101 Enterprises in New York; Olympia Press in Paris and later New York (with its Other Traveller series); Svea in Copenhagen; and dozens of others.[7]

The adult bookstores that sprang up in cities across the United States during the 1960s added gay sections. Because of the paperbacks' distribution system, however, by far the most important venues for gay readers to find gay pulps were the very stores in which they naturally shopped, even in rural areas of the country. Mass market paperbacks, unlike hardbacks and trade paperbacks, were distributed by the same vendors who put out magazines, and just like magazines, new paperback titles appeared at regular monthly or weekly intervals.[8] Once gay pulps became an established commodity, many of the books included mail-order forms at the back of the volume for anyone willing to trust the US postal service. In his account of *The Advocate*, the cultural historian Rodger Streitmatter notes that the paper's largest advertisements came "from mail-order companies specializing in homoerotic books."[9] Gay pulps were also reviewed in gay magazines and newspapers, such as the *Mattachine Review* (where Barbara Grier wrote under the pseudonym Gene Damon), *ONE* (with Joseph Hansen writing as James Colton), *Vector* (where Richard Amory reviewed a number of books in the early 1970s), *California Scene*, *Tangents*, and *Drum*. The Swiss journal *Der Kreis* also looked at American writers.[10]

Paperback books have always played an important role in the lives of gay and lesbian readers. From World War II until the early 1980s, the majority may have had "respectable" hardbacks on display in their dorm rooms, their apartments, or their homes, but they sought queer content among the paperbacks found on the ubiquitous paperback racks rather than hazard coming out of the closet in mostly family-owned bookstores or in public libraries. And now at the neighborhood convenience store or in the local five-and-ten, gays, like lesbians a decade earlier, could find Greenleaf Classics and Lancer Books cheek by jowl with Bantam Books and Signets.

Whether they bought the books or stole them, they read them avidly. And then, save for the bravest or those in like-minded city neighborhoods, they hid them away or destroyed them.

## THE PULP EXPLOSION

Perhaps the most amazing aspect of the gay pulp phenomenon is the sheer number of books appearing in such a relatively short time. Early liberation magazines such as *ONE*, *Der Kreis*, *Mattachine Review*, and *Tangents* had published gay short stories and poetry, but no one could have envisioned how many gay writers were waiting, eager to share their real-life experiences, ideas, and fantasies. From the beginnings the books explored an enormous range of genres, to the point that in many cases a pulp novel represents the first appearance of a genre in the history of gay literature. One finds action stories, boy-love stories, comedies (both campy and otherwise), coming of age stories, coming out stories, cop novels (a genre peculiar to the pulps), stories of decadence, detective stories, exposés, stories of family bonding, gothic novels, historical romances, horror stories, incestuous romances, initiation stories (a very rich field with all kinds of variants), love stories, melodramas, military stories, pastoral romances, picaresque novels, pure pornography, political novels, prison fiction, satires, school stories, S/M stories, sports stories, spy thrillers, supernatural tales, tragedies, wisdom literature, and both blue-collar and gray-flannel worker stories. There are far more short-story collections than is generally realized.

The wealth of material makes it difficult to generalize about these works. Take the matter of endings. Once writers realized that happy endings were possible, more and more books began to end on an optimistic upbeat. But unhappy endings continued to appear, even in Greenleaf Classics: murder, natural death, suicide (for example, Victor J. Banis's *The Why Not*, 1966; Chris Davidson's *Go Down, Aaron*, 1967; Dick Dale's *Gay on the Range*, 1967). There are unlikely conversions to heterosexuality (Lynton Wright Brent's *The Gay Bunch*, 1965). Identifying an author's corpus is not easy. The fact that many legitimately feared social and professional reprisals (and may have remained wary of possible legal repercussions) led the majority to publish under pseudonyms. Banis used as many as eleven. Many of the presses used "house names," which they routinely assigned to a genre regardless of who authored a work.[11] Although the majority of the books were written by gay authors, straight men and straight and lesbian women jumped into this new market when they realized it was a ready source of easy money.

Texts are sometimes corrupt. Some of the presses during the editing process proved remarkably incapable of changing their former attitudes toward homosexuality. According to the cultural historian John Howard, Publisher's Export Co. retained a marked homophobia even as it sought to cash in on the newly liberalized legal situation. He writes, "Pulp publishers like P.E.C. . . . skirted moral objections to queer content by packaging the narratives as socially responsible, cautionary tales. Homosexuality, they warned as they reworked authors' narratives, led to ruin. Editors forced these constructions on writers like [Carl V.] Corley [and] capped a morality play ending onto an otherwise unacceptable work of gay porn."[12] Greenleaf Classics swung just as far in the other direction. Since it saw its mission as supplying one-hand reads, it expected authors to comply. If they did not, the press simply commissioned someone to supply the missing sex scenes, sometimes with no regard to whether they fit into the context of the novel. Banis's 1966 mystery *Goodbye, My Lover*, for example, had two such scenes interpolated jarringly into the text.

Samuel Steward's memoirs, published in 1981, made it clear that piracy was also a part of the business. His 1970 novel *San Francisco Hustler*, written under his pen name, Phil Andros, was republished in 1975 as *Gay in San Francisco* by "Biff Thomas." The characters' names were changed, but curiously enough it contained the manuscript ending that the original publisher had cut.[13] Such a rewrite was far from an isolated incident. Dan Evans's story of a hypocritical vice squad unit, *Glory Hole* (1968), became Trock Bender's *The Gay Force* (1969). Alan Fair's murder mystery *The Boys in Olive Drag* (1968), along with the usual name changes, was moved from an army to a navy base in Jack Wood's *Navel Maneuvers* (ca. 1972). Throughout the 1970s and 1980s novels were routinely reissued using the original plates with the authors' names and titles changed.

Still, broad outlines of the period are beginning to emerge. The first true pulp star was Richard Amory, who published seven novels between 1966 and 1974. The importance of his first novel, *Song of the Loon,* was immediately recognized. If any one pulp novel is cited in a survey of gay literature, it is almost invariably Amory's (though the title is often incorrectly given as *The Song of the Loon*). In 1975 Hugh Honour casually dropped in an allusion to the novel (by title, without naming the author or indexing the reference) in *The New Golden Land,* his important survey of the impact of America on the European imagination. In 2011 Mark D. Jordan accorded the novel the same status as Vidal's *The City and the Pillar* and John Rechy's *City of Night* in his study *Recruiting Young Love: How Christians Talk about Homosexuality.*[14] Tom Norman, in his bibliography of erotic gay paperbacks, reports that an estimated thirty percent of the American gay male population read *Song of the Loon.* It received the dubious distinction of Amory's own publisher bringing out a hilarious parody, *Fruit of the Loon* by "Ricardo Armory" (1968). Amory's novel was the first gay work of fiction to serve as the basis for a gay film, directed by Andrew Herbert in 1970. For a special new edition published in 2005, Amory's son, Cesar Love, wrote a brief but illuminating biography.[15]

Amory was one of a coterie of writers based in the San Francisco Bay area that included Larry Townsend, Dirk Vanden, Peter Tuesday Hughes, Carl Driver, and Douglas Dean. Lou Rand and John Coriolan were also part of the scene. They were joined for a while by Samuel M. Steward. A good friend of Gertrude Stein and Alice B. Toklas, Steward has consistently been held in high regard by both readers and fellow authors. Writing under the punning pseudonym Phil Andros, the name of his hustler narrator, Steward's book career was supposed to begin with *$tud,* printed in 1966 by Guild Press for hardback release. But Womack was going through another bout of financial woes, so it did not become available until 1969, in a pirated paperback edition and finally a three-volume paperback and a limited hardback edition from Guild. In his memoirs, *Chapters from an Autobiography,* Steward discussed Andros's origins and the new and positive goals he was striving to achieve with the character. Steward has become the first pulp writer to receive the accolade of a full-scale biography, Justin Spring's *Secret Historian* (2010).

These San Francisco writers were largely college educated and widely read in American, British, Continental, and classical literature. They took pride in their craft and were serious about their role as artists. Moreover, they were keenly aware of the unique position they occupied in the history of gay writing. As a result, they became increasingly disgruntled with what they perceived as the editorial high-handedness of their publishers, particularly Greenleaf Classics. They went public with their complaints in 1970. In a series of interviews Amory attacked Greenleaf for insisting on one explicit sex scene per chapter, editing gay writers ineptly and illiterately without their permission, and making a fortune on books while paying its writers a five-hundred-dollar flat fee.[16] The writers were especially unhappy with editorial interference in their texts.

Writing in *The Advocate* in August 1970, Townsend reported: "Because of the difficulties in persuading standard publishers to produce books with frankly homosexual themes, most of us have been forced into the 'adult' or 'porno' market. None of us are overly pleased with this, as it restricts our range of expression." A month earlier, Amory had this to say in *Vector* magazine: "I was trying to widen the range of options open to homosexuals. . . . Is our art so completely at the mercy of third-rate, unimaginative, keyhole Victorians that we can't say what has to be said in an educated, sensitive fashion, *or even say it at all*?" And in an interview with Vanden for the newspaper *GAY* a few month later, Amory threw down the challenge: "Gay people have got to get together as the blacks have done, as the students have done, with our own *honest* literature, our own theatre, our own art—and we've got to decide who we are and what we want out of life."[17]

But another member of the San Francisco literary scene, Douglas Dean (the drama critic, actor, and director Dean Goodman), blamed gay readers rather than heterosexual publishers for skewing the development of a credible literature. In an essay published in *Vector* in May 1973, "Fuck Books or Gay Literature?," he praised one Greenleaf editor, Ginger Sisson, "a young woman of taste and high standards [who] wanted to do something worthwhile with gay literature." But the books she promoted, according to Dean, did not do as well as those containing the "raw, raunchy sex stuff," and so she was "eased out of her position." He continued, "There is no use in blaming the bosses for this. The dismissal of Ginger Sisson and the termination of a group of fairly decent writers for the Greenleaf stable can be blamed only on the readers, the gay public which didn't buy more of the books which Ginger and her writers turned out."[18]

Whatever the truth of the situation, had it not been for these heterosexual publishers, the advent of any kind of new gay literature would have had a longer wait. After the demise of Guild Press in 1972, three years passed before the next gay book publisher appeared: the aptly named Gay Sunshine Press. SeaHorse Press began in 1977, and Alyson Books arrived in 1980. Providing a counterbalance to his fellow writers' list of indictments, Banis, for one, remains grateful to Greenleaf Classics. He wrote in his 2004 memoirs that "in general these publishers were far more willing than most mainstream publishers to take a chance on books whose sales prospects were none too great," noting that this gave him "a freedom to write pretty much whatever I chose, a privilege usually known only to big name authors." And in a 2009 essay he went further: "We were now free to write not only all kinds of fiction in every genre, but—and this may have been the biggest breakthrough of all—we could write about real gay people in real situations living the kinds of lives gay men really lived."[19]

Earl Kemp credits Banis for being the catalyst that ultimately moved Greenleaf Classics into gay publishing. It brought out his innovative first gay novel, *The Why Not* (1966). This was swiftly followed by *The Man from C.A.M.P.*, which went on to become the first gay mystery series. There were ultimately ten *C.A.M.P.* volumes, all published under the house name Don Holliday; Banis wrote the first nine. He was the center of a pulp-writing clique based in greater Los Angeles. Among others, he was friends with the Walt Disney illustrator George Davies, who published his first pulp novels under the pseudonym Lance Lester. Davies was also the Ricardo Armory behind the notorious parody. Banis's lover at the time, Sam Dodson, published under a number of pseudonyms, including the house name Marcus Miller. Chris Davidson, according to Kemp, appeared out of nowhere and just as mysteriously disappeared, after turning out a whole series of respected pulp works. Banis was also on good terms with the mystery writer Joseph Hansen, who wrote pulps under the pseudonym James Colton. Hansen was also a longtime activist for homosexual rights and one of the organizers of the first gay pride parade in Los Angeles, held in 1970.

These are the only two literary circles that have come to our attention. Carl Corley worked alone in Louisiana. Despite his publisher's high-handedness, it honored Corley by bringing out three of his books in one volume, *Gay Trilogy* (1967), consisting of *My Purple Winter, The Scarlet Lantern,* and *A Fool's Advice.* There are yet other isolated writers whose works are remembered fondly by devoted fans. They include the New York–based Alexander Goodman (George Haimsohn), the science fiction writer Felix Lance Falkon (George H. Scithers), the unknown Jack Love, and the equally unknown Jay Greene, whose tragic vision has not deterred a remarkable following. James Barr, whose *Quatrefoil* (1950) remains one of the most im- portant postwar documents, published his last novel as a pulp: the far more adventurous romance *The Occasional Man* (1966).

Pulp publishers not only provided outlets for new works during this heady time of experimentation in the 1960s, they also reprinted a range of works such as Barr's government-censored *Quatrefoil,* Fritz Peters's *Finistère* (1951; briefly retitled *The World at Twilight*), and Jay Little's two extraordinary ventures into what the critic Roger Austen has snidely called "softcore pornography" (though he does credit them for making "a contribution of sorts by opening the bedroom door"): *Maybe—Tomorrow* (1952) and *Somewhere Between the Two* (1956).[20] These publishers recuperated *Teleny* (1893), publishing it in 1966 for the first time in the United States as "attributed to" Oscar Wilde. Despite the mystery of its authorship, the fact that it was written about, by, and for homosexual men makes its inclusion among gay pulps a bridge between Victorian and contemporary eroticism. Following the lead of Olympia Press, Greenleaf in 1967 brought out the first American edition of a translation of Apollinaire's *Les onze mille verges* (1907).

In 1970 E. V. Griffith edited an anthology of gay stories and poems for Greenleaf Classics, *In Homage to Priapus.* This collection gives us a sense of which authors were considered important at the time. Emphasizing the emergence of what he labeled "gay erotic realism," Griffith chose sixteen works of fiction. Only three date from before 1965: Lonnie Coleman's "The Theban Warriors," C. V. Howard's "A Very Important Call," and Stanley Kauffmann's "Fulvous Yellow." The other thirteen are by Andros (as Ward

Stames), Banis (one under his own name and another as Don Holliday), Corley, Goodman, Greene, Griffith himself, Allan James, Tom Lockwood, Julian Mark, James H. Ramp, Peter Randolph, and Rechy. Among the poems included is a sequence of four from Amory's *Song of the Loon*.[21]

*In Homage to Priapus* was one of sixty-two books in Greenleaf's 7" x 5" GL series. Because of its size, it would not have appeared with the mass market paperbacks on metal bookracks. It was the last occasion for pulp writing to make up the bulk of an anthology before Michael Bronski's *Pulp Friction* in 2003. In the 1974 collection *Different: An Anthology of Homosexual Short Stories*, Stephen Wright did include Hansen's "Snowfall," originally published under his Colton pseudonym, and four Phil Andros stories. "Snowfall" was reprinted in Peter Burton's *The Mammoth Book of Gay Short Stories* (1997). Selections from Andros, Lester, and Townsend were chosen by John Preston for *Flesh and the Word* (1992); excerpts from Andros, Townsend, Colton, and Lester (as Cardwell) appeared in the anonymously edited *A Century of Gay Erotica* (1998); and Simon Sheppard included excerpts from Amory, Andros, Banis, and Vanden in *Homosex* (2007).[22] But by the start of the 1970s the times were indeed changing, and the pulp writers of the previous decade began their long slide into obscurity.

## AFTER THE 1960s

Victor Banis has thought long about "the battle to legitimize gay themes" and the various writers' roles, including his own, in the fight. He recalls that, in 1967,

> we were just beginning to appreciate what was being won. It was a heady experience to come out from under the covers, to be able to go into a store and buy not one, but two, three, a dozen books, of whatever sort we wanted. Funny books, scary books, cookbooks, westerns, mysteries—they were all there. And so were we. We shopped. And cruised. And chatted. And began to perceive that we were far less alone than we had heretofore thought. And, yes, I do believe that it was here, as much as anywhere—among the beefcake

> covers and the campy titles and the astonishing variety of stories and themes that were suddenly there for us—that the sense of community, of oneness, that would soon lead to Stonewall and the Castro and the entire gay revolution, first took seed.[23]

It is a claim the historian David K. Johnson would agree with. In an article examining publications (particularly physique magazines) as part of the emerging gay consumer culture and its resultant politics, Johnson writes, "Content analysis of brochures, catalogs, magazines, and pulp fiction in the 1950s and 1960s shows . . . that consumer items provided a means for gay men to understand themselves as belonging to a larger community." He concludes that "the [Stonewall] riots were not the beginning of a movement—as they are often portrayed in the popular media—but the culmination of a gay consumer rights revolution."[24]

As gay liberation movements gained momentum in the 1970s, literature by, about, and for gay and lesbian readers became publicly celebrated for the first time. Not only did gay and lesbian presses come into existence, but mainstream houses became willing to publish works aimed at a gay-lesbian readership. Because of E. M. Forster's status, *Maurice* was, of course, snapped up by a major press and published in 1971. Likewise, Isherwood's *Christopher and His Kind* (1976), since it was by an established living author, serves as an even more striking example of the larger critical reinvention and reevaluation of gay writing that was occurring during the decade. Gordon Merrick began his extraordinary paperback career with *The Lord Won't Mind* in 1971. The novel had originally been published in hardback in 1970, with nothing like the escalating sales the paperback achieved. The same thing happened with Patricia Nell Warren's *The Front Runner* (hardback, 1974; paperback, 1975). Armistead Maupin gathered his first collection of *Tales of the City* in 1978. As such writers successfully blurred the division between mainstream and marginalized literature, theirs and similar works furthered the roles that 1960s gay pulps had performed.

Meanwhile, pulp publishers realized just how far government censorship had relaxed and how much they now had to compete with mainstream houses and small presses. As a result, they pushed for more and more sex, to the ultimate deterioration of literary quality. Lancer Books brought out Samuel R. Delany's bizarre excursion into pulp fiction, *The Tides of Lust* (1973). During the first half of the 1970s Midwood Books continued to publish works of varying merit by Jay Greene, Dallas Kovar, and newcomers Roger St. Clair and Michael Scott/Roland Graeme. Throughout the decade Surrey House (also called Surree and Surey Books) turned out traditional pulp novels of quality. The work of Tom Hardy, the pseudonym that Isherwood's actor friend Gordon Hoban used, is particularly outstanding. Surree's Blueboy Library series (1976–1977) represented the last true flourishing of gay pulps until the advent of Badboy Books in 1992. But the majority of the hundreds and hundreds of books churned out in the 1970s served as little more than masturbatory aids, their quality degenerating even further in the 1980s when publishers tried to compete with videotapes as erotic stimuli.

Unfortunately for the 1960s writers, this period of decline was the moment gay literary scholarship was coming of age. So there existed not only the obstacle of cultural historians' desire to divide everything neatly into pre-Stonewall and post-Stonewall, but also the understandable problem of critics having no sense of a need to examine such seemingly marginalized literature. For whatever reason, few pulp writers made the transition out of the pulps, and those who did largely covered their pulp roots. Hansen published his first Brandstetter novel under his own name in 1970. Banis left gay fiction and began a series of historical novels and suspense romances aimed at straight readers, largely women. Much later, in the 1980s, Samuel Steward and Vincent Lardo published gay mysteries under their own names as part of Alyson Books. Even later, Lardo and Thom Racina turned out straight thrillers. Some writers, such as Hughes, Greene, and George Davies (the latter under new pseudonyms), continued the pulp formula, and Townsend and William J. Lambert III remained true to their origins when they moved into trade paperbacks. Quite recently Banis, Lardo, Vanden, and Graeme have all returned to writing with renewed vigor. But they seem to be the minority.

What position do gay pulps occupy in the genealogy of gay literature? There is obviously a direct line of erotic writing from them through John Preston, Aaron Travis (Steven Saylor), and Lars Eighner all the way to their usurpation and reinvention as M/M romance for women readers in the present century. Writers such as Edmund White prefer to trace their roots to European models. But logically there must be more direct lines than are presently evident between pulps and that great middle ground of gay literature that is widely read but rarely examined by scholars. First fostered by independent presses and gay bookstores and then embraced by mainstream publishers and booksellers, this body of writing includes romances such as those by Merrick and Warren as well as mysteries, science fiction, trendy vampire stories. There are Charles Nelson's two military novels, the campy novels by Joe Keenan and James Earl Hardy, and the domestic dramas of Jim Grimsley and Jay Quinn. Pulps fought and won battles that post-Stonewall writers no longer had to engage in. They obviously fostered new expectations about the scope of gay fiction. But much work needs to be done to establish the links in the chains.

## GAY PULPS AND THE ACADEMY

The critical erasure of gay pulps paradoxically began in their very commemoration in early surveys and later encyclopedia articles. Beginning with Michael Perkins's study of modern erotica, *The Secret Record* (1976), on through Roger Austen's survey of gay American novels, *Playing the Game* (1977), James Levin's catalog *The Gay Novel* (1983), and Daniel Harris's *Rise and Fall of Gay Culture* (1997), pulps were essentially dismissed as erotica or pornography: in Austen's words, "more valuable as sociology than literature." Discussions of pulps in *Encyclopedia of Homosexuality* (1990), *The Gay and Lesbian Literary Heritage* (1995), and *LGBTQ America Today* (2009) follow suit.[25]

It was not until David Bergman's essay "The Cultural Work of Sixties Gay Pulp Fiction" (1999) that a new attitude began. In it he argues that Banis and Amory were united by a "desire to break with the stereotypical treatment of gay men and [an] attempt to articulate a different discourse on homosexuality." Susan Stryker's lavishly illustrated survey *Queer Pulp* (2001) stood out on the shelves of bookstores. Michael Bronski's anthology *Pulp Friction* (2003) brought selections from gay pulps back into print, and his headnotes offer astute observations, including his realization that "thinking of all gay fiction after the war up to the Stonewall riots as a separate literary category was a mistake." He adds, "I would now argue that the very concept of 'gay fiction' is most usefully understood as a post-Stonewall invention, one that serves a specific political function." The surveys offered in *Routledge International Encyclopedia of Queer Literature* (2006) and *Queers in American Popular Culture* (2010) are more nuanced and generally affirmative about the place of gay pulps in American literary history.[26] Whitney Strub's essay elsewhere in this collection places this scholarly evolution into a larger context.

Until now, the only full-length study of gay pulps has been the collection of essays edited by Drewey Wayne Gunn, *The Golden Age of Gay Fiction* (2009). Illustrated with reproductions of pulp covers, it offers Tom Norman's introduction to his bibliography, Philip Clark's account of Guild Press, Earl Kemp's reminiscences, memoirs by Banis, Jack Evans, and William J. Lambert, and essays about Colton (by Josh Lanyon) and Banis (by Fabio Cleto), as well as surveys of science fiction (by Rob Latham), crime novels (by Gunn), supernatural and horror stories (by Dave Doyle), and westerns (by Neil DeWitte).

Despite this growing attention, most people probably continue to think of gay pulps as artifacts rather than as texts. Stryker's color collection led to a boom in reproductions of campy covers as refrigerator magnets, postcards, address books, and even framed prints. Richard Dyer earlier surveyed examples of paperback covers from 1949 through 1966 in "Coming Out as Going In," an essay accompanied by black-and-white reproductions in *The Matter of Images* (1993). And Ian Young in 2007 published his survey *Out in Paperback: A Visual History of Gay Pulps.* All three contain useful information about the books' contents, but their focus is iconic, not textual, and may create a different kind of misunderstanding of the work of gay pulp fiction in the development of gay culture.[27]

Researchers are aided by four bibliographies. Tom Norman compiled the most inclusive list, *American Gay Erotic Paperbacks* (1994).[28] Ian Young in *The Male Homosexual in Literature* (1975; rev. ed. 1982) included a selective number of pulp novels (often with authors' pseudonyms decoded), thus beginning the process of determining which works are worthy of attention. Neither bibliography is annotated. Two specialized bibliographies that include pulp novels, however, are annotated: Eric Garber and Lyn Paleo's *Uranian Worlds* (1983; rev. ed. 1990), a bibliography of science fiction, fantasy, and horror, and Drewey Wayne Gunn's *The Gay Male Sleuth in Print and Film* (2005; rev. ed. 2013), in which he specifically argues for the importance of gay pulp to the development of the mystery genre.[29]

It is not easy to study gay pulp fiction. The earliest books in particular are quite scarce. Given that only one state had decriminalized homosexual acts at the time they appeared, early buyers routinely destroyed the books for fear of being found out. When 1960s pulps do come on the market nowadays, they are often quite expensive; the esteem that pulp covers have received has especially driven up prices for the rarer books. A number of academic libraries have begun to build collections, but their holdings are rarely if ever available through interlibrary loan, and fear of cracking the spines has so far prohibited photocopying.[30] But given the lesbian model for recuperation of authors and texts, obviously such problems are not insurmountable.[31]

## THE LESBIAN PULP FICTION MODEL

Lesbian and gay paperback originals both first appeared in Fawcett's Gold Medal series, but lesbian pulps, for reasons that remain speculative, had a fuller, richer development in the 1950s. Tereska Torres's *Women's Barracks* (1950) is generally credited with being the first pulp novel to include lesbian relationships; it gained special notoriety when it was singled out by a nervous House of Representatives committee during the Cold War as an example of the way paperbacks promoted moral degeneracy. It sold well, prompting Gold Medal to follow up with *Spring Fire* (1952) by Vin Packer (Marijane Meaker). Her book is often cited as the first true lesbian pulp novel since its plot focuses squarely on the relationship between its two protagonists. Although some lesbian novels were written by men (some by gay men) posing as women, a significant number were written by women. Besides Meaker, important lesbian pulp authors include Clare Morgan (Patricia Highsmith), Artemis Smith (Annselm Morpurgo), Ann Bannon (Ann Weldy), Valerie Taylor (Velma Narcella Young), and various pseudonyms used by Marion Zimmer Bradley.

A sense of exposé—what Scott Herring terms "literary slumming"[32]—infiltrated their plots and permeated their covers. Lesbian culture is portrayed as exotic, shadowy, and tragic; plots include prostitution, rape, orgies, incest, suicide, and insanity. Lesbian sexuality often exists as a voyeuristic thrill for male characters (who "redeem" the femme from the lesbian lifestyle at the end of the novel) and for implied male readers. (Something of the same happened in contemporary gay novels, in which the errant male was saved by a woman and marriage; for example, *Man Divided*, by Dean Douglas [1954].) Many critics claim that the lesbian books were, in fact, written primarily for heterosexual men as a sexual thrill, with the plot devices editors insisted on—the tragic ending, the sex scenes, male redemption—catering to their tastes. No hard evidence seems to exist to verify these claims one way or the other.

Because these books had the same distribution network as the rest of mass market paperbacks, the intended, and primary, audience may well have been lesbians themselves. As with gay novels, the tragic or "redemptive" endings may have been as much about avoiding government censorship as they were about appealing to the sensibilities of straight men. Most of what we know about reading practices at the time comes from anecdotes by lesbian critics remembering their experiences before Stonewall. For many of them it was "survival literature"—the only public source about the codes and existence of urban lesbian communities. To use lesbian pulps as a how-to guide, however, required distinctive reading practices. The classic method, as recounted by Stephanie Foote, was to stop reading before the last chapter in order to avoid the undesirable ending.[33]

Unlike gay pulp fiction, lesbian pulps have become an integral part of the larger story of queer culture and literature. Lesbian literature as a whole was canonized within the larger context of 1970s feminism. Because women's writing had largely been dismissed as inferior, feminist critics questioned established aesthetic standards and sought to devise new models to understand and appreciate lesbian literature, including pulp fiction. Lesbianism's cultural role in the 1970s as the ultimate expression of feminism meant that lesbian literature had a broader reading public to sustain it—lesbian critics made a case that such writing was not just about lesbians but also important in general considerations of gender and sexuality.

Early critics may not have approved of lesbian pulps' melodrama, voyeurism, and tragedy, but they recognized the genre's importance in the construction of lesbian identity and its encoded messages about the existence of lesbian culture. This led to the creation of a number of critical apparatuses that have ensured its survival. Early on, the Lesbian Herstory Archives made the decision to preserve copies of lesbian pulps, and this collection has become one of its best known and most used. Naiad Press, founded in 1973, reprinted a number of lesbian pulps; since the closing of Naiad, Cleis Press and the Feminist Press (in its Femmes Fatales series) have continued to keep key texts in print. And a rich diversity of articles and books have given serious critical attention to this genre.[34]

Theories of masculinities have never had the cultural impact that feminism has. Gay literary critics seem to focus more on outing traditional canonical writers, such as Herman Melville and Henry James, than on recuperating lost literature. Nor have gay critics questioned traditional aesthetic categories as much as their feminist counterparts have. As Forman Brown, Lonnie Coleman, and myriad others can attest, pulp authors are not the only gay writers to have been relegated to obscurity.

## NEW READINGS, NEW QUESTIONS

The present collection brings together a diverse range of scholars, methodologies, and reading strategies to interrogate the importance of 1960s gay pulps. The evidence that these essays amass amply demonstrates the significance of gay pulps for gay literary history, queer cultural studies, and, more broadly, book history. The twelve authors undertaking this exploration themselves represent a diversity of disciplines: American history, art history, creative writing, English studies, film criticism, gender studies, photography, and Spanish literature. From their cross-disciplinary investigations, it becomes apparent that gay pulp fiction arises from and appeals to distinctive but broader-ranged writing and reading communities than has hitherto been assumed, ones that beg for systematic analysis and discussion. The first three essays address broader topics; the rest focus on individual writers. The essays are arranged in chronological order by the publication dates of the writer being discussed.

The diversity of the dozens of texts discussed here shows how the very label "gay pulp fiction" obscures a complicated reality. The books differ dramatically in themes, techniques, and interests. Reading these essays, one senses that from satire to serious social commentary, from affirmative romance to masochistic dread, these writers seem united only by their salacious covers and their critical neglect. It is even more sobering when one realizes that the essays in this collection cover only the barest sliver of the overall production of gay pulps in the late 1960s.

The detailed readings of gay pulp novels presented here suggest that embarrassment and squeamishness about "fuck books" have blinded critics to the actual features of these texts. The question of literary value has been under debate for decades, as feminism, ethnic studies, and popular culture studies have highlighted the biases and cultural assumptions that underlie such judgments. Book history, in particular, has emphasized the contingent nature of literary merit; one writes for a particular reading and writing community, which has its own standards for determining worth. Gay pulp is infinitely more complex, diverse, and valuable than the dismissive cultural critics that Whitney Strub surveys in his essay have appreciated. And the line between trash and art, as James Gifford's proem to the volume suggests, is more porous than much literary criticism has allowed. Gifford points to the larger Cold War paperback book revolution as an example of this cultural miscegenation, as well as the highbrow literary allusions that populate gay pulp.

Several authors trace connections between gay pulp and more highbrow literary traditions in Spain, France, England, and the United States. Both Gifford and Ann Marie Schott mention the way authors let drop various kinds of literary allusions. Schott profiles a pulp writer with connections to Paris expatriates. Beth Bouloukos shows not only that *Song of the Loon* has firm literary antecedents in the Spanish pastoral novel, but also that a thorough knowledge of that tradition should cause critics to rethink any dismissal of the novel's language. Randall Ivey connects Banis's novels to both American and French traditions. Jaime Harker's discussion of Isherwood's incorporation of plot and structure of gay pulps into his last novel suggests future avenues of inquiry for literary criticism of canonical gay writers. Almost certainly, unexpected revelations await scholars once they start exploring pulp archives.

Many of the essays show that, long before the Internet, gay pulps' cultural influence was enormous. Strub traces the connections between Mattachine activists and distributors of gay pulp, complicating the activist/consumerist divide that so often animates debates about gay politics by showing how much more porous that imaginary line was than subsequent histories have admitted. Philip Clark's discussion of the reach of the Guild Press to both urban and rural areas shows that notions of "gay community" were always virtual as well as physical; gay Internet culture, much as it has been derided by some gay activists, grows directly out of the mail-order businesses of the 1960s. The importance of such virtual fantasies for political action is one contribution gay pulp can make to assessments of gay liberation.

One such contribution is the function of pulps in creating modern gay identity. Clark has the most thorough investigation here of this role; he shows that H. Lynn Womack's gay publishing empire insisted on the acceptability of gay desire, and that his writers (like so many other pulp authors) protested sodomy laws, fought religious prejudice, and insisted on freedom and sexual liberation. The role of pulps in building gay identity and community is also important in the essays by Pamela Wojcik, Schott, Ivy, Harker, Gunn, and Jeremy Fisher. Some writers, like Vanden (see Gunn's essay), made the coming out process central to their novels. Others, like Banis (see Ivey's essay), took gay identity as a given. Ivey also shows that Banis and other pulp writers used "fairy" stereotypes humorously and affectionately, while other writers, as Gifford, Gunn, and Schott demonstrate, explicitly rejected anything smacking of effeminacy, prioritizing traditional masculine identities. But Schott's discussion of the fraught masculinity of the Phil Andros stories also shows how complicated, and potentially retrograde, such an embrace of "real masculinity" could be. Collectively, these essays uncover a rich, often transgressive, and unusually defiant gay community in gay pulp, one engaged in a debate about the nature of gay identity and community that is as sophisticated, in its own way, as later debates in gay liberation and queer theory.

To truly appreciate the gay pulp reading community, scholars must gain a greater understanding of the experience of the original readers. A number of essays, especially those by Gifford, Gunn, and Fisher, use personal reading experience in revealing and touching ways. Clark's essay shows that rural readers made up a large percentage of the original community.

Those readers, as both Gifford and Strub suggest, became a key constituency in the more open and activist gay communities of the 1970s. The gay sexual culture of cities imagined in many gay pulps may, indeed, have contributed to the migration that fueled gay liberation activism. And gay pulp, though an American phenomenon, could become a conduit across national boundaries, as Fisher's discussion of one writer's exportation to Australia via a pulp reprint demonstrates. It is astonishing how many copies of gay pulps somehow migrated to England, at least to judge by the number offered for sale online today.

To determine the impact of gay pulps more fully, we need oral history projects before this generation passes on, similar to the surveys of lesbians' pre-Stonewall reading habits that have yielded much useful information. Such an endeavor may be complicated by the fact that, for many, gay pulps were a guilty pleasure. Isherwood derided the books, even in his own semiprivate journal, but he read them voraciously and with pleasure. Certainly gay news journals need to be combed for reviews and interviews from the time. We may even hope that someone will uncover a large file of fan letters tucked away in one of the gay archives, though fear of obscenity laws may have led publishers to destroy such documentation.

Likewise, more needs to be unearthed not only about the publishing houses themselves, but about marketing specific books. Some of the essays collected in *Sin-a-rama* (2005) provide some general insight but little detail and practically nothing about gay and lesbian novels. Some of the essays included here—those by Strub, Clark, Schott, and Reed Massengill—map out some of this territory, but so far no one has located and explored publishers' files, if indeed any still exist. Exact sales figures thus remain unknown. It would be almost impossible to estimate how many books were stolen by readers unwilling to face the cashier, or how many were obtained in a coverless state.[35] Though the general contours of many aspects of gay pulp publishing can be discerned, much remains unknown about what was clearly a major publishing phenomenon.

The editors, the contributors, and University of Massachusetts Press hope that the present collection will start a fruitful dialogue among scholars. During the 1960s there emerged two distinctly different publishing paths in the United States: the established mainstream route and the more adventurous and risky paperback original route. Until now these have been largely seen as diverging roads, and scholars have been generally content to take the more traveled fork. But until gay pulps gain close scrutiny and a true appraisal as literature, as contributors to the sense of identity and community, and as an outlet for otherwise stifled expression, it is our belief that it is impossible to make valid generalizations about the scope of post–World War II gay literature, including post-Stonewall writing.

## NOTES

1. For example, Felice Picano, in *Art and Sex in Greenwich Village: Gay Literary Life after Stonewall* (New York: Carroll & Graf, 2007), writes: "The portraits of gay men and lesbians they offered—although virtually always leading to suicide, institutionalization or (assumed) celibacy in the priesthood—were fairly accurate to what we expected from gay-themed books" (13). Justin Spring, in *Secret Historian: The Life and Times of Samuel Steward, Professor, Tattoo Artist, and Sexual Renegade* (New York: Farrar, Straus & Giroux, 2010), holds that "they were, for the most part, badly written tales of loneliness, alcohol, and psychic defeat, often concluding in suicide or murder (or both)" (ix). Both are wrong, as essays in this collection amply demonstrate.
2. Edgar Box was, of course, Vidal's pseudonym for his murder mysteries. The sources for these figures are Noel I. Garde, *The Homosexual in Literature: A Chronological Bibliography, circa 700 B.C.–1958* (New York: Village Press, 1959), along with a supplement prepared by Village Press of books published in 1959; and Marion Zimmer Bradley, *A Complete Cumulative Checklist of Lesbian, Variant, and Homosexual Fiction*, first published in 1960 (n.p.: Emereo Publishing, [2012]).
3. See Roger H. Tuller, "'A Subject of Absorbing Interest to Mankind': U.S. Supreme Court Obscenity Rulings, 1934–1977, in *The Golden Age of Gay Fiction*, ed. Drewey Wayne Gunn (Albion, NY: MLR Press, 2009), 135–40; and Whitney Strub, *Perversion for Profit: The Politics of Pornography and the Rise of the New Right* (New York: Columbia University Press, 2011).
4. Charles Kaiser, *The Gay Metropolis, 1940–1996* (Boston: Houghton Mifflin, 1997), 125. It would be interesting to know how Jay Little's two much more explicit and quite positive novels, *Maybe—Tomorrow* (1952) and *Somewhere Between the Two* (1956), and their publisher, Pageant Press, escaped federal censorship.
5. See Philip Clark, "The First King of Pornography: H. Lynn Womack and Washington, D.C.'s Guild Press," in Gunn, *Golden Age of Gay Fiction*, 87–95, and his essay elsewhere in this volume. Hal Call and six others formed Pan-Graphic Press in San Francisco in 1954; although it published a number of books, later established the Dorian Book Service, and was tied into the Adonis Bookstore via Call,

its primary function was to publish the *Mattachine Review.* It seems to have published its last book in 1964. See James T. Sears, *Behind the Mask of the Mattachine: The Hal Call Chronicles and the Early Movement for Homosexual Emancipation* (New York: Harrington Park Press, 206), 300–302 and passim.

6. Earl Kemp, "Strolling through Tumescent Town," in Gunn, *Golden Age of Gay Fiction,* 104. Kemp has created an ezine, *e.I* (http://efanzines.com/EK/index.html), which contains much information about Greenleaf Classics and its writers.
7. Tom Norman, *American Gay Erotic Paperbacks: A Bibliography* (Burbank, CA: privately printed, 1994), 3–4, revised as "American Gay Erotic Paperbacks: A History," in Gunn, *Golden Age of Gay Fiction,* 80–81. To confuse matters for bibliographers, these firms often modified or completely changed their names. Adding further layers of complexity, most houses had a whole series of imprints, sometimes identifying the parent house, sometimes omitting it. Thus Greenleaf Classics, often abbreviated to simply Greenleaf, is only the most common name for several series published at the same San Diego address. Norman lists the following: Adult Books (1967–1968), Adonis Classics (1975–1985), Ember Library (1967), Gay Novel (1973), Greenleaf Classics (1966–1968), Greenleaf Library (1969–1970), Late-Hour Library (1967–1968), Leisure Books (1965–1967), Nightstand Books (1967–1968), Phenix Companion Books (1967–1968), Pleasure Readers (1969–1973), and Sundown Readers (1966). Even Olympia Press might be Ophelia or Traveller's Companion, in addition to The Other Traveller. One must also remember that presses did not always separate their gay, lesbian, transgender, and straight books into separate series, as a quick look at Graham Holroyd's *Paperback Prices* (Chattanooga, TN: iGuide Media, 2003) will confirm.
8. For a good discussion of the different distribution systems used by hardback and trade paperback publishers and mass market paperback publishers, see Richard Curtis, "The Rise and Fall of the Mass Market Paperback," available in two parts at http://curtisagency.com/blog/2010/06. There are many histories of American paperbacks easily available online; for example, Oliver Corlett, "A Short History of Paperbacks," *IOBA Standard: The Journal of the Independent Online Booksellers Association* 2.3 (Winter 2001), available at www.ioba.org/standard/2001/12/a -short-history-of-paperbacks/.
9. Rodger Streitmatter, *Unspeakable: The Rise of the Gay and Lesbian Press in America* (Boston: Faber & Faber, 1995), 88. See also David Bergman, "Selling Gay Literature before Stonewall," in *A Sea of Stories: The Shaping Power of Narrative in Gay and Lesbian Culture: A Festschrift for John P. De Cecco,* ed. Sonya L. Jones (New York: Harrington Park Press, 2000), 43–52.
10. Tyler Alpern and Brad Confer have begun indexing many of these early journals; see *Tyler and Brad's Index to Early Gay Publications & Periodicals,* www.tyleralpern.com/sitemap.html. On *Der Kreis* see Hubert Kennedy, *The Ideal Gay Man: The Story of "Der Kreis"* (New York: Harrington Park Press, 1999), 36–50.
11. See the lists of authors and pseudonyms compiled by Earl Kemp in *Sin-a-rama: Sleaze Sex Paperbacks of the Sixties,* ed. Brittany A. Daley et al. (Los Angeles: Feral House, 2005), 284–87.
12. John Howard, *Men Like That: A Southern Queer History* (Chicago: University of Chicago Press, 1999), 206.

13. Samuel M. Steward, *Chapters from an Autobiography* (San Francisco: Gay Fox Press, 1981), 116; Norman, *American Gay Erotic Paperbacks*, 6; Norman, "American Gay Erotic Paperbacks: A History," 84.
14. Hugh Honour, *The New Golden Land: European Images of America from the Discoveries to the Present Time* (New York: Pantheon, 1975), 244; Mark D. Jordan, *Recruiting Young Love: How Christians Talk about Homosexuality* (Chicago: University of Chicago Press, 2011), 109–12. See also Byrne R. S. Fone, *A Road to Stonewall: Male Homosexuality and Homophobia in English and American Literature, 1750–1969* (New York: Twayne, 1995), 274–75; and Gregory Woods, *A History of Gay Literature: The Male Tradition* (New Haven: Yale University Press, 1998), 161.
15. Norman, *American Gay Erotic Paperbacks*, 3; Norman, "American Gay Erotic Paperbacks," 80–81; Cesar Love, "Biography of Richard Love," in *Song of the Loon*, by Richard Amory (Vancouver: Arsenal Pulp Press, 2005), 215–17.
16. These interviews have been reprinted as appendixes to Amory, *Song of the Loon*, 219–47.
17. Ibid., 236 (Townsend), 220 (Amory), 247 (Vanden). Townsend also mentions his disagreements with Greenleaf in an interview with Michael Rowe, in Rowe, *Writing Below the Belt: Conversations with Erotic Authors* (New York: Richard Kasak Books, 1995), 341. Amory, Townsend, and Vanden turned to Olympia Press, where Frances Green was an editor, as did Banis and Hansen.
18. Douglas Dean, "Fuck Books or Gay Literature?," *Vector*, May 1973, 17. Townsend was less happy with Sisson; see "Me and Maurice," *e.I* 4.5 (Oct. 2005), http://efanzines.com/EK/eI22/#townsend.
19. Victor J. Banis, *Spine Intact, Some Creases: Remembrances of a Paperback Writer* (2004), rev. ed. (Rockland, MD: Borgo Press, 2007), 162; "The Gay Publishing Revolution," in Gunn, *Golden Age of Gay Fiction*, 121. Banis's memoir was originally published by Edizioni Culturali Internazionali Genova.
20. Roger Austen, *Playing the Game: The Homosexual Novel in America* (Indianapolis: Bobbs-Merrill, 1977), 178–84, quotation on 178.
21. E. V. Griffith, ed., *In Homage to Priapus* (San Diego: Greenleaf Classics, 1970).
22. Stephen Wright, ed., *Different: An Anthology of Homosexual Short Stories* (New York: Bantam, 1974); John Preston, ed., *Flesh and the Word: An Anthology of Erotic Writing* (New York: Plume Books, 1992); Peter Burton, ed., *The Mammoth Book of Gay Short Stories* (New York: Carroll & Graf, 1997); *A Century of Gay Erotica* (New York: Masquerade Books, 1998); Simon Sheppard, ed., *Homosex: Sixty Years of Gay Erotica* (New York: Carroll & Graf, 2007).
23. Banis, *Spine Intact*, 165.
24. David K. Johnson, "Physique Pioneers: The Politics of 1960s Gay Consumer Culture," *Journal of Social History* 43.4 (Summer 2010): 870, 888.
25. Michael Perkins, *The Secret Record: Modern Erotic Literature* (New York: Rhinoceros Books, 1992), 213–34; Austen, *Playing the Game*, 212–19, quotation on 219; James Levin, *The Gay Novel: The Male Homosexual Image in America* (New York: Irvington, 1983), 246, 250–51, 252–53, 264–65, 268, 297; Daniel Harris, *The Rise and Fall of Gay Culture* (New York: Ballantine, 1997), 134–59; Daniel Eisenberg, "Pornography," in *Encyclopedia of Homosexuality*, 2 vols., ed. Wayne R. Dynes (New York: Garland, 1990), 2:1025; Edmund

Miller, "Erotica and Pornography," in *The Gay and Lesbian Literary Heritage: A Reader's Companion to the Writers and Their Works, from Antiquity to the Present*, ed. Claude J. Summers (New York: Henry Holt, 1995), 258–65; Robert Nashak, "Sadomasochistic Literature," in Summers, *The Gay and Lesbian Literary Heritage*, 622–26 (see also www.glbtq.com/literature/sadom_lit.html, where the author's name is listed as Robert Wood); Michael G. Cornelius, "Pulp Fiction, Gay," in *LGBTQ America Today: An Encyclopedia*, ed. John C. Hawley, 3 vols. (Westport, CT: Greenwood Press, 2009), 3:967–70. Georges-Michel Sarotte, *Comme un frère, comme un amant* (Paris: Flammarion, 1976), and Stephen D. Adams, *The Homosexual as Hero in Contemporary Fiction* (Totowa, NJ: Barnes & Noble, 1980), ignore pulp fiction altogether, and Fone, *A Road to Stonewall*, and Woods, *A History of Gay Literature*, mention only Amory.

26. David Bergman, "The Cultural Work of Sixties Gay Pulp Fiction," in *The Queer Sixties*, ed. Patricia Juliana Smith (New York: Routledge, 1999), 26–41, quotation on 33; Susan Stryker, *Queer Pulp: Perverted Passions from the Golden Age of the Paperback* (San Francisco: Chronicle Books, 2001); Michael Bronski, ed., *Pulp Friction: Uncovering the Golden Age of Gay Male Pulps* (New York: St. Martin's Griffin, 2003), quotation on 6; Fabio Cleto, "Pulp Fiction, Gay," in *Routledge International Encyclopedia of Queer Culture*, ed. David A. Gerstner (New York: Routledge, 2006), 467–69; Sarah Boslaugh, "Gay Pulps," in *Queers in American Popular Culture*, ed. Jim Elledge, 3 vols. (Santa Barbara, CA: Praeger, 2010), 2:123–38.
27. Richard Dyer, "Coming Out as Going In: The Image of the Homosexual as a Sad Young Man," in *The Matter of Images: Essays on Representations* (New York: Routledge, 1993), 73–92; Ian Young, *Out in Paperback: A Visual History of Gay Pulps* (Toronto: LMB Editions, 2007). See also such websites as *Gay on the Range: An Archive of Gay Paperback Artwork from the 50's and 60's*, www.gayontherange.com/; and *120 Days of Sodom(y)*, http://120daysofsodomy-vintagegaypulp.blogspot.com/.
28. Norman credits the catalogs periodically published in the 1970s and 1980s by the book dealer Elysium Fields for helping him establish his bibliography. (Bolerium Books has begun to take on something of the same function today.)
29. Ian Young, *The Male Homosexual in Literature: A Bibliography*, 2nd ed. (Metuchen, NJ: Scarecrow Press, 1982); Eric Garber and Lynn Paleo, *Uranian Worlds: A Guide to Alternative Sexuality in Science Fiction, Fantasy, and Horror*, 2nd ed. (Boston: G. K. Hall, 1990); Drewey Wayne Gunn, *The Gay Male Sleuth in Print and Film: A History and Annotated Bibliography*, rev. ed. (Lanham, MD: Scarecrow Press, 2013).
30. Significant holdings are archived at University of British Columbia, Brown University, University of California–Davis, California State University–Northridge, Central Connecticut State University, Cornell University, the Madeline Davis Gay, Lesbian, Bisexual, Transgender Archives of Western New York (in Buffalo), Duke University (where Gunn's pulp mystery collection has found a home), the Kinsey Institute at University of Indiana, University of Louisville, Michigan State University, University of Minnesota, New York Public Library, New York University (Fales Collection), the ONE National Gay and Lesbian Archives (now part of the University of Southern California Libraries), Quatrefoil Library (Minneapolis), San

Francisco Public Library, University of Saskatchewan, University of Toronto, George Washington University, and University of Wisconsin–Milwaukee.

31. Bill Warner, owner of GLB Publishers, began the Gay Writers History Project to make available ebooks of noted early pulp writers. He chose to begin with Amory, Banis, Coriolan, Burton Lewis, and Vanden, before poor health forced him to abandon the project.
32. Scott Herring, *Queering the Underworld: Slumming, Literature, and the Undoing of Gay and Lesbian History* (Chicago: University of Chicago Press, 2007).
33. Stephanie Foote, "Deviant Classics: Pulps and the Making of Lesbian Print Culture," *Signs: Journal of Women in Culture and Society* 31.1 (Autumn 2005): 176.
34. See for example, Yvonne Keller, "Pulp Politics: Strategies of Vision in Pro-Lesbian Pulp Novels, 1955–1965," in Smith, *The Queer Sixties*, 1–25; Joan Nestle, *A Restricted Country* (San Francisco: Cleis Press, 2003); and Katherine V. Forrest, ed., *Lesbian Pulp Fiction: The Sexually Intrepid World of Lesbian Paperback Novels, 1950–1965* (San Francisco: Cleis Press, 2005). See also Morgan Gwenwald and Micki Trager, curators, *Queer Covers: Lesbian Survival Literature*, Lesbian Herstory Archives exhibit, 1993, www.lesbianherstoryarchives.org/exhibits.html#queer.
35. As with all mass market paperbacks, distributors received credit for unsold pulps by tearing off the covers and returning them to publishers as evidence that the books had been destroyed. But often they were not destroyed, and one can still find such coverless books on the market.

# Proem

## *HOW TO READ GAY PULP FICTION*

James J. Gifford

How can I take this book seriously?

After spending so much of my academic career in ferreting out gay texts of the past, looking for coded references to homosexuality in books that have long been forgotten, why am I even looking at a yellowing and brittle paperback from the 1960s called *Idylls of the Queens*? Such texts are disposable, I thought, the remnant of an era that trashed gay sensibilities by reducing them to the salacious writing that you'd find on a 42nd Street newsstand kiosk. And even if one *did* hide copies of the Marquis de Sade and *The Pearl* at the back of one's bookshelf—well, those are *old*. Are these relatively recent pulps really worth my time? How could they be? They could not say anything to me.

I was wrong.

The more I read in *Idylls of the Queens*, which is a 1968 Greenleaf Classics anthology of fifteen short stories by one "Carl Branch" (clearly a nom de plume),[1] the more I realized that something quite different is going on from what I had expected. And I should've known better.

Thanks to graduate school, I am familiar with Steven Marcus's *The Other Victorians*, a study of nineteenth-century pornography, not to mention

Janice Radway's *Reading the Romance*, a close look at the phenomenon of the Harlequin bodice-ripping paperback, a genre that shows no sign of aging after decades of jaw-dropping sales. Both analyses dignify the bluest and trashiest (I thought) of genres by recognizing their success—for they *were* successful productions—as psychological and sociological if not exactly proper literary phenomena. So I took pause. Was I really labeling 1960s gay pulp as subliterary because I had become an academic prig? I know all about canonicity, and the process of glorification of some works as good, over others, is really at heart a subjective thing. My own research involves the recovery of early American gay-inflected writing, so what right have I to canonize *those* texts as sacred and dismiss a very successful strain of gay writing—namely, pulp fiction—that was active from the 1940s well past the 1980s? After all, any Greenleaf title had easily outsold the meager five hundred copies of Edward Prime-Stevenson's *Imre: A Memorandum* (1906), which I idolize as the first great American gay novel. Both productions had their readership; and the story of American gay writing is far from complete.

Not to mention my own knowledge.

Back to *Idylls of the Queens*. The stories read easily and are mostly westerns, with an occasional military-themed one. What brought my guard down and struck me at once, though, is that each story is far from the lascivious and oversexed text I had expected. In fact, all are instead optimistic, "proper," and even romantic. Two men meet, usually thrown together by the most arbitrary of circumstances, fall in love, forge a bond, and plan on staying together. When the cowboys in particular fall in love, the bond is often referred to as "marrying up," a term which reverberates to a reader in 2012 who has just married his life partner after a surprising marriage-equality victory in New York State. But more than that, it is the *tone* of these stories that proved an eye-opener.

Usually Branch's heroes find themselves adrift, to put it kindly, isolated, as the stories begin, in some kind of nowhere state, whether on a ranch or a road or even in a jail cell, and though often ambitious, set to live life woodenly. They are men in their mid-thirties who are stoically trying to deal with the hardships of life. Until love steps in. And that's *love*, by the way, not lust.

*Imre* was significant in its own day as the first known American novel in which two men end up happily together; but by the 1960s it seems that there were dozens of homosexual novels in which the same Hollywood ending was a given. Both Edward Prime-Stevenson and E. M. Forster, writing in the closet in the early twentieth century, foresaw an age when such unions would be acceptable, and these gay pulps from decades later seem a fulfillment of sorts. It is difficult for modern readers to imagine there was a time in gay literary history when unhappiness and psychopathology, if not an unhappy ending, was the norm for gay characters. Suicide or rejection or disgrace was usually their lot. Such is the example in *A Marriage Below Zero* by "Alan Dale" (1889). Even when the gay relationship seems relatively stable and happy, the structural and cultural demands of the day insisted that two men could not stay together at the story's conclusion, as in Bayard Taylor's *Joseph and His Friend* (1870) and Frederick W. Loring's *Two College Friends* (1871). Indeed, after *Imre* up until the period after World War II, the few American novels with gay characters (excepting perhaps Henry Blake Fuller's ambiguous *Bertram Cope's Year* (1919) and Forman Brown's roman à clef *Better Angel* (1933), written under the pseudonym Richard Meeker) simply did not conclude with their heroes safely and happily in each other's arms.[2]

But the paperback boom that began in earnest during that war proved a boom for gay writers as well. Michael Bronski and Drewey Wayne Gunn have mapped out the terrain, and the many gay pulp titles that started appearing with greater and greater frequency seem to attest to the fact that not only were there more working gay authors on the scene than ever before, but also many more gay readers. David Leavitt and Mark Mitchell's anthologies have testified that early gay texts were often "passed hand to hand" from one gay reader to another.[3] Prime-Stevenson's writings, under the pseudonym of Xavier Mayne, were personally distributed to friends and acquaintances or sold only at "particular" bookstores in large European cities and even in New York. How remarkable, then, is the leap, within decades, to finding gay books mixed in with heterosexual racy titles at practically any newsstand, and all this before the great demarcation of Stonewall. While gay historians continue their focus on authors such as

Fuller and Carl Van Vechten and Hart Crane as they hopscotch their way along the great irregular arc of American gay writing, where each title seems a distinctive and isolated breakthrough in gay publishing, it now seems clear that there were many more titles available after World War II, and widely so. Had I been sleeping not to realize that these pulps were a major and underappreciated part of this trend? Throughout the second half of the twentieth century gay fiction transmuted itself, and production snowballed. While the gay characters and titles that appeared irregularly during the 1920s and 1930s tentatively showed their faces without any seeming reference to one another, the arrival of gay pulp fiction was explosive.

Yes, the authors of pulps were as anonymous as the writers of *Imre* and *A Marriage Below Zero*, or *The Story of a Life* (by "Claude Hartland," 1901); and yes, paperbacks were surprisingly as guarded a format, in some ways, as earlier books that were published abroad or privately or via a medical press. Once purchased, paperbacks could easily be stripped of their covers and stowed anonymously in coat pockets and under book piles. But more than the format, something else was going on in the type of fiction that was being written. Very gradually there was a shift in the style of gay writing as well. Certainly many of these pulps bear lurid titles (*Man into Boy* and *Faggots to Burn!*) and include melodramatic plots, but others, such as the *Idylls* I was holding in my hand, are full of everyday people and everyday situations—only the heroes are gay. Instead of the odd, idiosyncratic, even pathological gay people that characterized such widely heralded novels as *The Fall of Valor* (1946) and *The City and the Pillar* (1948), pulps tended to show gay people who were more like people you would be apt to run into on the street, anywhere.

And they were being sold for the most part in the open air! For even if they were relegated to kiosks in the adult section, such newsstands existed practically everywhere.

I continued *Idylls* with a new appreciation. Different thoughts kept occurring to me as I read. There is more than a little self-conscious hokey-ness in the men's western patois (one story is called "Pancakes and Pulkrytood"), and sometimes the language is curiously quaint ("Chick Sale" meaning "outhouse," for example). But there are many literary references as well. Isn't that Alfred Lord Tennyson being lampooned in the book's title, after all? One story, called "Disinherited," begins with a sonnet that the hero has written, no less, and later on the muscly military policeman quotes the poet A. E. Housman. The stories are peppered with references to *Sturm und Drang* and Praxiteles, but the author apparently saw no anomaly even when his characters speak, as they often do, with an uneducated twang. Such references would seem to be accessible only to college-educated readers, which suggests he was writing for a broad audience.

Remarkably, these stories have a strong morality attached to them. Branch misses no chance to allow his characters a chance to lecture on not losing hope, the dangers of sexual repression, and the difference between love and lust (love "is a grim dedication, a demanding hunger which is seldom fed"; "When you love someone you want to do something for *him*. When you're *in* love with them, you want them to do things for *you* too"). His lovers don't bed each other until there's a promise of fidelity—and this in a pulp! Branch shows us an interracial gay relationship in "Fallen Sparrow," in which a black nurse is berated by a white patient for his constant self-belittling racial comments. "Us minorities. We must stick together!" he says.[4] I occasionally winced at the obviousness of Branch's frequent use of symbolism. Several stories take place near foothills called the Superstitions. The hero in "The Quest" has a large red itchy spot on his chest that keeps growing, and it won't go away until he declares the truth about his love for another man (the one place in the collection where Branch avoids strict realism). The eponymous hero in "Kissing Bug," in the simplicity of his country background, grows up kissing every boy and man he meets, and his straight neighbors accept it as part of his personality. As I read story after story, another prejudice fell by the wayside: that the heroes (and readers!) of pulps must've been uneducated and sleazy themselves.

The collection reveals that Branch felt under some compunction to stay true to a formula, just as Harlequin romances do, even if each tale has a plot quite distinct from its brothers. The writing often is witty, and if the tales follow an obvious formula, Branch never hesitates to create characters that are psychologically consistent and credible. The final pair of stories in *Queens* is a *coup de maître* in that they tell the same story but from the opposing sides of the two lovers. Always, the emphasis is on *romance*, not sex—something else that surprised me. Also astonishing in the pairing of these same-sex couples is the heavy suggestion of Fate, for in this book men do not meet each other when they are on the hunt in gay bars or haunts. The idea is rather that partners find each other by Fate, willy-nilly. In this, Branch harks way back to *Joseph and His Friend*, in which the two heroes meet each other accidentally and form an almost immediate bond. Love at first sight is hardly remarkable, but the emphasis is decidedly on believable events to track the chance meeting of the two people, though there is occasionally just enough of fantasy in them to be titillating. In the middle of the night a doctor's car runs into trouble on a lonely road, where he is rescued by a handsome wrangler on a horse ("Line Shack"). Two men share a foxhole and fall in love ("The Need"). A man newly out of jail spends the night at a Catholic monastery ("Jail Bird"). A drug user finds sympathy from the hospital orderly who helps him through a night of detoxing ("Fallen Sparrow"). The message invariably is: Hang in there—you will meet someone yet. And out of nowhere the Right Person steps in. Although several of these couples are forthright in declaring their attraction, there are a few pining over undeclared love. But true to the formula he writes by, Branch concludes each story with the heroes leaping into bed together. Interestingly enough, however, they don't get there until they plight their troth. For example:

> "Say what you mean, Ard," said Tom softly.
>
> "I mean, I love you! I have from that first day when you took me in and said, 'You are very welcome here!' "
>
> "And I loved you from that moment. I left my vocation for you, and I've waited so long . . . so long . . . for you to tell me!"
>
> "Then come here, Red Wolf, and let us devour each other!"[5]

Also surprising is that none of the gay men evinces any stereotypes. They are for the most part straightforward about who they are, seeing themselves as part of the spectrum of human nature, the way God created them. Most often the straight people around them accept them that way, too. There are supportive parents, friends, a friendly postman, even Granny in "The Quest"! Further, there are no derogatory terms to describe being gay. No flouncing or bouncing or mincing in this book, though the cover art may reveal effeminate eyes or poses.[6] Instead, the author uses masculine prototypes—the cowboy and the military man and the farmer—as his gay heroes. (It reminds me of Prime-Stevenson's insistence that the hero of *Imre* be an outstanding soldier.) These bastions of virility are war heroes, marines, cattle farmers, salt-of-the-earth types. Many long to start a spread and create a home for themselves, to settle down ideally with a partner. The World War II vet appears so many times in these stories that clearly the author had a special empathy for them, for their sense of isolation and their longing to connect. In 1968 veterans were the perfect image of men who had been badly used and shown the worst that humanity can inflict on one another. They become the ideal types who long to love men, not fight them. It is interesting that in the midst of the Vietnam War, Branch could create sympathetic and manly heroes out of military men.

And though there are some unsavory situations in the collection (a military lighthouse keeper who sexually traps the men assigned to him; a sailor who tries to kill himself), the most remarkable attribute of the majority of the gay men we meet is a sense of their *kindness*. The story "Disinherited" traces the nightly rounds of a tough but compassionate MP as he searches through a single night for down-and-out and victimized sailors, only to wind up falling in love with the would-be suicide he's saved. Instead of bringing the book down on men often victimized by their own naiveté, the macho MP is kind and helping, non-condemnatory, anxious to salvage bad situations and restore to the luckless their dignity and sense of self-worth. "South Forty" tells the story of a gay couple who nurse a cattle rustler back to health, and find him a partner and a new life in the process. It's actually rather touching. A sense of brotherhood pervades *Idylls*. Men kid each other, watch out for each other, keep their eyes open for possible partners for their friends. One cowboy readily suggests that the hero meet a pal of his, a good friend with whom he'll likely get along. When a marine stumbles on two soldiers arm-in-arm out on duty, he shrugs, "Well God Bless! Glad someone has found something in this screwy war!"[7] In another story, a father unwittingly (or not) becomes the means for his son and another man to get together.

Am I making too much of this one book, chosen pretty much at random? How could *Idylls of the Queens* be representative among so many gay pulps? Is it just the English teacher in me typically overanalyzing?

I think not.

From what I know of the literary past, gay authors have had a history of coopting what genres they could, in the hope of getting their voices on record. Homosexuals grabbed at the case history format early on, for instance, to tell their stories (*The Story of a Life; Imre*), because the age of dynamic psychology gave them access to a new literary structure. Westerns, too, with their all-male cast of characters, were easy venues to express male-male feelings (Theodore Winthrop's *John Brent,* 1861; Owen Wister's *The Virginian,* 1902). Belles-lettres, always written with specific and limited audiences in mind, could be coopted too, Fuller's *Bertram Cope's Year* (1919) being an example. With the mass marketing of paperbacks, how quickly gay writers assimilated *that* medium. If mainstream publishers were only gradually beginning to accept homosexuality in novels (and then grudgingly and often with restrictions), why not use the freer medium of the paperback original? Were some pulp novels pornographic? Of course. But *Idylls of the Queens* shows that at least some authors used the platform as a way to romanticize, even normalize, gay feelings. The positive portrayal of same-sex relationships was stunning to me in this 1968 collection. *Idylls* exhibits all the happy endings that Forster and Prime-Stevenson had only dreamed about. And I had picked this book at random.

If I were to name a gay literary production from the past that is closest in tone and spirit to *Idylls of the Queens,* it would be Charles Warren Stoddard's *South Sea Idyls* (1874), and not just because of the title. In that collection of homoerotic tales, most of the stories feature the loving relationships of Stoddard himself with a number of native boys he encountered on his travels through Pacific islands. Their time together is always brief and edenic. But they all end unhappily, with the ever-fickle author taking his leave of the heartbroken boys. Although Stoddard had to be circumspect about specifics, readers in the know clearly understood what kind of love he was really talking about. The joyous freedom of the island culture and the laissez-faire attitude toward sex they represented fit Stoddard perfectly. Years later, Carl Branch writes in a similarly joyful fashion, with an open and liberated attitude toward sex—*except* that his lovers bond for life. The jump from *Idyls* to *Idylls* is ninety-four years: it's an eon when you're talking about American gay literature.

I always thought that the number of gay-themed books before Stonewall was provocatively and annoyingly small, each one like a rare jewel set in a crown. Now I realize that some pulps of post midcentury America shone like glitter around such "canonical" titles. Indeed, many of these pulps may be jewels themselves. Am I saying that *Idylls of the Queens* is great literature? I am not sure. But is it and its brothers worth investigating? The answer is definitely yes.

Because pulps are often sexually explicit, and since that is the impression that enters one's head even at hearing the word "pulp," I thought I would be remiss (having lost my pulp virginity, so to speak) if I didn't take a look at an example as part of my self-introduction to gay pulp fiction. Obviously such pulps were written with both provocative as well as money-making aims in mind. But were such pulps, as gay authors handled them, merely pornographic, or were they genuine erotica? I am not sure the line of demarcation is clear, or even if there is one. But I assume erotica has a more literary bent, handling sexual formulas cleverly and maybe even including ideas, themes, and purposes, as any literature might. Could there be any redeeming features if an author tells a salacious tale?

I picked up *The Fag End* by Dick Dale (1969), also a Greenleaf production.[8] The author's name is too good not to be a pseudonym, and the title is an obvious pun. If, as I have heard, some authors had to tolerate publishers' adding sex to their already formulated tales, Dale's writing did not seem to have been submitted to such editorial intrusion. The book was pretty nonstop when it came to sexual action: explicit scenes did not look like mere decoration layered onto a predetermined story. In fact, the more I read, the more I—surprisingly—felt that sex was integral to the plot.

Briefly, the story revolves around two mid-teen boys, Jim and Tommy, who meet each other "by Fate" and gradually develop strong feelings for each other. They attend a Sunday School camping trip overseen by the Reverend Leonard Smith, who is an amalgamation of all one's worst fears about the ministry. Sex-obsessed and a pederast to boot, Smith resembles Robert Mitchum's Reverend Powell in the 1955 film *The Night of the Hunter*, with his evil focus on two children, but he more anticipates the clichéd and sex-riddled Reverend Peter Shayne (played by Tony Perkins) in *Crimes of Passion* (1984). Dale shows us (in detail) just about every character's sexual initiation; but Jim's, at the hands of a muscle-bound stevedore, is the only one with a saving grace. The older man is careful not to abuse the boy, though Jim clearly wants more. Smith's initiation, in a flashback to years before, is not so happy, however, as his partner turns on him when it's over. Thereafter, we are to understand, Smith longs for reciprocal and loving feelings with a partner, something he is unable to find, though he looks hard enough and even fathers children. This rejection turns him into an evil man who eventually turns to boys as sexual objects as a way to find an experience that will make up for his first loss. Young Frankie, his son, complicates matters, as both he and his father focus on Jim as their object of desire. But Jim faces the minister down in the book's strongest scene, and the story closes with Jim and Tommy finding romance with each other, and the elder Smith somehow at peace with his demons.

I have probably dignified this story a bit more than it deserves. The book is full of typos and misprints, suggesting a rush job, whether by author or printer. The story's heavy insistence on sex, however, does not disguise some deeper ideas. As a cautionary tale, *The Fag End* certainly delivers. For all its insistence on portraying teenage sex, the Reverend Smith is a loathsome figure, obsessively caught up with his own devils, subverting religion into an unholy dominance over any boys he can. Pederasty is certainly not shown as admirable in this book, and in fact Smith suffers greatly for his predilection, which, it is suggested, was a conscious choice on his part. Dale's rationale for Smith's behavior is weak at best, but there is no denying that the book's examination of his psychopathology is eerily fascinating. Although the purple prose might repel some readers, the progress of events keeps one turning pages. (Or at least it did for me.) In that sense the book sidesteps a charge of pornography, wherein to my mind plots are merely decorative devices. Still, *The Fag End* is certainly no *Tom Jones.*

Though explicit, the description of burgeoning sexual feelings seems truthfully portrayed, and in its way Dale's book captures the sexual struggles and desires and feelings of some aspects of growing up gay. If Mark Twain had been truthful enough, some of this material might have easily been put into *Huckleberry Finn.* Though we may all have such sexual thoughts, it is easy enough to contemn an author who dares to set them down. I sidestepped the sex to try to find similarities between this book and

*Idylls of the Queens,* for there are echoes. For one thing, there is a strong element of Fate in the meeting of the two friends. They find each other and immediately and inexplicably each is drawn to the other. They overcome obstacles and stand up for each other. And by the story's end they are in each other's arms. Oddly, there is a strong emphasis on kindness and thinking about the other person in both books. But the mere thought of sexual feelings in those not of legal age (not to mention pederasty) could be a sufficient turn-off for many readers. It is almost as though the author has incongruously chosen some of the diciest material he could in order to tell a moral tale. For the predator villain is punished (perhaps cured), and the two boys learn that their love and respect for each other trump every other temptation, that *sex and love go together.* That is perhaps the most surprising thing I take away from *The Fag End.*

Bizarrely, except for the overt sexuality, the tale reminds me of Edward Prime-Stevenson's early boys' book *Left to Themselves* (1891). In that work, which the author himself later admitted (in his 1909 nonfiction work *The Intersexes*) couched homoerotic undertones, we see two boys of the same age as Jim and Tommy as they meet, become friends, go through a series of adventures, and wind up in each other's company for life. Indeed, when a tramp attacks the younger boy, the older bravely steps in to save him, just as Jim confronts the Reverend Smith. Both stories have as their focus the relationship between two boys and how they learn to care for and assume responsibility for each other. That also seems to be the backbone of *The Fag End.*

So I leave Dale's book with a confusion of feelings. The sexual explicitness is strong, but weirdly enough the moral message is equally strong. The material is not always attractive, but by book's end there seems to be a *point* (besides titillation) to it. Pederasty is distasteful to most people, especially in an age when the Catholic clergy seem to be daily fighting such charges in the news, but we have to admit that pederasts exist. Whether they deserve pity or prosecution, the condition is part of the human spectrum. If, as I believe, the author of *The Fag End* embedded scruples in his tale, only the individual reader can decide whether they redeem the scurrilous prose that conveys the story.

It is impossible for me to contextualize gay pulp erotica within the tradition of erotica in general, although that would be an interesting undertaking. Steven Marcus years ago remarked that he had discovered very little gay pornography in his look at the Victorian era.[9] Whatever was there was folded into generally heterosexual stories. When did American gay literary porn make its first appearance? What was the first pulp to provide gay sex-specific scenes? If *The Fag End* is typical of that tradition, is it fair to say that gay erotica has a moral backbone to it that erotica in general does not have? Does such intended lewdness represent another step in the history of American gay writing? Or are such productions better studied by a psychologist rather than a literary critic?

The sheer number of volumes from Greenleaf Classics and similar presses says something. Clearly there was an audience, and the public availability of such works seems startling in retrospect to one who thinks of the 1950s and 1960s in terms of the old television sitcom *Happy Days*. *Idylls*, *The Fag End*, and other pulp titles were right out in plain sight at newsstands. I can remember seeing them! Suddenly, it occurs to me how much easier it was for gay men of that time to find out about homosexuality than it was for earlier generations, who had to hunt for subterranean and medical texts, for brief mentions in novels like *David Copperfield* or books of poetry. To think of such novels for sale in Dubuque and Oklahoma City! For such pulps were available pretty much everywhere, apparently. Such new connectivity among gay readers is astounding to consider.

At least some of the pulp books that I had despised (or worse, thought nothing of) were in reality the fodder for Stonewall, nothing less. These books added to a consciousness that homosexuality was as widespread a phenomenon as the 1948 Kinsey Report had suggested. Further, gay men could see themselves represented happily and (yes) lustily and not alone and still basically moral; and how could that not add up to a sense of strength in numbers and self-esteem? The queens who fought back at the Stonewall Inn in 1969 were brave, to be sure, but in many ways they were standing on the shoulders of the pulp writers who had preceded them. These pioneers were laying the groundwork that helped gay men realize a positive self-image. Their books were loudly proclaiming to their readers that they had the right to love and settle down, an equal entitlement to live and not be ashamed.

And now, having read my first pulp fiction (*and lived!* as a pulp cover might exclaim), maybe I can give a bit of advice to readers who are wondering whether they too should try one. Here are a few tips:

(1) *Come to the work with an open mind.* Give the book a break. Do not assume that every pulp is a piece of sleaze or an undiscovered masterpiece. Let those presumptions go. Give the book the chance to be a good read. Keep a sense of humor and listen to what the story has to say.

(2) *Be conscious that each book is a product of its time.* All books have publication dates. Try to recall what stage of gay life generated the story you're reading. In the present day, where homosexuality is proud to stand up and be counted, remember that your forebears had to be more circuitous about themselves. Keeping gay lives hidden was commonplace, and still is with some people. Try to see how this book reflects that sense or, more likely, struggles against it. Be grateful you do not live then, if nothing else, but do not be patronizing. See where this book is coming from.

(3) That said, do not be surprised if it still has a few things to say to *the present-day reader.* Romance, as the song goes, "is never out of date." The dynamics of finding someone and making him your own never fails to be fascinating. The author of the pulp you're considering may well have a new or clever way of telling an age-old story. Or even something new about yourself. (And unfortunately sexual predators are not likely to go away either.)

(4) *A pragmatic note: you may have to spend some money.* Pulps have become collector's items, and some can command quite a hefty price. Or you can sample Michael Bronski's anthology of highlights in his Pulp Friction (2003). And I must warn you that this may become a compulsive hobby. (Now that I think of it, why am I urging you to buy the very copies of the works that I will soon be hunting for?)

(5) *Above all, enjoy the freedom that this pulp represents and sends down the decades to you.*

And what about me, you may ask. Will I go on and read other pulps? Let me just say this: Carl Branch, I discovered, also wrote two other Greenleaf titles that I found on the Internet: *A Few of the Boys* and *All Shades of Gay.* They just arrived in the mail today.

# NOTES

1. David D. Irwin, executive director of the Quatrefoil Library, has suggested that Carl Branch may be a pseudonym for the writer James H. Ramp. See *Gay Bookworm* 4.6 (Nov. 1989): 4–5, available at www.qlibrary.org/quatrefolios/Quatrefolio%201989%20 November.pdf.
2. For examples of multi-author recuperation efforts for pre–World War II American writers, see James Gifford, *Dayneford's Library: American Homosexual Writing, 1900–1913* (Amherst: University of Massachusetts Press, 1995); Devon W. Carbado, Dwight A. McBride, and Donald Weise, eds., *Black Like Us: A Century of Lesbian, Gay and Bisexual African American Fiction* (San Francisco: Cleis Press, 2002), 1–105; A. B. Christa Schwarz, *Gay Voices of the Harlem Renaissance* (Bloomington: Indiana University Press, 2003); Axel Nissen, ed., *The Romantic Friendship Reader: Love Stories between Men in Victorian America* (Boston: Northeastern University Press, 2003); Gifford, ed., *Glances Backward: An Anthology of American Homosexual Writing, 1830–1920* (Toronto: Broadview Press, 2007); Nissen, *Manly Love: Romantic Friendship in American Fiction* (Chicago: University of Chicago Press, 2009); and Christopher Looby, "The Gay Novel in the United States, 1900–1950," in *A Companion to the Modern American Novel, 1900–1950*, ed. John T. Matthews (West Sussex: Wiley-Blackwell, 2009), 414–36.
3. Michael Bronski, ed., *Pulp Friction: Uncovering the Golden Age of Gay Male Pulps* (New York: St. Martin's Griffin, 2003); Drewey Wayne Gunn, *The Gay Male Sleuth in Print and Film: A History and Annotated Bibliography* (Lanham, MD: Scarecrow Press, 2005; rev. ed., 2013); Gunn, ed., *The Golden Age of Gay Fiction* (Albion, NY: MLR Press, 2009); Mark Mitchell and David Leavitt, eds., *Pages Passed from Hand to Hand: The Hidden Tradition of Homosexual Literature in English from 1748 to 1914* (Boston: Houghton Mifflin, 1997); Leavitt and Mitchell, eds., *The New Penguin Book of Gay Short Stories* (London: Viking, 2003); Mitchell, ed., *The Penguin Book of International Gay Writing* (with an introduction by Leavitt; New York: Penguin, 1995).
4. Carl Branch, *Idylls of the Queens* (San Diego: Greenleaf Classics, 1968), 46, 89, 91.
5. Ibid., 33.
6. The cover is reproduced in Gunn, *The Golden Age of Gay Fiction*, 228, and on the website *Gay on the Range: An Archive of Gay Paperback Artwork from the 50's and 60's*, www.gayontherange.com/a-z/.
7. Branch, *Idylls of the Queens*, 120.
8. Dick Dale, *The Fag End* (San Diego: Greenleaf Classics, 1968). The cover (which has little relationship to the actual novel) is also reproduced on the *Gay on the Range* website. (In fact, it is another novel by Dale that lends the site its name.)
9. Steven Marcus, The Other Victorians: A Study of Sexuality and Pornography in Mid-Nineteenth-Century England (New York: Basic Books, 1966), 261.

# Historicizing Pulp

## GAY MALE PULP AND THE NARRATIVIZATION OF QUEER CULTURAL HISTORY

Whitney Strub

The year was 1966. Writing for the homophile magazine *Tangents*, book critic Barbara Grier lamented, "It seems clear that the era of good Lesbian paperbacks is about over," the rare high-quality works driven out of sight by the profusion of tripe unleashed as obscenity laws fell by the wayside. Meanwhile, only a few months later, the gay magazine *Vector* celebrated the publication of Richard Amory's pulp novel *Song of the Loon* with "Well, here 'tis! The book you've all been waiting for," calling it an "erotic fantasy" of "great literary merit" that portended a fusion of gay pulp and gay pride.[1]

Several decades later, the tables had turned. Lesbian pulp fiction was perceived as integral to the emergence of modern lesbian community and identity—a "sort of 'how-to' of lesbian lust," the "closest thing to a Dewey decimal system for dykes," "poised on the threshold of a feminist vision of lesbian identity," as three scholars phrased it. The place of pulp authors Ann Bannon, Vin Packer, and Valerie Taylor in the lesbian pantheon was uncontested, and it was difficult to imagine a comprehensive lesbian history that did not account for the writing, circulation, and reading of lesbian pulp fiction as a critical force in fostering awareness and providing a social roadmap to midcentury lesbians. Certainly the valorization of lesbian pulp maintained a critical awareness that the legal, social, cultural, and political contexts of the Cold War era mandated mixed messages that blurred lesbian-friendly themes with sensationalized and homophobic content, but historians gave lesbian readers credit for ably navigating the textual disarray, reading against the grain, long before critical theorists coined that phrase, to selectively create meaning.[2]

As lesbian pulp caught the eye of historians, gay male pulp receded to the background. In roughly three decades of gay history written inside and outside the academy, gay pulp occupied the most tenuous of margins, almost never receiving the close, attentive treatment accorded its lesbian sibling. Some of the reasons for this omission are obvious. As an oppressed group, gay men nonetheless benefited from male privilege in a patriarchal society that afforded them greater access to the means of cultural production. Gay culture-work was thus more widely dispersed across the arts and media than lesbian efforts, making lesbian pulp more prominent in a cultural landscape of necessity less expansive than that of gay men (for instance, with the one exception of Dorothy Arzner, almost no lesbians—much less women altogether—worked as filmmakers in the first half-century or longer of the cinema). Because of the rich gay tradition in film, art, and literature, no necessity to emphasize pulp ever developed; with an iconography extending from Murnau to Warhol to Baldwin, aesthetics alone suggested that the admittedly purple prose of pulp fiction could never compete with the astonishing richness of more culturally legitimized gay contributions. Moreover, many of the great battles over free speech in gay history had been fought over films and magazines, bestowing historical importance to works on the frontlines of the legal struggle for gay equality but again leaving pulp fiction—affected by censorship and obscenity law but rarely taking center stage in memorable courtroom dramas—in the dustbin of historical memory.

That the social circulation of gay pulp merits historical inquiry is beyond doubt, regardless of its aesthetic quality (which arguably varied as widely as did lesbian pulp). Having proved lucrative for many years, including to some distributors with key links to gay rights activism, and having imparted imagery, characters, narratives, and eroticism to multiple generations of gay men and other interested observers, gay pulp fiction is simply a fact of the queer past. Why, then, has it gone so overlooked, even as the recovery of that past emerged as a major scholarly project beginning in the 1970s? In addition to the reasons I've mentioned, gay pulp fell between the cracks in the periodization of gay history. The homophile era, lasting from the early 1950s to the Stonewall rebellion of June 1969, relied on a model of respectability to gain acceptance in a violently hostile society. This bid for mainstream tolerance meant downplaying the role of anything that reinforced homophobic images of gay life—and pulp novels, with their lurid seediness, ran that risk. When Stonewall ushered in the newly sexualized, politically radical gay liberation movement, the often young activists who claimed to speak for it fashioned the movement as a break from a closeted gay past, and this rupture consigned much of the era that laid the groundwork for gay liberation behind that closet door. As hardcore gay porn won a triumph of the visual in the 1970s, pulp resided in its shadows, held down by an occasionally expressed baggage of "past"-ness that made it seem a relic in the face of the proud gay bodies onscreen.

Historians have done much to puncture the myths and narratives of both homophile and liberationist eras, with sophisticated critical analyses of the intents and use-values of those constructions. Pulp has remained at the margins of these efforts, however. While I make no particular claims for the merits of pulp beyond its undeniable social importance as a set of texts with a wide gay readership, both eras in question marginalized pulp, and historians in turn often left that marginalization unchallenged. With pulp increasingly understood as a crucial feature of gay cultural history, the convoluted dialectic between gay culture and politics—two terms with malleable semantic borders, to say the least—can be better understood. In other words, pulp provides a telling window into how gay historicity has self-consciously evolved over time.

## THE HOMOPHILE ERA

### UNDERWRITING THE MOVEMENT, WRITTEN OUT OF THE MOVEMENT

The great historiographical debate over the pre-Stonewall homophile movement centers on the role and function of respectability in activism and ideology. While historians unanimously agree that respectability marked and even in some ways defined the homophile era, contestations over the meaning of that framework have differed widely. One effect of this has been to perpetuate, in some ways, a narrativization of the homophile era that was inscribed during the era by the movement itself, with the borders between proper political activism and the disreputable nascent gay consumer culture of pulp fiction and physique magazines overstated in ways that downplay their intimate connections.

For instance, John D'Emilio's pioneering 1983 work on the homophile era, *Sexual Politics, Sexual Communities,* devoted separate chapters to the development of the pioneering Mattachine Society and its internal struggles as it forged a homophile agenda, and to the cultural realm of film, literature, and other media, where threats of censorship and obscenity prosecutions loomed large and thus structured queer expression in a multitude of ways. D'Emilio laid out the classic critique of homophile activism, detailing its "retreat to respectability" as the Mattachine moved from a radical underground group with sweeping social analysis that went beyond sexuality alone to a more moderate body with mainstream, assimilationist goals. D'Emilio rightly pointed out that utilizing "respectability" as an organizing principle necessarily meant abandoning radical critiques of Cold War nationalism and also carried with it connotations of hegemonic identity categories of middle-class, gender-normative whiteness that hampered homophile inclusiveness. Coming from an avowedly Marxist standpoint, D'Emilio's indictment of respectability pinpointed the Mattachine's shift from a class analysis of homosexuals as a distinct, oppressed social minority to one of homosexual "normalcy" in which only object-preference distinguished homosexuals from average Americans.[3]

All subsequent work on gay American history was heavily indebted to

D'Emilio's pathsetting study, but interpretive challenges gradually emerged, most strikingly in the work of Martin Meeker and Marc Stein, both of whom sought to refine the critique of respectability by more concretely situating it in the interplay between homophile activism and Cold War homophobia. In his 2001 article "Behind the Mask of Respectability," Meeker asserted that "a thorough reconsideration is now in order" of homophile respectability. "Rather than being a cowardly retreat," Meeker argued, homophile respectability constituted "a deliberate and ultimately successful strategy to deflect the antagonisms of its many detractors."[4] Favoring open visibility over the early communist-inspired secret cell organizing, for instance, was simply a smart tactic in the red-scare 1950s, not a craven gesture of complacency. Likewise, Stein's rich community study of midcentury gay and lesbian Philadelphia formulated the concept of "militant respectability," emphasizing the courage embodied in such homophile actions as the first gay-rights protest picket in 1965.[5]

Gay pulp fiction made few appearances in these narratives. Stein's study included a lengthy and brilliant examination of the Philadelphia activist Clark Polak, an entrepreneur whose magazine *Drum* (discussed later in this essay) aggressively "linked sexuality and politics in new ways."[6] Focusing on Polak's pictorial boundary-pushing, Stein left less examined his Trojan Book Service, a distribution unit that disseminated pulp fiction as well as more "reputable" works across the nation. Meeker's congruent reinterpretation of homophile practice located a similar link, in that two of the Mattachine's leaders, Hal Call and Don Lucas, ran a separate but concurrent publishing operation, the Pan-Graphic Press, whose Dorian Book Service likewise offered a slate of material that emphasized intellectually or aesthetically credible works but nonetheless included pulp as well. More interested in the anticensorship politics of the book service, Meeker said little about its frequently pulpy offerings.

While it bears stressing that the nature of Stein's and Meeker's projects mandated no particular necessity for highlighting pulp, especially since Call, Polak, and their associates served as somewhat disengaged distributors rather than more hands-on editors or publishers of pulp, the thread that their work jointly reveals but avoids emphasizing is the crucial role of pulp fiction in literally underwriting homophile activism. Frequently disparaged or simply disregarded by the official machinery of the movement, pulp fiction nonetheless supplied a source of revenue that links it more directly to the movement than its organizations preferred to acknowledge. The homophile movement did little to publicize this aspect of its operations, however, a deliberate distancing that effectively shaped historical memory.

Depending on the semantics of "pulp," one might assert not only that gay pulp fiction in fact predated the homophile movement, but even that it arose independently of the paperback revolution that spawned the proliferation of dimestore genre novels in the 1930s and 1940s.[7] By World War II an underground infrastructure of story-sharing existed, fueled primarily by desires outside the reaches of the capitalist market system. Often openly pornographic, going well beyond anything allowed for in hetero- or homosexual literary realms of the time, these stories were passed from man to man in mimeograph, typescript, and even handwritten form. Ranging in length from two quick pages to several dozen, these stories anticipated much of the iconography of pulp (sailors, rooming houses, eroticized police officers, high school athletes, etc.) but, because of their surreptitious and frankly illicit nature, made none of the concessions that market-based publishers found necessary due to obscenity laws. Proudly queer and highly graphic, the stories often celebrated public sex, group sex, and assorted other transgressive behaviors. "There Is No Harsh Detergent in the Blood of the Lamb," a nine-page typed story (undated, but circa 1950) details an archetypal trip to the big city; traveling by bus from Shelbyville, Indiana, to New York City, the unnamed narrator hears about a "gay rooming house on West 56th Street" from "a queen on the bus." Arriving, the narrator meets a "nice Puerto Rican kid" and says of their encounter, "I had never sucked an uncircumcised cock before and it was great." The slightly confused recipient mistakes desire for hustling and leaves ten dollars, inspiring the narrator to begin charging for his services. The story climaxes as the narrator sets up camp in a sixth-floor bathroom, fellating all who randomly enter. Before long, a line develops, and men arrive "from all over the building to the john to get their cocks sucked by the hustler—for free!" With that uncoupling of desire from the commodity market, the pleased narrator concludes.[8]

As that example shows, these proto-pulp stories evinced no indication of shame, pathology, or any of the other afflictions projected onto gay identity at the time. As they circulated, the stories reflected an awareness of history, with "Suppressed Scenes from the Memoirs of Fanny Hill" calling attention to the long-deleted "sodomitical" elements of the otherwise hetero-inclined smut classic. Others took an epistolary form that may or may not have been nonfictional; a 1947 example simply begins "Dear Bob" and proceeds to detail a sexual encounter between two men on "the evening before the Syracuse–Colgate football game." After dispensing with their female companions, the two men use the comparative measuring of their "pricks" as a pretext for quickly escalating contact in which "we fooled around until he suggested a fuck—up my ass." Laced with a realism worthy of Henry Miller's heterosexual tales, the tale continues: "We had to stop while he got some K-Y and in a minute I felt his cock in my ass-hole."[9]

Reproduced, traded, modified, and even annotated, these stories circulated for decades, a nexus of illegal expressions of desire facilitating precisely the communication networks upon which community-formation rests. "I could not have forgotten that you were interested in trading stories whenever it could be conveniently arranged," one man about to travel to San Francisco wrote another in 1962, suggesting they share bibliographies in advance to better size up their options. The letter-writer had "a couple more good ones which I have lent to a friend," and added "I am working on the acquisition of two or three good ones." Thomas Waugh has powerfully shown how the trading and sharing of gay visual erotica forged collective solidarity, legitimized desire, and constructed identity in the pre-Stonewall years, and clearly the same argument applies to the multiplicity of stories that traversed the nation through the mail system and traded hands in person, as gay men sought one another out and refined, classified, and articulated the varieties of queer desire embodied in the various stories.[10]

Much the same could be said of commercial pulp, with the qualification that its mediation by the various regulatory bodies (postal authorities, obscenity laws, publisher/distributor demands, etc.) embedded in the "free" market resulted in discernibly toned-down levels of raunch. The other essays in this collection, as well as those of its predecessor *The*

*Golden Age of Gay Fiction*, speak to the ways gay men frequently relied on pulp for all of the purposes I've mentioned. Gay books, in general, were rife with complexities at both the textual and the distributional levels, which were not always in sync. Michael de Forrest's *The Gay Year*, for instance, might "not demonize homosexuality," as Michael Bronski writes, but when it was published by the Jack Woodford Press in 1950, the company's titular head (a pseudonym for author Josiah Pitts Woolfolk) "blew his top" over being associated with "a fag book."[11] That gay men could extract from such books what they needed paralleled the contemporaneous efforts of lesbian readers, who routinely disregarded unhappy endings and anti-gay psychobabble to make their own meanings.

If profit motives targeting the exploitation of the homosexual niche market drove much gay pulp publication, the genre nonetheless remained intimately linked to the homophile movement. Hal Call took great pains to keep Pan-Graphic Press and its subsidiary, Dorian Book Service, organizationally distinct from homophile groups, but still dedicated them to buttressing the movement. "Everything Pan-Graphic Press does," he wrote in a 1960 letter, "is with the aim of supporting Mattachine and the homophile movement." He and cofounder Don Lucas kept the press privately owned, but devoted over 50 percent of its time to unpaid Mattachine service, including the printing of the *Mattachine Review*.[12] Even with a protective institutional distance to insulate the Mattachine from charges of disrepute, Dorian Book Service remained confined to a certain veneer of respectability by the prevailing standards of obscenity. "We attempt to avoid 'sex trash' reading," Call explained in private 1960 correspondence, adding that "we absolutely do not mail or handle any work declared obscene."[13] Not even that caution would protect Dorian from legal harassment, as when Washington, DC, customs officials seized several physique magazines headed to it from Europe in 1962.[14]

Nonetheless, neither respectability nor state persecution could stop Call's project from profiting off the sensationalized marketing of gay pulp fiction, which provided too lucrative a market to pass over. The July 1963 booklist offered by Dorian's *Book Quarterly* contains an indicative roster of openly tawdry pulp sanctified by no meaningful stabs at socially redeeming value whatsoever. The anonymously written *Male Bride*, a "scorching novel," detailed the "desperate yearnings" of the homosexual "twilight world of desire and dreams." Other titles skirted the border between pulp fiction and pseudo-scientific case study; Matt Bradley's *Homo Hill* (and sister volume *Lesbian Lane*) employed obvious pulp titling tropes to frame purportedly true reporting "in a manner to appeal to the sidewalk voyeur." While the effect was one of apparent pulp nonfiction, the format carried an intended use-value. "These two books don't really damn homosexuality and its expression," the booklist blurb promised, explaining that "as nonfiction documentaries, containing pulp histories, their timber is presumed to be too tough for the censor's axe." This confluence of pulp thrills, legitimizing form (or subterfuge), and antihomophobic presentation typified the Dorian method.[15]

As Call and Lucas harnessed pulp to underwrite homophile ends, the movement itself kept a cautious distance. *ONE*, an offshoot of internecine Mattachine factionalism, validated homophile tactics when it won a landmark Supreme Court case in 1958. Having been withheld from the mails on grounds of obscenity, the magazine persevered despite losing at every rung of the judicial ladder, finally appealing to the highest court in the nation, even though it found little legal support even from such free-speech defenders as the ACLU, still then complicit in governmental homophobia. In celebrating its victory, though, *ONE* took a careful posture, accepting a normative superstructure in which "it can be agreed that being 'against smut' is entirely praiseworthy, but first we must find out what 'smut' is." *ONE* offered no definition, relying on unstated but evident premises that distinguished its reputable, political stance from that of tawdry, lurid pulp and physique material.[16]

*ONE*'s position was not without its convolutions, but it navigated them ably within the constraints of homophile respectability. When the *Los Angeles Times* published an attack on smut in early 1961, *ONE* responded with a defense of free speech that delicately avoided endorsing the material at hand. Its author, Dale Mallory, wrote that "literary merit is a virtue generally lacking in the [pulp fiction] paperback novels being attacked," and he repeatedly emphasized that his rejection of censorship should not be confused with an endorsement of the "trash" that was "somewhat depressing" to acknowledge as popular among the reading public (and, though Mallory treaded carefully around the distinction, among the gay counterpublic much more susceptible to such anti-smut campaigns).[17]

In assessing pulp directly, which it infrequently but periodically did, *ONE* took a measured approach. Reviewing the anonymous novel *All the Sad Young Men* in 1962, Edward Denison chided it for wallowing in the "lurid aspects of the gay world," but found redeeming values in the ways the text of the book chafed against its sensationalized graphic design; while the back cover called it a tale of "lost souls," in fact, Denison noted, this was "somewhat misleading" as the novel charted pleasures and companionship alongside moral decline. Ultimately, Denison dismissed the novel but acknowledged its entertainment value. In a similar manner, writing a year earlier, the lesbian pulp author Ann Bannon, in a survey titled "Secrets of the Gay Novel," attributed "special strength" to novelists in their use of character and narrative to shape reader perception. Bannon avoided sanctimony, knowing quite intimately the market pressures that compelled even well-intended authors to "manufacture a little excitement" in their stories. The danger, though, was that "the prose will get a little too hot and the picture will become perverted beyond all connection with reality." Without being counterbalanced against humanized, three-dimensional representation of gay life, this "pure hack work" was, Bannon contended, "doing vicious harm to homosexuals everywhere." Bannon avoided naming names, though her article clearly favored conventionally literary writing over the sleazier sort.[18]

The *Mattachine Review* complemented *ONE* in representing the dominant face of the homophile movement, although the two publications' respective editors felt sizable hostility toward each other, which sometimes came through in the pages.[19] While *ONE* hardly neglected gay literature, the *Review* offered more expansive book reviews, covering everything from the latest psychology monographs to numerous gay and lesbian novels in almost every issue. Its stance toward gay pulp fiction began on a distinctly disparaging note, softening over time but rarely approaching endorsement. Like *ONE*, it tended to commend the more reputable aspects of pulp, chiding the cheap thrills. Jay Little's novel *Somewhere Between the Two* actually appeared as a hardback from a vanity press (a choice that probably indicates the higher esteem hardbacks had), but it has all the qualities of a pulp (a status it assumed in 1965). It won a harsh review in 1956 for the "predictable interval" at which sex scenes appeared. The critic, Richard Mayer, complained that such scenes "are described in explicit, even alarming detail, in words of unmistakable meaning and fancy language, much of which I am convinced has no meaning whatsoever." Even in acknowledging that the novel "does report accurately the way a great many homosexuals live," Mayer reminded homophile readers that it had "no literary merit."[20]

Deborah Deutsch's pulplike *The Flaming Heart* (which also appeared as a hardback in 1958, and then as a pulp in 1966), a 1959 review suggested, failed at achieving full pulpiness ("not quite as effectively salacious" as most) but managed to be "not quite as submoronic as others" in the genre—which was the extent of reviewer Jack Parrish's praise. By 1962 the *Mattachine Review*'s position on pulp had settled into bemused condescension; Roger Davis's *Always Love a Stranger* was described as simply "another of the run-of-the-mill, undistinguished but quite readable and enjoyable homosexual novels appearing as paperback originals."[21] Barbara Grier's "Literary Scene" column of the 1960s (written under the pseudonym Gene Damon) offered staggeringly comprehensive surveys of gay and lesbian literature, and periodically included brief but substantive discussions of gay pulp. Discovering Robert Chessman's 1960 novel *The Park Jungle* in 1964, for instance, Grier warned, "Don't be overly put off by the hideous tasteless covers still used by the 'sensation' paperback houses . . . [because sometimes] a garish front on a paperback original from a lower rate publishing house hides a really good book." Chessman's episodic novel, set in and around New York's Central Park, won Grier's praise for its effective use of place and "very well-drawn characters."[22]

Even in praising Chessman's book, however, Grier clearly set it apart from the mass of undifferentiated pulp fiction forming the dim backdrop against which it shone. Other homophiles of the decade agreed. Writing in *Vector*, published by San Francisco's Society for Individual Rights, James Ramp mused, "Why do we read homophile literature?" Concerned "only with books which dignify the Community and love," Ramp valorized the literary aspirations of several hardcovers while excluding pulp from his notion of "homophile literature." *Vector* carefully policed homophile boundaries throughout the decade. When it gave Richard Amory's massively popular *Song of the Loon* a positive review in 1967, it acknowledged the "four letter words that 'nice' people find horrifying" but qualitatively distinguished the book from pornography on grounds of "the pace, style, poetry of passionate description and the awareness of nature," all of which bore "great literary merit." The next year, responding to a commission on pornography and obscenity established by the Lyndon Johnson administration, a *Vector* reader asserted that "any connection" drawn between porn and homophile activism constituted "a disservice to the movement and an affront to the majority of homosexuals who are not interested in pornography," written or pictorial. Even with Stonewall about to explode, the homophile movement maintained the mantle of respectability.[23]

In this context, some publishers kept a cautious distance from the movement, even while supporting its aims. H. Lynn Womack, a publisher outside formal homophile auspices, published both pulp fiction and physique magazines through his Guild Press. Though trafficking heavily in pulp, Womack's Guild Book Service also delivered such wares as Walter Ross's novel *The Immortal*, a transparent retelling of James Dean's life, with, in the service's own words, "sex as the dominant theme." Attempting to spice up the book for a gay audience, the service's sales pitch read, "Our hero, upon being chided for alleged associations with faggots, remarked, 'God, man, why pass up a whole sex?' " As Womack served up such prose with a smirk, he made no attempt to valorize the works on which he profited (which was pilloried in the *Mattachine Review*, whose reviewer noted that *The Immortal* "sometimes gets gruesome in detail. . . . That kind of reading, it seems, has become popular these days"). While the Guild Book Service carried serious works by John Rechy, Donald Webster Cory, Jean Genet, and Hubert Selby, its very first bulletin in 1963 announced that such literature would coexist with "a certain amount of trash" for its readers. "This will be described for what it is," the bulletin continued, "and no pretense made that it is anything other than something with which to kill an otherwise dull evening."[24]

Despite his lack of acclaim from homophiles, Womack went on to secure the next major gay Supreme Court victory, when his right to send physique magazines through the mails was upheld by the Court in 1962, in *Manual Enterprises v. Day.* Though the court held its nose at the "dismally unpleasant, uncouth, and tawdry" nature of Womack's wares, it asserted that homoerotic representations must be held to the same standards of obscenity as hetero-oriented erotica.[25] A landmark precedent by any standard, *Manual Enterprises* would later support arguments for the relevance of physique magazines to gay history, but because Womack's pulp operations had not been the primary target of government persecution in the case, pulp again garnered little acclaim.

As these events were happening, Call and Lucas were wise to keep Pan-Graphic and Dorian distinct from Mattachine—partly in terms of self-interest, since one privately expressed reason was to secure the stability of their positions amid the tumult of mid-1950s internal homophile politics, but also because efforts to weld homophile activism to the presumed sordidness of pulp fiction and physique photography ended poorly for Clark Polak, the first to fully attempt that union. An engaged member of regional homophile groups, and also the operator of the pulp-friendly Trojan Book Service and publisher of the erotic/political magazine *Drum*, Polak found himself in tension with the East Coast Homophile Organizations (ECHO) for his efforts.

Even those such as Polak, willing to capitalize on pulp, had little of warmth to say about it. While Trojan's catalogs offered panoplies of textual pleasures, with the salacious "erotic case histories" of the pulp-apotheosis *The Tortured Sex* listed next to works by Isherwood, Cory, and other more reputable titles, *Drum* took a militant stance toward sexual rights, most notoriously in its groundbreaking publishing of full-frontal nude photographs in 1965, to that point unheard of in an erotic context.[26] "The free sale and display of literature designed for homosexual pleasure," Polak claimed, "serves to improve the well-being of the community through the promotion of happier citizens in addition to heralding the emergence of less repressive societal attitudes."[27]

Neither Polak's profiting from pulp through the Trojan Book Service nor his effort to demystify sex through open erotic expression found much favor from the organized homophile movement. Indeed, ECHO unceremoniously expelled Clark's Janus Society in 1965, finding his efforts detrimental to the respectable homophile project.[28] In denying physique magazines a place in the homophile movement, the Mattachine Society of Washington explained, "They try to cater simultaneously to physical and intellectual interests—which should remain separate." Its conclusion that "a distinction must be made between the serious and the pleasurable" applied as easily to pulp as physique—though the fact that the Mattachine did not bother explaining so was itself telling.[29] Even as the sexual revolution began, public representations of gay sexuality remained caught between movement imperatives and a youth generation informed less by Cold War strictures than the increasing permissiveness of the 1960s. Neither camp embraced gay pulp fiction; to the homophiles it carried the threat of disrepute, while to the younger generation (about to coalesce around the idea of gay liberation), ironically, it would carry the cultural baggage of the homophile movement.

The Stonewall-era Mattachine Society of New York (MSNY) reflected the tensions (and cultural hierarchies) of late-homophile thought. MSNY's executive director, Dick Leitsch, continued to frame the group's primary function as that of "a protective agency" in mid-1968, listing its achievements in the political and legal arenas to a physique photographer who wrote inquiring about lawyers who might guide him through current obscenity laws. Far from taking a critical stance toward the man's photography, though, Leitsch asked whether MSNY might pass along models to him, since the group also received frequent requests from models for photographer contact information.[30]

While Leitsch embraced visual representation of the naked male body as part of the homophile agenda, his stance toward pulp novels remained one of disdain. In 1967, when an entrepreneur requested to license MSNY's name to create the Mattachine Book Service, Leitsch and the governing board skeptically agreed. By 1968, though, their minds had changed, and a discernibly irate Leitsch sent a letter to the book service's manager discontinuing their relationship. The service's list, he complained, "consisted of nothing but trite, trashy, lurid, sensational material which could not help but give the Society an image different from the one we have tried so hard to build." Even this material, Leitsch continued, might be acceptable were it balanced by "the standard classics, or the new and important books on homosexuality," but in appealing strictly to "the lowest common denominator of intelligence and taste," the book service did a disservice to its namesake. Drawing a firm distinction between the "patrons of 42nd Street bookshops," who might support the service, and Mattachine members, who "are above average in taste and intelligence, and cannot be appealed to on the low level your service is trying to appeal to," Leitsch went beyond policing the public image of his group to make unfounded assumptions about its members. When the book service disregarded MSNY's repeated notices, an incensed Leitsch demanded the New York District Attorney's office prosecute for fraud in July 1969—two weeks after Stonewall—invoking Mattachine's "honest, decent and respectable" reputation.[31]

The discrepancy between Leitsch's friendly stance toward explicit photography and his hostility toward "trashy" novels suggests an emerging notion of gay pride, one in which erotic interest in the visual representation of the naked body was assimilated into that pride, whereas tawdry pulp novels simply reflected poorly on their sad, lonely readers. In the homophile tradition, Leitsch also conflated political self-positioning with personal proclivities. Respectability had been devised along instrumentalist lines of self-preservation in a violently hostile world, but Leitsch blithely mapped it onto homophile activists' erotic interests, simply locating the Mattachine Book Service's line beneath them. Pulp fiction had no purchase in this economy of desire, which continued to privilege culturally ennobled articulations of eros ("classics," presumably possessed of "intelligence and taste"), while tacitly—and inconsistently—endorsing visual erotica, unburdened by the historical baggage read into pulp.

Leitsch's stance reflected the tensions of the homophile movement by the late 1960s, as it tried to accommodate both the respectability framework and the imperatives of sexual revolution announced by Polak, devising an implicit cultural hierarchy of erotica. In the months and even years before and after Stonewall, this effort to contain desire within the confines of respectability grew increasingly untenable. As the steady weakening of obscenity laws helped generate a veritable flood-tide of smut across the nation, both verbal and visual pornography accelerated their march toward open hardcore. The proper death knell of homophile respectability was arguably not Stonewall, but rather the 1967 opening of the Adonis Bookstore in San Francisco, which marked the transformation of Hal Call from movement architect (in his suit-and-tie 1950s Mattachine leadership role) into smut-entrepreneur guru.

By the mid-1960s Call openly "preferred erotica to the old maid of Mattachine," and publication of the *Mattachine Review* languished after 1964. With Adonis, Call went well beyond anything undertaken by the Dorian Book Service earlier in the decade; while much of his attention focused on just how engorged the penises of his naked pictorial models could grow without incurring legal action from the authorities, Adonis also carried various magazines and pulp novels, combining Leitsch's vaunted classics with more tawdry fare.[32]

Call's openly and unapologetically pornographic endeavor climaxed with the addition of the CineMattachine in 1973, a small adult theater grafted onto the Adonis Bookstore. While by that point the younger generation had abandoned "homophile" as an organizing term and adopted the gay liberation mantle, Call continued to proudly present himself as executive director of the Mattachine Society in his correspondence with San Francisco's chief of police. This belated convergence of homophile organization and smut was intended to capitalize on the Mattachine legacy (well into the 1970s, Call continued to invoke the organization in CineMattachine advertising), but it also brought to surface how sheerly instrumentalist the respectability framework had been: discarded by its very progenitor as soon as the cultural shifts of the sexual revolution allowed, it functioned as a sheltering awning against the harsh investigative spotlight of Cold War homophobia, not as the constitutive substance of homophile aspirations.[33]

Leitsch's presumptions notwithstanding, homophile activists had never disavowed their diverse erotic interests, merely policed the public appearance of them in the name of expediency. By the time this was obvious, in Adonis or CineMattachine or any number of comparable endeavors, the obsolescence of the homophile movement in the eyes of the burgeoning gay liberation movement rendered any substantive public discussion of the issue moot. This history would be lost in the reconfiguration of gay activism set in motion by Stonewall, as the homophile era gave way to a gay liberation built on a new historical narrative. Pulp invisibility would be one of the few constants to hold during this shift.

## THE STONEWALL MOMENT
### FROM HISTORICITY TO HISTORIOGRAPHY

The Stonewall rebellion of 1969 did not emerge out of a vacuum, but rather crystallized several trajectories already in motion, most notably the youth-led rebellion against the confines of homophile respectability. Almost immediately, though, Stonewall took on iconic status, representing a radical break with the old activism. For gay liberation activists, informed by the strains of the 1960s—black nationalism, radical feminism, sexual revolution, youth culture, and so forth—the homophile movement could only be read as part of a conformist Cold War 1950s. Without question reductionist and ahistorical, this perspective nonetheless proved the window through which respectability as a tactic became legible for the younger generation, which read it primarily through its obsolescence to their own experience. Thus, almost immediately with the formation of the Gay Liberation Front (GLF) in 1969, the politics of respectability were retroactively assigned qualities of complacency, meekness, and "closetedness," a conceptual innovation designed by gay liberationists to distinguish their "coming out" process of public openness and visibility from the perceived shame and secrecy of their forebears.

That all of this distorted the past to read it through the prism of the liberationist present has been well noted by historians, who compellingly argue that this backward projection of the closet was anachronistic at best, given that earlier generations had long "come out" into the gay world but avoided public pronouncement to the straight world for reasons ranging from the lack of a need to the material reality of state-inflicted violence or incarceration.[34] Yet the kindest words Carl Wittman's 1970 "Gay Manifesto" could find for homophile groups was that "reformist or pokey as they sometimes are, they are our brothers."[35] The effect of this revisionist history on pulp was largely—but tacitly—to consign it to the homophile past of "the closet." That pulp had held an ambivalent relationship at best with those groups mattered little; what appeared most obvious to gay liberationists is that both bore the stigma of the closeted past—a collapsing of "past" into "closet" necessary for a movement that envisioned itself emerging sui generis from the rebellious energy of the gay youth generation for whom Molotov cocktails at Stonewall superseded the suits and ties of homophile pickets.

In this framework, the blatant coding of Cold War gay pulp—the "twilight," "shadows," sideways cover-art glances, and other tropes that so clearly signified queerness at the time—ceded ground to direct and unambiguous declarations of gayness. The art historian Richard Meyer has shown that the GLF "positioned visibility . . . as a key component of its broader mission," in a way that privileged visual markers of queerness as the standard-bearers of gay liberation.[36] As a result, the culture workers who assumed primacy around the Stonewall moment were largely filmmakers, particularly erotic filmmakers; what "serious" literary authors had been to the homophile era, proud pornographers were to the liberation era, when the asserting of gay sexuality into the public sphere took a place of centrality, in response to both homophile desexualization and the still violently homophobic dominant culture.

Thus Pat Rocco, who shot and screened the first openly gay erotic films at the Park Theater in downtown Los Angeles in 1968, was often feted by the gay press. In short films like *A Very Special Friend*, *The Performance*, and *Disneyland Discovery*, Rocco celebrated a playful, boyish, but assertively gay sexuality, in part by situating his (generally naked, or imminently so) male characters in public space, a cinematic act of place-claiming that deployed visual evidence to make undeniable the gay presence in a variety of Los Angeles areas, from Hollywood Boulevard to Griffith Park to even Orange County's bastion of normalcy, Disneyland. The gay press responded by positioning Rocco as a break from a past whose vestiges still lingered. "Though the gay life has been much liberated in recent years," Jim Kepner wrote in a 1970 *GAY* article, "too much homosexual art still carries an overlay of guilt and shame. Rocco's work does not."[37]

The weakening of obscenity laws over the course of the 1960s resulted in public screenings of both straight and gay hardcore porn by the dawn of the 1970s. Where Rocco stopped at naked frolics, Wakefield Poole explicitly linked his 1971 breakout hit *Boys in the Sand* to the liberationist project. Following its star, Casey Donovan (whose Robert Redford–like looks helped draw attention to the film), through a series of sexual encounters on Fire Island, the film adopted a policy of maximum visibility, depicting its sex scenes in graphic, unsimulated detail. Poole distanced the film from the seamier side of gay culture ("There are no forced acts, no sadism, no degradation element," he said), and framed it as a political effort. "The whole time I made the film," he explained, "I thought of the gay lib slogan, Gay Is Beautiful." And indeed, when *Gay Activist* claimed in 1972 that "most American pornography, gay and straight, is peculiarly unliberated," it made an exception for *Boys.* The history of gay pulp lay enveloped in the unexplicated interstices of that peculiar unliberation.[38]

Rounding out the heroicized triumvirate of filmic gay eros was Fred Halsted, whose 1972 *L.A. Plays Itself* delved further into kinky sadomasochism than Rocco or Poole. Halsted expertly capitalized on willful perversity to claim the mantle of gay liberation's counternormative drive and used movement language to describe his filmmaking process. "Making the film was my liberation," he said, "my coming out of the closet." With a prominent ad-blurb from John Francis Hunter of the Gay Activists Alliance and Halsted's remarkable success in forcing the *New York Times*'s hand by refusing its usual "all male cast" label to win the first use of "homosexual" in the paper's movie ads, *L.A. Plays Itself* came to represent the liberationist ethos for many.[39] Halsted even became the literal voice of gay porn cinema's self-narrativization as the narrator of the 1973 hardcore history lesson *Erotikus,* which chronicled the emergence of gay hardcore with copious clips.

No pulp author emerged to parallel the filmmakers in prominence and political valorization. The liberalization of obscenity law had allowed fiction, like film, to grow increasingly graphic, but written texts found themselves in the shadows of beefcake magazines and cinema—a triumph of the visual that paralleled GLF's stance. Richard Amory, arguably the first celebrity pulp author of liberationist circles, capitalized on the success of *Song of the Loon* to expand the novel into a trilogy, but by 1970 he was convening other pulp authors for a panel to discuss the "plight of gay novelists," while fellow pulp writer Dirk Vanden accused Greenleaf Classics of leading the "Fag-Exploitation" game on multiple levels. A disillusioned Amory agreed, comparing the editors to "classic dirty old men selling fuck-pictures in dark alleys" who lacked compassion for, or even interest in, gay issues. Amory staked a clear position, arguing that "jackoff books have a valid place in our literature" but wanting to incorporate "social and political content" alongside the sex—something his publisher fought against. Insisting that gay novels should be "*put out by a gay publisher,*" he reflected the material constraints of pulp; unlike the filmmakers who controlled rights over their work (at this point—arguably because gay porn had not yet taken shape as an industry), pulp novelists remained beholden to straight financial interests.[40]

To be sure, gay publishing firms still existed, though not always with reputations distinctly better than their straight peers. Womack's Guild Press, for instance, deeply alienated Samuel Steward by binding him to a contract and then leaving his classic-to-be "Phil Andros" hustler novel *$tud* unpublished for three years.[41] In the late 1960s, Guild capitalized on faltering obscenity laws by issuing cheap chapbook editions of the old typescript sex stories that circulated in earlier decades. Offered with plain covers bereft of artwork—whether as a stylistic throwback to the plain-wrapper era or a budget-cutting device by Womack is unclear—the Black Knight Classics series billed itself as "classics from the homosexual underground," with titles like *Boxing Camp*, *The Boys of Muscle Beach*, and *A Crack in the Wall*. Each opened with an introductory manifesto titled "The Meaning and Value of Homosexual Literature," which claimed that "these stories are not devoid of social importance, and they were not padded with 'social significance' in order that they might be legitimately sold. They always had something important to say about the human condition, even while they also aroused and amused"—which served both to ward off possible prosecutors and to assert political significance.[42]

In recontextualizing "closet"-era smut as proto-liberationist cultural agitation, Black Knight Classics smartly assessed the tenor of the times. What had once been of necessity covert could now circulate with impunity, and

Guild even tactically intervened in the stories to adjust them to the era. *I Found What I Wanted* had circulated as an untitled twenty-six-page story in earlier decades, its graphic descriptions of "plung[ing] my cock deeper into his hot mouth and nearly gag[ging] him" inconceivable at the height of Cold War repressiveness. While the story in its earlier form (which quite likely had multiple permutations) already ended on an unrepentantly gay note, with "fresh out of high school" Bill Jones going from "dread[ing] the thought that I could be a fairy, a queer, a pansy, a fruit" to ultimately embracing long-term companionship with his partner ("I still get a tremendous thrill out of seeing him step from the shower dripping wet," it originally ended), the 1969 Guild version tacked on a somewhat gratuitous, but timely, final reflection: "I lay back in my bed and said, 'Well, if you are gay, might as well accept it as a fact. If God allows guys to love each other and be sexually attracted, it must be natural even if society doesn't approve of it!' "[43]

Guild's bid for liberationist approval ran up against market forces, however. The glut wrought by the late-1960s smut explosion weakened Guild's commitment to a gay focus; as an editor wrote to an aspiring gay pulp novelist in 1971, the press was "looking for manuscripts of heterosexual nature at this time," due to the "oversupply of homosexual type novels on hand."[44] While surely appreciated by veterans of its era, the series never drew the attention of its filmmaking contemporaries.

When Steward's *$tud* was finally published, it joined Amory's work in the tiny pulp canon. But Steward, an idiosyncratic tattoo artist with a doctorate in English, refused to align himself with gay liberation. Though he had first begun writing the Phil Andros stories in the 1960s to counter the dismal vision of John Rechy, and though the first Andros story published in the United States appeared in the activist-minded *Drum*, Steward kept a frosty distance from the movement. Even when an *Advocate* editor enticed him to review pulp novels in the mid-1970s, Steward "accommodated him—but grimly," according to his biographer. Steward's reviews were hardly celebratory, and he referred to the major pulp publishing houses as churning out "unbelievable excrement."[45]

The liberation-era gay press featured pulp authors and sometimes incorporated their voices into the movement imaginary. Most continued to perceive themselves as only tenuously included. Speaking to *GAY* in 1970, Dirk Vanden outlined his view of a more imaginative pornography, but when asked what the next step should be, called for "more respect for the readers. And the authors themselves, who have been misunderstood and mistreated by publishers too long."[46] Likewise, the S/M novelist Larry Townsend wrote in *Vector* the next year that the bar was rather low to success as a gay pulp author—a mixed blessing, with "success" a very relative term. Douglas Dean (the pseudonym used by Dean Goodman), three years later, insisted, "I'm not a snob. I have nothing against pornography, per se. The fuck books have their place." He could not, however, disguise his resentment over his own thoughtful novel *Return Engagement* being outsold by *Clint Wins His Letter*, a sex-filled pulp "without any story line or central theme."[47]

That same year, 1973, a gay liberation conference in New Jersey reflected split opinions on pulp. For one participant, Tina Mandel, "most badly-written gay books" (presumably pulp), lapsed into a "closet mentality" on account of their "masochistic state of mind." For another participant, though, cheap paperbacks, with their embrace of gay lust *and* identity, constituted "some of the most positive literature for homosexuals." While a report published in *GAY* presented both sides, its title favored the former: "Closet Novels Called Dangerous." With "closet" loosely defined, its application continued to extend toward representations deemed backward-looking or politically untenable.[48]

Meanwhile, the liberationist celebration of sexuality did not always equate to comfort with its commodification. Suggestions that pornography in fact countered true sexual liberation ran back to critiques by such intellectuals as Herbert Marcuse and other members of the Frankfurt School of the media and capitalism's capturing of the worker body. While this did result in criticism of the porn filmmakers (though the most common complaint was simply inflated ticket prices), it played out most palpably in print media spheres. Craig Rodwell's Oscar Wilde Memorial Book Shop in New York City provides a key example. When it opened in 1967, Rodwell's refusal to carry smut fit then-reigning homophile notions. Disparaging "dirty old men" in a 1968 interview, he said "they wander in, look around and in about 30 seconds are on the street again." Interested "only in good and serious material," Rodwell—like his Mattachine peer Dick Leitsch—drew an unfounded distinction between presumptively young and clean-minded homophiles and the "DOMs," as he called them.[49]

As the 1970s took shape, Rodwell embraced gay liberation, rearticulating his position in its new terms. Rejecting porn for reducing gayness to "totally sexual phenomena," Rodwell found many supporters over the decade. One man seeking to emulate the Oscar Wilde Memorial Book Shop in San Francisco wrote Rodwell for advice, bemoaning the "trashy gay sex novels" that "don't instill a sense of pride in a gay person." When the owner of the Stonewall Memorial Bookshop in Chicago contacted Rodwell in 1977, he complained that many people assumed his was a porn bookshop. Rodwell congratulated him and endorsed his efforts over a competitor, which Rodwell called "a sexist dump" for selling gay smut. Another fan wrote from Madison, Wisconsin, also hoping to open a "non-pornographic" gay bookstore.[50]

When these men invoked "pride," they assigned it a specific, post-Stonewall meaning, one that certainly applied most meaningfully (or easily) to a relatively affluent, educated, urban demographic. Adherence to this form of "out" pride was requisite for inclusion in gay liberation. Thus, when the magazine *Christopher Street* published a 1977 cover story on Nazi persecution of gays that might be read as erotic, flyers went around Greenwich Village calling for a boycott; "They are *using* gay liberation as a vehicle for the expression of a detestable genre of pornography," it read.[51] In short, new standards of conduct and expression had been developed; more sexual, oppositional, and diverse than those of the homophile era, they nonetheless amounted to a normative regime of "liberated" propriety. Pulp fiction, while rarely excoriated, was also marginal at best to this cultural construct. Superseded by visual porn on one end, tainted by the vestigial traces of "the closet" on the other, treated poorly by publishers, critics, and bookshops, pulp continued to exist as a cultural orphan.

Certainly gay pulp laid claim to liberationist credibility. Blueboy Library, published out of Santee, California, put into practice some of the ideals advocated by Richard Amory with its pulpy, erotic novels whose explicit sex scenes were invariably prefaced by declarations of political sentiment. Unlike the boilerplate Black Knight Classics statements, Blueboy's introductions always related to the book in question. The introduction to Murray Montague's *Security Risk* (1976), named after the coded term used to dismiss gays and lesbians from federal employment during the Cold War, reminded readers that "homosexual civil rights are still at issue in this, a country representing itself as the beacon of liberty to the rest of the modern world," and linked anti-gay politics to the earlier efforts of "McCarthy and his ilk." Sydney Harper's sexed-up police thriller *Two, the Hard Way* (1976) began with an introduction suggesting that it "might well be viewed as an argument for an end to discrimination in public employment from the standpoint of individual sexual preference"—and then supplied extensive sexual thrills alongside its message.[52]

Certainly these issues pertained to gay readers; Cold War anti-gay policies still lingered, and the question of gays serving on police forces remained a heated issue, with homophobic LAPD chief Ed Davis continuing to declare himself "appalled" that the Los Angeles City Council would consider mandating nondiscrimination regarding sexual orientation as recently as 1975.[53] Yet pulp continued to fall outside the auspices of the developing gay canon. When *Gay Activist* surveyed "paperback gays" in 1979, it still privileged the culturally legitimized higher-brow output of Baldwin, Rechy, Vidal, and others. Both Larry Kramer's *Faggots* and Andrew Holleran's *Dancer from the Dance* appeared in 1978, making it a banner year in gay fiction; as those two authors and several equally prominent contemporaries formed the Violet Quill, self-consciously cultivating an image of gay literary renaissance, they distanced themselves from the past in typical liberationist fashion. They "did not know or care very much about the novels of the late 1940s and early 1950s," their chronicler explains, nor did pulp figure into their reflexively generated genealogy.[54]

Another key moment of gay canon-formation occurred with the publishing of Roger Austen's *Playing the Game: The Homosexual Novel in America* in 1977. Austen's exhaustive study of gay representation ranged from the nineteenth century to the 1970s, but found little space for pulp. When he did discuss the field, Austen employed a curiously anomalous armchair psychoanalysis not applied to other texts, which he generally read quite deftly. While he took the dismissive liberationist party line toward "middle-class Mattachine accomodationists," his discussion of Jay Little harked back to the *Mattachine Review*'s scolding tone, as Austen read Little through his work, blithely declaring that Little's poorly written sex scenes reveal that "the author is quite obviously compensating for past frustrations through the ploy of wish-fulfillment fantasy." The greater nuance and sympathy Austen showed toward other authors made such assessments as much political as aesthetic, like the Violet Quill's devising a particular sense of liberated historicity in which pulp had little apparent place.[55]

As pulp's historical significance remained marginal, gay filmic porn again rose to prominence as the 1980s dawned. While the years after Poole's and Halsted's hardcore landmarks had witnessed an undeniable flattening of hardcore horizons as the genre lapsed into more formulaic product, the feminist antiporn movement emerging from the late 1970s put gay men on the defensive. Antiporn feminists targeted pornography as a cultural tool of women's subjugation, promoting an objectification that facilitated patriarchal rape culture. But their analysis often sprawled beyond heterosexual smut to include gay porn, which they accused of perpetuating similar structures of spectatorship. When *Gay Community News* interviewed the antiporn leader Robin Morgan in 1979, she pulled no punches, arguing that "men, whether heterosexual or homosexual, have a vested interest in pornography" that made lines of sexual orientation less important than phallocentric modes of objectification.[56]

Many gay men found this critique threatening in the ways it offered the homophobic mainstream culture an ostensibly progressive framework on which to hang further anti-gay policies. Indeed, by 1984 the same newspaper was blaming antiporn feminism for "the arrest of nearly 3500 Gays in adult bookstores and elsewhere" in the past three years. With the battle lines thus drawn, gay scholars launched impassioned defenses of gay porn that returned it to the center of gay history, as an illicit, historically suppressed record of desire.[57]

Visual porn bore the brunt of feminist antiporn arguments (although Andrea Dworkin did single out the homoerotic, albeit homophobic, smut novel *I Love a Laddie* in her 1981 manifesto *Pornography: Men Possessing Women*), and as a response powerful gay defenses of cinematic porn emerged, distinguishing the oppositional history of gay smut from the oppressive history of heterosmut. With Thomas Waugh developing the argument of his 1985 *Jump Cut* essay into an astonishingly wide-ranging 1996 monograph on gay male visual erotica from the dawn of photography to Stonewall, filmic and photographic gay smut were firmly entrenched in the gay historical memory as integral parts of the genealogy of gay identity and desire. Once more, pulp fared more poorly, earning no such political merit badge.[58]

The formal recognition of gay history as a legitimate field of study developed against this backdrop of 1980s sex wars. While such public historians as Jonathan Ned Katz had pioneered the field in the prior decade, it was the publication of John D'Emilio's *Sexual Politics, Sexual Communities: The Making of a Homosexual Minority in the United States, 1940–1970* in 1983 that truly forced the academy to open its doors, with the social capital and research funding that entailed. D'Emilio, writing from a liberationist perspective, took a critical stance toward the homophile movement's politics, but in other regards his book accepted the manufactured distinction between the movement and pulp/physique culture. In this respect, the homophile era succeeded in cultivating and perpetuating its own historical narrative; while *assessments* of the respectability framework would vary, its place of centrality would not, dominating the historiography for decades. D'Emilio gave glancing attention to gay fiction, crediting the burgeoning genre with the cultivation of "the sense of belonging to a group" in a hostile era, but when he turned to the seamier side of paperback fiction, his discussion of pulp was devoted to lesbian novels, with only a quick nod to Richard Amory's *Song of the Loon*. Barry Adam's *Rise of a Gay and Lesbian Movement* had even less to say on the matter.[59]

In breaking new ground, these early works laid the template for much of the LGBT history to follow, particularly in the separation of activism from culture. In the first two decades of scholarly gay history (the 1980s and 1990s, roughly), pulp fiction made recurring cameo appearances, suggesting its historical significance, but rarely received sustained treatment. Some of the best social histories of queer communities grounded pulp in the material conditions of gay life. George Chauncey's pivotal 1994 study, *Gay New York*, noted the "flurry of gay-themed novels" appearing between 1931 and

1934 (when the end of Prohibition foreclosed a somewhat tolerant attitude toward gay urban life). With such titles as *Twilight Men, Butterfly Man,* and *A Scarlet Pansy,* these books clearly portended the future of gay pulp, but Chauncey was unable to fully examine them (or the reading practices of their consumers) in his expansive book, acknowledging in a footnote that these novels "deserve more study."[60] John Howard's *Men Like That* (1999) undertook some of that study, with a striking recovery of queer southern fiction, returning to Jay Little's two 1950s novels to argue that they "established New Orleans as a queer urban hub in perpetual reciprocal relationship with adjacent rural populations"—that is, a valuable slice of gay social history independent of its aesthetic quality. In his sustained examination of the Mississippi pulp novelist Carl Corley, Howard offered both methodological ruminations on the detective work needed to track such marginal figures and also an attentive reading of Corley's unheralded oeuvre as a window into southern gay identity.[61]

Such moments aside, most queer scholars showed particularly little interest in gay pulp, tending to devise a genealogy of modern gay literature that privileged precisely those aesthetic qualities through which the emergent gay canon could be constructed as a mirror of the professoriate itself. Thus richly allusive, densely written, theoretically informed books were consistently highlighted over those more ephemeral works whose ubiquitous placement in catalogs and newsstands bespoke their place in the developing gay imaginary. James Baldwin, Tennessee Williams, Christopher Isherwood, and their later peers received extensive examination, while such contemporaries as Victor J. Banis earned little notice. David Bergman's 1991 study of gay literary self-representation disregarded pulp, as did Reed Woodhouse's *Unlimited Embrace: A Canon of Gay Fiction, 1945–1995* (1998). Though Woodhouse's canon was expansive enough to include Boyd McDonald's pornographic 1970s zine *Straight to Hell,* it ignored pulp; for example, in support of its observation that Baldwin's well-regarded 1956 novel *Giovanni's Room* "had its predecessors," it named only John Horne Burns, Gore Vidal, and Fritz Peters, omitting the various lower-brow pulp works that nonetheless surrounded *Giovanni's Room* in its material circulation.[62] Ben Gove, in examining the works of John Rechy, Larry Kramer, Andrew Holleran, and others in his 2000 book *Cruising Culture,* did note the influence of pulp in "shaping their fantasies and understandings of promiscuous sex," but then once more moved the genre "beyond the scope of this study." Christopher Nealon, in a remarkable 2001 study of queer affect before Stonewall, balanced a chapter on physique culture against one on lesbian pulp, thus eliding gay pulp entirely.[63]

By the late 1990s, with both the sex wars of the 80s and the generational tensions of the liberationist era fading from immediate tangible memory, efforts to recuperate the pulp past began moving into greater prominence. Daniel Harris's *Rise and Fall of Gay Culture* (1997), for instance, offered an incisive chapter on gay pulp and porn, including a look at the poorly written but graphic "populist" gay smut—"cranked out on ditto machines by such clandestine operations" as Esoterica Press and 7 Zephyrs Press in the 1940s and 1950s, printed in Tijuana and then smuggled into the United States. Harris's attentive look at the evolution of gay smut novels even charted the use of language from the "gentler, almost touchy-feely verbs" of *Song of the Loon* and its pre-Stonewall peers to the "concussive, high-impact verbs" of more explicit later pulp novels, in which the "newly militarized, gay liberation asshole . . . actually fucks back," no longer being a passive (and euphemistic) "delicate, quivering flower" of yesteryear. Harris's nuanced assessments paid thoughtful heed to the gains and losses of this transition, and recovered presses otherwise absent from the historical record, drawing a link between pre-pulp pornographic typescripts and the proliferating pulp market.[64]

Bergman corrected his earlier oversight with an excellent 1999 essay, "The Cultural Work of Sixties Gay Pulp Fiction," which suggested that "class prejudice obscures the positive images of pulp fiction"—that is, the absence of the qualities and tropes that serve as calling cards for scholarly recognition had led to the collapsing of its *aesthetic* worth into its *historical* significance. Surveying the pulp landscape of the 1960s, Bergman argued for a revaluation based on its congruence with several tenets of still-developing liberationism, from *Song of the Loon*'s vision of nonmonogamous gay companionship to the ways Banis's *Man from C.A.M.P.* series exposed "the arbitrariness of homo/heterosexual boundaries."[65]

Susan Stryker and Michael Bronski expanded on this, publishing pivotal pulp explorations in books whose covers, and sometimes internal images, emphasize gay pulp's exteriors. Stryker's *Queer Pulp* (2001) uncovered entire taxonomies of pulp, incisively noting that one reason gay fiction historically tended to branch into pricier hardcovers on one side and the seamier corner of the pulp market on the other was that it lacked the "vast middle ground" of non-gay readers that drove mass market publishing; in other words, the straight men who helped drive the lesbian pulp fiction with their prurient leers found little counterpart in the audience for gay fiction, which tended to draw an exclusively gay readership.[66]

Bronski's *Pulp Friction* (2003) reflected a sea change from his 1984 historical investigation *Culture Clash: The Making of Gay Sensibility.* There, his chapter on gay porn had, in the spirit of the times, valorized it as performing an "important political function"—but it had nothing to say on pulp, even though the chapter opens with a quote from the 1954 novel *Gay Whore.* Two decades later, Bronski had reassessed gay cultural history, concluding that pulp's great significance had gone almost completely overlooked. Bronski held accountable both homophile respectability *and* post-Stonewall liberationist disparagement of the "closeted" past for this historical elision and, in a powerful introductory essay and selected samples from various gay pulp novels, sought to rectify it. He insisted that using aesthetic merit as a yardstick of historical significance was at odds with the substantive agenda of social history, which was more about the circulation of texts and the meanings they took on in specific historical contexts. Building on existing analyses of lesbian pulp, he admitted that "they vary in form and tone, and certainly their literary quality ranges from high to idiosyncratically low, but each of them exhibits a rebellious, radical urge as they bring the possibility, and pleasure, of same-sex eroticism to a world that is both fascinated by and fearful of it." *Gay Whore* reappeared, but was now presented as part of an important shift: "What had been hidden was now visible." Jay Little, Richard Amory, and Carl Corley all appeared in *Pulp Friction,* forming a virtual counter-canon based less on conformity to the standard criteria of literary worth than the sheer discursive resistance of articulating forbidden desire.[67]

When Martin Meeker published *Contacts Desired: Gay and Lesbian Communications and Community, 1940s–1970s* (2006), he began the process of restoring pulp to the social history of the homophile era. While restricting his close textual studies to lesbian pulp, Meeker emphasized the symbiotic relationship of the Dorian Book Service and the Mattachine Society, with the former unbound by the respectability requirements of the latter and thus free to print and voice more provocative material. At the same time, Marc Stein's meticulous reconstruction of the life and activity of Clark Polak in Philadelphia emphasized the direct link between the pulp-peddling Trojan Book Service, which "defied the politics of respectability," and Clark's homophile work with the Janus Society, noting that Polak invested his profits from the book service in order to "support activities that were more consistent with his commitment to 'operate beyond reproach.' "[68] These works combined new archival research with analytical models that finally moved beyond homophile autohistoricization to situate its respectable public image in a broader history of gay politics and culture. In an article published in 2009, Jaime Harker further interrogated the line between "literary" gay fiction and what Christopher Isherwood once called "fagtrash," noting that verbal content was only one aspect of a book—and that in the pulp market, even Baldwin, Vidal, and Isherwood himself could be easily repackaged and literally turned to pulp.[69]

A year later, David Johnson's work on midcentury gay consumer culture built on these foundations to powerfully challenge distinctions between gay politics and consumer culture. While scholars often position activism and consumerism as antagonistically related, Johnson argues that it was in fact "the very rise of a gay consumer market that helped provide the rhetoric and construct the networks that fostered gay political activism."[70] Focusing predominantly on physique culture, Johnson also weaves pulp publishers into an ongoing project that promises a unified theory of gay "activism," writ widely, with an analytical framework sharply attentive to the internal dialectics between and among consumerism, community, identity, and political activity, in which reading pulp and joining the Mattachine Society can be situated as complementary activities.

All of this work portends a further integration of the writing, reading, and circulation of pulp texts into the narrative and memory of gay history. Complementing the scholarly efforts, recent research outside the academy has shed fascinating light on Samuel Steward and Jay Little, though much ground remains to be covered; the life and career of Wallace de Ortega

Maxey, an early Mattachine member turned prosecuted pulp publisher, for instance, has received minimal attention but provides an intriguing example of a further intersection between homophile activism and pulp. And while Steward's biographer, Justin Spring, found inspiration for his project in Brown University's gay pulp archive, such holdings remain drastically underutilized. Back in 1977, Roger Austen suggested that "fuck books" might "deserve a separate study," but that "the great problem is locating a sufficient number to provide a representative view."[71] But with gay erotic and pornographic stories now collected in various archives across the country, materials are available for further study.[72] As historians continue to challenge the narratives handed down by both homophile and gay liberation activists, it stands to reason that new conceptualizations of the past will energize further study of its overlooked nooks and crannies. Pulp's prose may be purple, but it helps tint the face of a broader lavender history.

## NOTES

Research for this essay was supported by a Martin Duberman Visiting Scholars fellowship at the New York Public Library, for which the author is very grateful.

1. Gene Damon (Barbara Grier), "The Lesbian Paperback," *The Ladder*, June/July 1969, 19 (reprinted from *Tangents*, June 1966); anonymous review of *Song of the Loon*, by Richard Amory, *Vector*, April 1967, 7.
2. The quotations are from Suzanna Danuta Walters, "As Her Hand Crept Slowly Up Her Thigh: Ann Bannon and the Politics of Pulp," *Social Text* 23 (Fall/Winter 1989): 90; Yvonne Keller, " 'Was It Right to Love Her Brother's Wife So Passionately?': Lesbian Pulp Novels and U.S. Lesbian Identity, 1950–1965," *American Quarterly* 57.2 (2005): 398; Diana Hamer, " 'I am a Woman': Ann Bannon and the Writing of Lesbian Identity in the 1950s," in *Gay and Lesbian Writing: An Anthology of Critical Essays*, ed. Mark Lilly (Houndmills: Macmillan, 1990), 70. These are merely some examples of the quite extensive bibliography of scholarship on lesbian pulp.
3. John D'Emilio, *Sexual Politics, Sexual Communities: The Making of a Homosexual Minority in the United States, 1940–1970* (Chicago: University of Chicago Press, 1983), 75–91. A second edition of *Sexual Politics, Sexual Communities* was published by University of Chicago Press in 1998.
4. Martin Meeker, "Behind the Mask of Respectability: Reconsidering the Mattachine Society and Male Homophile Practice, 1950s and 1960s," *Journal of the History of Sexuality* 10.1 (2001): 79, 80.
5. Marc Stein, *City of Sisterly and Brotherly Loves: Lesbian and Gay Philadelphia, 1945–1972* (Philadelphia: Temple University Press, 2004), esp. 226–58.

6. Ibid., 234.
7. On paperbacks, see Kenneth Davis, *Two-Bit Culture: The Paperbacking of America* (Boston: Houghton Mifflin, 1984).
8. "There Is No Harsh Detergent in the Blood of the Lamb," n.d. (ca. 1950), Gay Erotic Stories (collection no. 7668), box 1, Division of Rare and Manuscript Collections, Cornell University Library, Ithaca, NY.
9. "Suppressed Scenes from the Memoirs of Fanny Hill," n.d. (ca. 1950), and "Dear Bob," Nov. 14, 1947, both in Gay Erotic Stories, box 1, Cornell University Library.
10. Bill Houston to "Charles," Feb. 5, 1962, Calvert Bowman Papers (collection no. 7318), box 1, folder 25, Division of Rare and Manuscript Collections, Cornell University Library; Thomas Waugh, *Hard to Imagine: Gay Male Eroticism in Photography and Film before Stonewall* (New York: Columbia University Press, 1996).
11. Michael Bronski, "Back to the Future: Recovering Our Gay Literary Past," in *The Golden Age of Gay Fiction*, ed. Drewey Wayne Gunn (Albion, NY: MLR Press, 2009), 23; Jay Gertzman, "The Jack Woodford Press: Bestsellers at the Army Base, the Drug Store, and the Tourist Bookstore, 1946–1959," *Journal of Popular Culture* 40.1 (2007): 41.
12. Hal Call to Paul Snow, June 30, 1960, box 3, folder 19, Harold L. Call Papers, Coll. 2008-010, ONE National Gay and Lesbian Archives, Los Angeles (hereafter cited as Call Papers).
13. Hal Call to G. A. Gregory, April 2, 1960, box 4, folder 13, Call Papers.
14. "Customs Backs Down," *Dorian Book Quarterly*, Oct. 1962, 2 (copies of this publication are held in the periodicals section of the ONE National Gay and Lesbian Archives). After its seizure of the Swiss homophile magazine *Der Kreis*, the customs office reversed itself in the wake of the US Supreme Court's *Manual Enterprises v. Day* opinion.
15. Dorian Booklist, *Dorian Book Quarterly*, July 1963, 2–3.
16. *ONE, Inc. v. Olesen*, 355 U.S. 371 (1955); William Lambert, "Editorial," *ONE*, April 1958, 4. For more on *ONE*'s obscenity travails, see Whitney Strub, "The Clearly Obscene and the Queerly Obscene: Heteronormativity and Obscenity in Cold War Los Angeles," *American Quarterly* 60.2 (2008): 373–98.
17. Dale Mallory, "Pornography They Say . . . ," *ONE*, May 1961, 8, 9.
18. Edward Denison, review of *All the Sad Young Men*, *ONE*, Nov. 1962, 22–23; Ann Bannon, "The Secrets of the Gay Novel," *ONE*, July 1961, 6, 9, 8, 10. Denison was a pseudonymous reader-turned-contributor; see Craig Loftin, ed., *Letters to ONE: Gay and Lesbian Voices from the 1950s and 1960s* (Albany: State University of New York Press, 2012), 208–9.
19. On intra-homophile tension, see C. Todd White, *Pre-Gay L.A.: A Social History of the Movement for Homosexual Rights* (Urbana: University of Illinois Press, 2009).
20. Richard Mayer, review of *Somewhere Between the Two*, by Jay Little, *Mattachine Review*, Oct. 1956, 32. The novel was published first in hardback (New York: Pageant Press, 1956), and then in paperback (New York: Paperback Library, 1965).
21. Jack Parrish, "Playing the Game from the Grandstands," *Mattachine Review*, May 1959, 18; Noel Garde, review of *Always Love a Stranger*, by Roger Davis, *Mattachine Review*, Sept. 1962, 25. *The Flaming Heart* was published in hardback (New York: Bruce Humphreys, 1958) and later in paperback (New York: Paperback Library, 1966); *Always Love a Stranger* was a paperback original (New York: Hillman Books, 1961).
22. Gene Damon [Barbara Grier], "Literary Scene," *Mattachine Review*, Nov.–Dec. 1964,

29–30. Although Grier was not aware of it, *The Park Jungle* (n.p.: Chariot Books, 1960) is actually an abridged version of *Park Beat*, a hardback by Reginald Harvey (New York: Castle Books, 1959). Just to confuse matters further, the paperback's copyright is held by Hyman Lindsey.

23. James Ramp, "Books," *Vector*, March 1965, 6; anonymous, review of *Song of the Loon*, by Richard Amory, *Vector*, April 1967, 7; comment by "B.B." in Larry Carlson, "The Anatomy of Pornography," *Vector*, Jan.–Feb. 1968, 17. James H. Ramp himself published at least four short story collections in paperback (1966–1967) and one pulp novel under the pseudonym Ross Hossannah (1965), though the last may be a pirated edition.
24. Guild Book Service, Bulletins nos. 10 and 1 (n.d.), H. Lynn Womack Papers (collection no. 7441), box 2, folder 22, Division of Rare and Manuscript Collections, Cornell University Library (hereafter cited as Womack Papers); John Logan, "The Light Went Out, but the Shadow Remained," *Mattachine Review*, July 1958, 22. On Womack, see Rodger Streitmatter and John Watson, "Herman Lynn Womack: Pornographer as First Amendment Pioneer," *Journalism History* 28.2 (2002): 56–65, as well as Philip Clark's essay on Womack and the Guild Press elsewhere in this volume. *The Immortal* was published in hardback (New York: Simon & Schuster, 1958) and paperback (New York: Pocket Books, 1959).
25. *Manual Enterprises v. Day*, 370 U.S. 478 (1962), at 490.
26. Trojan Book Service advertisement, *Vector*, April 1966, 11.
27. Clark Polak, "The Story behind Physique Magazines," *Drum*, Oct. 1965, 15. *The Tortured Sex*, by John S. Yankowski and Hermann K. Wolff, was published by Hollo-way House (Los Angeles, 1965).
28. Stein, *City of Sisterly and Brotherly Loves*, 244.
29. Mattachine Society of Washington, "Washington Section," *Eastern Mattachine Magazine*, Nov.–Dec. 1965, n.p.
30. Dick Leitsch to Frank Cole Jr., July 15, 1968, Mattachine Society, Inc. of New York Records, reel 5, New York Public Library (hereafter cited as MSNY).
31. Dick Leitsch to Albert J. de Dion, Feb. 1, 1968, and Leitsch to Lothar Genge, July 17, 1969, both in MSNY, reel 11.
32. James Sears, *Behind the Mask of the Mattachine: The Hal Call Chronicles and the Early Movement for Homosexual Emancipation* (Binghamton, NY: Haworth Press, 2006), 520, 526.
33. Hal Call to Donald Scott, Sept. 14, 1973, box 4, folder 40, and CineMattachine flyer, May 1976, box 4, folder 33, Call Papers.
34. For effective dismantlings of the "closet" as historically grounded hermeneutic, see George Chauncey, *Gay New York: Gender, Urban Culture, and the Making of the Gay Male World, 1890–1940* (New York: Basic Books, 1994); and Michael Sherry, *Gay Artists in Modern American Culture* (Durham, NC: Duke University Press, 2007), 105–9.
35. Carl Wittman, "A Gay Manifesto" (1970), reprinted in *Out of the Closets: Voices of Gay Liberation*, ed. Karla Jay and Allen Young (New York: Douglas, 1972), 341. On gay liberation, see also Terence Kissack, "Freaking Fag Revolutionaries: New York's Gay Liberation Front, 1969–1971," *Radical History Review* 62 (1995): 104–34.
36. Richard Meyer, "Gay Power circa 1970: Visual Strategies for Sexual Revolution," *GLQ* 12.3 (2006): 447.

37. Jim Kepner, "The World of Pat Rocco," *GAY*, June 1, 1970, 10. See also Whitney Strub, "Mondo Rocco: Mapping Gay Los Angeles Sexual Geography in the Late-1960s Films of Pat Rocco," *Radical History Review* 113 (2012): 13–34.
38. Donn Teal, "Wakefield Poole Adds New Dimension to Porn," *Advocate*, March 1, 1972, 17; John Maiscott, "Parker Tyler Meets Casey Donovan," *Gay Activist*, April 1972, 18.
39. Donn Teal, "Halsted's Porn," *Advocate*, May 10, 1972, 21–22; *L.A. Plays Itself* advertisement, *Gay Activist*, April 1972, 23. See also William E. Jones, *Halsted Plays Himself* (Los Angeles: Semiotext(e), 2011). Arsenal Pulp Press has announced Cindy Patton's *L.A. Plays Itself* as forthcoming in its Queer Film Classics Series.
40. Larry Townsend, "Plight of Gay Novelists," *Advocate*, Aug. 19, 1970; Dirk Vanden, "Coming Together" (originally published in *GAY*, Oct. 26, 1970), reprinted in Richard Amory, *Song of the Loon* (Vancouver: Arsenal Pulp Press, 2005), 235–47, quotations on 235, 239, 244, 246, 225.
41. Justin Spring, *Secret Historian: The Life and Times of Samuel Steward, Professor, Tattoo Artist, and Sexual Renegade* (New York: Farrar, Straus & Giroux, 2010), 329.
42. All of the Black Knight Classics cited here were published in 1969 (Washington, DC: Guild Press), and all books in the series carried the identical introduction (quotation on 14).
43. *I Found What I Wanted* (Washington, DC: Guild Press, 1969), 47, 16, 79; earlier untitled and undated typescript version, Calvert C. Bowman Papers (collection no. 7318), box 1, folder 29, Division of Rare and Manuscript Collections, Cornell University Library.
44. J. J. Proferes to David Schmierbach, Oct. 1, 1971, Womack Papers, box 2, folder 3.
45. Spring, *Secret Historian*, 306, 324, 368–69.
46. "Sodom and Tomorrow," *GAY*, March 18, 1970, 17.
47. "Larry Townsend Talks about His Life as a Gay Novelist," *Vector*, Oct. 1971, 40; Douglas Dean, "Fuck Books or Gay Literature?," *Vector*, May 1973, 17. *Clint Wins His Letter* was by Lester Lance (George Davies).
48. Peter Hadley, "Closet Novels Called Dangerous," *GAY*, June 7, 1971, 12. My thanks to Wayne Gunn for the Dean and Hadley citations.
49. Tony Guild, "Unique Homophile Bookshop," *National Insider*, May 5, 1968.
50. Craig Rodwell, "Oh, Pornography," undated typescript (c. 1972), box 1; Richard Boyle to Rodwell, July 7, 1972, box 1; Rodwell to Gene Jankowski, May 23, 1977, box 2; David Smith to Rodwell, Aug. 30, 1977, box 2; all in Craig Rodwell Papers, Manuscripts and Archives Division, New York Public Library.
51. "Boycott Christopher Street Magazine" flyer, n.d. (1977), Rodwell Papers, box 2, folder "1977."
52. Murray Montague (Jerome Murray), *Security Risk* (Santee: Blueboy Library, 1976), 6; Sydney Harper, *Two, the Hard Way* (Santee: Blueboy Library, 1976), 4.
53. Ed Davis to Robert Stevenson, Jan. 16, 1975, City Council File no. 74-2967, Los Angeles City Archives.
54. Bill Schoell, "Paperback Gays, Part Two," *Gay Activist*, June–July 1979, 11; David Bergman, *The Violet Hour: The Violet Quill and the Making of Gay Culture* (New York: Columbia University Press, 2004), 46.
55. Roger Austen, *Playing the Game: The Homosexual Novel in America* (Indianapolis: Bobbs-Merrill, 1977), 220, 179.
56. Jill Clark, "Interview: Robin Morgan," *Gay Community News*, Jan. 20 1979, 11.

57. Robert Halfhill, "On Anti-Porn Efforts and Gay Male Separatism," *Gay Community News*, May 26, 1984, 5.
58. Andrea Dworkin, *Pornography: Men Possessing Women* (New York: Perigee Books, 1981), 36–42; Thomas Waugh, "Men's Pornography: Gay vs. Straight," *Jump Cut*, March 1985, 30–35; Waugh, *Hard to Imagine*. See also Richard Dyer, "Male Gay Pornography," *Jump Cut*, March 1985, 27–29. *I Love a Laddie* was by Greg Anderson (n.p.: Continental Classics, 1970).
59. D'Emilio, *Sexual Politics, Sexual Communities*, 32, 134–37; Barry D. Adam, *The Rise of a Gay and Lesbian Movement* (Boston: Twayne, 1987).
60. Chauncey, *Gay New York*, 324, 450.
61. John Howard, *Men Like That: A Southern Queer History* (Chicago: University of Chicago Press, 1999), 197, 192–220.
62. David Bergman, *Gaiety Transfigured: Gay Self-Representation in American Literature* (Madison: University of Wisconsin Press, 1991); Reed Woodhouse, *Unlimited Embrace: A Canon of Gay Fiction, 1945–1995* (Amherst: University of Massachusetts Press, 1999), 35–36.
63. Ben Gove, *Cruising Culture: Promiscuity, Desire and American Gay Literature* (Edinburgh: Edinburgh University Press, 2000), 4, 5; Christopher Nealon, *Foundlings: Lesbian and Gay Historical Emotion Before Stonewall* (Durham, NC: Duke University Press, 2001).
64. Daniel Harris, *The Rise and Fall of Gay Culture* (New York: Hyperion, 1997), 134, 147, 149.
65. David Bergman, "The Cultural Work of Sixties Gay Pulp Fiction," in *The Queer Sixties*, ed. Patricia Juliana Smith (New York: Routledge, 1999), 27, 35.
66. Susan Stryker, *Queer Pulp: Perverted Passions from the Golden Age of the Paperback* (San Francisco: Chronicle Books, 2001), quotation on 98.
67. Michael Bronski, *Culture Clash: The Making of Gay Sensibility* (Boston: South End Press, 1984), quotation on 161; Bronski, *Pulp Friction: Uncovering the Golden Age of Gay Male Pulps* (New York: St. Martin's, 2003), quotations on 9, 195.
68. Martin Meeker, *Contacts Desired: Gay and Lesbian Communications and Community, 1940s–1970s* (Chicago: University of Chicago Press, 2006), esp. 54–59; Stein, *City of Sisterly and Brotherly Loves*, 251 (and 226–86, more broadly).
69. Jaime Harker, "'Look Baby, I Know You': Gay Fiction and the Cold War Era," *American Literary History* 22.1 (2009): 199.
70. David K. Johnson, "Physique Pioneers: The Politics of 1960s Gay Consumer Culture," *Journal of Social History* 43.4 (Summer 2010): 870.
71. Spring, *Secret Historian*, ix; Austen, *Playing the Game*, 196–97. Brooks Peters uncovered much about the life of Jay Little in "A 'Little' Romance," *An Open Book* blog, March 1, 2010, www.brookspeters.com/2010/03/a-little-romance/. While that site is down as this book goes to press, a summary can be found at http://neglectedbooks.com/?page_id=325.
72. See the introduction to this volume, n. 30.

# "Accept Your Essential Self"

## THE GUILD PRESS, IDENTITY FORMATION, AND GAY MALE COMMUNITY

Philip Clark

J. Edgar Hoover was troubled. There had been a steady increase in sex crimes in the United States, including forcible rape, which Hoover tied to what he saw as a concurrent increase in commercially available pornography. On January 1, 1960, the FBI director issued a letter to all law enforcement officials, instructing them to move against "unquestionable [*sic*] base individuals" who were spreading obscene literature, comic books, photographs, and "salacious magazines." What, Hoover wanted to know, was being done to protect America's youth "against the tainted temptations of muck merchants"?[1]

In less than two weeks' time, on January 13, the first obscenity indictment—thirty-one counts—was handed down against Herman Lynn Womack for sending physique magazines through the US mail. A second indictment, another thirty-five counts, came on December 8, 1960, months after Womack had been convicted on the first set of charges but before the appeal of his conviction was heard.[2] In bringing criminal charges against

Womack, the director of Manual Enterprises and its subsidiaries, including Guild Press Ltd., postal inspectors were following the postal service's standard enforcement procedures for U.S. Code Title 18, Section 1461, which provided for fines and imprisonment of anyone who knowingly used the mails to ship obscene materials. This was routine; in 1961 alone, there would be 377 convictions under the law.[3]

The legal fight H. Lynn Womack raised against his conviction and the gay media empire he subsequently launched upon winning his case, however, was anything *but* routine. The son of Mississippi sharecroppers, Womack had earned a PhD in philosophy from Johns Hopkins University and had taught, beginning in 1953, at universities and colleges in Washington, DC, and Virginia.[4] In 1958, he had begun taking over publication of the magazines *TRIM* and *Grecian Guild Pictorial* from their founder, with the intention of cornering the field of physique magazines.[5] These magazines, billing themselves as male strength and health periodicals, were finding an expanding market among gay men eager for photographs of the mostly undraped male body. Inaugurating more than a decade of fighting legal actions against him, Womack took his appeal in the case of *Manual Enterprises v. Day* all the way to the US Supreme Court.[6] Writing in 1962 for a 6–1 majority, Justice John Marshall Harlan ruled that, although Womack's magazines were "dismally unpleasant, uncouth, and tawdry," they did not rise to the level of obscenity as marked out by a new legal test, that of "patent offensiveness."[7]

Justice Harlan further wrote that "the magazines are not, as asserted by petitioners, physical culture or 'body-building' publications, but are composed primarily, if not exclusively, for homosexuals, and have no literary, scientific or other merit"—but at the same time, the understanding that "the magazines are read almost entirely by homosexuals" was a key factor in their failing to rise to the level of patent offensiveness. Harlan argued, "It is only in the unusual circumstance where, as here, the 'prurient interest' appeal of the material is found limited to a particular class of persons that occasion arises for a truly independent inquiry into the question whether or not the material is patently offensive"—the very test that was used to declare Womack's publications not obscene. As a result, materials appealing to homosexuals could no longer be declared prima facie obscene.[8]

The ruling boosted Womack's confidence that he could publish and distribute materials marketed to gay men with relative legal impunity. Following this victory, he was no longer content selling only physique magazines. The 1964–65 catalog for the Guild Book Service, the gay mail-order house he founded after the *Manual Enterprises* decision, provides an overview of his developing concepts. The book service, he wrote, was founded "in the spring of 1963, in response to the insistent demands of patrons of Guild Press, Ltd."—a step that was "taken reluctantly [because] there was considerable concern as to whether or not a special interest field such as ours could succeed financially," but that was met with an "overwhelming" response. Womack outlined extensive intentions for his "highly organized, efficient, and expanding service." Not only did the Guild Book Service offer its clients "hardcover books, paperback books, nudist magazines, cologne and records," but Guild Press would also be "launching a publishing program that will reprint every serious work relevant to this special interest field" and would "solicit original manuscripts, poetry, novels, short stories, serious scholarly works, anything relevant to our field; these will become part of a publishing program that is already launched."[9]

In creating such a vast marketing empire directed at gay men, Womack became a publishing pioneer.[10] Other than the small Pan-Graphic Press in California, Womack was—through the Guild Press and its related enterprises, Potomac News Company, Media Arts, and 101 Enterprises, Inc.—the first publisher to market his materials exclusively to gay men.[11] Womack advertised his books, magazines, and other products aggressively, using a mailing list that included at least forty thousand names.[12] The range of materials offered outstripped that of any similar businesses of the early 1960s: pulp novels, short stories, nonfiction books, magazines (both physique and other niche-interest magazines on a variety of gay-related topics), one of the earliest gay travel guides, book reviews and recommendations, and a male pen-pal service, the Friend-to-Friend Club.

All these various Guild Press publications, by operating together to present arguments about the ubiquity and normality of gay men and gay life, striking out rhetorically against religious, medical, and government views of gay men as deviates, and celebrating gay sex and the male body, contributed to the formation of a positive personal gay identity. These materials also provided a pathway for gay men to connect to a larger gay community in both physical and imagined forms. Guild Press's activities thus served as important steps in the emergence of a new attitude about gay life in the mid-twentieth century.

## THE WORLD GUILD PRESS INHERITED

The second set of charges brought against Womack alleged that between August 15 and November 10, 1960, he had used the US postal service to mail "obscene, lewd, lascivious, indecent, filthy and vile pictures and books," along with advertisements about where to obtain these obscene materials, not only to New York City and Washington, DC, but also to suburbs, small towns, and rural areas, such as Beverly Farms, Massachusetts; Hull, Massachusetts; Mooreland, Indiana; and Shamokin, Pennsylvania. The initial set of charges against Womack had followed a similar pattern: Chicago, Salt Lake City, and Baltimore were joined by such towns as Grace, Idaho; Accokeek, Maryland; Lincoln, Maine; and Butler, Pennsylvania. While gay men have traditionally been associated with large cities and urban areas, Womack's mailings make clear the wide geographic range over which men interested in gay materials were spread. Thus part of the success of Womack's mail-order business model came from his ability to reach potential customers in all areas of the country, not just urban settings where more concentrated numbers of gay-identified men might be found.[13]

For gay men living in isolated areas, viewing photographs and reading were among the few ways to connect to others who shared their sexuality. Julie Abraham has pointed out the crucial role gay literature played in early notions of gay identity and gay resistance, noting, "The pioneering sexologists and gay advocates were every bit as committed to literature as the urbanists of their generations." Citing the literary and critical output of Havelock Ellis, John Addington Symonds, Edward Carpenter, and Magnus Hirschfeld, Abraham notes the centrality of literature for an understanding of homosexuality, likely "because of the cultural authority of literature in the modern period."[14] Surveying mid-twentieth-century gay literature, John Loughery writes:

> As many cultural critics have observed, the role of books and writing in the development of an identity—prior to the age of television, at any rate—has often been of special significance to marginalized groups. Denied access in their daily lives or in public forums to any kind of validation, or even a knowledge of their history and the diversity of their contemporary experience, such groups will look to writers to fill that gap. For homosexuals, whose families and teachers are not likely to have much to say to them on the subject, the gay novels and plays encountered in adolescence and early adulthood can be vitally important and long remembered.[15]

These observations are supported by the many "I found it in the library" anecdotes in gay men's oral histories.[16] David K. Johnson uncovered the importance of novels like Robert Scully's *The Scarlet Pansy* (1933), Blair Niles's *Strange Brother* (1931), and Andre Tellier's *Twilight Men* (1931) to young gay men living in Chicago in the 1930s. Contemporary oral histories and research conducted by sociology graduate students at the University of Chicago revealed that "commercial rental libraries all over the city—not just in bohemian neighborhoods—were carrying one or more of the half dozen gay-themed novels available in the early 1930s," and that these books were checked out extensively. For example, "the proprietor of one rental library on Drexel Boulevard reported that all six copies of *Strange Brother* had been rented over one hundred times and were worn out," and another "had to establish a waiting list" for copies of gay-themed novels.[17]

Early nonfiction works about homosexuality also influenced the lives of leaders of the homophile movement of the mid-twentieth century. Harry Hay, the founder of the Mattachine Society, told his biographer that his first understanding of homosexuality came from reading Edward Carpenter's gay-rights apologia *The Intermediate Sex* (1908) after finding it in his town's library as a youth. Similarly, Jack Nichols, cofounder of the Mattachine Society of Washington, remembered that he "rummaged through the basement of an old bookstore and found a rare, mildewed copy of *Love's Coming of Age* [1896] by Edward Carpenter," adding "I found myself mesmerized by the exquisite spiritual intonations of its author. His gentle sophistication was, for me, my first communion with a great gay thinker."[18]

More widely available were books like the anti-gay, scandal-mongering *Washington Confidential* (1951) by Jack Lait and Lee Mortimer, part of a series the two published on crime in US cities. Such a book was easier to find in the 1950s than works by Carpenter or other early gay rights advocates. The tone of *Washington Confidential,* which titled its section about gays and lesbians "Garden of Pansies," was also more common than the "exquisite spiritual intonations" that Nichols found in Carpenter. Lait and Mortimer, who made liberal use of terms like "fairies" and "homos," gleefully reported that "more than 90 twisted twerps in trousers [were] swished out of the State Department" and mentioned a female State Department employee whose job was "to visit faggot dives, observe the queens in action, and ask them how they got that way." Nevertheless, one teenager, William B. Kelley, found a copy in his public library in Missouri and learned from it that gay men gathered in "leafy Lafayette Square, across Pennsylvania Avenue from the White House." In Washington on a trip, Kelley bought a physique magazine from a newsstand to make himself more obvious as a gay man and proceeded to cruise the park.[19] While such reports could show a reader like Kelley that there were others like himself and even where to find them, the era's standard hostile descriptions of a "marked twilight sex, unwelcome at home, pariahs afar" were no help to gay men seeking to craft a positive personal identity.[20]

Neither were other popular accounts of homosexuality. Throughout the 1960s articles specifically addressing homosexuality appeared in mainstream US magazines, such as *Harper's, Life, Look,* and *Time.* Major newspapers, including the *New York Times* and *Washington Post,* ran investigative reports looking at homosexuality. There were also several well-publicized books released by mainstream publishers, such as *The Sixth Man* (1961) and *The Grapevine* (1964), both by the journalist Jess Stearn, which purported to provide an inside look at the lives of gays and lesbians.[21] These articles and books range in tone from toleration and pity—Jean M. White, in a series in the *Washington Post,* asserted, "Homosexuals can have warm, tender feelings. . . . Yet their lives are usually a series of passing liaisons at the best"—to outright scorn, as when *Time* magazine's 1966 article "The Homosexual in America" concluded that homosexuality "deserves no encouragement, no glamorization, no rationalization, no fake status as minority martyrdom, no sophistry about simple differences in taste—and, above all, no pretense that it is anything but a pernicious sickness." These articles, in John D'Emilio's words, "imposed their interpretations upon the lives they portrayed and the subculture they described."[22]

As Larry Gross has written, "Ultimately, the most effective form of resistance to the hegemony of the mainstream is to speak for oneself, to create narratives and images that counter the accepted, oppressive, or inaccurate ones." This is exactly what the emergent gay and lesbian movement attempted to do during the 1950s and 1960s: to create a space, through the culturally respected medium of print, for stories written *by* gays and lesbians as opposed to those written *about* them. It was crucial to counter negative mainstream print narratives with an alternate, more authentic point of view; as Marc Stein notes, "published texts . . . had a breadth of circulation, a level of cultural authority, and a degree of material permanence that most other types of public and private utterances lacked." Indeed, Gross credits "the pioneering lesbian/gay press" with providing the "urban gay world [with a] growing self-consciousness in the decades prior to Stonewall."[23]

The majority of scholarly attention to this early gay and lesbian press has gone to the magazines and newsletters published by homophile organizations, including *ONE*, the *Mattachine Review*, and *The Ladder*. Rodger Streitmatter, in a discussion of the homophile movement press, points out that "particularly during the 1960s when virtually all of American society felt contempt for homosexuality, women and men with same-sex desires turned to movement publications to help them understand both their own feelings and the largely invisible minority group to which they rightly belonged." These "movement publications," produced by groups such as the Mattachine Society and the Daughters of Bilitis and largely written by gays and lesbians themselves, emphasized an informed, journalistic approach, presented factual information about gay and lesbian life, and occasionally struck a militant note, as when Dale Jennings, in the initial issue of *ONE*, spoke out against unjust police practices.[24]

There were, however, inherent limitations in the structure and aims of the homophile movement press. On a logistical level, the homophile press reached only a small number of gay people. *ONE* had a circulation of 5,000 in 1960, but this dropped to 3,000 by 1965.[25] The *Mattachine Review* was next largest at 2,200, while the lesbian-oriented *Ladder* had a peak circulation of 500 copies.[26] One possible reason for the low circulation numbers stems from the homophile movement's decision to present information in a journalistic way. It had its benefits in countering the sensationalism of more mainstream articles and books, but it also restricted the size of the audience. The historian Martin Meeker writes:

> The "serious nature" of the new language of homosexuality that [Hal] Call [the editor of the *Mattachine Review*] and others sought to interject into the overall discourse of homosexuality came from a perspective that was, in the most general terms, middle-class, white, and college-educated. Call, as a white, college-educated journalist, apparently believed in a culturally nonspecific language as the proper basis for objective reporting, which was to be the language of the *Review* but also the ideal language in which the media would address homosexuality. Yet, this language was inherently culturebound itself and thus marginally intelligible to many persons because of reasons as profound as race or as situational as sense of humor.[27]

Even readers who fit these categories and might most be expected to appreciate the homophile magazines could be underwhelmed by them. Newton Arvin, a literary critic and professor at Smith College in western Massachusetts, had "a lukewarm reaction" to *ONE* and the *Mattachine Society Newsletter*, describing *ONE* as "pretty tame" and the *Newsletter* as "terribly earnest and high-minded, as of course it should be, but a little solemn." Arvin, whose career would be destroyed by his arrest in 1960 for receiving magazines published by Guild Press, seems to have preferred the physique magazines, with their mildly coded sexuality and open display of the male body, to the controlled, serious discussion and reporting found in homophile publications.[28]

Homophile leaders, Meeker writes, "felt constrained from publishing the kind of information that gay men likely most desired: personal ads; names and locations of gay bars, baths, and cruising sites; and information about how to contact publishers of pornography (especially if the circulation statistics for 1950s male physique magazines are to be believed)."[29] Guild Press had no such compunctions. If homophile publications tended to avoid open discussion of sex or any suggestive visual content, aiming to project a "respectable" image and fearful of obscenity laws that could destroy them and send their editors to jail, Womack seemed to believe he could defeat all legal challenges, particularly after the favorable decision in *Manual Enterprises v. Day.* Guild Press's novels and magazines had few restraints in their subject matter, language, or illustrations.[30] They exploited interest in sex and the body to reach a wider audience while still delivering many of the same messages that the homophiles did in combating straight society's opinions of gay men, particularly as expressed by the government, the church, and the medical establishment. Beginning with a narrative of normality and ubiquity, Guild Press went on to construct a positive identity for its readers in the face of societal disapproval.

## WHAT FEELS NORMAL IS NORMAL

Womack began Guild Press by taking over the operation of the physique magazine *Grecian Guild Pictorial* in 1958. Founded in Virginia in 1953 as an organization selling physique photographs to "bodybuilders, artists and collectors," the Grecian Guild began publishing *Pictorial* in late 1955. From its inception, it attempted to assist its audience, whom it referred to as "one great brotherhood," in achieving a high-minded combination of physical, mental, and spiritual development.[31] Typical early issues combined photographs of Greek sculptures and young bodybuilders wearing posing straps with articles discussing bodybuilding, nutrition, physique art, Christian spirituality, and the philosophy of the Grecian Guild. Arguing that the ancient Greeks "felt that a trained, intelligent mind in a healthy, virile, beautiful body was the height of human accomplishment," the magazine's editors adduced classical Greek civilization to provide intellectual and moral support, along with a legal buffer, for its obsession with the young male body.[32]

Both Womack and Randolph Benson, the founder and original publisher of *Grecian Guild Pictorial,* were clear-eyed about the magazine's pictures being the reason their readers subscribed. In a March 1958 letter to Benson, Womack wrote: "GGP could never be accused of being anything other than lofty and inspiring. . . . [B]elieve you me, we're going to be so inspiring that it will make you sick. As a matter of fact, we should begin a campaign in GGP and TRIM [another physique magazine Womack published] along the lines of 'Make sure your Mother and Father read the same things that you read!' Seriously, I think that this matter of censorship [owing to pictorial content] can be handled without any trouble."[33] The strategy of wrapping its photographs inside an acceptable cover story was not only intended to help *Grecian Guild Pictorial* get past the watchful eye of US postal agents, but also provided Guild members with a justification for receiving a magazine full of nearly nude male photographs.

These early issues began a process, one that Womack continued, of helping members of the Grecian Guild audience craft a strong personal identity that took its power from the seeming ubiquity and normality of fellow Grecians and the idea of being part of a special group. Larry Gross notes that "the pinup publications," such as the *Pictorial,* "were an early form of community-building that provided, along with the bars, a rare venue for the cohesion of gay identity and the sense of community."[34] Starting with the second issue of the magazine, a letters section allowed readers to see that the geographic range of Guild members included locales from the largest cities to the tiniest towns. An article in the July 1957 issue, prompted by "numerous requests we have received for information on Guild members," claimed that "over half our members live in smaller cities, towns, and rural areas. They live almost everywhere—Novelty, Ohio; Nowata, Oklahoma; Truth or Consequences, New Mexico; Agana, Guam; Bangkok, Thailand."[35]

Not only did readers of the *Pictorial* learn that fellow Guild members spanned the continent and the globe, but they were also assured of those members' normality, as the editors provided statistics about ages and occupations and proclaimed: "[They] do not differ from the great majority of Americans. . . . [O]ur typical Grecian would be a 27 year old office worker or business employee living in Southern California. Close to typical would be a 30 year old executive in New York, or a 28 year old teacher in Chicago."[36]

In one early article, S. George Spillman discusses "the adjusted personality," telling readers, "The whole man, as defined by the Greek ideal, is one who seeks physical, mental, and spiritual perfection."[37] Being a Grecian, they were assured, means "I live a life that is open, for I have nothing to hide in darkness nor in secret."[38] Gay readers of the *Pictorial* were thus given an affirmation of identity and encouragement to lead healthy, open lives that were unseen in American society in 1957 outside the pages of small-circulation homophile magazines.

The Guild Press carried over emphases seen in *Grecian Guild Pictorial* into its fiction offerings, connecting stories to their readers' personal identities and to the idea that gay men were everywhere and lived regular lives. Guild Press fiction often used elements of the bildungsroman. Frequently, a young man—either gay or straight-identified at the story's opening and many times explicitly from a small-town background—begins to have gay emotional or sexual experiences and must attempt to integrate those experiences into his psychological and social identity. These characters achieve a level of verisimilitude by mimicking, in their physical and psychological movement, varying stages in the process of identity formation of their readers, some of whom left small towns for the big city and most of whom had to deal with the same process of coming out, either sexually or socially. Characters achieve varying levels of success in integrating homosexual experiences into their sense of self, accepting or resisting a gay identity and ties to other gay men, but a common motif is the protagonist's realization that homosexuality is widespread and a regular part of life.[39]

One Guild novel that quickly establishes its philosophy of the normality and ubiquity of homosexuality is Guy Faulk's *It's a Gay, Gay, Gay World* (1968), set in 1930s Los Angeles. Early on, its nameless protagonist says, "Another great big bunch of foolishness is that saying about 'this year's trade, next year's competition.' It ain't true—if you're queer, you're queer and you've been that way from the day you were born." The narrator then goes on to introduce the idea of variations of "queer" sexuality: "There is a hell of a lot of degrees of queerness and there are so many of us that even the word 'queer' isn't fair."[40]

Characters in other Guild fiction titles confirm these views, as when the commanding officer of a ship in *Navy Discipline Below Deck* (1970) has sex with two of his sailors and discovers that "the most surprising thing to me about the whole situation is the fact that less than an hour ago I was completely *straight.* I detested, but respected, queers and faggots and homosexuals. . . . Now I had to take one hell of a long look at myself before I could ever hope to pass judgement against someone else for such a similar reason."[41] The officer realizes he enjoys sex with men and proceeds, without guilt, to continue his encounter with the sailors and to set up future liaisons. In presenting enjoyment of gay sex as a possibility even for straight-identified men, this novella creates a zone of normality around homosexuality: anyone can engage in homosexual sex, and doing so does not have to induce a crisis. As the US Marine protagonist of *Any Man Is Fair Game* (1969) realizes, "a homo could be anybody—they had no mark or brand on them."[42]

This introduces a frequent motif throughout Guild Press books: if anybody could potentially have homosexual desires, then what *feels* normal to a character *is* normal. When questioned by a teenage sailor about whether the sex they are having is abnormal, a navy officer in *All the Studs at Sea* (1971) replies, "If it is then I must be queer because this is the first time I been happy for a hell of a long time!" While the officer does not commit himself to a gay identity until later in the novel, he delivers an early message to readers of the normality of their desires. A statement of justification that the officer makes to the sailor—"I hear that a lot of guys like to swing with other guys!"—is delivered in casual language, as gossip, confirming that gay sex is both common and natural: in short, not an issue for concern.[43]

Even Guild Press books with a more serious tone than *All the Studs at Sea* repeated this message about the naturalness of homosexuality, implying that readers should not worry about their sexual identity. Robbie, the only thoroughly likeable, self-possessed character in Alexander Goodman's *Handsome Is . . .* (1966), tells Tony, who is confused about his sexuality, "I'm not very different from anybody else. . . . I had a very good, uncomplicated childhood. Perhaps that's the unusual thing about me: in almost every way I'm normal and quite respectable—I just happen to like boys. And I'm not ashamed of it."[44]

This narrative of normality also appears in *Jerry and Jim* (1967), a classic bildungsroman in which Jerry grows up in a small town but comes to accept his homosexuality and even develop a level of political consciousness about it.[45] Directly after an interview with a psychiatrist about his homosexuality, Jerry hitchhikes and begins a sexual encounter with the driver who picks him up. As they kiss, "Jerry suddenly remembered the psychiatric interview: had he not said he wanted to give up the homosexual in him, to be 'normal'? It now appeared hopeless to give up his deviation—and besides, the 'deviation' was such a natural part of him that it was somehow false or a game to call it 'unnatural,' for if a queer was 'queer,' wasn't that in itself a contradiction of sorts? Was not a person a unit and responsible only to his own unique sexual nature?"[46] Tortured syntax aside, Jerry's ruminations are just another variant on the message readers would receive again and again from Guild Press's novels: that their sexuality, however "queer" it might seem to society, was a natural part of their identity.

## NOT A SIN, NOT A SICKNESS, NOT A CRIME

A major hurdle to justifying homosexuality as an identity and convincing a gay audience of its normality was the array of social institutions lined up against gay people at the time. Declared sinners by the nation's churches, categorized as mentally ill by the American Psychiatric Association, expelled from government and military service, and arrested by the police, gay men were under assault from all sides. Guild Press launched a counterattack against "the cruel hypocrisies of contemporary American society" and the notion of gay men as sinning, sick, or criminal.[47]

Beginning with the article "Spiritual Exercises" by the Reverend Robert W. Wood in the fourth issue, *Grecian Guild Pictorial* included regular contributions from men of religion. In addition to multiple appearances by Wood, who would go on to write the pro-gay *Christ and the Homosexual* (1960), the *Pictorial* added a column written by the Guild's national chaplain, the Reverend James A. M. Hanna, and featured an Episcopal missionary as "Grecian of the Quarter," including an accompanying physique photograph.[48] Although almost certainly valued by the editors as a socially convenient cover story for the photographs they published, the religious contributions served as an important counterbalance to the traditional religious depiction of gay men as sinners.

Attempts to achieve bodily, mental, and spiritual perfection were linked throughout the *Pictorial*, and even editorials that were not directly about religion used religious ideas to encourage readers to have a sense of self-respect. In the June 1959 issue, an unsigned editorial that may have been written by Womack told readers that in order to achieve happiness, "First of all, you must have respect for yourself. Remember that you were created in the image of God, and that there was a purpose in your creation. . . . [A]ccept your essential self."[49] For gay readers struggling with their sexual nature and labeled as sinners by mainstream churches, such a message of acceptance, linked to traditional religious belief, was a powerful tool in identity building.

One of Guild Press's authors, Guy Dandridge, launched a virtual one-man campaign to inform readers that being homosexual did not go against God. Dandridge's rhetorical assault against the church's traditional view of homosexuality begins in the opening pages of *Jerry and Jim*, his first novel for Guild Press. As Jerry sits in church and watches Jim in the choir, he "wanted the whole world to know of his strange love—especially in church where he was taught that God is Love, that Christ died for the outcasts and misfits of society as well as for the so-called respectable people." Although Jerry understands that he should be accepted by Christian society under the dictate that "God is Love," he knows that he cannot reveal himself and "silently cursed the unfeeling congregation for their everlasting hypocrisy." The novel's happy ending, in which Jerry concludes that he can "face his own image in a mirror . . . without remorse, without the former profound sense of inferiority" is all the more powerful for his initially mirroring the position of many gay readers who found themselves rejected by their church.[50]

Elsewhere in Dandridge's books, his characters come to feel accepted by God, even if not by the formal church or religious teachings. At the end of *Boys' Camp* (1971), a by-the-numbers erotic novel, Dandridge's protagonist, Eddie, a camp counselor, decides that his sexual encounters have not damned him; instead, he concludes "that God accepts me as I am, not as I would be. He understands the homosexual longing as He understands the more orthodox expression of human love. . . . God will look beyond and past convenient, earthly and relatively condemnatory concepts such as 'pederast' and 'sodomist' and 'pervert' and He will see only the person, above his particular brand of sex life." Eddie's ultimate "trust that God is my final and fair judge" bypasses for Dandridge's readers any social reproach of their homosexuality.[51]

Even common interpretations of Biblical passages used to condemn homosexuality are overthrown in Dandridge's *Ready, Willing, and Able* (1971), in which one character deconstructs the story of Sodom and Gomorrah for his listeners, delving into mistranslations of Hebrew texts and concluding that "the issue of homosexuality has often been seen in Biblical passages and stories in which the subject was completely unrelated" and that "America is still suffering from a massive hangover of Puritanism."[52] The lectures delivered by Dandridge's characters are summed up in the final line of the new ending Guild added to *I Found What I Wanted* when it published the anonymous story in 1969. After spending the entire book denying his homosexuality while engaging in every male-to-male sexual act imaginable, the narrator concludes he is gay and that "if God allows guys to love each other and be sexually attracted, it must be natural even if society doesn't approve of it!"[53]

By the 1950s and 1960s, America's religious narrative of homosexual-as-sinner had been joined in the public arena by a medical narrative of homosexuality-as-illness. D'Emilio observes that "the medical model played only a minor role in society's understanding of homosexuality until the 1940s," when inductees into the World War II–era US military were given psychiatric tests and "psychiatry emerged from the war with its status enhanced":

> Increasingly, Americans came to view human sexual behavior as either healthy or sick, with homosexuality falling into the latter category. Medical guides aimed at a lay audience expounded on the phenomenon of same-sex orientation and the possibilities of curing it. In the fifteen years after World War II, legislatures of more than

> half the states turned to psychiatrists for solutions to the problem of sex crimes, and they passed sexual psychopath laws that officially recognized homosexuality as a socially threatening disease. In the postwar era, medicine was moving toward parity with religion and law in structuring American culture's perception of homosexuality.[54]

Womack himself used the psychiatric view of homosexuality as an illness to avoid being placed in the DC jail system after his initial conviction for mailing obscene materials, insisting on a psychological evaluation and spending a brief period at St. Elizabeths mental hospital.[55] Many were not so fortunate as to choose entry, D'Emilio notes, "since some families committed their gay members to asylums." Others suffered brutal treatment; because the medical model of homosexuality implied the possibility of cure, "doctors experimented on their wards with procedures ranging from the relatively benign, such as psychotherapy and hypnosis, to castration, hysterectomy, lobotomy, electroshock, aversion therapy, and the administration of untested drugs." By the time Guild Press began publishing its books and magazines, psychiatry had "branded homosexual men and women with a mark of inferiority no less corrosive of their self-respect than that of sin and criminality."[56]

Gay men who wanted to approach a doctor to discuss their homosexuality also understood the social dangers involved. During his brief stint working for Guild Press, Richard Schlegel, who had been fired from a civil service job for being gay, made a public offer to provide confidential counseling to gay men. One of the requests he received was from a man in Stowe, Vermont, who told him: "I have had homosexual relations before and enjoyed it until after when I stop and try to look at my future. I do not dare see a doctor, as I live in a small town and if my employer found this out I would be fired. Any counseling you can give me will be greatly appreciated and needed."[57]

Facing these medical beliefs, their accompanying dangers of loss of liberty or livelihood, and the emotional toll of being labeled mentally ill, gay men found an ally in Guild Press's authors. Their characters' words and actions make clear their skepticism or scorn of both the sickness narrative and the psychiatrists who peddled it. In Goodman's *Handsome Is . . .*, Robbie is presented as the novel's most socially normative and self-confident character: he refuses to have sex for money; he insists on affection from his sexual partners, saying that he would "rather do without than go to bed with a boy who doesn't even like me"; and he tries to warn the protagonist, Tony, away from a sociopath. This increases the weight of his rather general statement that "I don't think homosexuality is a sickness, or even that it's an aberration. . . . I'm doing my very best to make myself the very best person I can."[58]

Other Guild Press novels are more specific in their criticisms. In *Jerry and Jim*, Jerry meets with Dr. Olson, a psychiatrist at the university hospital, but by the end of the novel he reflects that "he had begun his therapy sessions with Dr. Olson convinced that his 'queerness' was a matter of damnation, but with each torrid sex affair his conviction grew that homosexuality was a matter of having a different orientation from that of the ordinary person. He was not alone, for he had met many other gay guys, many of whom were completely admirable."[59] Sessions with Dr. Olson are no match for the pull of sexual desire, and Jerry's real-world experience with other gay men defeats medical theories about homosexuality as a sickness.

Psychiatric beliefs about homosexuality are also questioned in Gene Holland's *Boys in Love, with Other Boys* (1967), published by 101 Enterprises. Homosexuality was believed by many psychiatrists to be caused by environmental factors, with internal family dynamics, particularly overprotective mothers, a prime explanation. The narrator, Gene, raises this idea only to dismiss it:

> From the very beginning I knew I was different. When other boys went on long hikes and played baseball I stayed home reading books and gardening. My father always complained that I looked thin and sickly and "why didn't I go out to play like the rest of the boys?" Mother, on the other hand, liked to have me around the house. I was aware at a very early age that my parents didn't get along and my mother looked to me for the companionship and love she did not get from my father. Being an only child I felt this burden keenly. Perhaps, if my mother had had other children to fuss over, my life would have been different. I say, perhaps. Blaming mothers for homosexuality is too easy an out these days. Frankly, I can't remember a day in which I was attracted to girls instead of boys.[60]

This skeptical response to the usefulness of psychiatric theory in explaining homosexuality finds its match later in the novel when, after joining the navy and ultimately having his homosexuality uncovered, Gene confronts navy psychiatrists. After being "sent to a mental ward," first in Japan and then in California, Gene finds that "a fat, neurotic psychiatrist in his fifties took a great delight in listening to my case." Gene initially hopes "that there really might be some way out of my sexual desires through psychiatry," but instead he discovers that "the doctors were of no help": "All they did was take down the data I had given them without comment but with more than a few leers. The last doctor, the fat, erratic one, leaned back in his chair and then exposed himself. 'This thrills you, huh?' he asked. 'You like this, huh?' He took his limp organ in his hand and wiggled it at me like a bloated worm squirming on a hook. I said nothing and stared at a spot behind his ear."[61]

Gene's encounter dramatizes the unethical treatment gay men could expect to receive at the hands of the psychiatric profession and echoes, in its emotional resonance, the experience of many gay men with psychiatrists in the 1950s and 1960s. Although he enters with ideas of a cure for his homosexuality, Gene leaves saying, "I didn't know where I was going but, at least, I knew I wasn't going straight."[62] Guild Press's publications confirmed an idea expressed later by the historian Martin Duberman, in his memoir of psychotherapy in the 1960s, that "the endemic unhappiness [connected to homosexuality before gay liberation] reflected not on the inherent nature of homosexuality, but on the persecutions leveled against homosexuals by a hostile, intolerant heterosexual majority."[63] The press's message to readers was clear: psychiatry held no solutions and psychiatrists' opinions could be safely ignored.

Whereas many gay men had no direct contact with psychiatry, the antigay policies of the government and its police forces had a long reach. The homophile movement aimed to change public perception of homosexuality by speaking out about "social action, rights of expression and privacy, political protest, and, above all, citizenship."[64] In time, this emphasis on civil liberties gained traction in countering the narratives of sin, sickness, and crime, but in the early 1960s gays and lesbians were still second-class citizens in the eyes of their government. When Guild Press began in 1958, all forty-eight states still upheld sodomy laws criminalizing homosexual sex acts, and laws addressing employment discrimination against gays and lesbians were nonexistent, with the government's own civil service and its military expelling members on simple suspicion of homosexuality.[65]

Guild Press engaged in political protest in its publications throughout the life of the firm. Womack had, of course, felt the force of anti-gay prejudice in his arrest as the publisher and distributor of physique magazines, and his antipathy toward the government's institutionalized discrimination ran deep. One of the early books that the Guild Press made available to its customers was *Fear, Punishment, Anxiety and the Wolfenden Report* (1959), by a British psychiatrist, Charles Berg. As a psychiatrist, Berg held a number of the normative views of his day about homosexuality.[66] Still, in his opening essay, "The Wolfenden Report on Homosexual Offences," he excoriates Great Britain's Departmental Committee on Homosexual Offences and Prostitution (better known as the Wolfenden Committee, after its chair, Lord John Wolfenden) for its timidity in recommending that "homosexual behavior between consenting adults in private be no longer a criminal offence" but concurrently recommending increases in prison sentences for other types of homosexual activity, including those involving males between sixteen and twenty-one years old.[67] While some of Berg's pique related to the absence of a psychiatrist on the committee—he repeatedly claimed that they were attempting to adjudicate "complicated matters far out of their depth"—his analysis of the committee's reasoning and disbelief at the illogic in their not going further in decriminalizing homosexuality was among the era's stauncher defenses of gay men's right to live without fear of the law. Berg firmly stated: "Crime involves violation of other people's freedom and liberty (the sort of thing we tend to do to homosexuals just because they are homosexuals). Crime has not necessarily anything to do with homosexuality, but operates in every field of human activity, but it would seem that we tend to lose our reason when it comes to homosexuality, on account of our emotionally overcharged repressed conflicts."[68] It is unsurprising that Womack placed in his readers' hands Berg's humane arguments regarding gay men and the law.

Womack attacked US state and national policies toward gays more directly when he reprinted the pamphlet *Homosexuality and Citizenship in Florida* in 1964. Originally published by the Florida Legislative Investigation Committee, which had been formed "to investigate and report on 'the extent of infiltration into agencies supported by state funds by practicing homosexuals,'" and known colloquially as "the purple pamphlet" or "the Purple Report" because of its abstract purple cover, *Homosexuality and Citizenship in Florida* became a huge controversy for the Florida government.[69] Amid a report that included scare-mongering linking gays and lesbians to child molestation and warnings about "aggressive homosexuals" working for social change, the Florida committee printed a glossary of sexually explicit "homosexual terms" and photographs illustrating such practices as bondage and public sex at a glory hole, sparking outrage at the committee's use of public tax monies to fund its investigations and print the results. Guild Book Service's advertisement for the reprint claimed that, after the pamphlet was released, "the entire state of Florida was in a state of shock and once even the slightest recovery set in, the last thing anyone wanted was for this report to be circulated." Of course, Guild Press made sure it received much wider attention than it otherwise would have.[70]

These attempts to fashion a gay liberation consciousness on the part of its readers by focusing on government's anti-gay behaviors continued in other, more straightforward ways. In an editorial in the July 1964 *Grecian Guild Pictorial*, Womack made a direct call for action, arguing in favor of openly gay men and women being involved in government. In an opinion radical for its day, Womack declared: "The public view toward homosexuals and lesbians will have to change, as it has been changing in recent years. It will have to be more than acceptance—more like public approval. Homosexuals should be allowed to acknowledge their inclinations and be able to obtain public offices."[71]

By 1970, Guild Press was in full-throated outcry against a variety of civil rights violations, echoing the homophiles' emphasis on a civil liberties approach to changing society's laws. Some publications that were overtly sexual also included extensive essays with overtones of political protest, as when H. Erick Lester, in *Studies in Danish Male Homosexual Pornography* (1970), told his readers: "Homosexuals complain to the American Civil Liberties Union constantly about their rights being denied, by being dismissed from their jobs for no apparent reason whatever, or that their mail had been opened, or that they had been intimidated by Postal Authorities, and they have been led into entrapment by police officers posing as 'gay trade,' going as far as completing the homosexual act in order to institute an arrest!"[72]

After reprinting a letter from *Playboy* in which an anonymous gay man from Birmingham told about his arrest by the vice squad and described collusion between police, attorneys, and judges, Lester comments, "This letter is reprinted in its entirety for the sole purpose of pointing up the fact that such conditions exist not only in Birmingham, Alabama, but in hundreds of communities across the country, because of a narrow-minded community which cannot accept homosexuality as being a fact." He ack- nowledges both historic persecution—discussing censorship battles with the post office and "the days of the 'red herring,' " when McCarthyism de- stroyed gay government employees' lives—and the possibility of legal change ("now we find the government beginning to bend a little, and perhaps soon the rules will be relaxed completely").[73] Lester's book thus combined protest about the plight of gays and lesbians with hope for the future, assuring readers that they were justified in their identities and on the cusp of a social movement.

Womack took particular interest in protesting the military's treatment of gay servicemen. His home was around the corner from the historic Marine Corps barracks at 8th and I Streets SE in Washington, DC, and he maintained friendships with a number of young soldiers.[74] In 1970, Womack linked homosexuality, military service, and his publishing activities in an interview with a reporter, telling him, "I honestly believe if I do anything to advance the freedom of the press, I'll consider myself lucky. I'm not a martyr. But if homosexuals want a literature, they have a right to it. They pay taxes and die. A hell of a lot of them have died in Vietnam."[75]

Such anger at the government's policies, toward both censorship of gay literature and ferreting out gays in the military, appeared throughout Guild Press's publications. Reviewing the novel *The Case against Colonel Sutton* in 1964, Womack praised the author, who "expertly exposes a little-known but horrifying aspect of the US Army. He authoritatively shows the vast amounts of time and taxpayer's money the Army spends on idiotic queer-hunts, searching for anything possible to rid homosexuals from its ranks."[76] The opening essay in the 1970 magazine *Homosexuality in the Military* further attacked the military's anti-gay witch-hunts; J. J. Proferes, a frequent Guild Press author and former military serviceman, argued, "Those homosexuals serving honorably in the service of their country deserve more than they are receiving, for being part of a minority, they must suffer the slings and arrows of their buddies, but [more so] the harassment and intimidation of those so-called *authorities* who 'investigate' them!"[77]

Proferes accused military investigators of unethical practices in searching out homosexuality in the ranks and ridiculed their unwillingness to follow the findings of their own studies, which "reported in 1947 and 1961 . . . that homosexuals (a) top the average soldier in intelligence, education, and rating, (b) are law-abiding and hardworking, (c) perform 'admirably' as office workers, (d) try to be good soldiers, (e) 'are often exceptionally courageous in battle,' and (f) are often well-adjusted to their condition."[78] Proferes thus provided gay readers with ample evidence, backed up by their own government's findings, that a homosexual identity was no hindrance to their worth as people or effectiveness on their jobs.

This attack spills into Guild Press fiction. In the anonymous novella *Navy Discipline Below Deck*, a ship's commanding officer is aggravated at being required to investigate two of his best sailors as "suspected homosexuals" and protests, "I had some reservations about 'homosexual laws' in and out of service. . . . 'Homosexual laws,' for the most part, I felt, seemed to infringe upon human rights, and when Mason had presented his assumptions to me about these two studs, I immediately had an inner rebellious attitude . . . 'cause I felt he was looking for me to cash in on someone else's privacy and reap rewards of merit to the service for having uncovered a couple of queers aboard ship."[79] Borrowing arguments about privacy presented by the homophile movement, the commanding officer scoffs at and ends the investigation, even though he knows that the sailors are sexually involved.

One of the broadest Guild Press attacks against anti-gay civil rights violations and the government's treatment of gays as criminals was launched in Alexander Goodman's semifictional *A Summer on Fire Island* (1966). Published three years before Stonewall, the book was reprinted in 1968, a relative rarity for Guild Press publications, indicating its popularity. An innovative combination of fiction and reportage, the book affords an unusual look at 1960s life at the famed gay retreat off the south shore of Long Island, with the entire ending an extended argument for gay civil rights that prefigures the demands of the gay liberation movement. Goodman describes in his penultimate chapter a raid conducted by the local vice squad on gays in Fire Island's Meat Rack section, a raid in which he is arrested. All the gay men arrested ultimately plead guilty, fearing worse penalties and possible loss of employment if they fight the disorderly conduct charges against them, but Goodman knows that he "had not committed any offense against nature or public decency."[80]

Another arrestee proposes that gay visitors to Fire Island organize to hire a lawyer to fight future arrest cases. The scene ends with one man's angry call for gay resistance and solidarity:

> We queens are all cowards at the smallest sign of trouble. But it's time we woke up—before it's too late. In those big books up in Albany queers are criminals, not much different from thieves and murderers. Each time a faggot does what comes naturally to him he's committing a felony. We're all at the mercy of the Albany boys, and who knows what is in the future for us? How many queer-hunts are up their sleeves? Will we always say meekly "Guilty, Judge" and go off to jail or maybe to prison without putting up one bit of resistance? Shouldn't we think of some way to protect ourselves?[81]

At the close of the book, Goodman also demands the decriminalization of gay sex: "Many leading American judges and lawyers believe that it is time that the sex laws in every state be drastically overhauled. . . . These American jurists believe the ridiculous sodomy laws . . . should be wiped off the books. The radical change of state sex laws should be the first goal for all homosexuals who believe in the necessary improvement of their condition in this country." Earlier, in describing the Meat Rack, Goodman writes: "There was something just right about this quiet wood near the bay. It was a beautiful place, a beautiful place to make love, and I sincerely believe that the naked boys who made love there never in any way spoiled that beauty."[82] In striking out against sodomy laws and emphasizing the beauty and naturalness of gay desire and sex, Goodman identifies powerful tools for strengthening gay identity.

## SEX, IDENTITY, AND REVOLUTION

Goodman's ability to conceive and articulate the goal of ending repressive anti-gay sex laws derived from the increased openness of the broader sexual revolution. Goodman himself comments, "It is now common knowledge that the United States is now undergoing a sexual revolution. A new morality is dramatically changing the habits and customs of the nation. . . . Homosexuality is no longer a valid reason for one man to jeer at, or beat up another. It is no longer a forbidden topic which society hides with the skeleton in the closet."[83] In 2007 Jan Ewing, who wrote novels for Guild Press under the name Jack Evans, reflected that it was only in the 1960s that "women were allowed to talk openly about sex, which they were allowed to do after birth control, because all of a sudden it was an issue. Once women started talking about it, then we [gay men] were able to talk about it, too, and it became part of the general upheaval of the '60s . . . so we really latched on to that movement and went with it. We got very noisy."[84]

John D'Emilio has argued, "It would be a mistake to conclude that the sexual liberalism of the decade would automatically have included homoeroticism without the initiatives taken by gay activists." While D'Emilio refers specifically to the efforts of the homophile movement to influence social discourse and the mainstream press, gay men's popular culture, such as the pulp novels and magazines published by the Guild Press and others, were equally influential by allowing gay men to shape a positive sexual identity. D'Emilio acknowledges that "antihomosexualism pervaded American culture, and it infected the consciousness of gay men and women no less than heterosexuals," and that the homophile movement "took upon itself an impossible burden—appearing respectable to a society that defined homosexuality as beyond respectability." He adds, "In trying to accommodate social mores, DOB [Daughters of Bilitis] and Mattachine often reflected back to their potential constituency some of society's most condemnatory attitudes. Their criticisms of the bars and the gay subculture undoubtedly alienated many of the men and women with the strongest commitment to gay life."[85]

Many homophile leaders, trying to attract the support of straight society to the cause of gay civil rights, cringed at the idea of discussing or promoting the sexual in their publications. Dick Leitsch of the Mattachine Society of New York, in talking about Philadelphia's *Drum,* which included physique photographs and outsold any other movement magazine, complained, "It contains nothing likely to reach the public at large and move them to our side . . . and little that will attract any useful persons to the movement. . . . Its only purpose seems to entertain faggots, which is not one reason for this movement. If we're in business to entertain, then let's go the whole hog and provide drag shows, muscle movies, gay bars, dances and orgies!"[86]

Leitsch ignores the internal benefits for gay men in having their desire acknowledged in print and pictures and the possibility that this acknowledgment helped create a powerful and positive sexual identity. Such an identity could encourage those gay men, many of whom were fearful or physically isolated, to seek out others and create gay community. In considering the impact of the drawings of the gay artist Tom of Finland, whose works appeared in Guild Press's and other contemporary physique magazines, Micha Ramakers writes that Tom's drawings "provided immeasurable pleasure to several generations of gay men and, furthermore, offered what had seemed unattainable for many of them: tools for an affirmative identity."[87] Ramakers quotes Robert Pierce, an arts critic for the *Soho Weekly News,* who in a review of Tom of Finland's work called the creation of gay pornographic art in the 1950s and 1960s "an act of defiance and a covert assertion of self in a period when overt action could mean blackmail or prison and, in some extreme cases, mental institutions."[88] This statement does not go nearly far enough. Not only the creation of gay pornographic art (and writing), but also its consumption, was "a covert assertion of self."

The availability of imagery and stories that glorified sex and the male body had a galvanizing effect on the creation of a gay self-image. Frank, a gay man whose reflections were included in the book *Growing Up before Stonewall,* recalled his first homosexual encounters, which took place while he was married: "Although I had not had homosexual contact with a man previously, . . . there had been an inclination previously, because I had admired the male body and had bought magazines and so on. I didn't buy pretty girlie magazines, I bought boy magazines. And I simply said why should I—realizing that there would be a problem from the standpoint of my social life—why should I be unhappy in my sexual life. And that is really what determined me to get the divorce." The formation of a gay sexual identity, specifically spurred by his reaction to "boy magazines" and their imagery, caused Frank to leave behind his "normal" life and begin to learn "how people lived in a homosexual milieu."[89]

Once a gay identity was formulated, pictures and stories in gay popular culture also improved self-esteem. In an interview, the early homophile writer and activist Jim Kepner recalled: "Validating erotic images was extremely important to our liberation. As the gay press came into its own, the publications began to extol the many virtues of the beautiful male physique. They screamed: 'Yes, gay men are sexual. And, yes, we are proud of our desires.'"[90] Gay men reacted positively to the sexual gaze in gay publications, as when a reader of *Drum* wrote to say, "I'm glad to see an organization put sex back into homosexuality. Certain other organizations who shall remain nameless try to obscure the fact that we homos like to gratify our sexual desires."[91]

Michael Bronski has analyzed "the social regulation of mainstream culture" in relation to the homophile movement. He points out: "The only way to avoid persecution for homosexual activity was to keep it secret. Even this, however, was not enough. In the 1950s and 1960s in the United States, it was not unusual for police to arrest men and women, often in private homes, for actual or suspected homosexual activity. People who frequented more public places, such as bars, clubs, and parks, were routinely arrested and charged under a variety of laws. . . . These laws were used to regulate public manifestations of homosexuality with the objective of suppressing them completely or, at the very least, driving them underground."[92] Neither the homophile movement nor popular publishers like Guild Press accepted the treatment of gays and lesbians as criminals. What the homophile movement did accept, however, was the notion that the sexual side of homosexuality must be kept private.[93]

Indeed, the privacy argument was one of the central tenets of the new discourse of gay civil rights during the era, which held that the government should not regulate private behavior. Bronski argues, however, that mainstream heterosexual society of the time was unwilling to accept any "legal or social concept of privacy for homosexuals," noting that "in the absence of a 'right to privacy,' and in the context of the continued criminalization of all homosexual sexual activity, any public manifestation of homosexual identity—from holding hands to crossdressing to purchasing homosexually oriented material—could lead to arrest." Thus the homophile movement's emphasis on privacy was doomed to failure as a social strategy, since only "homosexual invisibility" would be accepted by the mainstream as "privacy."[94]

Guild Press's publications did not entirely reject the notion of privacy as a useful tool; the commanding officer in *Navy Discipline Below Deck*, for example, cites a basic right to privacy as a reason not to pursue the allegations of homosexuality against two of his sailors. But by aggressively promoting the pleasures of sex and the body—by publishing stories and displaying photographs that made gay sex and male bodies obvious and desirable—Guild frontally assaulted the homophiles' idea of sexual privacy as a strategy for assimilation. When Goodman complains, "Our modern civilization is so hemmed in by archaic laws and worthless customs. Sex is still a dirty word. A frightened world presses the lid on our pure animal desires," he speaks for all those gay men who felt oppressed by the "social regulation of mainstream culture" that Bronski notes. When Goodman describes the activities at Fire Island's Meat Rack and declares it a "place where a man can discover what he really is," a place "where man, as the superb animal he is, can freely give himself to his natural passions," he entices readers to discover and express the homosexual identity suppressed by straight society.[95] If an argument Howard Becker posed in 1965 in *The Nation*—that "sexual expression ought to be one of the 'inalienable' rights guaranteed to Americans"—was the theory, then writings published through Guild Press were supportive of both the theory *and* the practice.[96]

Because of their presence on newsstands, physique magazines were among the first publications to present gay sexual desire openly and thus challenge heterosexual insistence on gay invisibility.[97] The *New York Times* noted this disapprovingly in a 1963 editorial: "Newsstands offer a wide range of magazines and papers designed to appeal to inverted sexual tastes. These include many of the so-called body-building publications presenting, under the guise of physical culture, photos of scantily clad, heavily muscled men, and others peddling outright homosexual pornography in text and illustration."[98]

The *Times*, of course, missed the full extent of the mission of publications like *Grecian Guild Pictorial.* Carlson Wade's three-part series of articles about the ancient Greek Olympics (which ran shortly before Womack acquired the publication) serves as just one example among many of the *Pictorial*'s promotion of the healthy, naked male body as an ideal that could lead gay men toward identity formation and pride. Wade's descriptions linger on the "naked, slender, muscular" bodies of the Greek youths participating in the Olympic games and return again and again to the Greeks' cultural promotion of male nudity. This he compares to the Romans, who crushed Greek culture, "worshipped violence, destruction, and death," and after years of "debauchery . . . decreed that nudity was shameful." This contrast between what Wade characterizes as the civilized Greeks, illustrated by their love of the naked male body, and the barbaric Romans, shown in their destruction of the body, mirrors the confrontation between the magazine's gay readers, who aspire to the Greek ideal, and the straight moralists who saw the naked male body as "an instrument of debauchery and as an object of shame."[99] In this way, *Pictorial* readers were given historical backing for their erotic desires and could feel a sense of pride in being aligned with enlightened civilization.

Promoting desire for the male body and sexual activity with those bodies proceeded apace in Guild Press's fiction. Its general line of reasoning regarding sex was summed up by a character in Dandridge's *Ready, Willing, and Able* who "personally believe[s] that as long as any two people willingly indulge in any kind of sex relations with each other, it is their business and no one else's."[100] Guild Press's more specific mission can be seen most clearly in its series of chapbooks known as the Black Knight Classics. Three dozen in number, they were marketed as anonymous gay samizdat, stories passed from hand to hand in the early decades of the twentieth century, when they "could not be published in the United States without fear of imprisonment and harassment."[101]

Although some of the stories contain internal clues that indicate they were written near the time of their publication, some truly were based on older anonymous, privately distributed sources, and the stories were presented to readers as "genuine human . . . fantasy" coming from the "homosexual underground."[102] An introductory essay included in each of the Black Knight Classics argued: "These stories in this volume cause no one to degrade himself. If a man is stimulated by them, well and good. If he goes out and finds a male sexual partner after reading one of these tales, that proves only that the writing stimulated his imagination and desire. The point is: his sexual desire, inverted or 'normal,' is part and parcel of his humanity and cannot and should not be legislated out of existence by any censor, prude or literary sniper looking for 'prurience.' " In this manner, Guild Press launched a defense both of the homosexual stimulation to be found in its books and the homosexual action that might follow reading them.

Although the introduction to the Black Knight Classics positions them as fantasy, albeit fantasy that could spur gay men to go out and pursue sex with other men, advertising materials for the series deemed them "erotic realism." Ad copy claimed they offered a "truthful description of the basic sexual realities of life": "These books may seem harsh and brutal; the young men may seem bereft of moral standards; the characters may seem dominated by sex and obsessed by the search for the 'eternal ejaculation.' If these things seem true, it is for the simple reason that they are true. They depict, not the idealized world of homosexuality where the characters turn 'straight' or die a tragic death, but the real world where one sexual encounter can only be followed by another."[103] This definition explicitly rejects contemporary gay fiction that fulfills heterosexual fantasies of gay invisibility by ending in a psychological "cure" or death for the main character. While neither the Black Knight Classics nor other Guild Press fiction titles ignored the real-life social and physical dangers that could come from pursuing gay sex, their emphasis is more frequently on the beauty of the male body and the pleasure that can be gained from sex.[104] Here again, a positive view of gay sexual activity is extended to readers as a possibility in their own lives, strengthening their sexual identity.

The sheer volume of gay sex across the Black Knight Classics series normalizes its existence. The diversity of sexual action defies easy categorization, with sex occurring in all ways and in all places. In just one story, *Sailor '69'* (1969), sex takes place in bedrooms, at remote beaches, at parties, in cars while hitchhiking, and at glory holes in public restrooms, making sex seem ever-possible to readers.[105] The narrator engages in every type of gay sex with numerous men, both known to him and anonymous, before falling in love with a marine. Virtually all the Black Knight Classics end on similarly happy notes, with characters meeting a more permanent lover, accepting their homosexuality, or participating in or anticipating their next homosexual encounter.[106]

Along the way, characters in these stories laud gay sex in a variety of statements, and gay sex is both omnipresent and powerful in constructing an identity. In *The First Job* (1969), guests at the Manley Arms Hotel happily pursue whatever sex they are interested in, and the narrator, a new bellboy—who first claims, "I didn't think I could be an individual who would enjoy sucking another man's cock, fuck another man, or have him do likewise to me"—is initiated into gay sex. He ultimately discovers, through sex with both hotel guests and coworkers, that he has "grown to appreciate some of the beauties and pleasures that can be derived from having 'homosexual' tendencies. I loved what I was finding out about myself."[107]

What characters in Guild Press stories consistently find out, even if some of them do not initially see themselves as homosexual and have to lower what the narrator of *Under the Bridge* calls "the straight barrier," is that gay sex leads them to happiness. *Under the Bridge* (1969) sets up an alternate outdoor gay world, "difficult to find if you're going there for the first time," similar to the common motif of the greenwood in earlier homosexual literature. In this not easily accessed location, which has "enough room for a guy to do his own thing and at the same time feel sort of screened in and protected by the trees growing at the river's edge," several teenage and adult men from nearby towns meet to lounge, sleep, talk, brag, and have sex.[108] The loosely episodic story ends with a sixteen-page sex scene between the narrator and another man, in which they enter a relationship and no longer need to go to the secluded spot. In a world dedicated to declaring homosexual activity sinful or criminal, the Black Knight Classics and other Guild Press fiction celebrated gay sex as a pleasurable end in itself and possibly a preliminary to a deeper connection with other gay men.

## ONWARD TO COMMUNITY

Many scholars have documented the presence of gay communities, largely in urban areas, throughout the early twentieth century.[109] But for various reasons, including hesitancy on the part of those communities to be too noticeable and thus risk legal sanction by the authorities, their existence has not always been obvious, even to gays and lesbians living near them. In researching lesbian and gay Philadelphia, Marc Stein found that "word of mouth" was the method most often cited for "first learning about gay bars, clubs, and restaurants," a method also noted by historians looking at other cities.[110] For gays and lesbians not living near such communities, however, knowledge of their existence had to be gained through other means.

Guild Press contributed to growing awareness of gay communities through several types of publications. Meeker observes that "in an era when interstate travel was still cumbersome and long-distance telephone calls an event, print remained the dominant means for individuals to communicate with each other across great distances."[111] Guild's Richard Schlegel (using the pseudonym Rick Sampson) founded the Friend-to-Friend Club at the end of 1967. The club was a gay personals column masquerading as a pen-pal service, offering Guild's readers an opportunity to create their own community of like-minded gay men through letters. Gay pen-pal services had a fraught history, as their operators were open to arrest on charges that they were facilitating illegal activities, but by 1967 Womack felt certain that this would not occur.[112]

With its own magazine, *The Male Swinger*, and ads in *Grecian Guild Pictorial*, the Friend-to-Friend Club took off, receiving over five hundred letters in November 1968 alone.[113] The advertisements for correspondents came in from all over the United States and several foreign countries, and later issues of *The Male Swinger* added a special section for servicemen and veterans. The club also held out the possibility of in-person meetings; ads listed the correspondent's city, and some specified a desire for "companionship" or requested letters from members in the surrounding area. Especially for gay men living in small towns or rural locations, the Friend-to-Friend Club was a way to engage with other gay men without having to risk appearing in a known homosexual gathering spot, if they could even find such a place.

For readers who traveled or were unaware of nearby gay gathering places, Guild Press offered additional opportunities to connect to gay communities through its publication, beginning in 1964, of the *International Guild Guide*. Heavily advertised, the *International Guild Guide* was among the first widely distributed gay tourist guidebooks.[114] Ads for the guide queried, "Lost? Lonely? Bored? Too Embarassed [*sic*] to Ask?" and promised that "only those places where you will be welcome are listed."[115] From a ninety-six-page listing of bars, restaurants, bathhouses, and other gay community locations, mostly in major cities, the guide more than doubled in size by 1968 and included an increasing number of small cities and towns across the nation. In mapping what Meeker terms "a homosexual geography," Guild Press and the compilers of similar guidebooks

> knew that there were gay sites in small towns and large cities and that the commonalities they shared were far more important than their differences—that at the base, these were places where men could meet men and women could meet women for friendship, companionship, and sex. This image of the gay world shared by the compilers shows that they believed a sort of gay nationality existed but was waiting to be discovered by its members; by cataloging and mapping this nation, the publishers of these guidebooks not only told gay men and, to a lesser extent, lesbians where they could find others like themselves, but they provided them with evidence of the larger world, indeed the quasi-nation, in which they lived.[116]

Increased numbers of listings in the *International Guild Guide* indicate not only improved information gathering, but also the growth throughout the 1960s of the "quasi-nation" Meeker identifies. As more gays and lesbians came to self-identify as such, a larger number of commercial establishments began, at least in part, to cater to their business. As an example, for Washington, DC (Guild Press's headquarters), listings in the *International Guild Guide* grew from five in 1964 to forty in 1969, the year of Stonewall. While many of these establishments were short-lived or only partly gay or lesbian, the proliferation of listings indicates an associated growth in the community. Users of the guide were increasingly assured that there was a homosexual community waiting for them.

No guidebook listings of gay community sites, though, could help readers unable or unwilling to appear publicly in places known to attract homosexuals. Still, for gay men, Guild Press's fiction offerings allowed them to participate vicariously in gay community, thereby strengthening their commitment to a gay identity. One of the first Guild Press books that explicitly depicted gay community sites was *The Gay Coloring Book* (1964). Combining snippets of text with illustrations of scenes from the life of Percy, an effeminate young gay man, *The Gay Coloring Book* brought readers inside all-male social spaces, including gay parties, a gay bar, and the sexual cruising scene in a public park, a public toilet, an alley, and a bathhouse.[117] In this way, it served as its own kind of guidebook to gay community sites.

What *The Gay Coloring Book* showed in pictures, Guild Press novels illustrated with words. Gene, the protagonist of Ronnie Anderson's *Only the Weak Cry* (1969), leaves Wyalusing, Pennsylvania, and heads to New York City, where a new, older gay friend takes him to a gay party. Anderson's description of the party, including guests taking on female names, bantering with each other, and kissing, shows the existence and details of gay friendships and community to readers who had no firsthand knowledge. Similarly, Proferes's *Navy Blues* (1966) describes a gay bar in Virginia Beach, including the patrons' use of gay slang (for example, "browning queen") and information about how to indicate sexual availability.[118] These kinds of descriptions—of parks and bus stations, gay bars and restaurants—are staples of stories from Guild Press.

Perhaps the most detailed and remarkable novel along these lines is Bruce King's *Summer Awakening* (1967), published by 101 Enterprises, which illustrates one gay man's development of his homosexual identity on both a personal and community level. A bildungsroman taking place mostly in Washington, DC, King's novel follows the narrator, Allen, as he visits specific locations in the city, both real and fictional: a nightclub with drag performers; the California Kitchen, a popular real-life restaurant and cruising place; Lafayette Park, where he is warned to be careful of undercover police; and a lesbian bar, Margaret's. Throughout the story, readers are closely informed about gay community customs, including cruising instructions and gay slang (the police, for example, are referred to as "Lily Law"), and such potential social dangers as government investigations to root out gay civil servants and picking up rough trade. The entire novel serves as an introduction to gay communal life for readers either isolated from, or just beginning to venture into, the gay community.

Allen's first visit to a gay bar mimics the position of those readers:

> Allen looked around the room—he had never seen so many [gay men] under one roof—it was amazing, but gratifying!
>
> "Well, what do you think?" Fred asked.
>
> "I don't know. Are all these—" Allen stopped.
>
> Fred laughed. "Yes, they're the same as you and I."
>
> Allen was fascinated; it was a new world. There were dozens, even hundreds around just like him! How wonderful; how delightful! Allen continued to gape at the crowd. There were all sizes, shapes and ages sitting at the little tables around the room. He studied the faces—some wore dull, listless expressions; others were animated in affected rapture; most were just ordinarily expressive of their extraordinary conversation.[119]

By emphasizing the diversity and extent of the gay men in just one bar, King shows his readers the possibility of their finding a place for themselves within the spectrum of gay life. In this way Guild Press attempted to connect the larger gay community with the individual homosexual identities their publications helped forge and strengthen.

## A LASTING INFLUENCE

Guild Press would not have long to participate in burgeoning gay activism post-Stonewall. In April 1970, the FBI raided their offices in the Capitol Hill neighborhood as part of a coordinated, multi-city strike against producers of pornography.[120] Womack was charged with using underage models in Guild Press magazines. He was convicted and, on August 25, 1971, sentenced to two-and-a-half to seven-and-a-half years in prison, a sentence that was later reduced to six months.[121] Following his release from prison, Womack would move first to southeast Virginia and then to Florida, where his death in poverty in 1985 went unnoticed by the gay press.

That the significance of Womack and his publications was understood by the emergent gay liberation movement at the time of his arrest, however, is attested in an article published in *GAY*, the New York City–based newspaper edited by Jack Nichols and Lige Clarke, two former members of the Mattachine Society of Washington. The Gay Activists Alliance released a statement following his conviction that reads in part: "In view of the routine issuance of bond to murderers, thieves, narcotics dealers, and those guilty of other crimes with victims, we find outrageous the denial of bond to a publisher of books—ANY books—on the obviously specious ground that he is a 'danger to the community.' . . . We feel that not only has Dr. Womack not been doing harm to the community, but he has supplied a valuable service to the community and should be commended, not condemned. We, the homosexuals, know this and it is our community which utilizes the materials in question."[122] Those materials, by refuting society's prejudices and highlighting the existence of gay community, were one part of a path toward a more positive identity for gay men in the 1950s and 1960s, a path that has only begun to be mapped.

## NOTES

Material from this essay was presented in September 2012 at the conference "Radically Gay: The Life and Visionary Legacy of Harry Hay" and in October 2012 at the 39th Annual Washington, DC, Historical Studies Conference.

1. More on Hoover's actions can be found in David Allyn, *Make Love, Not War: The Sexual Revolution, An Unfettered History* (Boston: Little, Brown, 2000), 187–88. Hoover's letter to law enforcement can be found in the H. Lynn Womack Papers (collection no. 7441), box 1, folder 7, Division of Rare and Manuscript Collections, Cornell University Library, Ithaca, NY (hereafter cited as Womack Papers).
2. For Womack's initial indictment see "3 Indicted on Lewd Mail Charge," *Washington*

*Post*, Jan. 14, 1960. For his initial conviction see "Educator Convicted of Sending Obscene Literature through Mail," *Washington Post*, March 22, 1960. For the second set of indictments see "Ex-Professor Indicted," *Washington Post*, Dec. 9, 1960.

3. See Edwin A. Roberts Jr., *The Smut Rakers: A Report in Depth on Obscenity and the Censors* (Silver Spring, MD: National Observer, 1966), 60–72, for a contemporary report on the US post office's law enforcement division and its activities, including conviction statistics.
4. Details of Womack's education and teaching can be found in his 1957 curriculum vitae, author's collection.
5. Womack correspondence with Randolph "Randy" Benson, 1957–58, box 5, Womack Papers. For more on Womack's life, see Rodger Streitmatter and John C. Watson, "Herman Lynn Womack: Pornographer as First Amendment Pioneer," *Journal-ism History* 28.2 (Summer 2002): 56–65; and Philip Clark, "The First King of Pornography: H. Lynn Womack and Washington D.C.'s Guild Press," in *The Golden Age of Gay Fiction*, ed. Drewey Wayne Gunn (Albion, NY: MLR Press, 2009), 87–95.
6. For the text of the oral arguments in *Manual Enterprises v. Day*, see Leon Friedman, ed., *Obscenity: The Complete Oral Arguments before the Supreme Court in the Major Obscenity Cases* (New York: Chelsea House, 1983), 89–142.
7. Quotations are from the ruling *Manual Enterprises v. Day*, 370 U.S. 478 (1962). For a clear and useful, if anti-gay, contemporary discussion of the case's legal implications for the definition of obscenity, see Richard D. Kuh, *Foolish Figleaves? Pornography in—and out of—Court* (New York: Macmillan, 1967), 53–59.
8. The *ONE, Inc. v. Olesen* case (1958) had previously suggested that discussion of homosexuality did not necessarily qualify as prurient interest, but as Streitmatter and Watson note, its reasoning and message was vague since the ruling overturning *ONE Inc.*'s conviction gave no explanation of why the appeals court's decision was being vacated ("Herman Lynn Womack: Pornographer as First Amendment Pioneer," 62). For a contemporary view of *ONE, Inc. v. Olesen*, see Jim Kepner, *Rough News, Daring Views: 1950s' Pioneer Gay Press Journalism* (Binghamton, NY: Harrington Park Press, 1998), 264–69.
9. *1964–65 Guild Book Service Catalog* (Washington, DC: Guild Press, 1964), 4. The earliest known Guild Press publication was a hardcover reprint of British journalist Michael Davidson's memoir *The World, the Flesh, and Myself* (1962).
10. For more on the beginnings of this marketing to gay men, see David K. Johnson, "Physique Pioneers: The Politics of 1960s Gay Consumer Culture," *Journal of Social History* 43.4 (Summer 2010): 867–92.
11. Pan-Graphic Press was associated with the Mattachine Society and with the Dorian Book Service, run by activist Hal Call; see James T. Sears, *Behind the Mask of the Mattachine: The Hal Call Chronicles and the Early Movement for Homosexual Emancipation* (Binghamton, NY: Harrington Park Press, 2006), 292, 417. Potomac News Company and Media Arts were run by Womack. Although the exact nature of the relationship between Guild Press and 101 Enterprises is not fully known, there was extensive correspondence between Womack and the owner of 101 Enterprises, who used the pseudonym Nick Krysalka; see Womack Papers, box 2, folder 4. Because of this connection and because 101 Enterprises' magazines and, later, its 101 Books series of short novels were extensively marketed through Guild Book Service advertisements and publications, I am including them here in connection with Guild Press.

12. Womack claimed to have a clientele of over 40,000 individuals; see Womack's letter to TOM Men's Shop in Switzerland, Aug. 2, 1966, box 2, folder 47, Womack Papers. Between April 1966 and October 1967, Womack was sending out 30,000–37,000-piece mailings at the rate of one to two per month, although it is impossible to say whether each mailing was reaching all the same customers; for mailing statistics see box 1, folder 6, Womack Papers. While the size of mailing lists—to say nothing of book and magazine sales statistics—is notoriously difficult to determine with much accuracy, the abundance of evidence seems to suggest that 40,000 is a reasonable estimate for the size of the Guild Press mailing list. This may have grown considerably at a later point; in a 1971 obscenity trial, testimony indicated that Womack sold 80,000 copies of his magazine *Auto-Fellatio and Masturbation* alone. Sanford J. Unger, "Homosexual 'Cause' Seen as Issue in Trial," *Washington Post*, July 21, 1971.
13. For a recent assessment of the historic association of gay men with cities, see Julie Abraham, *Metropolitan Lovers: The Homosexuality of Cities* (Minneapolis: University of Minnesota Press, 2009). The grand jury indictment and list of charges against Womack are in box 1, folder 4, Womack Papers. One count in the second indictment alleged possession of "certain photographs of male nudes with intent to sell, give away, and exhibit to others." Co-indicted with Womack was Alfred J. Heinecke, a New Jersey–based photographer who emigrated to the United States after a period of confinement in Hitler's prisons as a Socialist. I am unaware of any scholarly attention to Heinecke's life or legal trials; for biographical details, see Alquin Images, Catalogue III (Winter 1986), unpaginated, George Fisher Papers (collection no. 7437), box 11, folder 9, Division of Rare and Manuscript Collections, Cornell University Library.
14. Abraham, *Metropolitan Lovers*, 42–43.
15. John Loughery, *The Other Side of Silence: Men's Lives and Gay Identities: A Twentieth-Century History* (New York: Henry Holt, 1998), 183.
16. In addition to those discussed here, a few representative examples, both gay and lesbian, can be found in John Howard, *Men Like That: A Southern Queer History* (Chicago: University of Chicago Press, 1999), 11; Peter M. Nardi, David Sanders, and Judd Marmor, *Growing Up before Stonewall: Life Stories of Some Gay Men* (New York: Routledge, 1994), 77, 86; James T. Sears, *Lonely Hunters: An Oral History of Lesbian and Gay Southern Life, 1948–1968* (Boulder, CO: Westview Press, 1997), 27, 99–100, 129; and Marc Stein, *City of Sisterly and Brotherly Loves: Lesbian and Gay Philadelphia, 1945–1972* (Chicago: University of Chicago Press, 2000), 195, 227, 270.
17. David K. Johnson, "The Kids of Fairytown: Gay Male Culture on Chicago's Near North Side in the 1930s," in *Creating a Place for Ourselves: Lesbian, Gay, and Bisexual Community Histories*, ed. Brett Beemyn (New York: Routledge, 1997), 97–118, quotations on 99–100. For more on these novels and others of the period, see Anthony Slide, *Lost Gay Novels: A Reference Guide to Fifty Works from the First Half of the Twentieth Century* (Binghamton, NY: Harrington Park Press, 2003).
18. Stuart Timmons, *The Trouble with Harry Hay: Founder of the Modern Gay Movement* (Boston: Alyson, 1990), 27–29; Nichols quoted in Sears, *Lonely Hunters*, 194.
19. Loughery, *The Other Side of Silence*, 198.
20. Jack Lait and Lee Mortimer, *Washington Confidential* (New York: Crown, 1951), 116–26.
21. See Martin Meeker, *Contacts Desired: Gay and Lesbian Communications and Community, 1940s–1970s* (Chicago: University of Chicago Press, 2006), esp. chaps. 3 and 4.

22. Jean M. White, "Those Others – III: Homosexuals Are in All Kinds of Jobs, Find Place in Many Levels of Society," *Washington Post*, Feb. 2, 1965; "The Homosexual in America," *Time*, Jan. 21, 1966; John D'Emilio, *Sexual Politics, Sexual Communities: The Making of a Homosexual Minority in the United States, 1940–1970* (Chicago: University of Chicago Press, 1983), 147.
23. Larry Gross, *Up from Invisibility: Lesbians, Gay Men, and the Media in America* (New York: Columbia University Press, 2001), 19; Stein, *City of Sisterly and Brotherly Loves*, 116; Gross, *Up from Invisibility*, 21.
24. Rodger Streitmatter, *Unspeakable: The Rise of the Gay and Lesbian Press in America* (Boston: Faber & Faber, 1995), 80 (quotation), 25–26.
25. Ibid., 76.
26. D'Emilio, *Sexual Politics, Sexual Communities*, 110.
27. Meeker, *Contacts Desired*, 55–56.
28. Robert K. Martin, "Scandal at Smith," *The Radical Teacher* 45 (Winter 1994): 7. Arvin's collecting of physique magazines, along with other erotic material, is detailed in Barry Werth, *The Scarlet Professor: Newton Arvin: A Literary Life Shattered by Scandal* (New York: Doubleday, 2001).
29. Meeker, *Contacts Desired*, 56.
30. Guild Press did avoid frontal nudity, owing to obscenity laws, until after the founders of the Minneapolis-based company DSI Sales were acquitted of obscenity in 1967 for mailing nudes. See "Male Nudes Not Obscene; DSI Acquitted on 29 Charges," *Advocate* 1.1 (Sept. 1967): 1. Regarding gay language, Guild published one of the earlier guides to gay slang, *The Guild Dictionary of Homosexual Terms* (Washington, DC: Guild Press, 1965).
31. "We Want You," *Grecian Guild Pictorial* 1.1 (Autumn 1955): 6–7.
32. "The Grecian Guild," *Grecian Guild Pictorial* 1.1 (Autumn 1955): 5.
33. Herman Lynn Womack to Randolph "Randy" Benson, March 29, 1958, box 5, Womack Papers.
34. Gross, *Up from Invisibility*, 222.
35. "Who Are the Members of the Grecian Guild?" *Grecian Guild Pictorial* 2.4 (July 1957): 4–5.
36. Ibid.
37. S. George Spillman, "Personality Strength through Mental Exercise," *Grecian Guild Pictorial* 2.1 (Jan. 1957): 8.
38. "I Am a Grecian," *Grecian Guild Pictorial* 2.1 (Jan. 1957): 15.
39. This transition from a small-town to a metropolitan area—what Colin R. Johnson terms "one of the few cultural narratives that bind us—the by-now familiar, indeed almost folksy, rural-to-urban migration narrative"—is a key element in queer theorists' critical discussion of metronormativity. Colin R. Johnson, "Homosexuals in Unexpected Places? An Introduction," *American Studies* 48.2 (Summer 2007): 5–8, quotation on 6; see also Judith Halberstam, *In a Queer Time and Place: Transgender Bodies, Subcultural Lives* (New York: NYU Press, 1995), 36–38; and Scott Herring, *Another Country: Queer Anti-Urbanism* (New York: NYU Press, 2010). Thanks to the anonymous reader of this essay who pointed me toward discussions of metronormativity. For discussion of twentieth-century lives in rural areas, see Howard, *Men Like That*; this includes analysis of gay fiction that does not involve a move to the city (189–220).
40. Guy Faulk, *It's a Gay, Gay, Gay World* (Washington, DC: Guild Press, 1968), 9. The

idea of "degrees of queerness" may also have more accurately reflected the self-identification of many readers of Guild Press material. For extended discussion of men who had sex with men without necessarily self-identifying as gay, see, among many other sources, Howard, *Men Like That*, 5–6, 12–15; and Barry Reay, *New York Hustlers: Masculinity and Sex in Modern America* (Manchester: Manchester University Press, 2010), esp. chaps. 2 and 4.

41. *Navy Discipline Below Deck* (Washington, DC: Guild Press, 1970), 58.
42. James J. Proferes, *Any Man Is Fair Game* (Washington, DC: Guild Press, 1969), 54.
43. Jack Evans, *All the Studs at Sea* (Washington, DC: Guild Press, 1971), 38.
44. Alexander Goodman (George Haimsohn), *Handsome Is . . .* (Washington, DC: Guild Press, 1966), 75.
45. Jerry directly connects the oppression of blacks and gays by American society, and the narrator links the social position of gays, integrationists, Communists, and liberals in the post-McCarthyist South. This level of direct political commentary is rare for Guild Press novels.
46. Guy Dandridge, *Jerry and Jim* (Washington, DC: Guild Press, 1967), 65.
47. Guild Book Service, Bulletin no. 43 (Feb. 1967), author's collection.
48. Robert W. Wood, "Spiritual Exercises," *Grecian Guild Pictorial* 1.4 (June–Aug. 1956). James A. M. Hanna's first contribution, "Thoughts on Our Creed," appeared in *Grecian Guild Pictorial* 2.3 (May 1957). The Reverend Robert H. Coleman was "Grecian of the Quarter," *Grecian Guild Pictorial* 1.5 (Dec. 1956).
49. "Who Are You?" *Grecian Guild Pictorial* no. 19 (June 1959): 10.
50. Dandridge, *Jerry and Jim*, 15, 148.
51. Guy Dandridge, *Boys' Camp* (Washington, DC: Guild Press, 1971), 154.
52. Guy Dandridge, *Ready, Willing, and Able* (Washington, DC: Guild Press, 1971), 117–18.
53. *I Found What I Wanted* (Washington, DC: Guild Press, 1969), 79; on the new ending see Whitney Strub's essay elsewhere in this volume.
54. D'Emilio, *Sexual Politics, Sexual Communities*, 17.
55. Clark, "The First King of Pornography," 89.
56. D'Emilio, *Sexual Politics, Sexual Communities*, 18. For one gay man's encounters with psychotherapy in the 1950s and 1960s, see Martin Duberman, *Cures: A Gay Man's Odyssey* (New York: Dutton, 1991). For a gay psychiatrist's reflections on the time period, see Dr. Charles Silverstein, *For the Ferryman* (New York: Chelsea Station, 2012). Numerous books by contemporary psychiatrists present the majority views of the medical community; Edmund Bergler, *Homosexuality: Disease or Way of Life?* (New York: Hill & Wang, 1956), is fairly representative.
57. Letter from L.L. to Richard Schlegel, May 16, 1967, Richard L. Schlegel Papers (collection no. 7306), box 1, folder 1, Division of Rare and Manuscript Collections, Cornell University Library.
58. Goodman, *Handsome Is . . .*, 75.
59. Dandridge, *Jerry and Jim*, 148.
60. Gene Holland, *Boys in Love, with Other Boys* (New York: 101 Enterprises, 1967), 15.
61. Ibid., 71.
62. Ibid., 72.
63. Duberman, *Cures*, 139.
64. David K. Johnson, *The Lavender Scare: The Cold War Persecution of Gays and*

*Lesbians in the Federal Government* (Chicago: University of Chicago Press, 2004), 190.

65. On government and military discrimination see Johnson, *Lavender Scare;* Randy Shilts, *Conduct Unbecoming: Gays and Lesbians in the U.S. Military* (New York: Ballantine, 1994); and William N. Eskridge Jr., "Privacy Jurisprudence and the Apartheid of the Closet, 1946–1961," *Florida State University Law Review* 24 (1997): 703–840.
66. Charles Berg, *Fear, Punishment, Anxiety and the Wolfenden Report* (London: George Allen & Unwin, 1959). Guild Book Service appears to have purchased an indeterminate number of copies of Berg's book, placed a Guild Press address label over the publication information on each title page, and resold them to its customers. A copy like this is in the author's collection. For Berg's views on homosexuality, see Charles Berg, M.D., and Clifford Allen, M.D., *The Problem of Homosexuality* (New York: Citadel, 1958).
67. Quoted in Berg, *Fear, Punishment, Anxiety,* 20. The Wolfenden Committee's report was released in September 1957, but its recommendation to decriminalize homosexuality between consenting adults twenty-one or older was not adopted until 1967. For contemporary discussion of the release of the Wolfenden Report, see Kepner, *Rough News,* 211–13, 246–47.
68. Berg, *Fear, Punishment, Anxiety,* 49.
69. Quoted in "Preface," *Homosexuality and Citizenship in Florida* (Tallahassee: Florida Legislative Investigation Committee, 1964). For a full discussion of the background of the committee, also known as the Johns Committee because of the leadership of state senator Charley Johns, and the effects of its various activities, see Sears, *Lonely Hunters,* chaps. 2 and 3; and Stacy Braukman, *Communists and Perverts under the Palms: The Johns Committee in Florida, 1956–1965* (Gainesville: University Press of Florida, 2012).
70. *1964–65 Guild Book Service Catalog,* 44. Even the advisory committee to the Johns Committee was aware of Guild Press's reprint of "the Purple Report" and "read background information on H. Lynn Womack" during their June 1964 meeting. See the reprint of the Advisory Committee's meeting minutes in Eskridge, "Privacy Jurisprudence," 835.
71. "Less Taxes for Bachelors!," *Grecian Guild Pictorial* no. 45 (July 1964).
72. H. Erick Lester, *Studies in Danish Male Homosexual Pornography, Vol. 2* (Washington, DC: Guild Press, 1970), 10.
73. Ibid., 14, 2.
74. Letters from some of these servicemen to Womack can be found among the Womack Papers at Cornell.
75. Quoted in James Griffin, "Dr. Womack and the Nudie Magazines," *Washington Daily News,* April 30, 1970. An illustration in one Guild Press book shows protestors carrying signs that read "Gay is Good!," "Gay Liberation Front," and " 'Fuck' Sounds Better Than 'Vietnam.' " See James J. Proferes, *Boys, Drugs, and Sex* (Washington, DC: Guild Press, 1970), 8.
76. Guild Book Service, Bulletin no. 19 (Feb. 1965), author's collection.
77. *Homosexuality in the Military* (Washington, DC: Guild Press, 1970), n.p. This publication, which appears to have been written entirely by J. J. Proferes, was one of several single-issue magazines put out by Guild in its last few years.

78. Ibid., n.p.
79. *Navy Discipline Below Deck,* 57–58.
80. Alexander Goodman, *A Summer on Fire Island* (Washington, DC: Guild Press, 1966), 107.
81. Ibid., 109.
82. Ibid., 115, 90.
83. Ibid., 111–12.
84. Jan Ewing, interview by author, Nov. 3, 2007.
85. D'Emilio, *Sexual Politics, Sexual Communities,* 245, 124–25.
86. Quoted in Stein, *City of Sisterly and Brotherly Loves,* 238.
87. Micha Ramakers, *Dirty Pictures: Tom of Finland, Masculinity, and Homosexuality* (New York: St. Martin's, 2000), ix.
88. Quoted ibid., 8–9; the original article is Robert J. Pierce, "Tom of Finland, the Case for Gay Art," *Soho Weekly News,* Feb. 6, 1980.
89. Nardi, Sanders, and Marmor, *Growing Up before Stonewall,* 127.
90. Quoted in Streitmatter, *Unspeakable,* 96.
91. Quoted in Stein, *City of Sisterly and Brotherly Loves,* 237.
92. Michael Bronski, *The Pleasure Principle: Sex, Backlash, and the Struggle for Gay Freedom* (New York: St. Martin's, 1998), 162.
93. For extended discussion of the drawbacks of the privacy argument as related to gay legal equality, see Eskridge, "Privacy Jurisprudence."
94. Bronski, *The Pleasure Principle,* 161, 162.
95. Goodman, *A Summer on Fire Island,* 87.
96. Becker quoted in D'Emilio, *The World Turned,* 30.
97. The role of newsstands in making gay materials available has yet to be fully explored. Jan Ewing recalled first finding Guild Press materials at newsstands surrounding Union Square in New York City in the 1960s; interview by author, Nov. 3, 2007. Donald W. McLeod discusses *GAY* magazine's attempts to achieve newsstand distribution in the United States in *A Brief History of GAY: Canada's First Gay Tabloid, 1964–1966* (Toronto: Homewood Books, 2003), 53–55. Meeker, *Contacts Desired,* 34, 50, discusses the homophiles' use of newsstands.
98. Quoted in Martin Duberman, *About Time: Exploring the Gay Past* (New York: Meridian, 1991), 241.
99. Carlson Wade, "The Greek Olympics," *Grecian Guild Pictorial* 2.5 (Sept. 1957): 38; Wade, "The Greek Olympics," *Grecian Guild Pictorial* 2.6 (Nov. 1957): 12–13.
100. Dandridge, *Ready, Willing, and Able,* 119.
101. All quotations in this and the following paragraph are from the anonymous seventeen-page introductory essay, "The Meaning and Value of Homosexual Underground Literature," included in all Black Knight Classics volumes.
102. For example, an earlier version of the Black Knight Classics' *I Found What I Wanted* can be found in Gay Erotic Stories (collection no. 7668), Division of Rare and Manuscript Collections, Cornell University Library.
103. Black Knight Classics advertisement, Village Books and Press, box 1, folder 1, Mail Order Erotica (collection no. 7634), Division of Rare and Manuscript Collections, Cornell University Library.
104. Some of the real-life dangers depicted in Guild Press fiction titles include appearances by the vice squad, military investigators, government investigators, blackmailers,

and rough trade (usually presented as gay men unable to accept their homosexuality who beat up their male sexual partners after the act).

105. *Sailor '69'* (Washington, DC: Guild Press, 1969).
106. Only four of the thirty-six Black Knight Classics (*After Hours, Give It Away!; A Night in the Hayloft; Off Duty Studs;* and *7 in a Barn*) do not end in this manner.
107. *The First Job* (Washington, DC: Guild Press, 1969), 18, 39.
108. *Under the Bridge* (Washington, DC: Guild Press, 1969), 63, 18–19. For a discussion of the greenwood theme, see Byrne R. S. Fone, "This Other Eden: Arcadia and the Homosexual Imagination," *Journal of Homosexuality* 8 (1983): 13–34.
109. One of the best known examples is George Chauncey's *Gay New York: Gender, Urban Culture, and the Making of the Gay Male World, 1890–1940* (New York: Basic Books, 1994). My essay has been influenced by the community histories presented in Beemyn, *Creating a Place for Ourselves.*
110. Stein, *City of Sisterly and Brotherly Loves,* 70. On other cities see, for example, the essays by David K. Johnson (Chicago) and Elizabeth Lapovsky Kennedy and Madeline Davis (Buffalo) in Beemyn, *Creating a Place for Ourselves.*
111. Meeker, *Contacts Desired,* 100.
112. See ibid., 23–26, for the history of gay contact clubs, and 56–59 for the Mattachine Society's internal debate about pen-pal services. In the second issue of his magazine *The Male Swinger,* Womack printed a facsimile of a March 1967 discussion in the US House of Representatives that revealed the Justice Department's unwillingness to prosecute cases of "traffic . . . in pornography through the mail between private correspondents." See *The Male Swinger* no. 2 (n.d.; 1968), n.p.
113. See letter from Richard Schlegel to Womack, Dec. 15, 1968, box 1, folder 69, Womack Papers.
114. For discussions of other such guidebooks, see Hugh Hagius, ed., *Swasarnt Nerf's Gay Guides for 1949* (New York: Bibliogay, 2010); and Meeker, *Contacts Desired,* chap. 5.
115. *1964–65 Guild Book Service Catalog,* 68–69.
116. Meeker, *Contacts Desired,* 224, 214.
117. *The Gay Coloring Book* (Washington, DC: Guild Press, 1964).
118. Ronnie Anderson, *Only the Weak Cry* (Washington, DC: Guild Press, 1969), 39–45; J. J. Proferes, *Navy Blues* (Washington, DC: Guild Press, 1966), 17–21.
119. Bruce King, *Summer Awakening* (New York: 101 Enterprises, 1967), 27–28.
120. Peter Osnos, "Womack Arrested Again as Obscenity Publisher," *Washington Post,* April 25, 1970.
121. "Ex-Professor Sentenced in Erotica Case," *Washington Post,* Aug. 26, 1971.
122. Quoted in Perrin Shaffer, "Guild Guide Publisher Jailed," *GAY,* Sept. 27, 1971.

# "Menus for Men . . . or What Have You"

## CONSUMING GAY MALE CULTURE IN LOU RAND HOGAN'S *THE GAY DETECTIVE* AND *THE GAY COOKBOOK*

Pamela Robertson Wojcik

When one mentions queer pulp, certain images come to mind: titillating garish paperback covers with men in tight T-shirts exchanging lurid glances, women in lingerie posing provocatively in duos, or three people in queerly triangulated relationships, set in various seedy locales—prisons, bars, and cheap apartments—with adjectives like "twilight," "strange," "odd," "forbidden," "unnatural," "bizarre," "tormented," and "secret" to describe the characters and actions within.

*The Gay Detective,* originally published in 1961 under the pseudonym Lou Rand, fits neatly into the queer pulp canon. Cover art from the original paperback shows a nude woman wrapped in a blanket sandwiched between two men in suits. A caption under the illustration reads: "Francis and Tiger had found out what they needed to know. The Trick now was to get the nude Vivien out of the bathhouse and to safety . . ." While the positioning of the woman, her nudity, and the caption would suggest a standard heterosexual triangle, with two men fighting over a women, the glances between the two men—and the curious bathhouse pink interior—suggest a different trajectory of desire. In 1964, when it was reprinted in hardcover as *Rough Trade*, the new title signaled its gayness in more coded terms than the first version, but described the narrative as "Handsome homosexuals on a rampaging orgy of gay lust and the sultry women who tempt them." The publisher restated the queer coding in its 1965 paperback-cover description as "a daring novel of handsome men caught in the violence of the twilight world of sex."[1]

But how do we account for Lou Rand's other major publication, *The Gay Cookbook*, published under the name "Chef Lou Rand Hogan"?[2] Rather than a torrid scene, its cover features a feminized man in queer attire—tight pants, pocket hanky, neck scarf, and an apron that says "hers" and has a big bow—holding a steak, somewhat limp-wristedly, over a grill. The cover identifies the book as "the complete compendium of campy cuisine and menus for men . . . or what have you." Describing its readers as "the androgynous," the book makes clear its intended audience and its camp tone, waggishly admonishing readers, "Don't bother to look it up, Maude. It means 'limp wristed.' "[3] Gay? Clearly. But not what we usually consider the stuff of pulp. The book is playful, not sensationalist; it is nonfiction, not a novel; and it places its gay character in the kitchen and at the backyard grill, not in the seedy milieu of urban subcultures. Rather than a "twilight world of sex," it promises "canapés, hor d'oeuvres [*sic*], aphrodisiacs," "swish steak," and "that old tired fish."

*The Gay Cookbook* invites us to expand our understanding of what constitutes gay male pulp. While pulp has come to signal certain genres—crime novels, detective fiction, sleazy romance—the term initially described a method of paperback production that enabled books to be printed on smaller pages and with smaller type, thus permitting them to circulate more easily as pocket books and through mail-order catalogs. The term "pulp" applied to both fiction and nonfiction titles, and while most paperback originals were written for the mass pulp market, others became pulp by virtue of packaging and distribution systems. It includes reprints of high culture literature (such as Radclyffe Hall's *The Well of Loneliness*, Carson

McCullers's *The Ballad of the Sad Café*, Tennessee Williams's *A Streetcar Named Desire*, and Emile Zola's *Nana*, which were repeatedly issued as pulps to attract new audiences), nonfiction tell-alls about underground cultures and subcultures (such as Christine Jorgensen's autobiography, and other books about transvestites, transsexuals, hermaphrodites, and other gender benders); and pseudo-scientific and other nonfiction titles that could be made to appear titillating (such as books about Leopold and Loeb or the Kinsey Report on male sexuality).[4] The larger category of pulp, then, signals not only certain genres, but cheap paperback culture generally, and it extends potentially to books that are not literally printed on pulp but deploy pulp marketing strategies and the exploitationist and sensationalist content associated with pulp titles.

Saber Press of Fresno, California, the original publisher of *The Gay Detective*, was a classic pulp publisher, operating on the "margins of respectability." As Susan Stryker and Martin Meeker note, Saber was owned and operated by Sanford Aday, a former pimp, and Wallace de Ortega Maxey, an ordained minister who was also an early member of the Mattachine Society. Saber sold a wide range of titles with "lurid, semi-sleazy topics" and "low production values." Aday and Maxey sold their books through mail order and, after repeatedly running afoul of the law, were convicted of distributing lewd material through the mail and served time.[5]

*The Gay Cookbook* was published in 1965 by Sherbourne Press, and then released in a new edition by Bell, a division of Crown Publishers. Like Saber, Sherbourne worked in the broader context of pulp, publishing ephemeral paperback books with sensational titles and cover art in categories such as astrology, how-to, sexual exposés, erotica, and parapsychology, and distributing their books through catalog and mail order as well as in newsstands and other retail venues. Among the titles on their list for the few years before and after *The Gay Cookbook* are *Sexual Stimulation* (Robert E. L. Masters, 1967), *Male and Female Sexual Deviations* (Michael S. Wolfgang, 1967), *Sex Offenders in Group Therapy* (Manning R. Slater, 1964), *Mr. Madam: Confessions of a Male Madam* (Kenneth Marlowe, 1964), *Confessions of a Male Prostitute* (John O'Day, 1964), *The Golden Age of Erotica* (Bernhardt J. Hurwood, 1965), and *The Male Homosexual*

(Kenneth Marlow, 1965).[6] Distributed alongside these titles, *The Gay Cookbook* would be consumed differently than if it were (and when it was) published by a more mainstream press or distributed alongside other cookbooks. Rather than taken solely as a variant of the cookbook genre, it would have been seen as participating in a broader project of exposing queer identities and practices.

Pulp fiction and nonfiction both operate on at least two levels simultaneously. On the one hand, they provide "outsider" or pseudo-scientific access to "deviant" and subcultural sexual worlds that could be marketed to straight readers. On the other hand, this material could provide knowledge of sexual subcultures and practices that gay and lesbian consumers might read, seeking clues and codes to subcultural practices. Several scholars have pointed out that while censorship concerns often led pulp fictions to denounce the homosexual desires they represented, they nonetheless functioned historically to acculturate gay men and lesbians into subcultures and were integral to processes of queer identification.[7] As Katherine Forrest writes: "The importance of all our pulp fiction novels cannot possibly be overstated. Whatever their negative images or messages, they told us we were not alone. Because they told us about each other, they led us to look for and find each other, they led us to the end of the isolation that had divided and conquered us. And once we found each other, once we began to question the judgments made of us, our civil rights movement was born."[8]

In addition to providing gay men and lesbians with a sense of belonging, Michael Bronski argues, pulps also functioned as "educational, self-help, and how-to manuals": "These books were the maps and signposts, the etiquette manuals and the foreign phrase books, for gay men entering the half-hidden world of homosexuality."[9] As David Johnson suggests, even anti-gay propaganda, like the homophobic diatribe *Washington Confidential* (Jack Lait and Lee Mortimer, 1959), which delineated the location of "degenerates" in DC parks, could function as a "virtual tour guide to the gay subculture."[10] Beyond the camp value of sensational plots and images, then, pulp fiction has been taken up as a record of what was possible and impossible to represent, as documents that helped produce pre-Stonewall imagined communities, as artifacts of oppression, and as relics of the closet. In this vein, Susan Stryker and Martin Meeker's introduction to the 2003 reprint edition of *The Gay Detective* emphasizes the book's function as a "veritable road-map to the inner dynamics of 'pre-liberation' gay culture" and, in particular, suggests a historical value in reading the book's thinly veiled allusions to public figures, public locales, and even the spatial arrangement of "commercial sexual activity" in San Francisco.[11]

*The Gay Cookbook* not only reminds us of the broader definition of pulp, but also points to the larger culture of gay consumerism that existed before Stonewall, in and through which the pulps circulated. As Bronski writes, "Gay male pulps were simply one of the more visible manifestations of a gay publishing, literary, and public culture that existed before Stonewall."[12] Theories of lifestyle generally highlight the "construction of identity through consumption practices, 'leisure-work' and domestic space." Rather than individual identities, lifestyle marks out classed identities and attendant "transformations in, and movements within, the social space of class relations."[13] As Johnson argues, pulp paperbacks, along with other mail-order items such as physique magazines, greeting cards, LPs, cologne, jewelry, and clothing, were covertly marketed to and consumed by gay men and lesbians, and their consumption mediated the production of queer social identities. Thus by purchasing gay-coded goods, including pulp and other publications, gay men expressed their identities and affiliations, while enacting a particular gay lifestyle: "The ability to purchase these items validated their erotic attraction to other men and provided particular class-based models for what it meant to be gay." Along with discovering themselves *inside* the books, gay men could self-identify through their purchase and consumption of these books, magazines, and other items; for example, Johnson mentions a young man carrying a physique magazine as a recognizable gay code when he cruises a "degenerate" park.[14]

While *The Gay Detective* and *The Gay Cookbook* might be seen as strange bedfellows—and most accounts of their authorship treat the cookbook as an oddity in relation to the crime novel—their joint circulation through mail-order catalogs, as well as their shared authorship, invites us to imagine them coexisting on the same bookshelf, in the same man's collection. In this light, we can read *The Gay Cookbook* alongside *The Gay Detective* in order to determine how each serves to acculturate men into a gay subculture and produce gay male identification.

Both *The Gay Detective* and *The Gay Cookbook* straddle the discourses of the closet era and those of emerging homophile movements. Taken together, the two books work similarly to, on the one hand, introduce a presumably hidden world and, on the other, suggest that the visible world is always already gay, with gay identities seen not as marginal to the dominant, but inherent to it. These works manage to engage gay identity as both different from straight culture and similar to it, without aiming for assimilation or normative definitions. At the same time, they provide very different "maps and signposts" to gay culture in the 1960s. While *The Gay Detective* charts a fluid, but macho, public world of sex and scandal, *The Gay Cookbook* portrays a world more stereotypically feminized, but less stereotypically domesticated.

## "GET HER"
### *THE GAY DETECTIVE* AND GENDER PARODY

In her analysis of gay detective fiction, Judith Markowitz characterizes *The Gay Detective* as "parody that turns hard-boiled fiction on its head" because it introduces a private detective "who has 'an unconsciously un-masculine air' and plays with stereotypes of gay men and lesbians as well as hard-boiled conventions." According to Linda Hutcheon, parody is "imitation characterized by ironic inversion."[15] It is repetition with critical distance that targets a text or art form, not life (as in satire). Parody, according to Hutcheon, distances the reader from the conventions of the original text or form by deploying the conventions of the form ironically, exaggerating the conventions of the form, or replacing the conventions with inversions. Markowitz views *The Gay Detective* as doing the last of these, insofar as the characters are "inversions" of what she views as the heterosexual norm of detective fiction. But thinking of the novel as parody in this sense seems to reinscribe the dominant and incorrectly assumes that all other detective fiction is "straight." Consider just the porn and blackmail ring in Raymond Chandler's *The Big Sleep*, the homoerotics of Chandler's *The Long Goodbye*, or the perverted fantasies of Jim Thompson's *Killer Inside Me*, and it becomes clear that the genre may be largely heterosexual but contains queer elements. (I am using "queer" here and throughout this essay in the sense Alexander Doty outlines as he attempts to account for a wide range of positions that are "non, anti-, or contra-straight." This sense of queerness includes gay- and lesbian-specific positions as well as non-gay and non-lesbian positions that nonetheless are in opposition to or at variance with the dominant, straight symbolic order.)[16] In contrast to Markowitz and more in line with my view, Stryker and Meeker argue that the book is "primarily a detective story" that will lead readers to wonder "whodunit and why."[17] In this sense, the book presents a gay variant on the detective plot, not an inversion of it.

While taking the book as a "straight" version of the detective novel, Stryker and Meeker, like Markowitz, view the book as camp. For Markowitz, its camp status seems to inhere in its "incongruity," and especially its inverted stereotypes. For Stryker and Meeker, the book is "hard-boiled camp" because of its queer characters and plot.[18] Acknowledging that camp exists in the "eye of the beholder," I would argue that *The Gay Detective* is less a camp novel in tone or manner than a novel that represents characters who camp, who represent camp behavior and adopt camp lingo, much as Mae West's characters did in her 1930s films.[19] Certainly *The Gay Detective* deploys camp. The characters in the novel are camp and enact camp critiques of their milieu and of each other throughout the text. But the novel itself is not presented as camp.

To make the distinction between a gay detective novel with camp characters and a gay camp parody, we can contrast *The Gay Detective* to *The Man from C.A.M.P.* series of ten gay pulp fiction novels, written largely by Victor Banis under the pseudonym Don Holliday.[20] *The Man from C.A.M.P.* subtly spoofs "Batman and Robin" and explicitly parodies *The Man from U.N.C.L.E.*, which began as a TV series (1964–1968) and spawned the spinoff *The Girl from U.N.C.L.E.* and two dozen novels between 1965 and 1968. *The Man from C.A.M.P.* operates within a pop camp milieu and tone. The name C.A.M.P., of course, adduces camp as an aesthetic, but the acronym is never explained in the books. A pro-gay agency, it is opposed by B.U.T.C.H. (Brothers United to Crush Homosexuality). Jackie Holmes, the detective at the center of the series, is a blond gay superspy with a killer poodle named Sophie. The books' titles parody specific well-known texts and express their camp sensibility through double entendres such as *Rally Round the Fag* (1967), *The Watercress File* (1966), and *The Son Goes Down* (1966). The covers, designed by Robert Bonfils, feature Jackie Holmes in comedically over-the-top costumes—such as toreador pants, tight yellow pants, ascots, and, frequently, underpants—with brightly colored backgrounds, especially in lavender and yellow.

In contrast, *The Gay Detective*, rather than a parody of detective fiction or a camp novel, can be seen as participating in a form of gender parody through its characterizations. Viewing gender constructions as performative acts, Judith Butler argues that parodies of gender norms can destabilize gender itself, to "render it thoroughly and radically *incredible*." In *The Gay Detective*, Hogan plays with gender by emphasizing the mobility of identity, gender performance, and the fluidity of gender roles, to show what Butler characterizes as the "contingency" of gender.[21]

First, the novel destabilizes identity through the characters' naming practices. In line with the book's emphasis on secret identities, we learn that Tiger Olsen, an ex-football star and car salesman who is hired by detective Francis Morley, is really named Clarence.[22] In dealing with his secretary, Hattie, Francis "often addressed her by such other names as came to mind at the moment," such as Bessie, Agatha, and Minnie.[23] Catching Tiger in bed with Vivien Holden, a female client, Francis refers to himself as Mother, answering Tiger's lame excuses with, "Yes, dear. Mother knows!" (67). In his memoir, Hogan identifies this practice of adopting false names as key to gay survival: "Because of the necessity to hide one's 'other self,' the vogue for 'stage names' came into being." He adds that when he worked onstage at Miss Brown's Pasadena Playhouse, he went first by the name Bubbles, then by Sonny. In his memoir, he refers to himself consistently as "Mother": "This 'name' thing was only a harmless bit, but it added some glamour to often unglamorous people, and it did protect the name of the 'girl' involved."[24]

In addition to playfully changing names, and thus unhinging the certainty of identity, *The Gay Detective* consistently shows identity to be a masquerade. When Francis and Tiger go undercover, for example, both men pretend to be gay tourists in order to gain access to the secret locales of the gay underworld. Even though Francis is coded gay in the text, he must perform a theatricalized version of gayness to succeed at the ruse: "Francis, who had again adopted his gayest manner, even to a slightly mincing step, loudly remarked, 'My gawd, dearies! There's nothing like this in Philadelphia' " (74). At another point, in a meeting with the police, Francis shifts from a camp mode of behavior to a more serious tone: "Francis, for the first time during the conference, abandoned his flippant attitude and took up where the captain had paused. 'Gentlemen, let's face it. Suppose we put it this way, and stop mincing words . . .' Strangely, and surprisingly to his listeners, his words were now clipped and sincere, and his tone distinguished by a dangerous steely quality that they had not heard from him before" (62). Francis thus shows himself aware of the codes of gay and straight behavior and able to adopt them at will, depending on context. This is not a performance of being in or out of the closet, in which he would play straight for one audience and gay for another, as he switches behavior dramatically in the middle of a conversation with police and he varies his gay performance significantly, even among his confidantes.

Further, not only Francis but also the straight-seeming Tiger perform differently in different situations. Tiger acts gay and drunk when undercover, and straight when at the police station and with Vivien. While this figures as standard role-playing for detective work, he also minces and acts camp in situations that are not related to his work as a detective. When Francis first hires Tiger, for example, and tells him he has a case for him, Tiger does a private performance of gayness for Francis: "Glancing around to be sure they were unobserved, Tiger put a hand on his hip and flipped his other wrist. 'And whoops to you, too,' he said with a boyish grin" (30). Near the end of the novel, Tiger again turns Francis's gayness back on him, saying "Get her" in response to one of Francis's remarks. But this time Francis assigns each of them a role: "Just for the record, Mr. Olsen, let me do the camping in this act. I'll make with the gay talk. You just be big and beasty, okay?" (131). Vivien, too, is shown to be masquerading when she appears as a fragile girl whom Tiger seduces "forcefully, manfully" in one chapter but discovers to be "wanton" and "mad" for rough sex in another (122). Masquerade in the novel neither masks nor reveals an "authentic" self behind the mask, but instead functions to emphasize the way in which identity is always already constructed through everyday performance. The masquerade can be heightened and theatricalized at times, but never escaped.

The emphasis on masquerade in *The Gay Detective* points to the instability and fluidity of gender categories in the novel. In part, the book points to gay identities as not fitting typical gender categories. In a drag club called the Bait Room, where Francis and Tiger go undercover, side doors are marked "Men," "Women," and "Us" (75). As Hattie ponders her new boss, Francis, she knows "only too well that the simple old classification of 'men and women' simply didn't cover the situation any longer" (11). When two decorators, Duke and Dixie, send a representative to Francis's office, he can't determine whether the person is a Duke or a Dixie and so the character is labeled "Duke (or Dixie)" throughout (19). A manicurist is, similarly, indeterminate, speaking in an "affected, lispy, little girl's voice" but not clearly identified as anything but "blonde" (18–19).

Beyond certain characters being indeterminate because gay or transgendered (in a loose sense), *The Gay Detective* marks spaces and people as fluid and porous, so that the city as a whole seems permeated by gayness and gender indeterminacy. Public spaces in the novel have dual or secret identities. Inviting Tiger to exercise with him, Francis takes him to what he describes as a ballet school but turns out to be a boxing gym—where Francis, proving his macho mettle, flattens Tiger (25–28). Near the beginning of the novel, the narrator takes the reader to Flanagan's bar, with its famous secret "Back Room" (4–10). There, select judges, lawyers, politicians, journalists, and businessmen gather. In addition to Tiger, who soon begins camping it up with Francis (while remaining resolutely hetero in sexual practice), the Back Room crowd includes the "bachelor" Senator Bruce Martin, later revealed to be tied in to the gay blackmail scheme and bath culture, and Captain Starr of the city's police department, who seems heterosexual but shows a deep familiarity with the Bait Room drag club, even identifying his favorite chorus girl as "the King of Queens. Now he's real pretty" (70). As Francis says, "Anyone knowing that much of the words and music is bound to have done the dance routines too!" (137).

## A QUEEN IN THE KITCHEN

### *THE GAY COOKBOOK* AND THE QUEER CONTINUUM

*The Gay Cookbook* shares some territory with *The Gay Detective*. Both establish the gay male consumer as a niche market and gay identity as a subculture with its own rules and mores. Both suggest—without being assimilationist—that gay identity is a significant and underacknowledged aspect of the overall population, more similar to than different from other variations. Both posit identity as fluid and porous. Because it is nonfiction and first-person, *The Gay Cookbook* is more deeply camp in its tone and address. The biggest difference, however, lies in the settings of the two books: *The Gay Detective* offers imaginary access to the public world of gay sexual subcultures, while the cookbook provides a window into gay domesticity and cooking discourse. *The Gay Cookbook* detaches the image of cooking and domesticity from married life; it also sexualizes cooking, tying it to seduction and a sexual identity, thus helping to construct a singles culture and prefiguring sexual liberation movements. Thus I will compare it not only to *The Gay Detective* but also to other cookbooks and cooking discourse.

In the preface to *The Gay Cookbook*, Hogan discusses the myriad cookbooks available, including regional, ethnic, family, and celebrity cookbooks, as well as cookbooks focused on certain foods, such as meat-only, or all-vegetarian, or recipes using Campbell's Soup. "In any case," he writes, "there seem to be new jazzy cookbooks for everyone, every type, every temperament. A mad, mad Editor has coyly suggested: 'Oh hell, May, why don't you people have a cookbook? After all, you're supposed to be "one-in-six," and that's a lot of cooking.' "[25] Deploying the popular one-in-six figure taken from Kinsey's *Sexual Behavior in the Human Male* (1948) for the percentage of men who, at one time or another, engage in homosexual activity, Hogan asserts a homosexual identity as being more or less similar to other types and temperaments; put another way, he suggests that homosexual activity might be like vegetarianism or a fondness for Italian food, representing a subculture or taste—or, more radically, that eating vegetarian or Italian, or acting gay, might be something many people do without necessarily considering themselves to be vegetarian or Italian, or always gay. Or, as Kinsey wrote when he introduced the Kinsey Scale of hetero- and homosexuality: "Males do not represent two discrete populations, heterosexual and homosexual. The world is not to be divided into sheep and goats. It is a fundamental of taxonomy that nature rarely deals with discrete categories. . . . The living world is a continuum in each and every one of its aspects."[26] Thus while Hogan asserts a gay identity, he also advances a more mobile or queer understanding of identity, similar to that found in *The Gay Detective.* Hogan pitches *The Gay Cookbook* to "the host (of whatever sex)" who wants to be "Queen of the Kitchen, whether man, woman, child or just undecided."[27] Here, gayness is not exclusively identified with one's sex or even one's "decided" orientation, but with a camp sensibility and a desire to be a queen, if only in the kitchen.

Certainly the cookbook addresses its reader as if he is a single gay man who will be entertaining primarily other men. Hogan says that the book is aimed at the man with "no 'little woman' to greet him at the door," and adds, making clear his lack of interest in such arrangements, no "customary whine about something or other" and "no smell of a scorching stew, either" (viii). The book hails not just gay men but, in particular, feminine gay men: readers are addressed as "girls," "bachelor girl (male or female)," "dearie," and "sissies," but most often given a female name, such as Winnie Mae, Pauline, Sue Ellen, Mildred or, frequently, May or Maude. In a typical example, in a chapter on fish, Hogan writes: "I know, Tessie, this may be dull-type material, but a girl is smart to find out what she can about what she's gonna eat—especially if she has to go out and find it, and then pay for it! Just be patient; sit there with your embroidery, and shut up!" (74).[28] Similar to *The Gay Detective*'s play with names, Hogan, himself a former drag queen, here, performs a verbal drag, enacting his own role as teasing feminized emcee and producing an androgynous feminized male reader.

*The Gay Cookbook* also feminizes its readership through its assumptions about the reader's lifestyle, and, in particular, the reader's lack of wealth. Throughout the book, Hogan attends to the economics of cooking and hosting: "Our slant is to the moderate-living person," he writes, one who might be saving up for "old age," or "to buy a Xmas present for Jim, . . . [or] for a new drag, etc.," and so he promises to "try to keep things economical" (3). In this vein, when Hogan discusses sherry, caviar, poultry, and so forth, he lists specific prices and debates the merits of cheaper versions or cuts. In a description of an ideal curry buffet, with Japanese silver bowls, fine damask cloth, silver or crystal salad bowls, and champagne flutes, he writes "Yes, my dears, real 'chi-chi' . . . but someone is bound to ask 'Who in the hell has all that silver and stuff?' Well, May, almost nobody"—and he recommends renting the service, to look "grand and gay" (39–40). This emphasis on economy differs from *The Gay Detective*, in which Francis is described as a wealthy man who could choose to be at leisure. But it echoes books aimed at single women, such as *Sex and the Single Girl* (1962) and *Saucepans and the Single Girl* (1965), both of which assume that working single women are on a tight budget, operate on principles of self sacrifice when alone, and engage "financial chicanery" or masquerade when entertaining.[29] This differs markedly from cookbooks and hosting manuals aimed at single heterosexual men, such as *The Esquire Handbook for Hosts* or *The Madison Avenue Cookbook* or *Playboy* magazine: all of these promulgate a view of masculine hosting as part of a sophisticated lifestyle, never mention concerns about the expense of parties or dinners, and seem to assume that the bachelor has a good income.[30]

*The Gay Cookbook* also aligns itself with the feminine in its attention to calories: In discussing the potato, Hogan argues against conceptions of them as fattening (212–13), but of mayonnaise-laden potato and macaroni salads he warns, "Sure, men like 'em, but are they ever fattening!" (28). This attention to calories aligns the gay cook with his female counterparts. In *Sex and the Single Girl*, for instance, Helen Gurley Brown advises women, "Keep an almost bare cupboard. *You* don't eat much"; and she offers very specific diet advice (up to how many grams of protein to eat a day) to achieve something like her slender figure.[31] By contrast, books aimed at straight men do not attend to the caloric content of meals. *The Gay Cookbook* differentiates between its feminized reader and the potential male eater of food when Hogan says that "men" like the fattening macaroni and potato salads—with the assumption that the men who eat them don't care about the calories, while the feminized cook might.

Another way in which the cookbook feminizes its reader is in its assumption of men as the Other. Sometimes, this involves remarking on masculine taste in a way that suggests it does not necessarily apply to the writer or reader: Hogan claims, for example, that "MEN like chili" (35) and introduces a recipe for macaroni and cheese by saying "Men LOVE it" (228). Marking the difference between the stereotypical male and his feminized male reader, he claims that Roquefort dressing appeals to "the physical hairy-chested type," but "some of us sissies just adore it too" (24). He advocates many recipes as man-pleasing. In the recipe for corned beef hash, for example, he proclaims, "Men adore real, genuine, honest to Gawd Corned Beef Hash; let's make 'em happy" (114). In this way *The Gay Cookbook* echoes books aimed at both single and married women that perpetuate traditional gender roles by emphasizing the importance of a woman's cooking as part of her domestic and marital obligations, or what Jessamyn Neuhaus describes as "the cooking mystique" that invests women's cooking with symbolic gendered meaning. According to Neuhaus and others, most midcentury cookbooks are aimed at white middle-class married women, and those women are told to cook for male tastes, not their own.[32]

*The Gay Cookbook*'s similarity to both single and married female cooking discourse marks the difference between its imagined gay male reader and the more exceptional heterosexual masculine cook, not only in terms of economics or attention to calories but also in style of cooking. According to several cookbook historians, female cookery and male cookery are distinguished from each other in three main ways: first, cooking by men is marked as a hobby, not as everyday life or routine; second, the food itself is masculinized (male tastes are seen as superior to women's, or certain foods as more appropriate to men—meat, for example, over salads, or cooking on an open grill over indoor cooking); and third, cooking is raised to an art form for men and the male chef's creativity is asserted over the female cook's more mundane recipe-following.[33] Heterosexual male cookbooks typically portray "men in the kitchen as epicures, as creative gastronomes, as hearty eaters with an appetite for the unusual."[34]

By contrast, women tend to be hailed as cooks interested in thrift, nutrition, and ease—as the obvious and necessary cook in the house, but with some recognition that they may take no joy in the role. (Thus the popularity among women of *The I Hate to Cook Book*, by Peg Bracken, first published in 1960).[35] The female cook is associated not with the exotic but with the use of prepared foods—which she must doctor to seem homemade and fulfill the mystique—and more routinized meals. Neuhaus, in her study of meatloaf recipes, for example, finds that meatloaf appears primarily in cookbooks aimed at women, not in male cookbooks, though it is typically characterized as food *for* men. These recipes for female cooks focus on using up odds and ends, or stretching the meat ration, or showing a woman's love and devotion by doctoring processed foods, and thus stretching her work (recalling Betty Friedan's view that suburban living expands the work of housewifery to fill the void).[36] By contrast, Neuhaus observes, on the rare occasions that meatloaf does appear in a male cookbook it involves exotic ingredients, expensive cuts of meat, and more work than recipes aimed at women—to register the meal as a gourmet variant on a lowly feminine recipe.

In opposition to this male/female contrast, *The Gay Cookbook* suggests many presumably feminine techniques and meals for its male but feminized readers. After giving a recipe for gazpacho, Hogan suggests that many canned soups are just as good, but he recommends doctoring the soup to make it more special, adding broth and tarragon to a canned tomato soup to match the standards of a "posh restaurant." Suggesting that readers "give the lowly meatloaf the once over," he offers a meatloaf recipe that is not exotic or based on fine cuts of meats, but instead relies on "extenders" like raw potato, oats, kasha, or rice, and includes a suggestion for a gravy based on canned mushroom soup (100–101). And, acknowledging that many men prefer a very basic salad of just salted tomatoes, he declares that he wants to "spare a few kind words for the Fruit Salad . . . it's swell"—thus aligning his taste with stereotypical female tastes (35).

But *The Gay Cookbook*'s gendering of the reader/cook as feminine, in opposition to the masculine eater, is troubled somewhat by the book's emphasis on sex and the instrumentalization of cooking for seduction. Hogan writes, "If the true way to a man's heart (what was that, again?) is through his stomach, then the many pearls of wisdom dropped here will help in making many trips to his best feature" (273). Thus *The Gay Cookbook* differs from *The Gay Detective,* which gingerly avoids scenes of gay male sex and offers only heterosexual sex in its pages, though it teases the homoerotic throughout. In instrumentalizing cooking for sex, *The Gay Cookbook* echoes both cookbooks aimed at single women and those aimed at single men. In these books, cooking is always primarily geared toward seduction. The single female cook, home alone, either doesn't eat, *à la* Helen Gurley Brown, or, as in *Saucepans and the Single Girl,* she eats TV dinners and undoctored canned soup. But she cooks for men. Brown advises women to have a shelf of extravagant spices to entice a man, because "They say you're a good cook."[37] *Saucepans and the Single Girl* offers menus to suit various men, including the Man in a Brooks Brothers Suit (Fondue), the Man in a Garret (Cornish Game Hens), and the Amorous Athlete (Beef Burgundy Flambé). Straight men, similarly, entertain with an eye toward seduction, but without giving in to or catering to feminine tastes. The *Esquire* guide, for example, suggests that the male's performative culinary efforts are geared primarily toward seduction—"a new twist on the old 'come see my etchings' routine."[38] *Esquire* also differentiates itself from the "standard womanly cookbook" and asserts its masculinity: "The world's greatest cooks are men. Since the beginning of time, he-men have always prepared the savory dishes that caress the palates of epicures of every nation. . . . You won't find doily tearoom fare here: no radish roses, no menus designed for their calorie content. [We have] concentrated on food of, for and by MEN."[39]

While all of these texts privilege male taste and aim at pleasing men by catering to male tastes, regardless of the object of seduction, each of them, in different ways, challenges the old-fashioned assumption about cooking being tied to the housewife in a single-family home. In the gay and straight variants, these cookbooks construct singles culture by positing an assumption of single domesticity, away from the family home and geared toward having nonmarital sex.

Thus, rather than simply ape the gendered roles of heterosexual marriage, *The Gay Cookbook* can be seen as intervening to produce a gay singles identity. Rather than simply feminizing gay men according to conventional gender stereotypes, Hogan dismantles those stereotypes. Against the model of the perfect suburban housewife as the ideal cook, he suggests: "No longer does the mistress of the house have a big range to stand over all day long, turning out those great home-style meals that started grandfather's ulcer. The 'mistress' of the house may not even live in a house but in a modern and compact (God Knows!) apartment. In fact, the 'mistress' may not even be a 'she' at all! Whoever and whatever our homebody is, she may just have to cope" (164). Just as when Hogan suggested that *The Gay Cookbook* might cross lines or locate queer affiliations across a wide range of types, here he undoes the assumption of female cookery, suggesting changing conditions in an urbanized world and changing roles in which the mistress may not be a she, but "whoever and whatever."

*The Gay Cookbook* has a parodic relation to both stereotypical femininity—witness the appropriation of feminine names and stereotypes—and stereotypical masculinity. Its cover, as I have suggested, parodies the association of men with outdoor cooking. Similarly, inside the book, Hogan parodies supposed masculine tastes. In his chapter on meat, for example, he troubles the supposed association between men and meat by overtly sexualizing it. After resisting a joke about gay men's dislike for fish, Hogan can't help but make a phallic joke about sausage, saying they come in "all sorts of shapes—and that is enough of that!" (73, 102). In his discussion of barbecuing, a form of cooking usually identified with manly cooking and masculine tastes, he undoes the presumed heterosexual associations of manliness. Noting that historically barbecuing was done over pits of fire, he says that "nowadays it all seems to be done with mirrors or something," and then digresses: "This reminds us, did any of you ever . . . er . . . 'work' in one of those mirrored rooms? Mirrors on the ceiling, the walls, everywhere? Gawd! You feel surrounded" (116). Over and over, sexual innuendo infiltrates the recipes and marks them as not only instrumentalized for sex but also as homoeroticized. In a chapter on poultry, for example, Hogan writes: "Grease the bird—(yes, that's what I said)—just oil it up with some oil or shortening or old bacon grease, or whatever (What? NO, you fool, not that!)" (147).

*The Gay Cookbook*, then, asserts a queer voice and queer readership, and, like *The Gay Detective*, posits sexual and gendered identities as somewhat fluid and permeable. Also like *The Gay Detective, The Gay Cookbook* asserts the presence of gay and especially feminized gay men without apology or self-loathing. Compare this to *The Man from C.A.M.P.* spinoff, *Sex and the Single Gay*, published two years after *The Gay Cookbook*. Modeled closely on *Sex and the Single Girl*, with chapters on clothes, grooming, decorating, meeting men, and ending an affair, this book offers self-help for men who want to "marry and settle, at least for a while." While proffering self-help in the form of "learn to like yourself . . . be the best friend you have," *Sex and the Single Gay* acknowledges that many gay men in 1967 are still, at a minimum, self-conscious, or worse, feel their life is a nightmare, or are even suicidal.[40] Pre-pride, however, the book accepts gay oppression and trains gay men how to live in the closet. Claiming that straight people "don't want to find out" and "it is your job to make this just as easy as possible for them," the book suggests that readers should not be "screamy," but "discreet." Not surprisingly, when the book turns to food, the author suggests buying a cookbook with manly "no nonsense" recipes, not trying to make the "lovely feasts in various women's magazines."[41]

We can see, then, that by contrast *The Gay Cookbook* and *The Gay Detective* both resist the discourse of the closet. While *The Gay Cookbook* speaks from inside a camp lingo and drag culture that will, post-Stonewall, register as a sign of the closet and thus as a mark of oppression, it speaks pre-Stonewall to an affirmative feminized gay identity, equal to other various identities, no more or less different than the rest. In certain ways, *The Gay Cookbook* and *The Gay Detective* can be stitched to homophile discourse of the period, which asserted the right to public association and aimed to bring positive representations of homosexuality into the mainstream, in a move toward being able to be out in public as homosexuals. *The Gay Cookbook* and *The Gay Detective* both "out" gay culture and put it on the table, as "one-in-six," part of the patchwork of identities that make up our broader culture.

At the same time, *The Gay Cookbook* could be accused of offering a regressive portrait of gay life, not only in its campiness and feminization of gay male culture—charges leveled against *The Gay Detective*, certainly—but, more importantly in its domesticity.[42] In locating gay identity in the kitchen, as opposed to the bars or other public spaces of *The Gay Detective*, *The Gay Cookbook* could be seen as participating in what William Eskridge has described as "the apartheid of the closet," a double standard in legal prosecutions of homosexuality between those homosexuals who relegated their sexuality to the privacy of their homes (and acted more or less straight in public) and those who brought their sexuality and gender into the public sphere.[43] But I would argue, and Eskridge agrees, that homosexuals had little privacy in their homes, as the illegality of gay sexual activity rendered the home vulnerable to police surveillance and scrutiny. In the first half of the twentieth century, as George Chauncey has amply demonstrated, gay male privacy could only be had in public because public spaces were historically less regulated than private ones. Therefore, gay men turned seemingly public spaces—bathrooms, tearooms, parks—into spaces for private sexual activity, and created codes and ways of inhabiting urban space that produced a gay map, visible only to those in the know. In terms of domesticity, boarding houses and residential hotels, like those operated by the YMCA, were, of course, popular among gay men. These residences put men into contact with other men, were not closely supervised, and—because guests were expected to socialize and take meals away from home—enabled secret lives. Later, as Chauncey argues, the apartment gave gay men access to greater privacy, space to entertain at home, and respectability. As a result, starting in the late nineteenth century when the bachelor apartment developed, and flourishing in the mid-twentieth century, gay enclaves (and, in some cases, all-gay buildings) came into being and made it "possible for a middle-class gay world to develop."[44]

Cooking, then, is only recently available to gay men as a result of greater privacy; and asserting the right to cook and entertain is an important step in producing gay culture that can be out in both public and private. In claiming gay space in the kitchen, *The Gay Cookbook* asserts a right to domesticity, not instead of or against a public gay presence on the streets and in the bars, but as private space. It is worth noting that when Hogan refers to his own cooking, he locates it squarely in what he calls Happy House.

Expanding our understanding of gay male pulp to include nonfiction books and broader practices of consumption, Lou Rand Hogan's two very distinct books, *The Gay Detective* and *The Gay Cookbook*, taken together suggest the ways in which different facets of the pulp market speak to and from gay culture to produce different "maps and signposts" of gay culture and identities. While both books open up an understanding of gay subcultures, they also speak to an awareness of gay culture within the heterosexual dominant and show, as Michael Bronski argues, that "homosexuality was very much in the public consciousness" and had permeated aspects of straight culture.[45] *The Gay Detective* presents a highly detailed but fairly standard map of mid-twentieth-century gay communities in relation to public spaces, such as the bars and baths that make up its milieu; *The Gay Cookbook* complicates this paradigm and reminds us of another side of gay life, related to domesticity and entertaining. *The Gay Cookbook* seems to characterize gay men as effeminate and camp, but *The Gay Detective* challenges this stereotype with its performative, but macho, heroes. If we separate pulp fiction, such as *The Gay Detective*, from the larger context of pulp, including such nonfiction works as *The Gay Cookbook*, and disentangle pulp from the broader practices of consumption, we lose some of the richness and diversity of gay cultures and history.

## NOTES

Earlier versions of this essay were presented at the conferences "Eating, Cooking, Culture" at the University of Wisconsin–Milwaukee and "Food Networks: Gender and Foodways" at the University of Notre Dame.

1. Lou Rand, *The Gay Detective* (Fresno, CA: Saber Books, 1961); *Rough Trade* (Los Angeles: Argyle Books, 1964), hardcover; (New York: Paperback Library, 1965), paperback. For reproductions of the pulp covers, see Susan Stryker and Jim Van Buskirk,

*Gay by the Bay: A History of Queer Culture in the San Francisco Bay Area* (San Francisco: Chronicle Books, 1996), 37. The back cover of the original (Saber) edition quoted Romans 14:14. A myth is being perpetuated on the Internet that it had a blurb describing its protagonist as "a fierce but fey private eye"; that "blurb" actually appears to be taken from a summary of the book in Susan Stryker, *Gay Pulp Address Book* (San Francisco: Chronicle Books, 2000).

2. See Susan Stryker and Martin Meeker, "Introduction: Mystery as History," in *The Gay Detective*, by Lou Rand (San Francisco: Cleis Press, 2003), vi–viii, for a brief biography of Lou Rand Hogan. According to them, he was a chef aboard the Lurline luxury liner, a chef at various posh San Francisco restaurants, and a personal chef for billionaires, as well as a member of the Royal Canadian Air Force. He published his memoirs, "The Golden Age of Queens," in six parts in the *Bay Area Reporter* in 1974 under the pseudonym Toto le Grand. The original manuscript (cataloged under Lou Rand) is available in the Len Evans Papers, Collection 93-8, Gay and Lesbian Historical Society of Northern California, San Francisco Public Library. He also wrote food columns for *Sunset* and *Gourmet* magazines as Lou Rand. According to the Social Security Death Index, Lou Hogan (no middle name given) was born on May 4, 1910, and died in August 1976 at his last address in Long Beach, California. In this essay I will use the name Hogan for the sake of consistency, but will use for citation whichever name is appropriate to the published text.
3. Chef Lou Rand Hogan, *The Gay Cookbook* (New York: Bell Publishing, by arrangement with Sherbourne Press, 1965), viii. For a reproduction of the original cover, see Stryker and Van Buskirk, *Gay by the Bay*, 48.
4. Susan Stryker includes all of the above in her compendium, *Queer Pulp: Perverted Passions from the Golden Age of the Paperback* (San Francisco: Chronicle Books, 2001).
5. Stryker and Meeker, "Introduction," ix–x.
6. Some of these titles are included in Stryker's *Queer Pulp* and in the online exhibit *The Pre-Gay Era in the USA*, which features homosexual rights organizations and publications from 1950 to 1969 and includes pulp nonfiction as well as pulp fiction; www.outhistory.org/wiki/The_Pre-Gay_Era_in_the_USA. Others I located through an online search.
7. See, for example, Yvonne Keller, "'Was It Right to Love Her Brother's Wife So Passionately?': Lesbian Pulp Novels and U.S. Lesbian Identity, 1950–1965," *American Quarterly* 57.2 (2005): 385–410; Meredith Miller, "Secret Agents and Public Victims: The Implied Lesbian Reader," *Journal of Popular Culture* 35.1 (Summer 2001): 37–58; Pamela Robertson Wojcik, *The Apartment Plot: Urban Living in American Film and Popular Culture, 1945 to 1975* (Durham, NC: Duke University Press, 2010), 218–22; and Stryker, *Queer Pulp*.
8. Katherine V. Forrest, "Introduction," in *Lesbian Pulp Fiction: The Sexually Intrepid World of Lesbian Paperback Novels, 1950–1965*, ed. Forrest (San Francisco: Cleis Press, 2005), xviii.
9. Michael Bronski, "Introduction," in *Pulp Friction: Uncovering the Golden Age of Gay Male Pulps*, ed. Bronski (New York: St. Martin's Griffin, 2003), 9.
10. David K. Johnson, "Physique Pioneers: The Politics of 1960s Gay Consumer Culture," *Journal of Social History* 43.4 (Summer 2010): 867.
11. Stryker and Meeker, "Introduction," xiii, xvi.

12. Bronski, "Introduction," 2.
13. David Bell and Joanne Hollows, "Towards a History of Lifestyle," in *Historicizing Lifestyle: Mediating Taste, Consumption and Identity from the 1900s to the 1970s*, ed. Bell and Hollows (Burlington, VT: Ashgate, 2006), 3–5.
14. Johnson, "Physique Pioneers," 870, 867.
15. Judith A. Markowitz, *The Gay Detective Novel: Lesbian and Gay Main Characters and Themes in Mystery Fiction* (Jefferson, NC: McFarland, 2004), 23; Linda Hutcheon, *A Theory of Parody: The Teaching of Twentieth-Century Art Forms* (New York: Methuen, 1985), 6.
16. Alexander Doty, *Making Things Perfectly Queer: Interpreting Mass Culture* (Minneapolis: University of Minnesota Press, 1993), 3. See also Pamela Robertson, *Guilty Pleasures: Feminist Camp from Mae West to Madonna* (Durham, NC: Duke University Press, 1996), 9–10.
17. Stryker and Meeker, "Introduction," xii.
18. Markowitz, *The Gay Detective Novel*, 24; Stryker and Meeker, "Introduction," v.
19. The quotation is from Susan Sontag, "Notes on 'Camp,'" in *Against Interpretation* (New York: Farrar, Straus & Giroux, 1966), 277. On Mae West's relation to camp see Robertson, *Guilty Pleasures*, 23–53.
20. See Lynn Munroe, "The Man from C.A.M.P.," and Victor Banis, "Paperback Virgin," both in *e.I* 2, no. 1 (Jan. 2003), http://efanzines.com/EK/e16/index.htm. For more on Banis, see Randall Ivey's essay elsewhere in this volume; he also comments briefly on *The Gay Detective*.
21. Judith Butler, *Gender Trouble: Feminism and the Subversion of Identity* (New York: Routledge, 1990), 141, 137.
22. Rand, *The Gay Detective* (2003 ed.), 8.
23. Ibid., 16–17, 44, 55, 108. Further page references will be cited parenthetically in text.
24. Rand, "The Golden Age of Queens," ms. 2–3.
25. Hogan, *The Gay Cookbook*, vii.
26. Alfred C. Kinsey, *Sexual Behavior in the Human Male* (1948; Bloomington: Indiana University Press, 1998), 639. Excerpts available at www.kinseyinstitute.org/resources/ak-hhscale.html.
27. Hogan, *The Gay Cookbook*, 3, 257. Further page references will be cited in the text.
28. The other female nicknames appear on pages 15, 25, 139, 24, 41, 58, 74, and 136.
29. Jinx Kragen and Judy Perry, *Saucepans and the Single Girl* (Garden City, NY: Doubleday, 1965), 12. See also Helen Gurley Brown, *Sex and the Single Girl* (1962; Fort Lee, NJ: Barricade Books, 2003).
30. *Esquire's Handbook for Hosts* (New York: Grosset & Dunlap, 1953); Alan Koehler, *The Madison Avenue Cookbook: For People Who Can't Cook and Don't Want Other People to Know It* (New York: Holt, Rinehart & Winston, 1962). In this regard, Hogan's cookbook articulates a different class relationship between gayness and food than the more upper-class queer connoisseurs of fiction described in Joseph Litvak's *Strange Gourmets: Sophistication, Theory and the Novel* (Durham, NC: Duke University Press, 1997). Here, economy trumps sophistication.
31. The quotation is from Brown, *Sex and the Single Girl*, 110.
32. Jessamyn Neuhaus, "Is Meatloaf for Men? Gender and Meatloaf Recipes, 1920–1960," in *Cooking Lessons: The Politics of Gender and Food*, ed. Sherrie Inness (New York: Rowman & Littlefield, 2001), 87–109. See also, for example, Sherrie Inness,

*Dinner Roles: American Women and Culinary Culture* (Iowa City: University of Iowa Press, 2001).

33. See Inness, *Dinner Roles* and *Cooking Lessons;* Neuhaus "Is Meatloaf for Men?"; and Neuhaus, *Manly Meals and Mom's Home Cooking: Cookbooks and Gender in Modern America* (Baltimore: Johns Hopkins University Press, 2003).
34. Neuhaus, *Manly Meals,* 217.
35. Peg Bracken, *The I Hate to Cook Book: 50th Anniversary Edition* (New York: Grand Central, 2010).
36. Betty Friedan, *The Feminine Mystique* (1963; New York: Norton, 2001), 345–46.
37. Brown, *Sex and the Single Girl,* 136.
38. *Esquire's Handbook for Hosts,* 11.
39. Ibid.
40. Jackie Holmes, That Man From C.A.M.P., as told to Don Holliday, *Sex and the Single Gay* (San Diego: Corinth Publications, 1967), 158, 10.
41. Ibid., 14, 15, 16, 73. *The C.A.M.P. Cookbook,* published in 1969, resembles *The Gay Cookbook* more closely. It adopts a similarly campy and slightly raunchy tone, uses feminine names to address its reader, and instrumentalizes cooking for seduction: "And away we go! Back to that little room. No, not that one—the one just on the other side of that place they call the dining area. . . . Now I'm sure you know your way around the other rooms, especially the one with the queen-sized you-know-what; but as I'm *prone* to mention from time to time, one of the ways to a man's heart is through his stomach which means you'll have to spend some time in the kitchen cooking." Lady Agatha in Conspiracy with Don Holliday, *The C.A.M.P. Cookbook* (San Diego: Phoenix, 1969), 1.
42. Stryker and Meeker detail some of the criticism of *The Gay Detective;* "Introduction," x–xii.
43. William N. Eskridge Jr., "Privacy Jurisprudence and the Apartheid of the Closet, 1946–1961," *Florida State University Law Review* 24 (1997): 703–838. Discussed in Nan Alamilla Boyd, *Wide Open Town: A History of Queer San Francisco to 1965* (Berkeley: University of California Press, 2003), 174.
44. George Chauncey, *Gay New York: Gender, Urban Culture, and the Making of the Gay Male World, 1890–1940* (New York: Basic Books, 1994), 158. Counter to this model, John Howard argues that, because of limited resources in terms of public space, gay men in the south experienced their sexuality primarily in the family home. This gay activity tends to be momentary and secretive, not producing an out gay home but participating in strategies of the closet. See John Howard, *Men Like That: A Southern Queer History* (Chicago: University of Chicago Press, 1999), 77. In a different vein, Nayan Shah argues that immigrant neighborhoods were often viewed queerly by middle-class reformers because their domestic arrangements did not fall into the dominant heteronormative familial structure but included women-run homes, homes with multiple families, and all-male homes. See Nayan Shah, *Contagious Divides: Epidemics and Race in San Francisco's Chinatown* (Berkeley: University of California Press, 2001), 77–104.
45. Bronski, "Introduction," 6.

# "Moonlight and Bosh and Bullshit"

## PHIL ANDROS'S *$TUD* AND THE CREATION OF A "NEW GAY ETHIC"

Ann Marie Schott

The gay pulps of the 1960s served as a liberating force for gay men, who for the first time saw mostly positive representations of gay sex and identity in their pages. Samuel M. Steward began writing gay pulp fiction under the pseudonym Phil Andros in the early 1960s and became a unique and abiding voice in the burgeoning genre. His 1966 story collection, *$tud*, follows a protagonist hustler, also named Phil Andros, through an episodic world of fetishism, sadomasochism, and miscegenation that pioneered such topics within the genre and legitimized new understandings of gay sex and identity. In his introduction to the 1982 abridged reprint of *$tud*, John Preston argues that Steward's writing was the "beginning of a new gay ethic," a bible of sorts for the "children of Stonewall."[1] But although Steward's may seem to be a progressive voice that anticipates the openness of gay liberation, I would argue that his hustler persona, Phil, is actually heavily invested in the norms of Cold War masculinity. Phil's queering of gay identity and his overessentialization of gender not only work to destabilize binary definitions of each, but also to reinforce those delineations. Steward held a "continuing ambivalence toward his fellow homosexuals—those for whom, presumably, he would be writing," and this ambivalence allowed him to criticize their lifestyles through a unique lens of removed intimacy.[2] In his writing, Steward decried the same elements of male homosexuality as did mainstream midcentury America, including effeminacy and out relationships between men, especially when those relationships resembled normative marital structures. In contrast, Steward was passionate about privately documenting his frequent sexual encounters with men of all ages and races and found his promiscuity to be an ideal manifestation of homosexuality. If *$tud* is the beginning of "a new gay ethic," as Preston argues, then it is a complicated ethic in which the marginal (gay) man, guarded by the distinction of trade, exhibits the fundamental perversities of American masculinity. Phil Andros employs trade as the ideal way to simultaneously embody and subvert the masculine ideal.

The stories of *$tud* carry with them a complicated and telling history. All but one of the eighteen stories were originally published in European magazines between 1963 and 1965.[3] They were collected in 1966 in a volume that, because of the publisher's financial problems, was warehoused for several years before being released in hardcover. A pirated pulp edition appeared in San Francisco in 1969. Only then did Steward's publisher, Guild Press, bring out a three-volume paperback edition—without an author's name of any kind. According to Steward, he received little financial compensation for any edition of *$tud*.[4] Although four of the stories were included by Stephen Wright in *Different: An Anthology of Homosexual Short Stories* in 1974, Andros's literary reputation remained largely underground. In 1981 George Whitmore, a member of the Violet Quill writing community, wrote an essay praising his writing for being "deftly constructed and entertaining," and Preston specifically applauded the collection's literary qualities in his introduction to the 1982 reprint.[5] This did not protect *$tud* from drifting into obscurity, however. As Michael Bronski makes clear in *Pulp Friction: Uncovering the Golden Age of Gay Male Pulps*, "one of the primary features of the paperback revolution was that the books were, in essence, disposable," so few of them are available today outside of anthologies or special collections.[6] As a character and narrator, Phil went on to "write" and star in five novels between 1970 and 1975, and Steward revealed himself as the author behind the hustler persona in his 1981 memoir, *Chapters from an Autobiography.*

The obscurity of *$tud* reveals something about the nature of its subject and the climate of midcentury American publishing standards. It also reveals something about the nature of the collection itself: that *$tud* exists, as it has always existed, in the liminal space between literary merit and pornography, between cultural legitimacy and artificiality. As Patricia Juliana Smith writes in her introduction to the collection of essays *The Queer Sixties*, "Marginal as they were in terms of social acceptability—and, in most cases, literary quality—pulps nevertheless were often the *only* source of gay or lesbian representation available to many queer subcultural readerships."[7] *$tud* is an anomaly in that it has seemed to transcend its backwards, illegitimate publication history and smutty reputation to achieve a remarkable resonance. It is literary in that it is John Rechy's *City of Night* (1963) reimagined and repurposed in order to challenge Rechy's additions to perceptions of queerness "in the popular imaginary."[8] Steward complains, "I'd read John Rechy's *City of Night* . . . but . . . Rechy's waffling attitude about his nameless hustler was annoying; I had the feeling he was holding back, afraid to reveal himself, carefully cultivating the icy center of his being and saving it for—what or whom? I didn't know."[9] *$tud*'s version of Rechy's "youngman," Phil Andros, "affirmed a gay lifestyle outside the bounds of heterosexual expectations" and thus established a new perspective for queer audiences that was funny, frank, and unapologetic.[10] In this way, Phil's unrestricted narration of his exploits seems a much more reliable artifact of midcentury queer masculinity. So Whitmore's question, "When does lit begin and porno leave off?" begs for a closer examination of this relic of queer identity and the complicated ethics bound within it.[11]

Although Steward had a nuanced idea of queer identity, he remained heavily invested in the veneration of masculinity that was called for by 1950s cultural conventions, even within gay communities. In his memoir, he elaborates on an idea gleaned from his work with Alfred Kinsey after the two met in 1949: "I learned . . . never again in my life to use the word 'normal,' which I once thoughtlessly employed in front of [Kinsey]. He jumped on me. . . . From that moment the word was sliced from my vocabulary, and replaced with something more exact, but clumsier, such as 'majority practice.' "[12] In *$tud*, Steward invents a realm away from "majority practice," and away from even minority (gay) practice. Every sexual act is somehow transgressive beyond the transgression of queerness and is thus made uber-queer. The liminal boundaries defined by transgression are challenged when those transgressions are themselves transgressed. The original transgression of homosexuality is thus reified in a Foucauldian sense, and homophobia is reversed, or expanded, to include the new enactment of queerness. Each encounter, however, is invested in some way in a larger binary of conventional gender dynamics, forming a logical contradiction of priorities. Steward at once attempts to create a likeable, strong narrative voice for homosexual men and to wryly reduce homosexuality to the shallow pursuit of orgasm. In so doing, he creates a space for queer identity within the framework of stereotype and marginality. Justin Spring, Steward's biographer, argues, "By approaching the subject of homosexual activity with openness and quiet good humor, [Steward] hoped to provide not only erotic entertainment, but also a basic enlightenment about the everyday nature of the non-relationship-oriented sexual encounters that had taken up so much of his life."[13] The stories that make up *$tud* offer a field of extreme sexual scenarios that defy even the most liberal understandings of queerness. In many ways, the complexity of the collection lies in the failure of logic, which is perhaps the logical fruition of queer theory.

Phil represents a series of contradictions that evidences this tension, which is still relevant in our conversations of queer and gay identities. He is devoted to the binary of normative gender and is constantly beefing up his masculine performance and denying any suggestion of femininity. But he is also perpetually subverting the masculinity he attempts to portray: he embraces the criminality of his actions, clearly reveling in his career as a hustler. The gay hustler seems the (perhaps tongue-in-cheek) answer to anxieties surrounding the questionable masculinity of gay men in the 1960s: as trade, Phil is allowed to be ultimately masculine, with ties to other men that are explicitly sexual, rather than homosexual or homosocial. He is also able to embrace other transgressions of the normative binary systems, such as miscegenation and sadomasochism, within the safety of sexual play. This occupation allows him to explore the perversities of "normal" American masculinity while remaining dissociated from the dangerous stigma of being an out homosexual man.[14] The social historian George Chauncey, in his study *Gay New York*, notes that "trade constituted a widely admired ideal type in the subculture" because of its secure location in the realm of socially sanctioned masculinity.[15] Overall, Phil contradictorily works to destabilize masculinity, even as he attempts to reinforce it. His sexuality, while always ambiguous, is never fraught. As he defines queerness through his own interactions with labels, definitions, performances, and perceptions, he illuminates the internal contradictions of Cold War gender and sexuality.

The publication of *$tud*, though delayed by monetary difficulties and other setbacks, happened at a perfect time to reflect the nation's anxieties surrounding gender, race, and sexuality. Although McCarthyism had faded by the time Steward began writing *$tud*, it had made a lasting impression on the culture of midcentury America.[16] Alan Nadel describes the pressures of the Cold War binary in his study *Containment Culture: American Narratives, Postmodernism, and the Atomic Age*. He argues that the "story of containment had derived its logic from the rigid major premise that the world was divided into two monolithic camps, one dedicated to promoting the inextricable combination of capitalism, democracy, and (Judeo-Christian) religion, and one seeking to destroy that ideological amalgamation by any means." America's emergence as a world power after World War II called for a redefinition of American identity in which the status of "normal" was both narrowly defined and critically important. This normal American identity was socially learned through "the pervasive performances of and allusions to containment narratives" and covered all aspects of appropriate gendered behavior.[17] As Bronski notes, "traditional ideas about masculinity, maleness, and male sexuality were profoundly altered by men's experiences during the war," and American men in the 1950s were "eager and extraordinarily anxious to redefine [themselves]."[18] Gender performance became crucial to the exhibition of good character and devout patriotism. In other words, an individual's inappropriate gender characteristics, within Nadel's model, would have been considered an act of treason to American democracy. This system reified conformity and complacence, leaving little room for interpretation or manipulation. Homosexuality was often conflated with gender inversion, and this conflation negated its viability as an identity. Although plenty of American men and women had been living outside of the accepted binaries of gender and sexuality for many years with little fallout, and even as queer pop-cultural iconography became more prolific in the 1960s, *$tud*'s Phil Andros remains heavily invested in the idea of "normal" masculinity and seems, paradoxically, to long for the containment of the 1950s.[19]

As the nation grappled with the challenge of defining and evaluating American manhood, gay American men grappled with the challenge of publicly defining their identities in a nation that considered them overly feminine, backward, deviant, and even traitorous. There were, in fact, subtle markers in these definitions that protected certain individuals from derogatory associations. Chauncey, who delineates some of the pre–gay liberation, indeed pre–World War II, subtleties that gave men like Phil a platform for subverting the Cold War binaries of gender and sexuality, notes that "many of the terms used in the early twentieth century were not synonymous with *homosexual* or *heterosexual*, but represent a different conceptual mapping of male sexual practices, predicated on the assumptions about the character of men engaging in those practices."[20] Throughout the first half of the twentieth century, these terms became popular among groups of homosexual men, and their subtleties were often understood in the larger culture as well. For example, the term *queer* was used to label a man with masculine gender characteristics and homosexual interests, while *trade* marked a man who embodied the masculine ideal of gender and who was sexually "normal" (heterosexual), but who would accept sexual advances from queer individuals. "*Trade* was also increasingly used in the middle third of the century to refer to straight-identified men who worked as prostitutes serving gay-identified men, reversing the dynamic of economic exchange and desire implied by the original meaning."[21] This seems to be the definition most closely in line with Phil's actions and self-perceptions. With such markers in place, a man could have sexual encounters with other men while still ascribing to the conventions of normative masculinity, thereby protecting his viability as an American man.

Like Steward, his narrator, Phil, is well-educated and sex-obsessed. The leather-clad pariah is as much tough guy as he is intellectual curio—which is to say his personality is carefully constructed by Steward to exist outside of normative American society as well as outside that society's understanding of queer culture. Phil is, therefore, too smart to be a whore and too butch to be a fairy; he is a hustler enigma. He is trade: a carefully constructed persona with the power to simultaneously communicate and challenge the nuances and mores of masculinity in the 1960s. *$tud* presents masculinity as an identity bound in artifice and homosexuality as a game of sorts, complete with its own rules, players, and penalties. Phil is distinctly aware of this game: he understands and criticizes it even as he participates in it. One of his most basic rules is "Know thyself, old fruit. And if thou canst not know thyself, know others. But at least—be well adjusted."[22] Although Phil certainly knows himself and others and manages to be surprisingly well-adjusted, he employs elements of artifice to protect himself from becoming *too gay*, from slipping into the realm of negative connotations of homosexuality he has absorbed from 1960s cultural norms. Again, Phil is nostalgic for the 1950s masculine ideal—for a time when men were men. He must contain his own sexuality by playing the game strategically and effectively, protecting himself above all others along the way. But even this containment is tongue-in-cheek, and his performativity is always ultimately exposed and self-aware, adding a complexity that was not only a coded nod to a potential gay readership, but a criticism of the burgeoning gay liberation identity of the late 1960s.

As a narrator Phil makes a point of communicating his intellectual pursuits and literary interests, as well as integrating a particularly smart brand of humor into every story. Unlike Rechy's youngman, for whom "being smart on the streets included pretending not to be," Phil uses his intellect as a tool of power, and is not afraid to display it prominently.[23] As he states at one point, "five minutes in a person's library can tell you more about him than a full course of digging through his itches on a psychiatrist's couch—provided you know your books" (110). Throughout the stories of *$tud*, Phil assumes a certain level of literary experience from his audience and expects that audience to consume his literary, philosophical, cultural, and scientific allusions as if they were examining the most intimate areas of his psyche. Literary allusions abound: the title of first story in the collection, "The Poison Tree," alludes to William Blake's poem of the same title. In another story, as Phil examines a stranger, he begins "to deduce as Sherlock might have" (151). When he meets good-looking older men, he wonders "what portraits were growing old in their attics" (137), alluding to one of Steward's most admired authors, Oscar Wilde.[24] A bit less expected are his allusions to Homer, Plato, Voltaire, Freud, Flaubert, Cummings, Wordsworth, Sandburg, and Shakespeare. These allusions, however, are as much a part of his constructed persona as his leather jacket, and their frequency marks ironically juxtaposed elements of narcissism and insecurity. Steward uses Phil's intellectualism to bend the expectations of his readers, who would assume a hustler to be desperately uneducated, or perhaps to have a certain amount of street sense or practical experience but very little literary knowledge.

Phil uses this performative intellect to manipulate or disarm the people and situations around him. In the same way that he is protected from being too gay by being incredibly masculine in appearance, his constant intellectual performance is a tool of power in his line of work. Even though it destabilizes the lowbrow working-man mystique, it allows him the comfort of dominance over other men, and Phil perpetually measures his cultural class against that of his clients. In the story "H2," he is excited to find a bookshelf in a client's apartment from which he is able to deduce, by browsing its contents, the man's entire professional and sexual history. He then uses this knowledge to manipulate the man sexually. Similarly, in "A Collar for Achilles" he meets a blond man and is excited by the man's potential ignorance, as it will reinforce his narcissistic obsession with his own intelligence: "He might have been as beautiful as the rosy-fingered dawn over the wine-dark sea, but he was sure as hell stupid. Everybody said so, and I hoped to be able to prove to myself that he was. That way he'd keep the tradition alive about blonds being beautiful but dumb, and I'd be able to maintain my admiration for the intellectual powers of the man I loved. Me." (168). Here, Phil is hoping for the same allowance of power, which he again uses to manipulate the man sexually. In a later story, "Arrangement in Black and White," Phil meets up with an older, wealthy man for sex. When he gets to the man's apartment, he observes the setting and decides that the man is his intellectual equal based on his taste in art: "There was a large Picasso of the Rose Period on one wall, a Modigliani on another. A sculpture by Epstein stood at one side of the room, in front of a floor-to-ceiling window looking over the dark lake." When confronted with the abnormality of a hustler noticing such finery, Phil simply says, "I'm an unusual hustler" (137).

Just as other parts of his persona will be deconstructed by hints of sarcasm or contradiction, however, so too is his brain power. During the same encounter, Phil misattributes a famous quotation and receives the requisite "polite flattery" that follows (139).[25] This moment playfully negates Phil's cultural pretensions to the reader and counterbalances the extremism of his intellectual obsession by highlighting its role in the greater performance taking place. The power dynamic in this encounter is gravely different from earlier encounters, and Phil finds himself unable to keep up with the intellect of his trick. He "couldn't think of anything else," and for the first time in a sexual scenario he covers his naked body with a dressing gown, as "somehow the place and the occasion made [him] put it on" (146). This is one of very few moments when Phil is vulnerable, exposed by the failure of his intellectual facade, and it works to further expose the artifice of his masculine persona. Without intellectual control, he feels exposed, and for the first and only time in the collection, admits aloud, "I'm homosexual" (142), foreshadowing his eventual submission to the inevitable pull away from conventional masculinity and into transgressive sexuality.

In addition to Phil's intellectuality, perhaps the most significant element of his persona is his status as trade. Phil is continually aware of the artifice of the leather-clad hustler persona and is always ready to expose the pretense of the leather scene and, in so doing, to expose the charade of his own identity. Of a fellow hustler, he observes, "He wore the [hustler's] 'uniform' as if it were his working clothes. . . . With the hustlers and the leather crowd you could generally tell it was all a masquerade, a drag, a play-pretend dressup costume party for itty bitty boys, with everyone more or less self-conscious" (200). Here, *$tud*'s narrator is negating his own masculine identity, as he too participates in this illegitimate, even silly, game of performance. He associates the hustler with drag, a campy performance of femininity, and degrades the hustler's performance of masculinity to the level of children's dress-up games. Steward once wrote of the leather scene that "the entire affair has become a ritual, a Fun and Games sort of thing, and in essence there is no difference today between a female impersonator or drag-queen and a leather boy in full leather-drag. Both are dressing up to represent something they are not."[26] Yet the hustler performance is integral to Phil's identity as trade, as it allows him to remain within the binary in which he is so heavily invested, even as he embraces the complexity of its artifice.

The status of trade is extremely important to Phil and his fellow hustlers, as it allows them to perform homosexual acts without relinquishing their masculinity and is somehow a more socially acceptable manifestation of same-sex desire. He is not perverting the normative marital structure by becoming romantically involved with another man, since his hustling allows only for casual sex with men who are merely his "clients." Phil is also able to keep himself emotionally removed from his partners, because his sexuality is his economic livelihood; thus his affairs with men are business, not pleasure, and this step of removal allows Phil the security in his masculinity that he needs to function within the strictures of conventional Cold War manhood. When Phil begins to be conscious of his own pleasure, he is instantly self-deprecating. In one instance, he thinks to himself, "More and more of late I'd been finding myself combining business and pleasure, or even sometimes forgetting about the business end of it. By this time next year, I thought wryly, I'd be a fruit in full flower" (200). This is an ironic coming-out that humorously deflects Phil's homosexuality with a self-deprecating feminine association.[27] Yet his fear of becoming a fruit is a very real anxiety. He is confronted with this problem in the story "Once in a Blue Moon," when he meets a young farm boy, Kenny, and is "afraid [he] might fall in love with him" (161). This is the only instance in the collection in which Phil allows himself to kiss another man. When he confesses to Kenny that he is a hustler, Phil is suddenly disgusted: "I felt very dirty, as if my body were coated and covered with the dried accumulations of saliva from all the tongues that had ever been placed on me, and the stiffened and flaking layers of semen that had been spilled on me. . . . I shuddered a little in the dark" (158). Here, it is the frequency and economic element of his encounters that disgusts him. He is conscious of being in a moment of pure affection with another gay man and finds himself ashamed of hustling. Again, this moment exposes the contradiction of Phil's character: he is invested in the gender binary of mass culture, but is ashamed of this investment when he feels genuine affection from or toward another man.

Phil is so caught up in this turmoil-inducing binary that he is unable to imagine a relationship between men that is not heteronormative or that does not follow the patterns and mores of conventional relationships between men and women. This is part of a larger culture of homophobia, bound in strict understandings of gender and sexuality that must assign each partner's role in a relationship as either passive or active against the foil of the other. Within this imagined normative framework, there is an inherent emasculation that occurs as one of the men in the relationship must logically act as the wife. This is problematic for the butch-obsessed Phil, whose anxiety is evident in the story "Sea Change." Here, Phil's otherwise butch friend Howie is emasculated when he enters a monogamous relationship with another man. Phil visits him months after the relationship begins, to find the former leather-clad factory worker keeping house for his partner and studying to be a beautician, or "hairburner." Phil's most horrifying realization is that Howie is "play[ing] the woman's part": he is keeping house, cooking, cross-dressing, and even taking a passive role sexually (212–13). As one of the few glimpses into long-term relationships between men in the collection, "Sea Change" becomes symbolic of Phil's anxieties of gender and sexuality and of the anxieties of the culture around him. Men who were trade or who cruised in bars were perceived as masculine, while those who established monogamous relationships with other men were assumed to violate gender conventions, with at least one man devolving into a wife. Of course, this story is problematic, since it essentializes gender, portrays the feminine as grotesque, and invalidates gay relationships. But it does so with a sharp irony that again at once voices and makes light of Phil's complex relationship with gender.

The most captivating example of the gender ethic of *$tud* is the story "The Easter Kid." It follows Phil on an everyday job—meeting a client who turns out to be just as consumed with artifice as Phil himself and thus gives him a wild ride through the game of gender performance. The client shows up on Easter with a cleverly fake name, Pasquale (derived from the Latin word for Easter), to match his tough-guy persona. Pasquale reflects Phil in every way, even down to the hustler uniform. He describes Pasquale's appearance in relation to his own: "We both had identical costumes on, from the black leather jackets and caps to the levis and boots" (34). But he trumps Phil's hustler "costume" by actually owning a motorcycle, a phenomenon rarely encountered at one of his motorcycle bars. Phil affectionately describes the leather bar scene: "It was fashionable that year to follow the patterns of moonlight and bosh and bullshit that passed for the kind of Fun & Games that the gay boys called sadomasochistic; and which were about as closely related to the real thing as a Woolworth diamond is to a 10-carat from Tiffany's" (32). Although Phil is able to see and analyze the performativity of the leather scene, he realizes that he is as much a participant as the other men involved. He is a player in the "Fun & Games" but has the illusion that his awareness of the artifice somehow gives him power and control over the scene. This description foreshadows Phil's eventual entrance into a very real world of sadomasochistic games that allows him to subvert normative gender expectations. As the collection continues, it is this artifice that must be melted away or turned on its head in order for Phil to find the ultimate satisfaction he craves.

After an initial introduction, the two men ride to Pasquale's hotel room on his motorcycle. Upon arrival, Phil discovers that Pasquale has become aroused by the trip through the San Francisco hills. Phil performs his usual duties, but finds Pasquale hard to satisfy. After several failed attempts at sex, Phil facetiously suggests, "We might wheel your bike in here. . . . I noticed that you got excited enough over that" (41). To his surprise, this suggestion excites Pasquale, and the two men wheel in the motorcycle and incorporate it into their sexual experience. Man morphs into machine when Pasqual has Phil tie him to the motorcycle and have sex with him. The bodies of the men are objectified and made inanimate in the ultimate act of artifice. A few days later, Phil learns from the bartender at the biker bar that Pasquale's peculiar request was a practiced bit that had been performed many times before. The bartender tells Phil that Pasquale "always picks up a stud who's hustlin', and rides him up to the Stanford [Hotel]. And he pretends he can't get excited. . . . And after a while he suggests the motorcycle bit, and you help him wheel it in. . . . 'At's the way he likes to get his kicks" (46). When Phil discovers that he has been played by a superior trickster, he is furious. He is accustomed to being the clever, manipulative hustler who can make a trick do whatever he wants. He says, "I hate being a patsy for anyone," and feels that being sexually manipulated feminizes him (47). Although Phil is acutely aware of the artifice of the leather scene, he seems to miss the irony of his situation. In a postmodern sense, Phil's authoritative voice is unreliable. Again, Steward seems to be nodding to a potential gay readership that could share the ironic revelation of such artifice without the knowledge or involvement of his narrator.

This story stands out as an introductory glimpse into Phil's gay ethic. Trade is represented as the utmost manifestation of subversive masculinity, but its effectiveness as such is limited by its own artifice. When one hustler hustles another, both are exposed and degraded.[28] Phil is able to move on from this embarrassing episode with little grief, however, and is finally able to laugh about it and continue his performance.

Perhaps the most pronounced element of the new (somewhat paradoxical) gay ethic contained in the pages of *$tud* is Phil's obsession with the body. He is constantly aware of the state of bodies—his own and those around him. His obsession with masculinity is tied intimately to this fascination, as he looks for the roots of gender in physical sex and locates his personal value and the value of others in the physical presence of their sexual bodies. Judith Butler has argued in *Bodies That Matter* that "once 'sex' itself is understood in its normativity, the materiality of the body will not be thinkable apart from the materialization of that regulatory norm. 'Sex' is, thus, not simply what one has, or a static description of what one is: it will be one of the norms by which the 'one' becomes visible at all, that which qualifies a body for life within the domain of cultural intelligibility." In a way, Phil's physical body and the bodies of other hustlers become a cultural currency of sorts. Not only are bodies bought and sold, consumed, enjoyed, and tossed aside, they are the markers of cultural existence in a system of normalcy that is otherwise quick to negate or complicate them. When individuals do not appear properly gendered, they are abjected, and "their very humanness . . . comes into question."[29] Again, in a culture that is quick to cast out queerness of any kind, it is essential that queer men cling to masculinity, even if that masculinity is performative.

Steward saw narcissism as "one of the important elements of homosexuality."[30] His protagonist constantly makes note of his own good looks, again taking a single characteristic to an extreme in order to place it in a larger context of social mores. Phil's narcissism is another manifestation of his gender anxieties: he is glorifying the characteristics that make him desirably masculine while simultaneously airing his own desire for maleness. In one story, Phil describes himself: "I looked in the mirror. It was a kind of hard sexy face that stared back at me. A lot of scores said that I was a dead ringer for the guy who played in the Bond movies, Agent 007, except for the hair. . . . Oddly enough, it was the sort of face I'd go for myself if I saw it on the street" (159–60). He is narcissistically his own ideal sexual partner and has convinced himself that he is as masculine as he appears, even as he ironically exposes his extreme vanity and attraction to men. Almost every element of Phil's carefully constructed persona is projected onto his physical body, and he uses the maleness of that body to confirm his subjectivity in a culture that threatens to objectify the feminine and abjectify the androgynous.

While Phil uses his own body to secure his place in the binary, he also looks outward, projecting his physical standards and class stereotypes on the bodies of the men he encounters. He often describes the men he sees as having working men's bodies; of a fellow hustler, he says, "His chest was tremendous, bulging. . . . His upper arms were at least eighteen inches around and his forearms were as brawny as those of Hercules" (166). He values the smell of "oil and leather and armpits" (39). The suggestion of muscle built from *real* work is tantalizing, as it assures a man's masculinity; his ability to perform a physical task to earn a wage is his enactment of the American dream.[31] A man's body is his currency in society and is his only confirming marker of maleness. Phil is a worshipper of bodies, and each body (like each man's bookshelf) is coded with ways to control it. To Phil, sex is a contest of bodies; it is another part of the game to be played, but this game is concentrated in the materiality of the bodies involved. Sex has no connection with romance or mutual satisfaction, but is instead a struggle of physical power between unconscious forces of the physical body. Phil explains this phenomenon in the story "H2":

> Considered objectively, the bed is a lonely battleground for attack and siege, assault and penetration. Of the two in combat, one is the victor, another the conquered. And once you are engaged on this battlefield, locked in mortal struggle until the miracle of the orgasm separates you from your opponent—you are absolutely alone. Neither money nor brains nor good looks will come to your aid. Your success as a lover boy depends on the workings of the secret muscles, the rustling come-and-go of the hidden blood, the silent snapping of reflexes and the unheard click of closing synapses—all functioning uninhibited and unhampered by thought, rationalization, and analysis—to produce the ultimate teaspoonful, the release of which deflates the arteries, slows the pounding heart, closes the pores, arrests the perspiration, and soothes the raw and gasping lungs. (112–13)

These "secret muscles" and "closing synapses" are given a mysterious, even sinister quality, and the body here is seen as an uncontrollable force in opposition with another, until the advantage of power is delivered (in the form of orgasm) to the most capable body. As Butler notes, "What constitutes the fixity of the body, its contours, its movements, will be fully material, but materiality will be rethought as the effect of power, as power's most productive element."[32] Thus the body becomes a landscape for the airing of countless issues, including gender, race, and violence, and sex becomes the battle between opposing forces upon that landscape. Even the book itself, at least in its pirated pulp form, became a marker of a certain transgressive physicality, its pages coarse and cheap, as did its status as pornography, a categorization that associates its subject with physical (sexual or masturbatory) rather than intellectual pursuits.

Phil is obsessed with the physical body because it is a marker of masculinity and thus a marker of cultural intelligibility, guaranteeing his station within the binary in which he needs to belong. But the physical body in *$tud* is often complicated by race. Much like the importance of gender in the stories, race serves as a marker of difference, reinforcing boundaries that Phil must either acknowledge or subvert. Five of the collection's stories deal specifically with mixed-race sexual encounters or relationships, and these intensify as the collection moves forward. David Bergman notes that "sexual desire, which is always at least about power, contaminates the representation of racial relations. The representation of the attraction that brings men of different colors together cannot help being regarded as racist, and . . . uncoupling desire from its representation is impossible." Phil's sexual appetite for black men at the chronological peak of the Civil Rights movement is on one hand progressive, as his physical affections cross boundaries of color and class.[33] But because Phil seeks out men of color to satisfy a certain appetite, race becomes a fetish and serves not as a marker of unity but as an exotic aesthetic choice. Dwight McBride explores these issues in his examination of the modern gay porn industry, in which portrayals of black men are often "operating on many of the most readily imaginable stereotypes about black masculinity." McBride argues that in the interracial genre of gay porn, white men mostly play a passive role to their more active, violent black counterparts, and that it is "this knotty interrelationship of power, desire, containment, and domination that is so well thematized in the function of black male bodies in gay porn."[34] This intermediation of white fetish helps to anesthetize the otherwise fearful element of black virility for white consumption.

Phil is quick to aestheticize black bodies, again relying on physicality as the locus of his affection, and perhaps playing into McBride's theory of white subjectivity in interracial porn. He explores this aestheticization: "Did I like them for that . . . intense sexuality? For their white teeth or their big dongs? Or did I like them for the exotic effect of the blackness of their handsome bodies against the white sheets . . . ?" (73). Here he not only aestheticizes them, but violently tears them into portions of bodies, into objects for consumption. Again, Phil is excited by the opportunity to transgress an acceptable norm, and the potential for criminality and violence is his main motivation. Continuing in the tradition of the romanticized Noble Savage, Phil has marked black bodies as objects of trade and consumption. By today's standards, many of Phil's interactions with black men are incredibly racist or paternalistic, and his miscegenation actually serves to reinforce the racial binary and to reconfirm boundaries of class.[35]

Phil's perceptions of black men's sexuality are often violent and troubling, and he associates this violence with racially motivated hatred toward him. The story "Ace in the Hole" chronicles Phil's relationship with Ace Hardesty, a black man in Dallas whom he meets while working in a hotel. Phil sees himself as the Desdemona to Ace's Othello, a comparison that makes Ace seem "darkly romantic" while also assigning normative gender associations to the men (71). What continues to be significant in this story is the presence of the body, the physicality of skin pigmentation, and all of the violence that comes from the intertwining of white and black bodies. Like many of his other tricks, Phil sees Ace as a purely physical being. But unlike the other men he encounters in the collection, Ace's physical appeal comes from his blackness, as is made clear in Phil's description of him. Phil sees him as a "coal-black Negro buck" who is "so black that the room lights turned blue when they reflected from his skin" (67). So his body is not only black to the extreme that it reflects blue light, but he is described as a "buck," a term that hints at the racist perception of black men as animalistic, wild, and virile. This is the seed of Phil's fascination with Ace's blackness, one that eventually develops into a dangerous racial tension between the couple.

Phil is acutely aware of the racial tensions of post-integration Texas and makes it clear that he is sympathetic. He experiences a "sample taste of black bigotry" the first time he goes to Ace's home and finds his landlady disapproving of a white man in her building (76). After this encounter, he is somehow better equipped to sympathize with Ace, a victim of racial oppression. He says of his black lover, "the indignities piled on him daily did not pass unnoticed," alluding to several instances of discrimination or verbal abuse that Ace endures in his daily life. Of such experiences, Phil says, "I learned from painful experience that it was not wise to be with him on the evenings of such days because he worked out his anger on me, sometimes very painfully. . . . A century's hates and customs do not disappear overnight" (78–79). The paranoia of racially motivated violence is highlighted in the benighted southern city of Dallas, and Phil is aware that his relationship with Ace is "the sort of business that [gets] you tarred and feathered and ridden out of town on a rail, or horsewhipped by the Ku Klux Klan" (77).[36] The southern sense of place is prominent for Ace, who affects a thick southern drawl in order to prove to local whites that he knows his place. Phil maintains a sense of security, however, and does little to camouflage his relationship with Ace. As the white partner of the couple, he is less responsible for sexual transgression.

Toward the end of the story, Phil begins to take Ace's violent sex as a sort of punishment for his whiteness, for his association by proxy with larger forces of systemic oppression and discrimination. Of course, this punishment is somewhat exciting for Phil, as well as for Steward, who often had consensual violent sex with black men in order to atone for his whiteness. In one of his journal entries of 1957, Steward describes this idea in more graphic terms. "Most of all at present . . . I enjoy [the black bodybuilder] Bill Payson. . . . It is his attitude of semi-cruelty, you might say, that I like; not cruelty exactly, but more a feeling of 'This is what you deserve, white boy; you scorn me because I'm a nigger, and here I am, shoving this big black tool right down in you, fucking you in the ass; that'll show you what I think of you' . . . and man—does he."[37] This is its own breed of discrimination; it not only eroticizes racial violence but falls back on centuries-old racist principles that characterized black men as animalistic, sexual, and violent. Phil sees black men as having a "look of the jungle" that is "pure sex" or as possessing "some ancient magic we whites could never learn" (143–44). Phil calls on such stereotypes for his own enjoyment and congratulates himself on being made an olive branch of (sexual) racial reconciliation. He is aware of this phenomenon, however, and wonders "if I hated myself so much for the percentage of queerness in me that I went to bed with Negroes to punish and degrade myself"—which seems a likely psychoanalytic motivation, though probably a bit too excusatory (73).

Another aspect of this phenomenon that is problematic is the narrative's portrayal of Ace and other black characters in the collection. Because he is written as a sexual conquest for Phil, his blackness is essentialized and eroticized, and he is only able to speak, to act, in the context of the fantasy in which he exists. Therefore, Ace becomes a vessel for the racially motivated sexuality that his character must embody. He is, in effect, a slave to the narrative that creates him. Even as he enacts his ultimate violence upon his white lover, who has become a helpless victim of his rage, he does so within the confines of erotic fiction and therefore at the whim of the white lover-victim. During a particularly violent argument, Phil describes the hatred he feels from Ace: "I had seen that look before—on the faces of southern whites as they looked at a Negro who challenged their feelings of superiority. It was the hate look, chilling, frightening, as venomous as that of a fanged snake, distilling its life into poison" (96). Ace has taken on the violent hatred of his oppressors, redirected it into punishment for their crimes, and directed that punishment at Phil. This is all part of the larger game of artifice and performance as Phil and Ace each perform their essentialized racial parts against the foil of the other.

The terminal scene of this relationship is quite appropriately a violent gang-rape, motivated by Ace's discovery that Phil has been seeing other black men for sex. Ace and several other black men tie Phil to a bed and rape him. The scene is incredibly disturbing, since it seems almost entirely racially motivated. Phil sees his rapists as "black shadows" or "dark voice(s)," and they call him only "Whitey" (98–100). Each party is disjointed and objectified, creating a distance that allows violence in the particular realm of racial dissonance. This is the last time that Phil sees Ace, and it marks a shift in the perception of Phil's attitude toward sex with black men. Where once he was intrigued about the ways that eons of racial conflict could enter his sexual life, he is now aware that being punished for his whiteness by black men has become a satisfying inevitability. But his satisfaction is mixed with anger and fear when he realizes he is no longer in control of the encounter and is no longer merely playing at submission. Phil's desire becomes more complicated as a result of this scene. Although the gang rape is traumatizing for him, he will seek out the pain of sadomasochism again and again with a black master and will discover that this complicated mix of pain and pleasure is his true, culminating desire. This racially charged sadomasochism is reminiscent of Tennessee Williams's 1948 story "Desire and the Black Masseur," in which the white protagonist, Anthony Burns, so desires physical abuse from a nameless black masseur that he is eventually broken and literally eaten alive in a scene that is hauntingly sweet and reconciliatory. In the same vein, Phil's answer to racial reconciliation lies with sexual violence, and "the answer, perfection, [is] slowly evolved through torture" (280).

In the final pair of stories in *$tud*, titled "The Blacks and Mr. Bennett" and "Color Him Black," Phil is given the opportunity "to become a 'slave' to a mysterious and unknown Negro, one of the leaders of the radical Black Muslims," Adam X. Although Phil is concerned that doing so will mean "abandoning [his] maleness, [his] assertive dominance," he eventually relishes the task (280). Again, Phil is tempted by the potential feeling of atonement. To Bennett, who is already employed as Adam X's sexual slave, he wonders, "Is it atonement . . . ? I never felt that angle of it because . . . I haven't any guilt feelings about Negroes in general"—to which Bennett replies, "Maybe it's atonement in the abstract. . . . You know, dying for the sins of the world" (282). In a moment that is again reminiscent of Williams's protagonist, Bennett compares interracial masochism with Christ-like sacrifice, a metaphor that is complicated at best. Like Steward, Bennett understands being dominated by black men as somehow racially progressive, as reparative for the crimes of his race. Even after Phil agrees to sexual servitude, however, he is unable to relinquish control for many months. After all, it is Phil's masculinity, the locus of his legitimacy, of his existence, that is at stake. He is finally dismissed as an unsatisfactory slave, but the story continues under the shadow of his inevitable return to Adam X's lair.

As Bennett says, this encounter, coupled with his relationship with Ace, makes him realize "the extent of the s/m elements" in himself. Bennett then wisely observes, "you ought never to use one term [sadism or masochism] without the other—they're so mixed up together in anyone who's like that" (282). Thus Phil Andros, the hardened hustler, relinquishes his role of power and returns to Adam X to confront the cocktail of "anger and anguish and desire" that can only be assuaged by total domination. His need for power, for control over his body and the bodies of others, has always harbored a twinge of desire for submission to a dominant force, and his resistance has only propelled him forward through an endless frontier of tricks. He realizes the futility of trying to conform to the strictures of American masculinity and is able to ultimately subvert the binaries of gender and race he has grappled with. When he does finally return to Adam X, he finds that Bennett has darkened the color of his skin and is passing as a black man. Bennett says of his change, "It's like . . . wearing a mask at a carnival. You let loose. All inhibitions gone" (194). His change is the culmination and reversal of essentialism—a white man becomes black in order to degrade himself and, in so doing, becomes liberated. The ultimate relinquishment of power in *$tud* is, of course, the relinquishing of the physical body. Although it is only suggested, Phil's return to Adam X in the collection's final scene is both a symbol of the relinquishment of his body and of the ultimate power and liberation he finds in doing so. He can only have the ultimate power he desires when he makes the decision to lose it.

The encounters and ideas of Phil Andros indeed reached more than "lonely old men living in hotel rooms," as the author joked of his readership.[38] Along with other gay pulps of this period, *$tud* presented, for the first time, a narrative of a non-normative lifestyle that was frank, humorous, and without the emotional strife or violent ends of earlier popular novels like Rechy's *City of Night*. Phil's obsession with physicality and his eventual submission to the world of sadomasochism and racial transgression evidence the tension between his strict investment in conventional masculinity and the contradictions and limits of that masculinity. Michael Bronski says of the late 1950s and early 1960s, "Neither best nor worst, it was simply the times as they were, and they were complicated, contradictory, and confusing, and—to our modern and postmodern contemporary sensibilities—often confounding and unnerving when focused on sexuality, sexual identity, and gender presentation."[39] The gay hustler is the perfect catalyst for grappling with these issues, and the collection's humorous delivery and self-criticism allow Phil (and Steward) to subvert masculinity and transgress boundaries of gender, race, and class even while reinforcing them. *$tud* is thus more than a dirty book intended to excite and titillate a gay male readership. Its concentration on elements of artifice and performativity and on the location of physical power in the material body show nuanced understandings of the issues of gender and race facing American men during the Cold War and beyond. The new gay ethic presented in its pages serves to further complicate understandings of "normalcy" and challenge the limits of queerness, all the while creating a warm, humorous space for the joyful dalliances of a gay hustler.

## NOTES

1. John Preston, introduction to *$tud,* by Phil Andros (Boston: Alyson Publications, 1982), 13, 12. Michael Bronski argues that early gay pulps "functioned pedagogically" to show gay men "how they might live their lives." Bronski, *Pulp Friction: Uncovering the Golden Age of Gay Male Pulps* (New York: St. Martin's Griffin, 2003), 8.
2. Justin Spring, *Secret Historian: The Life and Times of Samuel Steward, Professor, Tattoo Artist, and Sexual Renegade* (New York: Farrar, Straus & Giroux, 2010), 58.
3. See Spring, *Secret Historian,* 446–48. Sixteen of the stories first appeared in the Dutch magazine *amigo,* one appeared in the Swiss magazine *Der Kreis,* and one had its first publication in the book.
4. Phil Andros, *$tud* (Washington, DC: Guild Press, 1966); Phil Andros, *$tud* (San Francisco: J. Brian, 1969); Anonymous, *$tud,* 3 vols. (Washington, DC: Beaumont Classics [Guild Press], 1969). For a detailed account of the publication difficulties *$tud* faced, see Samuel M. Steward, *Chapters from an Autobiography* (San Francisco: Grey Fox Press, 1981), 116; and Spring, *Secret Historian,* 329–40. I appreciate an e-mail from Philip Clark about the Beaumont Classics edition.
5. Stephen Wright, ed., *Different: An Anthology of Homosexual Short Stories* (New York: Bantam, 1974), 35–83; George Whitmore, "Phil Andros," *Little Caesar* 12 (1981): 163–68, quotation on 163; see also David Bergman, *The Violet Hour: The Violet Quill and the Making of Gay Culture* (New York: Columbia University Press, 2004), 53–54. Six stories were omitted in the 1982 reprint to make for uniformly sized editions. Three of the omitted stories were reprinted in *Below the Belt and Other Stories* (San Francisco: Perineum Press, 1982) and one in *Different Strokes: Stories* (San Francisco: Perineum Press, 1984).
6. Bronski, *Pulp Friction,* 16.
7. Patricia Juliana Smith, ed., *The Queer Sixties* (New York: Routledge, 1999), xxi.
8. Ibid.
9. Steward, *Chapters from an Autobiography,* 113.
10. Smith, *The Queer Sixties,* xxii.
11. Whitmore, "Phil Andros," 165.

12. Steward, *Chapters from an Autobiography,* 99.
13. Spring, *Secret Historian,* 346.
14. It takes Phil most of the collection to actually admit he is homosexual; before then he frequently degrades himself, suggesting that he is less than "a real man," but without the "sissy taint" found in other, less masculine homosexuals. Finally, when he is experiencing a rarely candid moment with a client, he admits, "I'm homosexual. Or maybe as the good doctor in Bloomington said: 'Man's a sexual animal.'" Andros, *$tud* (1966), 34, 137, 142.
15. George Chauncey, *Gay New York: Gender, Urban Culture, and the Making of the Gay Male World, 1890–1940* (New York: Basic Books, 1994), 16.
16. Following World War II, during the late 1940s and 1950s, there was suddenly heightened importance surrounding American manhood as Senator Joseph McCarthy and other American politicians tried to contain the American household under the guise of an effort to combat the spread of communism and secure perceptions of American identity on a global stage. In so doing, they established a "normal" model for American men and women and created negative, often incriminating associations for deviations from that model. See Michael Sherry, *Gay Artists in Modern American Culture: An Imagined Conspiracy* (Chapel Hill: University of North Carolina Press, 2007).
17. Alan Nadel, *Containment Culture: American Narratives, Postmodernism, and the Atomic Age* (Durham, NC: Duke University Press, 1995), 3, 4.
18. Bronski, *Pulp Friction,* 13.
19. See Chauncey, *Gay New York,* for a history of the men and women who lived non-normative lifestyles long before the strictures of the Cold War. For a study of coded queerness in popular literature and culture during the 1960s, see Smith, *The Queer Sixties.*
20. Chauncey, *Gay New York,* 14.
21. Ibid., 70.
22. Andros, *$tud* (1966), 73. Subsequent page references cited parenthetically in the text refer to this edition.
23. John Rechy, *City of Night* (1963; New York: Grove Press, 1994), xiii.
24. In *Chapters from an Autobiography* Steward speaks of the importance of *The Picture of Dorian Gray* to his own education (29).
25. Phil attributes the quotation "An image of God cut in ebony" to Bishop Jeremy Taylor; it was actually written by the eccentric British historian and churchman Thomas Fuller (1608–1661).
26. Quoted in Spring, *Secret Historian,* 302.
27. Again, this association is potentially incriminating when considered in Nadel's containment binary.
28. This moment is not unlike the tender encounter between fellow hustlers youngman and Pete in Rechy's *City of Night.* The two sleep side by side, holding hands, and both feel so alienated and degraded by the event that they never speak again. The main difference between the stories and between the collections themselves seems to be the humor given to this hustler reflexivity by Steward.
29. Judith Butler, *Bodies That Matter: On the Discursive Limits of "Sex"* (New York: Routledge, 1993), 2, 8.
30. Steward, *Chapters from an Autobiography,* 81.
31. Spring notes that "Steward's fascination with rough trade was in fact part of a well-established tendency among middle- and upper-class homosexuals for taking their

sexual adventures with men of working or criminal class, whose masculinity may have seemed greater due to their more violent, less predictable natures." Spring, *Secret Historian,* 59.

32. Butler, *Bodies That Matter,* 2.
33. Bergman, *The Violet Hour,* 114. Citing Kobena Mercer's readings of race in the photographs of Robert Mapplethorpe, Bergman writes: "Mercer insists that all representations of race must be rigorously placed within their historical, cultural, and erotic contexts before they can be evaluated. An attitude that was progressive in the light of 1957 may be reactionary in 1967 and repulsive by 1987" (116).
34. Dwight McBride, "It's a White Man's World: Race in the Gay Marketplace of Desire," in *Why I Hate Abercrombie & Fitch* (New York: New York University Press, 2005), 102, 105.
35. Phil admires the extreme paternalism of his wealthy client Ben, whose black sexual servant, Lem, is literally the son of his former lover (147).
36. The prominence of violence in Dallas is made quite explicit as the two men flee from the city after a violent encounter that occurs on the same day as the Kennedy assassination.
37. Quoted in Spring, *Secret Historian,* 246.
38. Quoted in Preston, introduction to *$tud,* 12.
39. Bronski, *Pulp Friction,* 15

# Carnal Matters

## THE ALEXANDER GOODMAN STORY

Reed Massengill

The artist, photographer, and writer George Haimsohn (1925–2003) was a man of many talents and almost as many identities. Although he is remembered today primarily as the cowriter and lyricist of the campy Off-Broadway musical *Dames at Sea*—the little show that catapulted its fresh-faced ingénue, Bernadette Peters, to fame—Haimsohn had a substantially more varied career. Born in St. Louis, he served in the Navy during World War II and later graduated from the University of California at Berkeley, where his early poetry was published in the campus literary journal. His artistic interests extended beyond writing, however, and he moved to New York City in 1952 to pursue his creative endeavors. He rented a fifth-floor walk-up apartment on West 13th Street in Greenwich Village, and invariably he bragged to each new visitor as they trudged up the dark, narrow steps, "Anaïs Nin lived here before I moved in." Haimsohn occupied this space for the remainder of his life, and it was in this small garret apartment, with skylights and an outdoor roof deck, that all of his creations came to life.

Among those creations were his numerous alter egos. As a widely published physique photographer, he was known as Plato, in homage to the Greek philosopher. As a writer of gay fiction, he chose the name Alexander Goodman. Occasionally, for short magazine features, he used the names George Maxim or Gregory Maxim. For a particularly campy book, he adopted the name Peter B. Luvvly. When he decided late in life to write video reviews for the porn magazine *Manscape,* he did so under the name Vulcan. Some of his later, more graphic gay fiction was published under the name Jack Ranch. Yet despite the genre in which he was working or the name under which he did it, almost all his creative output was realized at his makeshift desk, at his cluttered kitchen table, or in his tiny bathroom, where as Plato he processed his negatives and hung them up to dry.

While it is his work as a writer under the pseudonym Alexander Goodman that is germane here, Haimsohn's life and work took several unpredictable turns before he became an important writer of gay fiction in the pre-Stonewall era. To understand the work, one must understand its creator, and in examining George Haimsohn's contributions to gay fiction as Alexander Goodman, it is essential to focus on three threads that were inextricably bound together in the development of his stories: sex, drugs, and, most important, his friendship with—and his conflicting feelings about—the gay entrepreneur and publisher H. Lynn Womack.

## A LIFE SPENT IN THE DARK

Although he occasionally worked at mundane office jobs to pay the bills, much of Haimsohn's time during the 1950s and 1960s was spent in the dark—going to movies, attending Broadway shows, and exploring the sexual freedom afforded him in New York City. His varied creative endeavors took root during this period, when he began to dabble more seriously in photography, collage art, fiction, and poetry. Although he used his camera to shoot a few nude or near-nude models—often young men he had picked up as hustlers—as the 1960s dawned Haimsohn decided to try selling photographs to earn some extra money. He was by that time well aware of the legal problems that plagued a number of New York City photographers, since their travails were often reported in the popular little physique magazines of the day. He opened a post office box at Old Chelsea Station to distance the photographs from his home address and decided to use the pseudonym Plato as his studio name.

During 1960 and 1961, Haimsohn photographed several models and submitted photos to established magazines such as *Tomorrow's Man* and *The Young Physique*. But it was a chance meeting with a beautiful young man at the Washington Square Park chess boards that proved life-changing for Haimsohn. Joe Cali was so striking that Haimsohn immediately was captivated by him. He asked Cali to pose for photographs and found that he was a serious, intelligent man who possessed much more than just a pretty face. When Cali undressed for their first session on Haimsohn's rooftop deck, the photographer knew that their meeting was kismet. Cali was 6'1" and weighed 170 pounds, with a naturally developed forty-six-inch chest that tapered seductively to a narrow twenty-eight-inch waist. Below the belt, Cali was equally well developed, with a girthy, pendulous endowment that complemented his movie-star looks. Haimsohn was smitten, and Plato had found his star model. "I did love him, in my way," Haimsohn recalled to me in 1997. "Every time I saw him I thought how lucky I was to have met him, to see him as often as I did. His beauty is so self-evident."[1]

Among the magazines to which Haimsohn submitted his early photographs of Cali was *Grecian Guild Pictorial*, one of a growing stable of physique magazines owned and managed by a former college professor, H. Lynn Womack (1923–1985). Womack was both a visual curiosity and an enigma to most who encountered him. A native of Hazelhurst, Mississippi, Womack was a twice-divorced white-haired albino. Although he had attended the University of Mississippi, he later transferred to George Washington University in Washington, DC, where he earned BA and MA degrees. Following a stint as a teacher and headmaster of several boys' schools in Maryland (including the John Carroll Boys School, Longfellow School for Boys, and Howell Academy), Womack resumed his education and earned a PhD in philosophy from Johns Hopkins University in Baltimore. He later taught philosophy at both George Washington University and Mary Washington College (now called University of Mary Washington) before launching his myriad publishing ventures.

Womack's umbrella organizations included Potomac Press and Guild

Press, Ltd., which during their heyday in the mid-1960s published a total of seven small physique magazines, each with slightly different audience appeal. In addition to the most established title, *Grecian Guild Pictorial*, these included *Fizeek*, *TRIM*, *MANual*, *Manorama*, *Vim*, and *The BIG Boys*. Womack had shrewdly purchased some of these publications, including *Grecian Guild Pictorial*, from their original (and often legally beleaguered) publishers, and along with them he also acquired the firms' mailing lists, photo files, and any other assets he might be able to exploit. Other magazines, such as *Manorama* and *The BIG Boys*, Womack launched on his own as a means of expanding his operations and leveraging economies of scale.

Womack also owned an extensive back catalog of physique photography, much of which he bought outright and inexpensively from the estates of deceased photographers or from those who had decided to exit the business because of their wrangles with police or postal inspectors. Unlike most physique magazine publishers, however, Womack owned his own printing plant and had developed extensive distribution capabilities. Equally important, long before the term "data mining" came into the vernacular, Womack shrewdly aggregated subscriber data from the various magazines to continually expand his customer list.

## "A" IS FOR ALBINO

Womack would come to be a pivotal figure—perhaps the most important figure—in Haimsohn's creative life during the 1960s. At the time the two became correspondents, Womack had settled into a "prison" sentence being served within the walls of a Washington, DC, mental institution. Following criminal convictions on numerous counts of mailing obscene material, Womack argued before the court at his sentencing hearing that because he was homosexual and because the American Psychiatric Association at that time categorized homosexuality as a mental illness, he should serve his sentence in secure confinement at a mental hospital rather than in a prison. The strategy worked, and Womack was confined to St. Elizabeths Hospital. Founded in 1852 as the Government Hospital for the Insane, St. Elizabeths is located on a large, bucolic piece of property overlooking the intersection of the Anacostia and Potomac Rivers. Here Womack lived in relative quiet, afforded a typewriter, a portable television, and other amenities that allowed him to continue his work without significant interruption despite his confinement. On New Year's Day 1962, Womack typed his first letter to Haimsohn and struck up what was to become a decade-long correspondence.

Womack's initial letter wasn't addressed personally to Haimsohn, but to his alter ego Plato, thanking him for submitting photos to the various Guild Press magazines. An avid letter writer, Haimsohn was encouraged when Womack's chatty, lengthy letters started arriving with regularity. Soon they were sharing confidences and trading gossip about the current goings-on in the physique publishing world. Of his entry into the field after more than a decade in the academic world, Womack wrote that it was "a complete accident":

> I had a great deal of money which I had made on the Over the Counter Stock Market. I was on the Board of Directors of three Corporations, directed their promotions, made a fortune out of each one of them, and shoved them into bankruptcy. I had invested $25,000 in a small holding company which five of my friends had each put $25,000 into. With this $150,000, we raised $600,000 of public money, stole as much of it as we could, and turned to stealing from each other. I soon saw that nothing would remain and decided that the printing business which the group had invested considerable money in was the only thing worth having. With a little effort and some real close swindling within the group (I paid off under the table to two other Directors to sell me the printing cheap and on credit), I took over the printing, left the group, and within 45 days the original corporation was in bankruptcy and I was launched in the printing business."[2]

At a time when Haimsohn often doubted himself as a photographer, Womack proved to be the one voice of encouragement. "You should do well in this business," Womack wrote in early January 1962. "Every photographer who runs his business as a business does well. Far too many run it as a hobby and are disappointed when the results are not what they anticipate. . . . The market for the work is here. With us working together, we should both make some money—the primary goal for both of us."[3] Making money on the photos was proving difficult for Haimsohn, however. As was the case with almost all the physique magazines, photographers were not "assigned" work, nor were they paid for their contributions; they received free ad space in return for the use of their photographs. Aside from the occasional mail orders he received as a result of the free magazine ads, Haimsohn never actually earned anything from the photos published in the magazines.

And while Haimsohn wrote repeatedly of his money woes and Plato's lackluster earnings, Womack was direct in his advice to shoot younger, better looking models. "Do not permit yourself to become discouraged," Womack wrote a few weeks later. "This is a tough business. The other photographers are not quite what you might wish they were, magazine editors are not always the nicest people in the world, models sometimes cause trouble, the public may not respond to a boy you were certain would make a great deal of money for you, and all kinds of other things could very well happen."[4] Womack knew a segment of his market had a particular appetite for young models, and he learned firsthand about the trouble and controversy they could cause. When Haimsohn once questioned whether the visible pubescence of some of the models who made the magazine covers was representative of Womack's personal preference and whether using them as cover models was in good taste, Womack shot back:

> Let us understand another thing; poor taste that makes money is perfectly justified as far as I am concerned and poor taste that that does not make money is inexcusable. . . . Look, I spent $15,000 going to the Supreme Court and winning with GGP as one of the books involved. I did not fight, spend money, go to jail, come to Saint Elizabeths to spend even one moment of my life living in fear of *anything.* There is no one who can do one damned thing about [the questionable cover model] Bobby Pell except his mother—and she would love for him to pose nude because they are devout nudists.[5]

Womack could be equally pointed when it came to Haimsohn's oft-mentioned financial woes. "I told you we would work with you to help get you out of the valley of poverty," Womack wrote him on November 27, 1962. "I must, in all honesty, tell you that I complained to [office manager] Angela [Grimmer] about her using 3 or 4 pix of your model 'Danny' in *Manorama* that is now printed. I told her that if you did not have better models than that, to give you notice that either better ones had to be forthcoming or I instructed her to forget you. I think he is pretty terrible."

Over time, Womack also demonstrated a similarly no-nonsense attitude about his own magazines, telling Haimsohn not to take occasional instances of poor printing, bad editorial placement, or typographic errors too seriously. "First of all," he wrote in March 1963, "I think anyone who takes most anything seriously is an ass. Arthur James Balfour once wearily remarked: 'Nothing matters much; very few things matter at all.' Now, the only thing that really matters about physique magazines is that they should sell (for the benefit of the owner) and that they should sell photographs (for the photographers). Apart from this, what eternal values are involved in them?" Although the words sometimes changed, Womack's overarching point was clear: he was in the physique business to make money, not for any artistic, cultural, aesthetic or political reasons. "I do not make up these magazines for my own amusement," Womack wrote a month later, "they have to sell."[6]

## PLATO EVOLVES INTO ALEXANDER GOODMAN

While Womack continued to place and publish Plato photographs in his various magazines, he also was candid with Haimsohn about his misgivings regarding the quality of the models Haimsohn was using. In a three-page letter dated March 11, 1963, Womack went to the trouble of listing all the Plato models that had been published in the Guild Press magazines to date, commenting on their individual attributes and shortcomings. "The point is this," Womack summarized. "The above list has little variety, it has a strong tendency toward the older type model, it has a tendency toward a certain maturity that represents neither smashing sex appeal nor great physiques." Increasingly, Womack encouraged Haimsohn to work on writing features for the magazines. Referring to a feature Haimsohn had recently submitted that was fast-tracked for publication in *Manorama*, Womack had written a few months earlier, "I would hold this up as an ideal article and urge you to write more like it. . . . Are you interested—able—have time for more writing?"[7]

Titled "The New Male Model," the article was attributed to Gregory Maxim, and Haimsohn was delighted to crank out additional features for the magazines. In short order, his creative efforts on Womack's behalf were evenly divided between photo submissions and text contributions. In addition to garnering some photo cover placements in *Grecian Guild Pictorial* and *Manorama*, Haimsohn contributed several "Grecian of the Month" features to the magazine, penned "The Grecian Scene" for another issue, and wrote occasional columns for *Manorama* titled "Camera Corner" and "Views and Reviews." These text pieces were the sorts of filler material Womack had himself provided when he had been on-site and able to do so, and his extended absence from the office created some editorial gaps during what Womack called the "dry spell." To help guide Haimsohn as he tossed around article and feature ideas worth pursuing, Womack articulated each of the magazines' graphic and editorial slants in a four-page letter on November 20, 1962, noting in particular that "GGP has as its ultimate goal being so staid that every faggot in the USA would put it on their coffee table without fear and so interesting that it will increase its audience while becoming thus established."

Between the encouragement Womack continued to offer in his letters and the more concrete satisfaction Haimsohn derived from seeing his articles in print in the magazines, his restlessness diminished and his creativity soared. With the additional help of amphetamines and marijuana, he spent some of his most fertile hours hunkered over his portable typewriter and fewer hours behind the camera. Haimsohn's creative outpouring as a writer was well timed; Womack was just then planning the expansion of his enterprise to include a gay book club, and in addition to acquiring existing titles to sell through his magazines and a catalog, he decided to publish new gay fiction under his Guild Press, Ltd., imprint. Thus was born Alexander Goodman.

Whether it was the effect of drugs, a short attention span, or his own peculiar genius, Haimsohn's efforts crossed genres, made use of his myriad talents both as a visual and literary artist, and kept him constructively occupied and amused. Haimsohn wrote and submitted a number of gay-themed books which Womack published under the pseudonym Alexander Goodman during the next half decade. These included short novels, collections of short stories, and campy compositions that were combinations of Haimsohn's verse juxtaposed with collages or stick-figure drawings. For a year or so, Haimsohn gleefully worked on a variety of projects all at once—photo shoots with models, short stories half-finished in the typewriter, sketchpads filled with jottings, notations, and lines of verse. All of this he did because of Womack's ongoing encouragement. The only problem was that there seemed to be very little money in these endeavors.

## THE STARVING ARTIST INCARNATE

After the initial fertile period was past and Haimsohn had polished and submitted a number of works for Womack's consideration, Haimsohn's letters became a near-constant lament about his money woes, the general lack of positive feedback from Womack about the stories, and indications that he was feeling ignored and unappreciated. "I really believe your anger at me and my last letter is guilt feelings about the way you've treated me," Haimsohn wrote in a letter dated March 13, 1964. "I've spent more time waiting for letters from you and [for] checks from you, and if I am more cautious now and do not send so much at a time, you can only blame yourself. If you would only do exactly as you say you will do, I would be quite satisfied."

Haimsohn made a valid argument. Getting encouragement out of Womack was one thing; getting a check from him was quite another. Although Haimsohn was always happy to receive the small checks that came in the mail when one of his features or articles was published, the more substantial payments for the more serious work he did for Womack seemed elusive. In the same letter, Haimsohn enumerated the work he had finished and submitted recently: "You have *The Gay Coloring Book* ($100 advance given); *The Gay B C's* (which title I like, $100 advance promised, but not given yet); *The Gay Little Prince* (nothing promised or given); article on traveling ($25 promised, not yet given); article on taxes (not accepted yet)."

Haimsohn then attempted to tease Womack with tidbits and descriptions of several additional projects then under way, mentioning that he had completed *Handsome Is . . .* ("A short novel. At present this artist friend of mine is doing a couple of drawings that I might show you"); *The Autobiography of a Camp* ("Done in squiggly style like *The Gay Little Prince*. Rather richer and longer than the first book. . . . Story of a typical queen and her various affairs"); *The Land of the Giant Faggots* ("A gay science fiction story with an Astronaut hero who likes boys, and with his handsome Astronaut idol takes a trip beyond the moon"); *The Rug Salesman* ("A short story"); and *My Trip Around the World*, about which Haimsohn wrote: "This could be 80 pages or 40 pages and requires at least 38 drawings. It is about a gay little queen whose Auntie had died leaving him a lot of money and a trip around the world. The rest of the story is about all of the boys with whom he has adventures (in 36 countries). It would need good drawings, showing all of the different national types, all as sexy and with as much innuendo as possible, as the text which is done all in couplets." When *My Trip Around the World* was later published by Womack's Guild Press, it included uncredited artwork by one of Haimsohn's friends, the pioneering physique artist Etienne (Dom Orejudos).

Still another project, *The Gay Psychedelic Sex Book*, was an easy sell to Womack, since it consisted entirely of Haimsohn's limericks and collages and it required merely setting the verse in type. Visually, the finished product looked like what it was—a loopy, amphetamine-induced lark. But the verses were for the most part more structured and thoughtful. Two examples:

> When the soft summer evening was dimming
> A young divorcee was out swimming,
> While her son on his knees,
> Somewhere in the trees
> Her muscular boyfriend was rimming.

> In this era when mass procreation
> Is a threat to the health of each nation
> The act of each queen,
> Though lewd and obscene
> Should be given a hearty ovation.[8]

Though the book was a lazy lark, it sold well from the Guild catalog, and Womack eagerly bought more of Haimsohn's work. Some of the additional stories Haimsohn had named to tease Womack were published under the

Alexander Goodman name, although a few were published anonymously or under the pseudonym Peter B. Luvvly. The Guild Press titles written by Haimsohn included *The Soft Spot* (1964), *A Sliver of Flesh* (1965), *Carnal Matters* (1965), *A Summer on Fire Island* (1966), *Mercenary Affections* (1966), *The Gay Psychedelic Sex Book* (1967), *Blaze of Summer* (1967), *The First Time* (1967), *A Sweet Gentle Boy* (1967), and *Happyland and Other Stories* (1968).

Though much of Haimsohn's output for Womack was more light than literary, he very much wanted to develop as a serious writer, and he continued to fret and rewrite his work at a pace that frazzled him. Womack's rather slipshod production values—the Alexander Goodman books generally were saddle-stitched sheets, sometimes haphazardly machine trimmed and somewhat lacking in visual finesse and design oomph—did little to assist in elevating Haimsohn's reputation. The effort put forth on Haimsohn's part, however, proved worthwhile despite Womack's production shortcomings. Even if his short stories and novellas have never taken their place alongside those of his contemporaries James Barr, Lonnie Coleman, Samuel Steward, or Richard Amory, Haimsohn's work as Alexander Goodman has merit. Haimsohn proved to be an adept stylist when it came to plot and structure, capable of building eroticism through intelligent pacing, and he was a particularly facile writer of dialogue.

Many of the Alexander Goodman stories had their roots in Haimsohn's own life as a single gay man in New York City. As an example, his short story "The Posing Session," in *A Sliver of Flesh*, recounts a day in the life of its protagonist, a handsome young man with few responsibilities who occasionally shoots physique photographs as a hobby. On a particularly beautiful morning, he heads for the gym in hopes of finding a model to shoot. At the subway platform he spies a young man with "ragamuffin Murillo features." He proposes a photographic session with the youth, only to find that he has landed himself in a situation that becomes increasingly uncomfortable as the boy demands more and more money for taking off additional articles of clothing and even charges him for a promise never to return when the photographer desperately tries to get him out of his apartment. Writing down some of his experiences, frustrations, and sexual encounters—and then embellishing and fictionalizing them, fleshing them out with dialogue—perhaps allowed Haimsohn to exorcise some of his own demons. Likewise, his lengthier *A Summer on Fire Island* drew upon his regular visits there during the mid-1960s, and the book's action was drawn from people Haimsohn knew—or observed—and actual events.[9]

## BRANCHING OUT

From the outset of their friendship, Haimsohn admired Womack not only because of the potential power the publisher held over his own creative output, but also because he perhaps mistakenly believed Womack had noble intentions in his fight against censorship and the legalized suppression of work targeted to a homosexual audience. Haimsohn even composed a poem about Womack—one of hundreds of unpublished poems—titled simply "Lynn":

> A peculiar Joan of Arc
> Round and white as a ball of snow
> Yet hard and braver than any man I know.
> He delights in finding dark corners
> And letting in fresh air.
> He works as though the land of Faggotry
> Was in his special care.
>
> He embarked on a solitary course, a mission
> To give the gay a voice.
> He says he was compelled,
> That it was really not his choice.
>
> But what a compulsion! What a peculiar goal
> That led him to stand alone
> Before the strongest powers in the world
> To defend with all his soul
> A naked boy.

Despite his admiration for Womack, Haimsohn's growing dissatisfaction with small advances and payments inevitably led him to seek out other potential publishers. In 1964, disillusioned with the lack of commitment from Womack, Haimsohn submitted his book *The Modern Fairy Tales* to the Minneapolis-based Directory Services Inc. (DSI) and received a warm and encouraging letter from one of its owners, Conrad L. Germain, offering to publish the book, or—if published by another firm—offering to purchase bulk quantities to sell through DSI's catalogs at the usual trade discount. Haimsohn also corresponded with the respected Swiss homophile journal *Der Kreis*. Rudolf Burkhardt (a pseudonym for Rudolf Jung), who was for many years an editor for *Der Kreis*, wrote Haimsohn about the possibility of republishing some Alexander Goodman stories. Burkhardt didn't want to deal personally with Womack, however. "I find it extremely difficult to write to Dr. Womack myself," Burkhardt wrote on June 7, 1967. "On the other hand (and granting that I'd like nothing better than to have you among my few contributors to my English section of *The Circle*) you might try to sound out Dr. Womack on the question of our publishing two or three of your short stories in German translation. (So far, I have translated three of them: 'Just Old,' 'A Dirty Story,' and 'Pictures You'd Be Proud to Show Your Mother.')"

Still, Haimsohn felt both friendship toward and an allegiance to Womack—although as the 1960s wound down those feelings grew increasingly strained. In the spring of 1967, following a futile trip to Washington to try to get Womack to write him a $300 check, Haimsohn wrote: "After last weekend I really felt that our friendship, our association was curdling, and it made me very sad, for you have helped me very much. I believe I've helped you too. I'm only at the beginning of my creative cycle. I feel my writing and ideas are getting better and better. But how do you think I feel when I'm paid less and less, when you ignore me more and more, when I increasingly learn that the Womack who purchases something is a different one from the one that pays?"[10]

In another letter from the same period, with the chip on his shoulder weighing ever heavier, Haimsohn wrote Womack on October 4, 1967, "I spent maybe a week in Washington doing *The [Gay] Psychedelic Sex Book*. It did surprisingly well for you. How well? It cost you $96.20—and you made how much from it? Is it unreasonable for me to think that when one of my books does well that I might get a little bonus out of it? After all this time, I am treated as a clerk, a 'hack,' not as the creative writer who has supplied more than half of the $3.00 books on display in the stores." A few months later, on December 9, Haimsohn wrote again: "*Perry Goldenberg* is still the best thing I've done. If you had published it and encouraged me —I would have written two more of the series, I'm sure. It would have sold better than all your other hardbacks put together—but more than two years have passed and it just sits there. Generally, your whole treatment of me discourages me, makes it more and more difficult for me to write."[11]

There is no evidence among Haimsohn's personal papers that Womack responded to these entreaties. On October 17, 1968, Haimsohn beseeched Womack, "Dear Lynn, DON'T YOU THINK IT'S RIDICULOUS TO LET ALEXANDER GOODMAN DIE? He was as much your creation as mine. Each one of his books sold well. They still sell but are fading. Just when he was at the peak of his talent, but promised to do better, you stopped publishing him." And in what may have been Haimsohn's last attempt to sway Womack as the 1960s came to a close, he wrote Womack on April 3, 1969, noting that he had written twelve books and two theatrical shows in the preceding four years. "I still am able to write twice as many books a year than you can publish. I really am not looking forward to being the world's greatest posthumous[ly published] homosexual writer."

## ALL ABOUT DAMES

The "shows" Haimsohn mentioned were whimsical flights of fancy with which he had entertained himself while Womack seemed to be actively ignoring him. Haimsohn's musical revue *The Psychedelic Follies* already was in development as he began work on *Dames at Sea*, a campy send-up of the brassy, toe-tapping 1930s-era Hollywood musicals. While *The Psychedelic Follies* was fully Haimsohn's creation, *Dames at Sea* was a collaborative effort; Haimsohn worked with Robin Miller on the book and lyrics, and James Wise composed the music. In the tradition of "the little show that could," *Dames at Sea* quickly became a cult phenomenon.

The success of the musical (originally subtitled "Golddiggers Afloat") surprised its creators and launched the career of its ingénue, Bernadette Peters, whose first top-billed starring credit, such as it was, was printed with Haimsohn's stick-figure drawings on the placemat "programmes" adorning the tables of its debut venue, Caffé Cino in Greenwich Village. The show ran there for 148 performances. In early 1969 it reopened at the Bouwerie Lane Theatre; audiences continued to grow, and after four months at the Bouwerie Lane the show moved to the larger Theatre de Lys (now the Lucille Lortel Theatre), where it enjoyed a lengthy run of 575 performances.

What had begun as a folly quickly spun into serious business when word-of-mouth and packed houses lured in the critics for a look-see. Laudatory reviews appeared in the *New York Times*, *Time* magazine, and other periodicals. Drama Desk Awards for the 1968–69 season went to Bernadette Peters for Outstanding Performance, Neal Kenyon for Outstanding Direction of a Musical, and to both Haimsohn and Miller for Outstanding Lyrics. *Dames at Sea* also won the Outer Critics Circle Award for Best Off-Broadway Musical that same year.

With the unexpected success of *Dames*, both Plato and Alexander Goodman disappeared at the end of the 1960s. Although his photographs were occasionally published and his Guild Press books were still in print, as the 1970s dawned Haimsohn, for the first time in his life, finally found some measure of financial stability. Not only did *Dames* draw crowds and earn money for its creators, but when the original cast album was released on LP by Columbia Masterworks Records in 1969, it too became a modest success. A production was mounted in London and enjoyed similar success abroad. As her own star rose and Bernadette Peters moved on to other roles, she was succeeded during the lengthy run of *Dames* by Bonnie Franklin, Pia Zadora, and Barbara Sharma. And while it isn't widely remembered today, NBC Television in 1971 broadcast a production of *Dames at Sea* starring Ann-Margret, Ann Miller, and Anne Meara in the three leading female roles. Character actor Fred Gwynne (better known to television audiences of that era as Herman Munster) also starred. The libretto and the score were published by Samuel French, and productions have been mounted in many countries in several languages.[12] Even today *Dames at Sea* remains a staple of high school, college, and community theater productions.

Haimsohn worked fitfully for several years to try to replicate the success of *Dames at Sea* with similar musical revues, but without success. He labored over rewrites and revisions to his earlier work, *The Psychedelic Follies*, but the material was too far outside the norm to find financial backers, so the production was a stillbirth. Haimsohn also struggled with the libretto for a musical titled *Johnny American*. He had slightly more success with his follow-up Hollywood musical spoof, *Zing!* It premiered at the Bucks County Playhouse in Pennsylvania on October 5, 1971, to generally good reviews (including one in the *Bucks County Gazette* that Haimsohn loved to boast and cackle over, headlined "Satire on Flicks Clicks in Sticks"). Although several of the reviews mentioned that the show was bound for Broadway, financial backers were not forthcoming and *Zing!* was never mounted in New York City. Like many of the short stories, poems, and limericks Haimsohn had written over the years, the script and notes for *Zing!* were added to one of the many growing piles of papers in his tiny apartment.

## "D" IS FOR DRUGS

Just as he had done when his photography work as Plato morphed into his fiction writing as Alexander Goodman, when Haimsohn became bored or unproductive in one medium, he simply got stoned and turned his attention to other amusements. While he coasted through the 1970s on the success of *Dames at Sea*, he continued to write fiction and limericks, take photographs, and even his little stick-figure drawings reappeared briefly. He illustrated several small volumes of his witty drawings, which were marketed as "Madcap Classics" by Perigee Books, an imprint of the Putnam Publishing Group. Now long out of print, Haimsohn's stick-figure illustrated paperbacks *The Bedside Faust, The Portable Hamlet,* and *Inside Romeo and Juliet* (all 1983) brought him a new way to leverage his artistic abilities and his wry wit. Haimsohn completed (but never published) additional titles for the series, including "The Confidential Carmen," "The Othello Coloring Book," "Cupid and Psyche Unexpurgated," and "The Etruscan Bathtub."

Although more than a few of his typewriters had been stolen by shady sex partners or vandals over the years, he continued to peck away at a series of new typewriters at his makeshift desk and write in often illegible longhand in his notebooks. For a time in the 1980s, he entertained the idea of getting a computer. "I may investigate learning one of those new machines," he wrote on his typewriter in an undated journal entry. "But I would rather not. I guess I would rather live as I was living, just day by day, not doing any particular work, being lazy, seeing shows, having sex. I guess sex has been my main occupation, always on my mind, and it is on my mind because I do so little else. And drugs sort of help it, ease things, but I have a feeling that might be slowing down too . . ."

Drugs always were a curiosity and a crutch to Haimsohn, who was eager to see what effects different drugs might have on his motivation and ability to write. In his Fire Island journal as early as July 1964, Haimsohn typed, "This will be the sixth time I have taken mescaline. It would take many books to describe fully my other moon journeys and the results that have come from them. Judith, who works at a chemical firm that makes drugs, said it is bad to take any drugs whatsoever, even aspirin. This is an old-fashioned idea and perhaps true. Just as it would probably be better not to travel anywhere, not to be queer, not to do anything experimental or unusual." Whether it was pills or peyote, skunk weed, hashish, or prescription pharmaceuticals, Haimsohn was an equal-opportunity guinea pig.

Drugs worked their way into his writing as well. In *The Gay Psychedelic Sex Book* Haimsohn had included this limerick:

A student who loved taking trips
With a reefer between his two lips
Sailed out of his mind,
Then woke up to find
A head was between his two hips.

Haimsohn's journals, notebooks, and reams of typed pages of random thoughts offer clear evidence of his problem, but it was not, in essence, a drug problem. It was a writing problem. Writing was never easy for

Haimsohn, and much of his extant output, in fact, consists of his perpetual rants and ramblings about his ongoing inability to write.

Frustrated with his sluggishness in recreating his earlier successes in the theater or publishing, Haimsohn's use of and dependency on drugs, anonymous sex, and video pornography helped him pass the time during the 1980s. He typed out accounts of his sexual adventures at the abandoned piers along the West Side Highway and at local gay bars. It was for a time during this period that Haimsohn, an almost maniacal fan and collector of video pornography, wrote porn reviews under the name Vulcan for *First Hand* and *Manscape* magazines (for which he was paid $35 per review), and occasionally he contributed book reviews as well. He even managed to sell the publishers some poetry ("Writing on the Wall," "The Leather Ball," "The Shy One," and "The Approach") as well as eighteen of his limericks, for which he was paid $100 for the four poems and $100 for the group of limericks. (He wrote the editor on September 1, 1986, "One hundred bucks isn't much for eighteen limericks but it's better than just letting them rot in a drawer.") The magazines also published some of his later attempts at erotic fiction under the pseudonym Jack Ranch.

Although Haimsohn's letters to his new editor, Lou Thomas, were amiable and chatty, Haimsohn and Thomas never developed a friendship or correspondence that matched (whether measured in length, frequency, intimacy, or visible level of frustration) the one he had carried on with Womack. "If you just happened to find a butch, intelligent, well-hung, muscular, socially acceptable college student who likes going down on middle-aged men, please send him along," Haimsohn jokingly wrote to Thomas in the fall of 1986.[13] Nor would their relationship last as long; Thomas died within just a few years, at the height of the AIDS plague, and Haimsohn noted in a passage in his journal dated February 10, 1990, that he was thinking about attending the memorial service. "Not that I'm anxious to go," he wrote. "I didn't know the man well. He was my editor for awhile, but that didn't turn out well because his checks for my stories and articles came so late (besides being so small). And I can imagine how dreary and awkward such a service will be. Gays are not good at being sad or serious. We try and avoid it. That's why growing old and gay is such a dismal prospect."

When he was determined to write, he turned to amphetamines to help him face the blank page in his typewriter. When he wanted sex, Haimsohn often chose marijuana both for its calming effect and because it helped tempt the hustlers and rough trade he preferred as sex partners to climb the five flights to his lair. When he was bored or wanted to sleep, he turned to barbiturates, pain pills, or—in a pinch—Tylenol PM. "Was at a point where there was nothing on the box I wanted to see, nothing I felt like reading or listening to, not ready to go out for a walk, couldn't nap," he dutifully wrote in one of his notebooks ("2-8-1990, 9:15 p.m."), "so I was wicked, I drank some vodka straight and took *two* sleeping pills." Another time, he noted, "Almost 11 P.M. Took Tylenol codeine pill for pain though I haven't had pain."

It was a cycle that proved unproductive and unhealthy, but for Haimsohn there seemed to be some small comfort in that predictability. He also preoccupied himself with a string of young hustlers who almost interchangeably brought him pleasure, caused him turmoil, cost him money, and served as the source of much of his journal material.

## THE SEX LIFE OF AN OLD MAN

Although he lived in a rent-controlled apartment and led a fairly Spartan existence, Haimsohn's financial situation was often precarious, although never quite dire, and he wrote frequently about his financial struggles. On February 8, 1990, he noted in his diary that he had spoken to an employee at Samuel French, the firm that published and represented *Dames at Sea*, who told him that his forthcoming royalty checks would total approximately $16,000 for British royalties and that the "semi-annual amateur check will be $25,618.11." With some confidence that he would not soon face bankruptcy, Haimsohn soldiered on, drafting stories and jotting down rambling ideas for new work. He spent much of his time writing out in longhand a series of scenarios he wanted to submit to the gay porn director Chi Chi Larue, for whom Haimsohn wanted to draft scripts for new videos. One such idea: "Young Genius—Tommy Edison, looks young—invents magic dildo, tries it on Hicky Jones from school, and Buddy Edison his brother in the Navy and his friend Steve. They steal it and take it to the barracks."

Despite having a reliable (albeit varying) income from *Dames at Sea* each year, Haimsohn fretted about his inability to control his habits and expenses. "For quite some time now I have been walking a very dangerous financial path," he wrote in his journal on February 13, 1990. "Aside from Social Security, which could never provide for more than my rent and utilities, I have been relying solely on royalties from *Dames at Sea*. The show has been bringing in royalties for 20 years now. Who knows when it might suddenly stop? Then again, it may go on forever." He lamented his addictions, such as they were, and though his math wasn't correct, there is no reason to doubt his assessment of his expense categories: "My biggest expenditure is for sex, namely [video]tapes and boys. In '89, say $15 for tapes each week, that's $1,000 a year, with boys—$75 (?) a week—$3,900 a year. So $5,000 a year for sex. Is that much?"

As the 1990s dawned, the sixty-five-year-old Haimsohn vacillated through emotional and financial highs and lows, with his moods and thoughts shifting from just-short-of-glorious to nigh-upon-self-pity. Having given up on the idea of learning to operate a computer, and too frustrated to sit hour after hour at a typewriter as he did when he was writing for Womack, Haimsohn increasingly scribbled in his journals and notebooks. He noted when he tried new drugs, as well as when he reverted to the proven pleasures of opium, ecstasy, or Ativan. His sexual adventures, conquests, and disappointments also were duly recorded. Some journal entries were scrawled out across several pages, while others were poignant in their brevity. On December 5, 1990, he wrote, "Victor sucked me three hours straight. I gave him $150 plus my microwave."

## THE RESURRECTION OF PLATO

Between 1993 and his death a decade later, Haimsohn enjoyed a surprising last-gasp resurgence of interest in his work. Several high-profile productions of *Dames at Sea* were launched—notably a Los Angeles production mounted by the Musical Theatre Company in 1995, and another in 2002 at the Goodspeed Opera House in East Haddam, Connecticut—and these and numerous smaller productions comforted Haimsohn that the musical still had legs and that the royalty checks would not cease coming anytime soon.

Far more astonishing to Haimsohn was the resurrection of interest in his earlier work as a photographer. In 1997, an extensive portfolio of Haimsohn's photographs was published in the Australian fine-art photography magazine *(not only) blue.*[14] This represented Haimsohn's first publication as a photographer in thirty years and earned him a check for $960, easily the largest single amount he'd ever generated as a photographer. Because he had known and photographed several members of Andy Warhol's Factory crowd, one of Haimsohn's images was included in a montage segment of a PBS *American Masters* documentary about Lou Reed (for which he was paid $250). And perhaps most gratifying of all, one of his portraits of the Warhol superstar Candy Darling appeared in a major retrospective, *The Warhol Look: Glamour, Style, Fashion,* at the Whitney Museum of American Art. Around the same time, browsing the books on display at A Different Light bookstore not far from his apartment, Haimsohn was shocked but pleased to find that two of his images had been reproduced in the book *My Face for the World to See,* a replica of Candy Darling's diaries that included her notes, letters, and ephemera from her personal collection.

The publication of some of Haimsohn's Plato-era images in *(not only) blue* led to broader interest in his male physique photographs and resulted in the inclusion of several of his male nudes and psychedelic painted images in two hardcover photography anthologies, *Uniforms* and *Male Bonding, Volume Two,* both published in 1998.[15] Later, a number of Haimsohn's images of his models Joe Cali and John Converse were included in a 2001 exhibition titled *The Muses* at the Leslie-Lohman Gay Art Foundation gallery space in New York City.[16] Haimsohn attended the opening reception and was thrilled to be included in an exhibition whose highlights included work by a number of important photographers, including George Platt Lynes, Skrebneski, Greg Gorman, Arthur Tress, Tom Bianchi, and Andreas Bitesnich. Much to his surprise, several of Haimsohn's prints sold, generating another $1,000 or so for him.

## DRIFTING AWAY

On January 17, 2003, Haimsohn collapsed on the street in front of his apartment and was rushed to nearby St. Vincent's Hospital, where he died following a massive aneurysm. He was seventy-seven years old. When his obituary appeared in the *New York Times* the following week, it not only noted his accomplishments with *Dames at Sea* and his other work as a writer, but also identified him publicly as the physique photographer Plato and as the author of gay fiction under the pen name Alexander Goodman.[17] His remains were cremated by his family and his ashes were scattered at sea.

The musical *Dames at Sea* will no doubt stand as the work for which Haimsohn is best remembered, but fortunately for a new generation, his photography has experienced a welcome revival in magazines, books, and exhibitions. Save for a fleeting appearance in a Greenleaf Classics anthology in 1970, none of Haimsohn's work as Alexander Goodman has been reprinted or anthologized, nor have his unpublished poems or short fiction been studied by scholars.[18] What we know today about Haimsohn's struggles as a writer, his relationship with H. Lynn Womack, and his photography, we owe in large part to the fact that a significant portion of his papers were preserved at the time of his death. Thanks to his notebooks, random typed pages, and his own garbled, handwritten notes and correspondence, we have a fuller, richer sense of the man, his struggles as a writer and photographer, and ultimately, his contributions to our cultural heritage.

Thirteen years before his sudden death, lamenting in writing about having fewer and fewer friends to tell his stories to, Haimsohn wrote specifically about why he kept his diary: "I would love for someone to read it, to be shocked by it. I have found in my life that few people care much about me, would really *want* to read about my life. When something of special interest happens to me, quite often there's no one to tell it to. So I tell my stories to myself—or let them drift away."

# NOTES

1. George Haimsohn, interview by author, July 5, 1997. Photographs of Joe Cali appear in Reed Massengill, *Uncovered: Rare Vintage Male Nudes* (New York: Universe, 2009). All letters and other personal documents cited in this essay were gifts to the author from George Haimsohn or his family and remain in the author's possession.
2. Womack to Haimsohn, April 16, 1963.
3. Womack to Haimsohn, Jan. 6, 1962.
4. Womack to Haimsohn, Jan. 21, 1962.
5. Womack to Haimsohn, April 8, 1963
6. Womack to Haimsohn, March 11, 1963, and April 16, 1963.
7. Womack to Haimsohn, Jan. 31, 1963.
8. Alexander Goodman, *The Gay Psychedelic Sex Book* (Washington, DC: Guild Press, 1967), n.p.
9. Alexander Goodman, *A Sliver of Flesh* (Washington, DC: Guild Press, 1965), 36–55, quotation on 40; Alexander Goodman, *A Summer on Fire Island* (Washington, DC: Guild Press, 1966).
10. Haimsohn to Womack, undated [March or April 1967].
11. Haimsohn's novel *Perry Goldenberg* was never published; he told me that some years later he sent his only copy of the manuscript to another publisher and never got it back.
12. James Waterman Wise, George Haimsohn, and Robin Miller, *Dames at Sea: A Musical Comedy* (New York: Samuel French, 1969); reprinted in *Return to the Caffe Cino*, ed. Steve Susoyev and George Birimisa (San Francisco: Moving Finger Press), 164–83; *The Vocal Book (Solos and "Chorus") for Dames at Sea* (New York: Samuel French, 1969).
13. Haimsohn to Lou Thomas, Nov. 2, 1986.
14. Reed Massengill, "Boys Gone By," *(not only) blue* 12.(Dec. 1997): 108–13.
15. David Sprigle, ed., *Uniforms* (Santa Monica, CA: FotoFactory Press, 1998); Sprigle, ed., *Male Bonding, Volume Two* (Santa Monica, CA: FotoFactory Press, 1998).
16. Photographs of John Converse also appear in Massengill, *Uncovered*.
17. Wolfgang Saxon, "George Haimsohn, 77, Dies; a Writer of 'Dames at Sea,'" *New York Times*, Jan. 25, 2003.
18. The anthologized story, "Life with Danny: Sketches – New York, 1964" (from *A Sliver of Flesh*), appeared in *In Homage to Priapus*, ed. E. V. Griffith (San Diego, CA: Greenleaf Classics, 1970), 170–80. For a discussion of some of Haimsohn's longer works as Alexander Goodman, including *A Summer on Fire Island*, see Philip Clark's essay elsewhere in this volume.

# Guerilla Literature

## THE MANY WORLDS OF VICTOR J. BANIS

Randall Ivey

On any list of classic gay pulp authors, Victor J. Banis will find his name at or very near the top. Using a variety of pseudonyms, among them Don Holliday, J. X. Williams (both house names used otherwise for heterosexual books), Victor Jay, and Jay Vickery, and only twice his own name, Banis published nearly sixty pulps between 1964 and 1970, books with both gay and non-gay content. The novels cover a wide stretch of fictional genres, including the historical novel, the science fiction–horror tale, and the detective story. What is more, through such a prodigious output, one that continues to this day, Banis was able to maintain a high level of writing quality, far surpassing most in the pulp field, to the point of being able to lay claim to a place in "legitimate" gay literature. From the beginning he demonstrated his skill at depicting a variety of characters and places and developing vital themes. While accepting the requirement for spicy sex scenes, which often resulted in contrived plots, Banis used the pulp genre as a means to explore serious issues for pre-Stonewall gay men (and women), among them personal and sexual identity and the need for community building at a time when isolation was more the norm than the exception for gay men coming to terms with themselves.

Banis can legitimately claim to be one of the "guerillas" of the field. His novels move well past the gay pulp formula of fake moralizing and teasing sex scenes to serious explorations of gay male identity and community. Lack of critical attention to gay pulps in general has concealed how writers such as Banis were mining and extending traditional gay tropes. But recognition of Banis's specific importance may have been hampered by his very achievements. His use of multiple noms de plume and his investigation of so many fictional genres have perhaps obscured the fact that a single writer was responsible for so much work, helping to deny Banis his place in any discussion of serious gay writing—a place he most certainly deserves if for no other reason than his role in breaking down censorship barriers. This oversight has been further abetted by overly identifying Banis with one of his creations, the widely popular Jackie Holmes, the larger-than-life Man from C.A.M.P.

Banis actually began his storied career in 1964 with a largely heterosexual pulp novel (sprinkled with lesbian content) published by Brandon House under the pseudonym Victor Jay: *The Affairs of Gloria,* a book virtually impossible to get hold of nowadays and one sorely in need of reprinting for its historical importance alone. It netted him not only notoriety but legal trouble as well. A subsequent obscenity trial involving the novel established Banis as a true hero of the First Amendment.[1] His role in it also indirectly helped convince another publishing house, Greenleaf Classics, to open a market for gay pulp novels.[2]

Banis's second novel, *The Why Not,* published by Greenleaf Classics in 1966 under his own name, was concerned entirely with contemporary gay life. Though a pulp novel, it should not be lumped into the same category as such works as *Mister Sister* and *Showbiz Suckers.* True, the famous front cover by Darryl Milsap leaves no doubt to whom the book was being marketed. It shows a pair of anonymous male legs, garbed in white trousers, angled in a fashion that suggests overt femininity, thus adhering to one of the traditional stereotypes about gay men. Behind the poser is a group of other men at a bar. But the old adage is more than true in this case: one cannot judge *The Why Not* by its cover. The novel's ultimate intent is neither titillation nor escapism. Though it remains extremely readable, it is not even written in the normal linear style of almost all gay pulps. If any gay pulp can lay claim to the mantle of "experimental novel," *The Why Not* is it.

The novel is a series of seemingly disparate scenes featuring a variety of characters who frequent the Why Not, a typical neighborhood bar of the period in Los Angeles, and it is set during a twenty-four-hour period in the lives of the denizens of the bar. Externally the Why Not is a nondescript place, but inside it provides the figurative glue that binds the various characters together. The dramatis personae include social climbers, drag queens, committed lovers, and searchers for love and for sex. If there is a protagonist, it is the interestingly named Jackie (a precursor to Jackie Holmes?), co-proprietor of the bar and a kind of "brother hen" to its patrons. Jackie is not without his own dilemmas. Along with a case of venereal disease, he is wrestling with the problem of devoting less time to the bar and more time to his young lover, Lon, who is jealous of all the time Jackie spends at the Why Not and even more jealous of Jackie's relationship with his business partner, Lindy. Perhaps the most memorable character in the novel is Queen Agatha, a drag queen living constantly inside her own delusions, who feels her charms receding with age; nevertheless she continues to attack life with the relish of a younger person and is in constant competition with her fellow queen Clara for attention. Other characters include Lee, a fading movie star who resorts to ambitious young men for his sexual satisfaction; Nicky, a blackmailing male hustler taking advantage of a closeted middle-aged businessman; and, perhaps most poignantly, Freddie and Walter, roommates, with Walter dealing with a case of unrequited love for Freddie and Freddie realizing too late how much he really needs Walter.

Banis tells their stories in unconventional ways, and he crafts each scene as a film editor might. He moves from past tense to present tense, from third-person omniscient to first-person narrators, but the reader is never confused because Banis captures the nuances of his characters' thoughts and speaking voices so well. What he achieves ultimately is the great sense of community among gay men during this pre-Stonewall period. In his essay "The Gay Publishing Revolution," Banis has written at some length about the ways in which gay people, following World War II, acted on the new choices offered to them by migrating to places like New York and San Francisco, cities more hospitable to those not living conventional lifestyles, and building vibrant communities that continue to exist. In contrast, Banis writes, heterosexuals making those same migrations, tearing themselves away from the rootedness of traditional home life, often found themselves alone and lonely.[3] As has so often been the case, gay men formed a network of friends and lovers that substituted for orthodox family life. *The Why Not* is one of the earliest fictional representations of such a network, and in that sense the main character of the book is not one person but the community as a whole.

One of the interesting aspects of *The Why Not*, as is common with all of Banis's early books, is that none of the characters wrestles with being homosexual. It is a given in each of their lives; they are more concerned with their attempts to find personal fulfillment within that reality. Surprisingly enough, this acceptance is not the norm of many of the gay pulps published during the same time frame. Even though they were written for an almost exclusively gay audience, many of their protagonists continue in the mode laid down by "mainstream" writers of being stifled by doubts and guilt over being gay in the first place. But in none of Banis's works does one find leading characters who hate themselves for being gay, or deny it strenuously, or attempt in some way to change their orientation. The only book that comes close is *Born to Be Gay* (of which more later), and even there the self-hatred comes not from the character's homosexuality itself but from the hard times he has in pursuing love and happiness as a gay man.

As a portrait of a gay demiworld, *The Why Not* invites comparison with the more renowned nonpulp gay novel published only a few years earlier, John Rechy's *City of Night* (1963). Rechy's first novel is the story of a male hustler who travels the nation in search of more than just rent and grocery money; his is also a spiritual journey, an attempt to find love and personal solace in places—that is, bars—where such commodities are in decidedly short supply. Rechy likewise experiments effectively with narrative progression. While *City of Night* does not, like *The Why Not*, move from narrator to narrator or point of view to point of view, it does bend the rules of traditional storytelling in its extensive use of flashbacks and its habit of switching between present and past tense (a characteristic throughout Rechy's subsequent work).

*The Why Not* bears even more comparison with later Rechy novels. *Numbers*, a 1967 follow-up to *City of Night*, takes place, like Banis's novel, within a twenty-four-hour period, as it follows hustler Johnny Rio's attempt to reaffirm his own sexual charisma by having sex with as many "numbers," or partners, as he can in one day's time. Such a race against the clock results in the kind of urgency that propels characters in *The Why Not* as they look for justification and happiness. Rechy's 1979 novel *Rushes*, set entirely during one night in a gay bar in a large, unnamed American city (the bar is obviously based on New York's notorious Mineshaft), is even more akin to *The Why Not*. All manner of characters show up during the evening: the attractive, the unattractive, the formerly attractive, the young seeking their first gay experiences, the proponents of the leather lifestyle—all motivated by the need to make connections, to reaffirm their beauty or their worthiness. *Rushes*, however, has a tougher edge than *The Why Not*. It becomes a portrait of the worst attributes gay men can display to one another (narcissism, snobbery, elitism about looks and age), and unlike *The Why Not* it does not end on a note of hope but one of despair and violence.

A still more relevant comparison would be to John Horn Burns's *The Gallery* (1947). It is even less a novel in the conventional sense, being composed of nine independent stories and ten interlinking chapters. The stories have in common some connection to the Galleria Umberto in Naples near the end of World War II, and the book's centerpiece, a long chapter titled "Momma," is set in an Italian bar located in the gallery. A haven for the local gay population as well as American and British officers and civilians, the bar is a virtual democracy in a country torn first by fascism and then by war. Like the denizens of Banis's Why Not, the patrons are allowed a few hours to "let their hair down": to cruise, connect, argue, wrangle over prices (if the target *d'amore* is rough trade), and reminisce over past erotic triumphs, until the MPs come in to break up the scene at sunrise. As Roger Austen remarks in his study of American gay novels, however, Burns paints his gallery with some circumspection. For instance, the goings-on in the story are viewed through the eyes of the bar's owner, a heterosexual woman who is "maternally *simpatica* as she stands by her cash register, taking an interest in each of her regulars."[4] Even with the threat of police crackdowns, the patrons manage to squeeze joy out of their nights in Momma's bar and in the process form, in a lesser sense, the kind of community one finds in *The Why Not.*

It was almost as though Banis had to get out a novel like *The Why Not,* one not catering particularly to popular tastes but casting a serious eye on American gay life in the mid-1960s, before he could let loose from his perfervid imagination a creation as uncommon as the denizens of the Why Not are common, his most popular character: secret agent Jackie Holmes, the "Man from C.A.M.P." Holmes would allow Banis a chance not only to entertain his readers but to give them a role model for not just surviving as gay men but actually flourishing. The Holmes books by Banis, all published by various imprints of Greenleaf Classics under the house name "Don Holliday" between 1966 and 1968, number nine: *The Man from C.A.M.P., Color Him Gay, The Watercress File, The Son Goes Down, Gothic Gaye, Rally Round the Fag, The Gay Dogs, Holiday Gay*, and *Blow the Man Down*. (A tenth Holmes novel, *Gay-Safe,* published under the Holliday pseudonym in 1971, was by another writer.) They depict the James Bond–like adventures of Holmes as he attempts to save the world from harm.

Besides the Bond novels and films, the other obvious influence on the Banis books is *The Man from U.N.C.L.E.,* a popular television show that began airing two years before the first Holmes book was published and ran until 1968. Other gay progeny of this show include Peter Leslie's *The Gay Deceiver* (1967), by one of the writers for the show; Don Rico's *The Man from Pansy* (1967); and A. Jay's *Hairy Chess,* subtitled *The Man from A.U.N.T.I.E.* (1964–1970s), the last a series of comic strips published in gay magazines.

Both the titles and the covers of the *C.A.M.P.* novels (all but one by Robert Bonfils) scream defiance in their recognition and exaltation of the stereotype of gay effeminacy. In this the *C.A.M.P.* books were not alone; similar stereotypes of gay effeminacy used not for derision but for humor and affirmation were to be found among pulps by Marcus Miller, Lance Lester, and Aaron Thomas, among others, at the same time. One of the most vivid pulp covers appears on Russ Sanders's *His Brother Love*, in which a fey character comes bouncing out of a doorway garbed in ballerina workout attire. Jackie Holmes emerges as the unquestionable leader of the pack. But behind his fey facade resides a man as resourceful and as indestructible as Bond at his best.

The chief difference between Bond and Holmes is that, while Bond is a magnet for beautiful women, Holmes is an up-front gay man, not in the least conflicted about his orientation. He is unapologetically gay, even joyfully stereotypical, with his elaborate blond hairdo and flamboyant outfits. He pursues his love objects as he does his nemeses—with great élan and lack of guilt, along with inevitable success—whether the target is a gay or straight man. His gusto for sex is epitomized by the wooden phallus he has erected in his home, one scored by notches indicating the number of his erotic conquests. They are many. His canine companion is a white poodle, as potent a symbol of effeteness as exists in the animal kingdom, but this one has razor-sharp teeth, and she is trained to kill with them. Holmes drives a ripe-red Bugatti, among other flashy vehicles, which only adds to his sense of carefree and ostentatious openness.

Jackie Holmes is not all show or braggadocio, sound and fury signifying little. He is the real thing when it comes to intrepid spying. He has at his disposal all the neat gadgets and gimmicks one would find in an Ian Fleming potboiler, as well as a deep knowledge of the martial arts and even a penchant for automobile tinkering. He is fearless in his mission, "the protection and advancement of homosexuals." He loves the United States as much as Bond loves Great Britain. In *Rally Round the Fag* he shows how much of a man (and a patriot) he is by donning the identity of a female double agent to help stave off a plot to start World War III at America's expense. The books are also funny; everything is done tongue in cheek, and the plots are wildly improbable. In the inaugural book, *The Man from C.A.M.P.*, for instance, Jackie Holmes must stop the insidious plan for world domination hatched by a gang of ruthless hairdressers. In *Holiday Gay*, Jackie finds himself pitted against a band of jewel-thieving midgets led by Holmes's arch-nemesis, Birdie Wingo.

The *C.A.M.P.* novels remain by far the most popular of Banis's works. In his memoir, *Spine Intact, Some Creases,* Banis says that only one other of his novels, *The Gay Haunt,* sold more than the individual Holmes books, eight of which sold over 100,000 copies each.[5] Although all have been reprinted in either handsome omnibus editions or as singletons, first editions of the paperback originals are hard to find and thus very expensive. The reasons for the books' popularity are obvious. When gay men bought pulp novels in the 1960s they sought entertainment and escapism (as did any other reader who indulged in popular fiction), as well as a mirror image of their own experiences. In the *C.A.M.P.* novels, Banis gave them both, and more. In his essay "The Gay Publishing Revolution," he wrote: "Jackie was not the first protagonist in a gay novel to be openly gay, but I feel he espoused that lifestyle in a way different and with more insistent pride than those who had gone before him. Jackie Holmes's frank and unashamed attitude toward his homosexuality was a dramatic change."[6]

In this way Jackie went far beyond an earlier gay character who appeared in print in 1961: Francis Morley, the protagonist of Lou Rand's *The Gay Detective* (reprinted in 1964 as *Rough Trade*), set in a fictionalized version of San Francisco called "Bay City."[7] Morley is a private detective, not a spy for an international organization like C.A.M.P. Like Holmes, however, Morley is a tough character. He bests his assistant, former football player and war hero Tiger Owens, in a boxing match to prove he is no pushover. And like Holmes he seems to live his life without giving a damn as to what anyone else thinks. But he is coy about his homosexuality; while certainly effeminate, he never comes right out and admits his predilection. It is taken for granted by those with whom he deals because of his mincing speech and mannerisms. Unlike Holmes, we never get an open glimpse of his private love life. (Indeed, the most explicit sex scene in *The Gay Detective* occurs between the burly Owens and the distraught sister of a homicide victim.) So despite Morley's stereotypical behavior, his true erotic and romantic preferences remain ambiguous.

For Banis, the publication of the *C.A.M.P.* novels had historical ramifications that went beyond just the emergence of a popular and highly visible gay character. "In a sense," he writes in that same essay, "gay pride could be said to have started with Jackie Holmes."[8] Indeed, the chief thesis of

Banis's essay is his intriguing claim that gay pulp novels helped galvanize gay men into organizing into a political bloc ready to fight for changes in American attitudes and laws, so that these books in a real sense paved the way for the Stonewall riots that would erupt in New York at the end of the decade.

But the writing of the *C.A.M.P.* novels, and his many other works, had a personal impetus. Banis recalls, "I felt that it was essentially dishonest to mostly ignore the positive elements of gay life. Even in the darkest days of the 1950s, homosexuals managed to have fun, to meet and fall in love, and in some instances actually launch . . . longtime relationships." He adds, "By 1965 I had become a gay activist. Like an increasing number of gays of the day, I had emerged from my closet and was proud to be who and what I was. I wanted to write something that would reflect this new attitude, something happy and positive."[9] David Bergman, in his article "The Cultural Work of Sixties Gay Pulp Fiction," echoes Banis's assessment of the Holmes books: "What I find remarkable is the unapologetic way in which Holmes discusses gay people. C.A.M.P. serves, not only to protect, but to advance gay people. While not rejecting straight people, it asserts that gays must look out for each other in a hostile, dominant culture." Bergman quotes Rich, Jackie's assistant, who tells a friend, "It gives me a feeling of worthiness to work toward a day when our kind of life and love will not only not be laughed at, but will have its rightful respect in the world."[10]

In his essay "Notes on C.A.M.P.," Fabio Cleto, an academic specialist on popular culture and an editor of Banis's work, places the *C.A.M.P.* novels in the greater context of the "camp zeitgeist" that swept the 1960s: the tendency to embrace, in movies, television, art, fashion, and lifestyles, anything remotely flamboyant, outrageous, effusive, colorful, and, well, gay. The term "camp" joined the greater lexicon thanks to Susan Sontag's famous essay "Notes on Camp," first published in 1964 in the *Partisan Review.* But Cleto sees this appropriation of the term "camp" and all it represents culturally as a kind of hijacking by straights of something not only created by gay people but used by gay people as a source of communication and identity. Jackie Holmes, not James Bond, is the true camp icon. Cleto writes:

> His adventures were in fact relished by those who did not have access to the culture and economic capital required by libraries and metropolitan bookshops, but only to newsstands. Jackie's C.A.M.P. Agency was a celebration of camp as the chief strategy allowing generations of queers to cope with a gloomy reality—by letting them find thrilling spectacles, self-fashioning theatrics, identity, and community in flamboyant parody, behind closed doors and in run-down bars, amid human debris and desolation. But Jackie himself did more than that. He showed the possibility—before Stonewall became plausible—of being gay and proud, to be at once a committed social activist and a gay Don Juan. He was someone whose license to look and be looked at advocated what in academic jargon is tagged as "second wave feminist theory," at a time when first-wave feminism was still articulating. Of all queer pulp images, name one who better qualifies as spy queen.[11]

All the *C.A.M.P.* novels, in terms of plot, are mysteries. Another detective story from that fertile year 1966, *Goodbye, My Lover*, is one of Banis's lesser efforts. It was published by Greenleaf Classics under the name J. X. Williams. Drewey Wayne Gunn, author of *The Gay Male Sleuth in Print and Film*, has argued for the importance of the book as the first American mystery to feature a gay amateur sleuth. Gunn also believes the unfolding of the main character's knowledge of his own sexual nature lends the book continuing relevance.[12] Here we have, at the beginning, a reticent, seemingly straight young man who, by the end of the novel, is willing to compromise even his body in order to solve the mystery of his friend's death.

The mystery itself is fairly negligible, as the killer is pretty obvious early on. A young man, Dennis Eastman, returns to Los Angeles from the Naval Academy back east. He is to meet his close friend and lover Linc Gardner to discuss the future of their relationship. It has been a year since they last saw each other. Linc is older than Dennis by about fifteen years, and he is also more worldly, having once had a promising career as a concert pianist that was stopped short by a freak accident that severely damaged his left hand. Dennis has a key to Linc's apartment and lets himself in, expecting to find his friend, but Linc is not there. A detective appears and informs Dennis that Linc was murdered by a hustler he picked up in a leather bar. Dennis is incredulous, knowing that Linc cared nothing for the leather scene. Later he is visited by Frank Davenport, another close friend of Linc's. Davenport tells Dennis that Linc underwent a drastic transformation in attitude and appetite in the year that he and Dennis were separated and that he actively sought out the company of the "leather crowd." A name surfaces: "Jeff," which Dennis believes belongs to Linc's murderer. Not accepting the official police theory, he initiates his own investigation into the murder and goes in search of this mysterious figure.

One would think the mystery would close with the revelation (and death) of Linc Gardner's killer. But it doesn't, and it suggests another reason critics may be unwilling to take Banis seriously as a writer. A curious sex scene is tacked on after the denouement, involving Dennis and a couple of other men. This joyous frolicking seems incongruous, considering what has just gone on for the last one hundred and fifty pages, and is totally out of keeping with the overall melancholy tone of the novel. Banis may have been forced to include the sex scene for the sake of commercial consideration. More likely, someone else inserted it into the novel, as a change in style would indicate. (It does not appear in the 2007 Borgo Press reprint.) Banis has written elsewhere about how publishers reworked his books on occasion to insert more sexual activity. He cites the first *C.A.M.P.* novel as an example: *The Man from C.A.M.P.* included at least one heterosexual sex scene that was excised from the 2004 reprint published by Haworth Press.

Banis would publish a number of mysteries in the 1970s under a variety of pseudonyms, and of late he has begun a series of detective novel featuring San Francisco homicide inspector Stanley Korski, with such titles as *Deadly Nightshade* (2009), *Deadly Silence* (2010), *A Deadly Kind of Love* (2011).

In the minds of many people gay fiction means city fiction. It is easy to forget how many significant American gay novels have small-town and rural settings. One thinks of such early classics as Richard Meeker's *Better Angel* (1933) and James Barr's *Quatrefoil* (1950). Both novels are distinguished by their positive treatments of the subject of homosexuality. *Better*

*Angel* begins in a small midwestern city and traces a gay man's coming to terms with himself both personally and artistically. *Quatrefoil* is the story of two naval officers in love and takes place partly in one of the men's small hometown in Oklahoma. Other notable titles include Hubert Creekmore's *The Welcome* (1948), set in a small Mississippi town, and Ward Thomas's *Stranger in the Land* (1949), the story of a New England small-town English teacher's fixation on a troubled young hustler.

Many of Joseph Hansen's gay pulp novels—such as *Lost on Twilight Road* (1964), *Strange Marriage* (1965), and *Hang-Up* (1969), all published under the pseudonym James Colton—have rural settings. Hansen's Brandstetter mysteries (1970–1991) also frequently move into the small coastal towns of Southern California, and Hansen draws their sleepy particulars with the eye of a skilled landscape artist. Another pulp novelist, Carl Corley, although much of his work is set in New Orleans, also portrayed small southern towns. *A Lover Mourned* (1967) is set in Corley's native Mississippi, in a town called Raymond, and features the kind of tragic ending all too present in pulps of the period; Corley's autobiographical *A Chosen World* (1966) chronicles a small town boy's attempts to be a writer and to discover and fulfill his nature as a gay man.[13] Even for those who accept their sexuality, being forced to live in environs naturally hostile to homosexuality creates dramatic tension in and of itself.

Banis has set many of his works in some of the world's most glamorous cities—Los Angeles, New York, Paris, Berlin—but he is also one of gay pulps' masters in depicting life in small towns (little wonder, as he himself is a product of such places, having grown up in rural Ohio). With sureness Banis limns the particulars of the small-town milieu: the soda shops, the high schools, the rundown motels, the movie theaters, the adjacent countryside, and most especially, the homes, where all manner of dramas take place. In particular one may cite his novels *Born to Be Gay* (1966), *The Bronze and the Wine* (1966), and *Man into Boy* (1968), all published by Greenleaf Classics.[14]

*Born to Be Gay*, published under the J. X. Williams pseudonym, is in many ways a rather conventional gay pulp. What sets it apart, in addition to its fine delineation of the small-town setting and of its main character, is

Banis's treatment of gay-bashing and internal homophobia, two issues that unfortunately continue to be as relevant today as they were in 1966. Terry Cabot is a rather stereotypical gay man, along the lines of Jackie Holmes, in his effeminate appearance and mannerisms. His main preoccupation is finding a love relationship grounded in deep friendship, the kind of "love of comrades" envisioned by Whitman—though one would be surprised if Terry has even heard of the poet, much less read him. (It is interesting that much of the sexual activity in the novel occurs in a Whitmanesque setting, in nature.) Terry is a loner at high school and is turned into a receptacle for casual sex by a gang of school bullies who take advantage of his orientation to relieve their own sexual frustrations. Terry acquiesces to their demands, finding minimal pleasure in the encounters, but remains frustrated in finding what he really needs: a lover, an intimate friend with whom he can share his life.

The only person who halfway fulfills this need is Bruce Tucker, the French teacher at the high school. He and Tucker strike up an after-school relationship in which they meet late at night at Tucker's home for sexual encounters. Terry cherishes any show of affection Tucker offers—a touch, a kiss. But Tucker turns out to be as selfish as the bullies who use Terry. When Terry confronts him with the possibility of taking their relationship beyond mere physical gratification, Tucker scoffs at the idea, asserting that he is no "queer" and doubting that such a thing as love can exist between two men (a stance also scrutinized in *Goodbye, My Lover*). Tucker is dating the school's young female English teacher, using her both as a cover for his homosexual activities and for the physical satisfaction she can give him.

Further frustration comes from Terry's relationship with Jack Lawson, a handsome school jock who possesses the qualities Terry seeks in a friend: kindness, affection, gentleness. At the beginning of the novel, it is unclear whether Jack is himself gay, although an overnight camping trip, in which the two boys share a tent, suggests that he may be. Then one night, outside Terry's house, Jack kisses him, confirming what the reader has suspected. It would appear that the much-put-upon Terry will finally receive the mutual pleasure and happiness he has been seeking. Not so: there will be no replay of Jay Little's *Maybe—Tomorrow* (1952). When Jack finds out that Terry has been servicing not only the French teacher but his erstwhile friends the bullies, he rejects him and storms out of his life. Terry wishes he were dead and considers suicide. But it must be emphasized: it is not because he is gay. He has grown tired of the harsh realities of living, the thwarted dreams and broken relationships, but never once does he wish to die because of his sexual orientation. He is, all things told, secure in that identity. When another character asks him why he does not pursue a relationship with a woman, he says he cannot, that it is not in his nature.

Interestingly enough, it is the novel's supporting characters who seem to be struggling with sexual identity. Tucker, the teacher, Monte Acheson, the chief bully, and his satraps Craig and the Barber twins—all engage in homosexuality with a selfishness and a brutality that suggest underlying needs. Neither Monte nor his buddies have girlfriends. They spend all their time together, roaming about the schoolyard and the small town like a pack of wildcats seeking diversion and destruction. During one moment of such brutality, in which Monte and Craig are taking advantage of Terry, threatening to expose Tucker to the school authorities if Terry does not give in to their demands, Terry turns to them and says, "You're queers too, just like me; but you'll never admit it. You don't want love. Just violence. But it'll catch up with you someday."[15] Needless to say, the remark does not go down well with Monte and Craig.

Terry's self-knowledge does not make him particularly heroic, at least not initially. He gives in much too much to the demands of the bullies and to his selfish French teacher. And there is one bit of gender confusion when Terry daydreams of being Tucker's "girl." But finally, near the end of the novel, Terry resolves to "act like a man" and to refuse the sexual onslaughts of his peers. Terry's acceptance of himself as a gay man and his willingness, by the novel's conclusion, to show courage are refreshing in the gay pulp atmosphere of the late 1960s, when too many of his contemporaries still agonized over their sexual identities and allowed themselves to remain victims.

*Born to Be Gay* is also notable as one of the more "sex drenched" of Banis's pulps. But the sex is not gratuitous, and Banis is skillful at suggesting more than he says. He does not resort to coy euphemisms. Nor does he use explicit language in his sex scenes, as would become the norm a mere two or three years later in the works of other pulp writers (and "mainstream" writers as well), once the Earl Warren Supreme Court handed down its liberal decisions concerning obscenity. Such freedom turned out to be a mixed blessing. While it gave writers more leeway in writing about sex, it also hurt the genre in terms of characterization, theme, and plot construction. By the time the 1970s rolled around, sex in all its explicitness became the raison d'etre of most gay pulps. In *Born to Be Gay*, however, the sex is a necessary component in drawing the characters and in showing sexuality as a means of power and control.

*The Bronze and the Wine*, yet another production from the fertile year 1966 and one again attributed to J. X. Williams, is one of the author's most accomplished works of fiction in terms of characterization and plot structure. The leading character, Glen Sanford—unlike Terry Cabot, who has accepted his sexual identity from the very first page—undergoes a painful journey to discover who he really is and what he actually wants. What we have here is a genuine coming out story, although not the typical post-Stonewall versions. The leading character is not a teenager or preteen but a grown man who has been married and who has established himself in a career.

Once again the setting is a small-town high school. Glen teaches English with some competence but not much passion. He is a decent man who discovers one morning that he no longer has any sexual interest in his wife, Ann. Indeed it is hard for him to remember the last time he did lust after her. This lack of interest tells more on his wife than it does him; Ann is ready to leave him for good, and makes preparations to do so after yet another failed attempt in bed. Glen claims to love her, but he is not terribly upset at the idea of her departure. His interests are focused elsewhere, on a troubled student at the high school named Jerry Allen, who evinces the potential to be a good student but refuses to put forth the effort.

Jerry is handsome but withdrawn from his teachers and other classmates. "An artist would have sighed at the delicate beauty of the sullen face," the narrator tells us, describing his "gracefully molded form" that would have attracted a sculptor. Sanford is no sybarite lecher along the lines of Bruce Tucker in *Born to Be Gay.* He would never dream of exploiting his students for their sexual possibilities. Thus he finds himself surprised to be suddenly intrigued by the boy, to whom he has previously given no thought at all, nor has he considered any plight the boy might be going through. But sympathy for Jerry is now awakened in him, "a sympathy perhaps springing from his own inability to come to terms with life."[16] When Glen discovers that Jerry is interested in classical literature, he tries to cultivate that interest, hoping to win the boy's trust.

At the beginning he is unaware that his interest in the boy is anything more than pedagogical. Gradually he becomes more physically and emotionally attracted to Jerry. When he gives the boy a lift home and casually places his hand on Jerry's knee, however, Jerry becomes irate and storms out of the car in great resentment. The reader later learns that Jerry has been forced by his mother into a life of male prostitution. (The mother also prostitutes herself and is a favorite of Jerry's schoolmates.) He is thus convinced that men are only interested in him sexually, and this bitter conclusion raises a barrier to any sort of loving, intimate relationship between Jerry and Glen. As for Glen, his homosexuality comes as a surprise to him, but not one that drives him to drink or to contemplate suicide. He wrestles with the notion, but not to the degree that it becomes agonizing. And when he takes full control of that knowledge, he uses it as impetus to save Jerry from his tawdry existence and to show him love for the first time in his life. The source of Glen's pain is not being gay but establishing a relationship with someone who seems so very much out of reach, even lost for good.

Before the end of the novel they consummate their relationship sexually. Banis describes the act allusively and makes no judgment about the difference in the characters' ages or a possible power differential. Rather, he makes it clear that their relationship is positive, helping Jerry find the intellectual and emotional stability that he has lacked. Such a nonjudgmental stance on the part of the author, fairly typical of the pulps throughout the 1960s and 1970s, may pose a problem for today's readers, given the pedophile scandals that have rocked education and the Catholic church, not to mention the general American discomfort with adolescent sexuality (despite the iconic status that *Queer as Folk* achieved). Though understandable, it is a shame, for *The Bronze and the Wine* is a beautifully written work.

*Man into Boy* (1968), published under the pseudonym Jay Vickery, also makes use of a small-town setting, but one quite different from those of *Born to Be Gay* and *The Bronze and the Wine.* For one thing, it is set in the Northeast rather than the Midwest. More important, its goings-on place it closer to a village in *The Twilight Zone* than to some quaint habitat imagined by Thornton Wilder. The title is misleading—perhaps the ploy of a publisher trying to suggest a more salacious story. The narrator, a very young man, is a beachcomber who falls in love with another youth who, one moon-bathed evening, emerges unbidden from the ocean. We know nothing of this beloved other than that he is beautiful, and once again the art of the sculptor is evoked to describe this beauty: "Here before me was the work which I had no less created. In my every dream, my endless fantasy, I had envisioned this magnificent creature of the sea and moonlight, moving toward me as he did now, slowly and with the grace of a rippling wave."[17]

They become passionate lovers instantaneously, without knowing each other's names or anything else. The narrator names his new love Eros, and Eros calls the narrator Psyche to complete the allusion. In describing their wild abandon on the beach, Banis uses fairly explicit language, in a way he does not elsewhere. Their intimacy frustrates the narrator, however. He yearns to know more about Eros, not only his real name but the reason he cannot appear in full daylight, why he seems to exist during the day in a state of darkness or semidarkness. And why does he need injections of a certain formula to remain healthy? He learns that Eros's family rents a home on the beach, and little by little he is able to piece together something of the other boy's identity. A trip to Boston provides him with the information that Eros is the son of a prominent scientist, Dr. John Iverson. But when he inquires after young Iverson, he is met with perplexed, even incredulous looks from Iverson's colleague, a kindly fellow scientist, and from Iverson's wife.

The reader gradually realizes that the tale is a variation of the Jekyll and Hyde story transplanted to New England and played out between a pair of adolescent boys whose relationship is completely homosexual, of quite a different order from the latent homosexuality many have read into Robert Louis Stevenson's story. Eros is not the son of distinguished Professor John Iverson but John Iverson himself, fifty-three years old but grown young and beautiful again with the help of an experimental drug, which he must continually ingest if he is to remain young (hence, "man into boy"). As in Stevenson, the good doctor perishes at the end, in this case from a heart attack caused by his strenuous work. The narrator is left with the memory of Eros to sustain him. The novel's ending is ambiguous: the narrator knows he cannot remain in his hometown, but it is unclear where he is headed. Will he go to the water in search of his beloved Eros?

Banis renders the whole narrative in a lugubrious prose style most uncommon among gay pulps, giving the novel almost operatic dimensions. The only other practitioner of such a self-conscious and verbally intricate approach is Carl Corley in his novels of gay life in New Orleans, but Banis's is a more skilled and sophisticated presentation than Corley's. The style fits the febrile romanticism of the story. The Jekyll/Hyde theme is appropriate also. But whereas Stevenson's original paradigm has been seen as a negative allegory of homosexuality—the seemingly "normal" individual who by day lives an ordinary life but at night, in the dark, takes on the dimensions of evil and goes seeking unsavory pursuits in unsavory places with unsavory people, only to resume his "normality" come the next day—here homosexuality is not in the slightest equated with evil. These two boys love each other very much, accept the fact, and expect others to do the same. Love is the issue, and the identity of the specific beloved, not the nature or the naturalness of the type of love.

*Man into Boy* also has an antecedent in Wilde's *The Picture of Dorian Gray*. Besides similar plot devices, both *Man into Boy* and *Dorian Gray* share an almost excessively romantic view of life, one in which it is appropriate, if not entirely requisite, to throw everything else away for the sake of love (*Man into Boy*) or pleasure (*Dorian Gray*).

*Man into Boy* was one of Banis's early forays into the world of fantasy and horror. He would return to the genre repeatedly throughout the remainder of the 1960s and into the early 1970s. *Three on a Broomstick*, published under Banis's Don Holliday pseudonym (Greenleaf Classics, 1967), is as campy as anything one would find in an episode of *Bewitched*, and the cover, again by Bonfils, is a true classic.[18] *Devil Soul*, by "Victor Jay" (Belmont, 1970), and *The Vampire Women*, by "Victor Samuels" (Popular Library, 1973; a collaboration with Banis's lover, Sam Dodson), deal specifically with the macabre, the former containing more than a hint of homoeroticism.

*The Gay Haunt*, also by "Victor Jay" (Olympia Press, 1970), the last of Banis's gay fiction for two decades, is a romantic/erotic/comic ghost story obviously inspired by Noel Coward's *Blithe Spirit*. Paul is a former writer who has thrown away his artistic inclinations for life in the corporate jungle. To help insure his climb to the top, he has become engaged to the daughter of his company's boss. Paul's erstwhile lover, the deceased Loren—who choked to death on a diamond!—returns to stop this charade by putting Paul into a series of situations that shows he is just as gay now as he was when he and Loren lived together. These comic set pieces not only provide lively verbal slapstick, they also showcase some of Banis's best sex scenes. The novel is also notable—and still relevant politically and psychologically—because it highlights the whole issue of "gay deactivation," the notion that gay men and women can be "cured" of their erotic and romantic preference. Paul insists he is no longer gay, even as he keeps proving the contrary to the reader over and over.

Banis has recently returned to the horror genre with such books as *The Blood of Love* (2010) and *Dead of Night* (2011), and to science fiction with *Angel Land* (2008).

Banis's first foray into historical fiction was the excellent *Gay Treason* (Greenleaf Classics, 1968), published under the J. X. Williams pen name. Its drama unfolds in the glittering European capitals of Paris and Berlin on the eve of World War II.[19] Banis continues to explore the theme of personal identity, but here it is not sexual identity but rather national identity and how much of one's national identity one is willing to renounce for the sake of love and personal survival. Jean-Louis Phillipe is a world-renowned opera singer enjoying his life of fame and fortune. He is adored by his fellow Frenchmen and Frenchwomen, and he is now preparing for his first performance of Bizet's *Carmen,* which is sure to be another triumph. He owns a beautiful villa right outside of Paris. And he enjoys the devotion and sexual favors of a handsome young valet named Armand.

Trouble is brewing in paradise, however, whether the oblivious Jean-Louis senses it or not. The news is abuzz with talk of war between France and Germany, and when it is official, when war does ensue between the two countries, Jean-Louis treats the whole matter rather cavalierly. The conflict becomes real and personal to him when his mother, who lives with him and who is herself German-born, decides to return to her native country to visit family. Jean-Louis protests the visit, but the mother will not be daunted and leaves anyway. Weeks pass without word from her, until Jean-Louis decides he must follow her to Germany to find out if she is alive and safe. He uses a type of French underground to get to Germany, but he is captured soon after his arrival by German officials.

The book contains exploitive elements typical of the pulps. They involve, early on, the sexual dallying of Jean-Louis with his servant Armand. These are not terribly explicit scenes, certainly no more detailed or scabrous than those offered up in the works of the time by Mailer and Updike. These sexual interludes provide moments of great happiness and pleasure for both, among the few instances of such in the entire book. Later on, Jean-Louis is essentially raped by a Nazi underling in his apartment. This instance of brutality is consistent with other violent confrontations in Banis's books: the bullying in *Born to Be Gay,* the exploitation in *The Bronze and the Wine,* the fatal gay bashing (of a heterosexual, as it turns out) in *The Why Not.* It is a staple of the genre, exploitive in most cases, but in the hands of someone more skilled and conscientious, such as Banis, it becomes an equation of sex with domination and exertion of power—in this case a lowly Nazi soldier is able to make himself "better" than a world-famous singer by sodomizing him.

Along with *The Bronze and the Wine, Gay Treason* is one of Banis's most accomplished pulp novels. Banis would continue writing historical novels during his nonpulp phase in the 1970s and the early 1980s. He returned to the genre in 2007, when he published *Longhorns*, a novel of gay love set in the traditional Old West. But his first essay remains one of his strongest efforts in the genre. Indeed, if the exploitive elements typical of the pulps were removed, *Gay Treason* could easily sit on the shelf with any Book of the Month Club selection.

In the vast corpus of gay male pulps, Victor J. Banis's work stands out for its innovations, its creditable restlessness, its confrontation with serious themes and issues, and its entertainment value—for certainly there is much pleasure to be found in the pages of all his books.[20] One can find, especially in *The Why Not* and the *C.A.M.P.* series, seeds of gay consciousness and community that would, a mere few years later, explode with the Stonewall Inn riots. Banis is a consummate storyteller who has as his chief concern not mindless orgasms or oversized genitalia but serious issues of identity, the price of love and desire, and the cost of self-preservation. He is a clear-eyed realist who has avoided the sentimentality that adheres to much gay pulp fiction of the same period. Like other gay writers publishing in the 1960s—John Rechy and Christopher Isherwood, Jay Greene and Joseph Hansen, Stanford Friedman and Donald Windham—he knows that life affords only fleeting glimpses of happiness, not whole and permanent views, and those glimpses must be purchased at a price. Overall, Banis projects a tragic vision in his work, not because his characters are gay but because they are human beings. This vision, along with his many other admirable qualities, gives him a rightful place at the table of gay literature.

## NOTES

1. For a detailed accounted of the obscenity trial in Sioux City, Iowa, involving *The Affairs of Gloria* and Banis's acquittal see Victor J. Banis, *Spine Intact, Some Creases*, ed. Fabio Cleto (2004; rev ed., Rockville, MD: Borgo Press, 2007), 116–26. From *Gloria*, Banis went on to author many more pulp paperbacks than the ones detailed here, the majority with gay themes. In 1970, however, he turned his talents to heterosexual romances, tales of the supernatural, and adventure yarns, most signed with female pseudonyms. From 1980 to 2006 he published little, but in 2007 he returned in full

power, publishing detective stories, romances, and horror tales, all signed with his birth name. If his themes have been diverse, so have his bases of operation; born in Pennsylvania, Banis grew up in rural Ohio and has lived in Alabama, California (both Los Angeles and San Francisco), and West Virginia, where he currently resides.

2. Greenleaf publisher Earl Kemp has described their fateful meeting in "Strolling through Tumescent Town," in *The Golden Age of Gay Fiction,* ed. Drewey Wayne Gunn (Albion, NY: MLR Press, 2009), 105–7.
3. Victor J. Banis, "The Gay Publishing Revolution," in Gunn, *Golden Age of Gay Fiction,* 114–16.
4. Roger Austen, *Playing the Game: The Homosexual Novel in America* (Indianapolis: Bobbs-Merrill, 1977), 108. Austen calls "Momma" "one of the most brilliant pieces of gay writing in English of this century" (107).
5. See Banis, *Spine Intact, Some Creases,* 151.
6. Banis, "The Gay Publishing Revolution," 120.
7. For more on Rand and *The Gay Detective,* see Pamela Wojcik's essay elsewhere in this volume.
8. Banis, "The Gay Publishing Revolution," 120.
9. Ibid.
10. David Bergman, "The Cultural Work of Sixties Gay Pulp Fiction," in *The Queer Sixties,* ed. Patricia Juliana Smith (New York: Routledge, 1999), 34.
11. Fabio Cleto, "Notes on C.A.M.P.," in Gunn, *Golden Age of Gay Fiction,* 149.
12. Drewey Wayne Gunn, conversation with author, July 11, 2011.
13. See John Howard, *Men Like That: A Southern Queer History* (Chicago: University of Chicago Press, 1999), 206–9.
14. Philip Clark's essay elsewhere in this volume reflects on the critical literature that has begun developing about the nature of the lives of gays in cities and in rural settings.
15. J. X. Williams, *Born to Be Gay* (San Diego: Sundown Reader, 1966), 153–54.
16. J. X. Williams, *The Bronze and the Wine* (San Diego: Corinth Publications, 1966), 22.
17. Jay Vickery, *Man into Boy* (San Diego: Adult Books, 1968), 9.
18. The cover is reproduced in Gunn, *Golden Age of Gay Fiction,* 212.
19. J. X. Williams, *Gay Treason* (San Diego: Greenleaf Classics, 1968). An interest in Nazis seemed a gay trend at the moment, in both pulp and nonpulp fiction. Chris Davidson published *Go Down, Aaron* in 1967, Ursula Zilinsky published *Middle Ground* in 1968, and Jean Genet's *Pompes funèbres* was finally translated into English in 1969.
20. Because of space limitations only a fraction of Banis's prodigious output, even in the 1960s, has been covered here. Extensive bibliographies can be found on Banis's website, www.vjbanis.com/bibliography.php, and in *Spine Intact,* 359–66.

# Shepherds Redressed

## RICHARD AMORY'S *SONG OF THE LOON* AND THE REINVIGORATION OF THE SPANISH PASTORAL NOVEL

Beth M. Bouloukos

When I first read *Song of the Loon*, I couldn't help but think how amused Juan Goytisolo, Spain's most famous gay novelist of the twentieth century (and the greatest living Spanish novelist, gay or straight, according to Carlos Fuentes), would have been with Richard Amory's novel had he read it when it came out in 1966. Amory conceived of *Loon* as a gay American version of famous sixteenth-century Spanish pastoral novels. One of Goytisolo's books, *Count Julian* (1970), also looks to past literary genres, first defacing Francoist nationalism and religious icons, then reclaiming history. Of course, *Loon* could never have been accessible in Spain in the 1960s or early 1970s because of state censorship; Goytisolo himself had long been self-exiled by this point, and his own books were not available in his homeland until after Franco's death.

Why was Amory drawn to the pastoral rather than to updates of the fairy tale or of medieval romances of chivalry, as so many of his contemporaries in Spain were?[1] To answer the question, it is helpful to look at the evolution of the pastoral and the way it eventually reached early modern Spain. The tradition began in the third century BCE with the Greek bucolic poets and continued into the first century BCE with the most famous examples of the genre, Virgil's eclogues. Virgil and, before him, the Hellenistic Greek poet Theocritus developed "the device . . . of referring to topical subjects, and contemporary characters, under pastoral cover."[2] (Amory adopted this convention when he incorporated the popular and timely 1960s theme of free love into his updated pastoral.) Throughout the first two centuries CE there were several notable pastoral poems and romances in both Latin and Greek, arguably the most important of which is Longus's *Daphnis and Chloe*, and then there was a long lull in the production of works in this tradition until the twelfth century. From this point up until the late fifteenth and early to mid-sixteenth century, when Spain (and Portugal, to some extent) took over the genre, Italy dominated its use and development (from 1160 until about 1500), with Dante, Petrarch, Boccaccio, and Lorenzo de' Medici being the most famous figures producing pastorals of one type of another. But it was another Italian writer, Jacopo Sannazaro—the author of *Arcadia*, written 1480–1496, with the first complete edition published in 1501—who probably had the most substantial influence on the two great early-modern Spanish writers of pastoral novels, Jorge de Montemayor and Gaspar Gil Polo. There were three printings of the Spanish translation of Sannazaro's *Arcadia*, in 1547, 1549, and 1578.[3]

Because of the fervor with which the Spanish reading public consumed *Arcadia*, Montemayor published *La Diana* in 1559. It made the pastoral the most popular type of fiction in Spain. *La Diana* tells the story of one Sireno, who becomes distressed on learning of the marriage of his beloved Diana. He goes to the wise Felicia looking for help, and she gives him a magic potion, which has the effect of turning his love for Diana into indifference. Diana herself is unhappily married and remains so at the end of the romance. The plot, however, is merely an excuse for extended discussions about the nature of love. One can imagine that people in sixteenth-century Spain liked it and the rash of pastoral novels that it inspired for the same reason that popular culture became obsessed with *Sex in the City* in the late 1990s and early 2000s: Who can resist an idealized landscape with plenty of leisure time to discuss love, beauty, desire, and the inevitable heartbreak and joy that ensue when these elements are combined?

Montemayor promised a sequel that was never delivered. Instead, the story was continued by other writers, most notably Gaspar Gil Polo. In his *Diana Enamorada* (1564), Diana meets a shepherdess, Alcida, who offers to cure her unhappy state of mind.[4] Diana prefers the pain of love to being cured of it. Diana's husband appears and falls in love with Alcida, who is engaged to another shepherd. These lovers too call upon Felicia. But Gil Polo's wise woman offers no magic potions; rather the complications are resolved through other means.

As had been true throughout the long international tradition lying behind the Spanish pastoral novels, the genre was characterized by "its amplitude and its absorption of literary and cultural innovations nurtured in the courts of Spain in a century in which Spanish literati profited enormously from their relations with the rest of Europe, especially from Italy."[5] This rich, millennia-long heritage of reinvention gave writers the ability to comment on current political and social circumstances while never naming names, maintaining a sense of distance. Since Amory was writing his pastoral as a closeted gay man in a period still reeling from McCarthyism, that detachment from his political message must have been another welcome element of the genre. For Richard Love—Amory's real name, the pseudonym obviously creating yet another layer of distance—craved a space where he could fantasize about the possibility of a gay Arcadia.

Thus we can easily see why Amory would be drawn to the Spanish pastoral. The Spanish pastoral's advancement of androgyny might have caught Amory's attention as well, although one thing is sure: Amory was interested in the pastoral genre for its potential for homoerotic encounters, part of its tradition from the beginning, and for its treatment of utopian ideals. Along with the inherently attractive elements of the genre for creating a gay-themed novel, the fact that Amory based his first book on Spanish pastoral fiction also has as much to do with his personal biography as it does with literary history. According to Amory's son, Cesar Love, in a biography written for the 2005 Arsenal Press edition of the novel, his father studied anthropology in Mexico during the early 1950s, and in the early 1960s began working toward a master's degree in Spanish at San Francisco State University, which he received in 1965, the year before *Loon* was published. He then continued studying Spanish in the PhD program at the University of California–Berkeley.[6] It is not surprising that Amory would read these two foundational Spanish pastoral novels as part of his studies, as most graduate students continue to do during their required coursework. Describing the genesis of his first novel in a June 1970 interview in the gay magazine *Vector,* Amory recalled that while he was he was working on his master's degree he "somehow got turned on to Gasper Gil Polo's *Diana Enamorada* and took off from there."[7]

In spite of *Loon*'s enormous popularity in the 1960s and 1970s and its enduring influence (marked by the success of the Arsenal Press edition, which has gone into a second printing), it appears that no critic has ever taken Amory's claims seriously and understood the novel in terms of what it really is: an ingenious reworking of Montemayor's *La Diana* and Gil Polo's *Diana Enamorada.*[8] In this essay I will, for the first time, chart the ways in which Amory appropriates the structure and characters of the famous Spanish pastorals while undermining their themes and also the sexual values and constraints of Amory's own time. In the process, Amory breaks down "bipolar, transitive relations," which Eve Sedgwick laments as the basis of what we have come to call "Theory."[9] Perhaps like all polarities, the binaries that Amory interrupts are gendered and culturally loaded; they include the distinctions between active and passive, monogamy and polygamy, and artifice and nature. Many of these are very much in place in the pastoral works that Amory was reading, but perhaps his inscription of the works of these "fathers" (*pastoral* also carries this meaning) illuminates the genre's ability to trouble scholars and to interrogate its own conventionality.

In judging the literary significance of Amory's book, many critics seem to share the opinion of James Levin, who, in his 1983 study *The Gay Novel,* describes *Song of the Loon* as "hardcore pornography." Levin's categorization of the novel as pornographic seems outdated even for 1983, but it continues to be the label used.[10] Admittedly, all of the encounters in *Loon,* sexual and otherwise, might seem gratuitous and lacking in artful construction if one reads the text without a working knowledge of its sources. If Spanish pastoral novels are anything, they are without a doubt excessively gratuitous and contrived.

Just as did the critical response to Amory's novel, the first serious discussion of the Spanish pastoral genre among scholars in the United States raised the issue of narrative quality. In 1892, when Hugo A. Rennert published "The Spanish Pastoral Romances" in *PMLA*, he described Montemayor's *Diana* (and similar works) as having "serious defects" in construction and form:

> Many of its incidents are loosely interwoven; there is a lack of cohesion; the narrative is sometimes involved, and is often interrupted by long digressions, so that one loses the thread of the main story, and the interest flags. This want of logical development, the failure to properly subordinate the various incidents of the story, and thus hold the attention of the reader, is a fault conspicuous not only in the "Diana," but in all Spanish romances of its class. Many of the incidents of the "Diana" are quite improbable, and its beauty is often marred by an excessive sentimentality, at times bordering on the ridiculous.[11]

These kinds of shortcomings, noted without attention to literary convention or to possible contemporary cultural implications, have also been lamented in Amory's novel. The perceived deficiencies of *Song of the Loon* are, however, "deficiencies" of the originals, or rather, parodic elements that Amory appropriated in his own culturally subversive literary project.

Rennert made it clear that Spanish pastoral novels were, by turn-of-the-century standards, not very good. The Spanish pastoral style did not fare well by 1960s standards either, which may be the first reason why Amory's rendition did not attract much real literary attention. With the popularity of the *nouveau roman* and the *nueva novela* in Latin America, the focus on radical novelty in formal elements came to the forefront of literary fashion. Despite the occasionally disconnected and digressive nature of *Song of the Loon*, it seemed strangely traditional and thus out of keeping with current taste. Today we are seeing a return to some traditional forms of narrative, with a focus on a newness in content that derives from an author's ability to traverse the traditional separations between literary and pop culture. Because of this reappropriation of classic narratological techniques, scholars, one hopes, will revaluate past works such as Amory's that have been marginalized because of their lack of formal innovation.

That *Song of the Loon* was published by Greenleaf Classics may also explain the lack of genuine critical interest in the novel. Like other books from Greenleaf it was branded a pulp novel, worthy of a brief read and a pass-on, but hardly of serious scholarly analysis. Today the novel remains lumped in the genre of 1960s gay pulp fiction. It is a "niche" text, marginalized by its assumed use of cheap titillation devoid of literary value. Michael Bronski works to overturn these conceptions in his introduction to the 2005 Arsenal Press edition of *Loon:*

> *Song of the Loon* was a first: a paperback original soft-core porn novel—more accurately labeled, by today's standards, erotica rather than porn—that didn't merely have literary aspirations; it had actual literary merit. Even Greenleaf Classics, a publisher not known for its literary impulses, emphasized the novel's high-tone qualities on the jacket copy and described the book as "a mystical blend of elements from Hudson's *Green Mansions,* J. F. Cooper's *Leatherstocking Tales* and the works of Jean Genet." Forgetting the fact that there is only a small kernel of truth in this description (there is little of Hudson's late-Victorian sentimentality here, and almost none of Genet's harsh vision of anguished salvation), the reality is that Richard Amory wrote a completely original and dazzling novel that marked a turning point in the evolution of gay literature.[12]

Like summaries of Netflix films or descriptions of literary texts by medieval catalogers and scribes, the account given of Amory's novel on the back cover of the Greenleaf edition makes us wonder whether the editors did more than skim the work they were summarizing. In a passage preceding this one, Bronski correctly attributes the "inspiration" for Amory's work to pastoral novels. Amory's book does represent something vastly new for the genre of gay literature, but it does so through a wholly unoriginal structure.

Indeed, Amory appropriates the structure, characters, language, and setting of Montemayor's and Gil Polo's texts, and this appropriation repeats one of the essential gestures of the Spanish pastoral novel itself. As John

Cull notes in his study of the genre, "Renaissance pastoral has been called a palimpsest: literally one text written over another."[13] Amory invoked this approach and the particular texts he inscribed when asked about his writing process for the novel: "The *Diana* is one of those highly erotic and extremely artificial sixteenth-century Spanish pastorals, which are usually laid in a cloud-cuckoo-land that the author is pleased to call Arcadia, and I thought it would be a perfect vehicle for a gay novel. After I changed the setting to the Oregon wilderness and costumed the *zagales* [shepherds] as mountain men and cowboys and Indians, the next two novels [in the *Loon* trilogy] practically wrote themselves."[14] These novels "practically wrote themselves" because they already existed; Amory had a framework for his writing before he even began. As he explained, his version of Arcadia would be the Pacific Northwest of the United States and his shepherds would be white trappers and Native Americans. As we will see, however, the Spanish pastoral novel is merely the skeleton on which Amory fleshes out his modern manifesto on love.

The subtitle of Amory's novel is "a gay pastoral in five books and an interlude," and this structure is taken directly from Spanish pastorals: segments of prose with interpolated poetry, grouped into sections known as *libros* or books.[15] Not only did Amory copy this general structure, but he also imitated the specific types of poetry found in the original sources: *coplas, ovillejo, égloga pastoril,* and *glosa*. In the *Vector* interview, Amory recounted some of his process for writing the poems in *Loon:*

> Near the end of the book there is a poem in *vers libre* that is technically what they call a *glosa* in Spanish—very popular in the Renaissance. What you do is take, say, a quatrain as a point of departure and then write four strophes, each one ending in a line of the original quatrain. Some of them are done on the *Ave Maria* or the *Credo* and so on and get to be terribly sacrilegious, so I took the first four lines of Whittier's *Snowbound*—you know "The sun that brief December day / Rose cheerless over hills of gray, / And darkly circled gave at noon / A sadder light than waning moon," and proceeded to turn it inside out into a fuck poem that would have curled poor old John Greenleaf's hair, by making each line of the quatrain refer back to a previous sex act between Cyrus and Ephraim. This was no mean trick, mind you, but of course the editor had never heard of *glosas* or *Snowbound,* and

> hardly ever of strophes and stanzas, so out of some entirely extraneous considerations which I can't fathom, they excised two of the sex acts leading into the poem, thereby spoiling my elaborate build-up and rendering the poem meaningless. This is sheer Yahoo-ism, and it took a lot of the fun out of the whole thing, and I'm still jangling.[16]

Even if Amory's editor at Greenleaf—more interested in sales than literary value—revised some of these poems, disrupting their original meter, their poetic forms remain discernable. That the characters in *Loon* sometimes sing the poems or set them to music reinforces their connection to the sixteenth-century sources.

Along with the structure, all the characters that appear in Amory's novel can be traced in part to their sixteenth-century sources. Ephraim MacIver, the protagonist, embodies Diana in characterization and situation; both are legendary beauties with three primary suitors. The first of Ephraim's suitors is Singing Heron, with whom he shares the "pure and honest love" that also characterizes Diana's relationship with her first admirer, Sireno. After Singing Heron departs, Ephraim encounters Cyrus, his eventual long-term partner, just as Diana meets and marries Delio after Sireno leaves her. Diana is also courted by Silvano, whom she abhors, and, not surprisingly, Amory includes a character, named Montgomery, who is Silvano's counterpart. Montgomery mistreats Ephraim, and the beginning of the narrative is concerned with the protagonist fleeing from his unwanted suitor.

It is interesting to recall here that Diana is not actually the protagonist of *La Diana;* she does take on a greater role in Gil Polo's continuation, and Amory picks up the story from there and makes his Diana the pivotal center of the narrative. Out of all the characters, we can imagine that Amory selected her as his prototype because Montemayor implies that she is not chaste. In Book IV of *La Diana*, the characters pass by a sign in Felicia's palace that reads:

> Whoever enters here must look at how he has lived
> and if he has guarded the gift of chastity;
> and she whom he loves or has loved well,
> look whether she has changed because of another man,
> and if she has not lost the faith and has conserved that first love,
> she may enter into Diana's temple.[17]

At this point in the narrative, Diana has not yet actually appeared in person, but Sireno takes the opportunity to interject that Diana would not be able to make this oath as she has gone against all the laws of "buen amor," which highlights the irony of her name.[18]

Amory, however, reinstates Diana (Ephraim) to a high moral stature. The goddess Diana was known for her pureness and chastity; she also refused to marry, even though she had many suitors. The character Diana in the Spanish pastoral taints her purity by marrying someone she doesn't love. Amory's eradication of monogamist marriages reestablishes the figure of Diana as pure in deed, because the new culture to which Ephraim subscribes holds that it is possible to love (both physically and spiritually) more than one person at the same time. The 1960s version of the tale releases "Diana" and the others from the burden of unhappy marriages without love. In the sixteenth-century romances, copious tears are often provoked when one character falls in love with someone who is already married to another; in most of these romances the amorous relationships are characterized by extreme melancholy and inequality. Amory remedies this by doing away with traditional monogamy and curing the unhappiness that dominates the pastoral genre. Amory's reworking of Diana's identity thus renders his novel a pastoral in the truest sense of the tradition: the authors of pastorals often took characters from long-forgotten sources and reworked their identities to fit the contemporary values they wished to express.

It might seem, initially, as if Amory's adaptation takes a misogynistic turn since he does away with female characters completely. In the Spanish pastorals, the women are truly active, intellectual characters on a par with the male characters. One could easily misconstrue the absence of women in Amory's novel as a serious affront to the second-wave feminism of his generation, but Amory foresaw this criticism and deliberately justified his decision in the *Vector* interview: there are "no women," he noted, "because they bring in a whole host of secondary problems that I didn't want to deal with; (at the time, as I recall, everybody was embroiled in questions as to the genesis of homosexuality, and it was fashionable to throw the blame onto Maw, poor Maw; I consider such preoccupations a total waste of time, and besides, they usually end up as a bitchy put-down of women)."[19]

If Amory takes women out of his novel, he does not do so in order to negate the progress that the Spanish pastorals had made in terms of female characters and their role in literature. In light of his justification, it would seem that he is more interested in critiquing dominant conceptions of masculinity. In *Loon,* there are seemingly overly macho characters like Cyrus—with his intimidating stature, bold courage, and MacGyverish handiness—but as his character develops, we see that he also has characteristics typically associated with women, such as tenderness and sentimentality. Along with this rejection of masculine/feminine binary oppositions, Amory does away with the stereotype of male-male sex as operating within a static pattern of discrete and mutually exclusive active and passive roles.

The secondary characters in Amory's novel also correspond to sixteenth-century characters, most notably the sage Felicia, who in *Loon* becomes Bear-who-dreams. In Book One of the novel, the reader learns about the premise of Ephraim's journey: he has set out to find a celebrated figure named Bear-who-dreams, who represents a sort of prophetic shaman. Ephraim's first love, Singing Heron, explains to him at the end of Book One that "you will never be at peace until you have seen the wise man," and that "you must be rid of the shade that haunts you," which can only happen through contact with Bear-who-dreams.[20] This "shade" that darkens Ephraim's life comes from the constant torment of his memories of Montgomery and the fear he lives with that his authoritative, controlling ex-suitor will find him.

The trajectory of the *libros* in Amory's novel reflects that of *La Diana* in that it charts the journey that the characters undertake in order to find the dwelling place of a legendary sage. In Montemayor's novel "the first three [*libros*] deal with the pilgrimage to the palace-temple; the fourth centers on Felicia's abode; while the last three represent the resolution of the love conflicts of the pilgrim-shepherds."[21] In Amory's novel, the first three books follow Ephraim as he searches for Bear-who-dreams' cave and encounters a group of young men at Eagle Camp, a lodge close to the cave (just as the shepherds meet a group of nymphs in a meadow near the Temple of Diana), and the fourth begins with Ephraim finding the cave. The fifth and final book resolves the amorous conflicts in the novel; as Ephraim is the only main character, Amory easily and quickly ends the novel in a single book. Anyone who has read *La Diana* would be thankful to Amory for doing away with the need for two concluding books.

Frederick de Armas notes that Book IV of *La Diana* is "the axis of the novel," and Juan Montero concurs.[22] Book Four of *Loon* is also the central point that the other events in the novel rotate around. Ephraim spends the first three books looking for Eagle Camp and Bear-who-dreams, and like the shepherds, this provides him the opportunity to share his story. In Book Four, Ephraim finally finds Bear-who-dreams, who induces Ephraim's "medicine dream," which will cure him of his malady. In the literal sense, Bear-who-dreams provides a *dream* for Ephraim. Likewise, as RoseAnna Mueller notes in her edition of Montemayor's romance, the sage Felicia offers "felicidad": "Felicia is the dispenser of happiness"; she is "mature and wise, in contrast to the young lovers of the Diana, who are immature and confused."[23] Bear-who-dreams is also an older, judicious figure who leads the other characters to greater happiness.

Both sages offer a magical substance to the younger characters to alleviate their woes. In Amory's adaptation, we might liken this "medicine dream" to a clichéd 1960s vision quest, but it also spoofs Felicia in *La Diana,* as she is a sage who concocts remedies to cure the lovesick.[24] Montero explains that Felicia's name "evokes the idea of happiness and [she] appears from the beginning as a sage who takes it upon herself to remedy the evil that loves causes."[25] In Amory's novel, Ephraim attempts to cure himself of his love-related problems with a visit to Bear-who-dreams; this wise man helps to ease the depression that Ephraim's relationship with Montgomery inflicted on him. Felicia's magical drink cures the characters but without providing any greater understanding of themselves; they merely fall asleep and wake up healed, having forgotten their former loves. Bear-who-dreams' remedy, on the other hand, helps Ephraim to overcome his tormented feelings for his ex-boyfriend through self-realization.

The climax of *Loon* comes in Book Four after Ephraim's interaction with Bear-who-dreams. As with the temple in *La Diana,* those who wish to gain access into the sage's realm must prove their worthiness: "The enclosure is only accessible to those who overcome a trial that gauges the chastity and fidelity of love."[26] In this "prueba de amor," as they are referred to in chivalresque novels, Bear-who-dreams does not judge Ephraim's chastity and loyalty but, rather, poses a series of questions intended to determine whether Ephraim's development has reached a sufficient level for him to understand the ways of the Society of the Loon (comprised of gay men who are linked by their approach to loving, respectful nonmonogamy). This definition of love sharply contrasts with the ideals of courtly love displayed in *La Diana*, where "buen amor" connotes chastity outside of marriage and monogamy within marriage. Even though it is possible to view the sixteenth-century novel as erotically charged—as Amory does in his reading of *La Diana*—there is no consummation of this energy in the same explicit direction in which Amory pushes the romantic situations in his narrative. Neoplatonic philosophy fuels the Spanish pastorals, but Amory asserts that love can be both exceptionally carnal and transcendent.

Along with the differing requirements for entry into these sacred realms in the two novels, the actual spaces themselves diverge in their metaphorical significance. Montero notes that in *La Diana* Felicia's castle expands on the theme of nature versus artifice. For example, the narrator describes the entryway of the palace as seemingly more part of nature than the work of human hands.[27] This comment, however, seems unwarranted, and the reader is left to wonder what exactly about the *chapitel* (arched entrance) could be confused with something that was not produced by a human. Even with the inclusion of the description of the palace gardens, the metaphor fails to describe the complex relationship between nature and artifice. Furthermore, when we see this metaphor in relationship to the bucolic topos of country versus city/court, the palace undermines the most basic premise of the pastoral. As de Armas observes, "The very structure of Montemayor's fiction seems to negate the supremacy of the countryside. The shepherds must journey to Felicia's palace to precipitate a resolution to their amorous difficulties since their natural environment had merely provided a forum for their distress."[28] In this way, the palace in *La Diana* ultimately fails in regard to its metaphorical usefulness, since it never provides any insight into the nature-versus-artifice debate, nor does it serve to expand on the theme of idealized life in nature. The pastoral is based on happiness being found in nature (what is natural is real and true), whereas in Montemayor's version the cure for suffering is found in what represents the height of artifice.

The council chamber at Eagle Camp in *Loon* better develops the nature/artifice metaphor, as it inhabits a space somewhere between pure nature and human artistic creation: "Among the trees were a scattering of tents, and in the center, a permanent wooden council chamber. The sides and roof were formed of carefully hewn slabs of cedar, carved and painted with designs reminiscent of the Indian blankets Ephraim has seen in [the village of] Astoria."[29] Here we have a manmade structure, but it is not pure artifice in the sense that the natural elements are not manipulated to the point that they cannot be recognized as such. With the inclusion of the lodge, Amory sets in motion a series of metaphors that culminate in an allegory that challenges binary dichotomies such as nature/artifice.

In Montero's description of the castle in his edition of *La Diana*, he goes on to say that Montemayor's source may be the allegorical and supernatural castles of the Middle Ages and the Renaissance. Although the council chamber in *Loon* resonates with a "peaceful darkness inside," it does not seem otherworldly nor does it have a special spiritual charge.[30] This cedar lodge appears to begin an important metaphor that Amory expands on with the inclusion of Bear-who-dreams' cave. Rather than develop this theme solely through a discussion of the council chamber, Amory integrates one of the most important elements of Gil Polo's *Diana Enamorada:* the sacred cave. That is, in Gil Polo's continuation of Montemayor's tale, he opts to center his narrative around a cave rather than an enchanted castle.[31] This "emblem for natural art," as de Armas defines the cave, more aptly represents the nuanced relationship between nature and art. De Armas observes, "The cave may have been shaped by powerful natural forces. . . . Even if the cave was shaped by man, it was carved in a way that so closely resembled natural means, that the artifice escapes the viewer."[32] Amory purposefully makes his reader think anew about artifice by adding cave paintings to the metaphor, so that now the reader is confronted with another level of complexity: paintings (artifice) are directly overlain on the cave (nature).

It should again be stressed that, as with every pastoral, Amory's work incorporates various genres, and the cave epitomizes this generic hybridity. In the section on Ephraim's prophetic dream-vision, Amory draws on early modern mystical narrative by the likes of San Juan and Santa Teresa. De Armas addresses this in his article on Gil Polo's version: "A cave is an emblem of what the Christians call the interior paradise of the soul."[33] The cave becomes a symbol of the core toward which the mystic must travel in order to reach a type of noetic understanding of the divine. While Gil Polo might also allude to this mystical tradition in his use of the cave, Amory explicitly frames Ephraim as a wayward soul in search of something greater than himself. To emphasize this point, Amory has Ephraim enter into his vision quest naked and fasting, in the true style of a medieval or early modern penitent monk. The dream is structured by Ephraim's interaction with different bodies of water, first a stream and then finally a lake. After he is led farther on his path by the stream, "before him was a lake, deep blue, almost purple. . . . [S]uddenly, before his eyes, the lake drained away leaving a huge blue hole."[34] If we take water as a metaphor of otherworldly knowledge, as it is in the mystic tradition, we know that this is Ephraim's moment of spiritual enlightenment and that the water (that is, noetic understanding) is no longer external but part of Ephraim himself. The lake has "drained away" and transferred itself to Ephraim's soul.

Amory's writing also highlights and extends patterns in the sixteenth-century language of Montemayor's and Gil Polo's pastorals. The artificiality with which these characters speak in Amory's novel is on par with the "excessive sentimentality, at times bordering on the ridiculous" and "peculiar and distorted sentences" of the Spanish versions.[35] This, and no mere penchant for outlandishness, leads Amory to produce what we might tend to perceive as overstuffed dialogue and garish metaphors, such as "And you, Ephraim, walk in handsomeness always," or "his eyes, like chips of obsidian." The extent to which Amory captures the bombast of sixteenth-century Spanish pastoral language is in fact one of the novel's most successful elements.

Most of the characters in the sixteenth-century pastorals do not speak as if they were actually unlearned country shepherds. Cyrus, much like all the counterfeit *pastores* in the source texts, is not *really* a simple outdoorsman, but a cosmopolitan intellectual in moccasins and a trapper's hat; he recounts at length his studies of French philosophy and the Greek and Latin classics in a highly articulate level of discourse. Amory takes this linguistic camouflage a step further, however. The transcodification here moves from the courtly language dressed in pastoral garb to the idiolect of 1960s gay pulp fiction characters outfitted in the fashion of fur trappers and Native Americans. The speech of Amory's characters has a marked carnivalesque quality, and Amory utilizes this type of language in order to add yet another level of artifice to his narrative. This purposefully antiliterary language is one more reason why *Song of the Loon* may have been overlooked in terms of its literary quality.

Amory's coopting of these elements of the Spanish pastoral novel, as well as forging those that are barely emerging in American mid-1960s erotic pulp novels, results in a socially minded subversion of tropes. If we take the novel genre to be a form that uses generic standards to bring about something new, something *novel,* then Amory's work most certainly succeeds, as it proposes a modern vision of gay love and of relationships in general. His choice to do this via a utopian framework makes perfect sense given the historical moment he was living in. Utopian settings have a long history in literary works in the United States, and it would be fruitful for a literary scholar to put Amory's novel into that context. It would also be productive to look at it as a reflection of the times in which it was written, a pivotal political moment in American history. It novel seems to reflect the spirit of the Berkeley Free Speech Movement; this was also the era that saw race riots begin to spread across the United States. Amory's generation (and later Amory himself) was fighting for and dreaming of a more inclusive country. All this becomes even more interesting in contrast to Muller's argument that the Spanish pastoral does not project forward to an idealized place, as the word "utopian" would suggest, but looks to a purer past that has faded away.[36] Amory, however, does not conceive of the western frontier as a lost gay world; rather at this particular moment in his life, I believe, he *is* dreaming of what the future will bring for gays in the United States, and this genre allowed him to project a *fantastic* vision of that in literary form.

# NOTES

1. Examples include Carmen Martín Gaite's *El cuarto de atras* (1978), Esther Tusquet's *El mismo mar de todos los veranos* (1978), and Ana María Matute's *Primera memoria* (1959).
2. Amadeu Solé-Leris, *The Spanish Pastoral Novel* (Boston: Twayne, 1980), 18.
3. My summary of the pastoral tradition necessarily presents a much simplified history. For a more detailed analysis (in English—there are many others in Spanish) of the progression of the pastoral, leading up to its popularity in Spain, see Solé-Leris, *The Spanish Pastoral Novel* (the primary basis of my description here), and Dominick Finello, *The Evolution of the Pastoral Novel in Early Modern Spain* (Tempe, AZ: Brepols, 2008). Solé-Leris has a more extended discussion of the persistence of bucolic themes in Spanish cultural productions throughout the Middle Ages, which may have influenced Spanish readers' favorable reception of Sannazaro's *Arcadia*.
4. Gaspar Gil Polo, *Diana Enamorada*, ed. Francisco López Estrada (Madrid: Castalia, 2000).
5. Finello, *The Evolution of the Pastoral Novel*, 13.
6. Cesar Love, "Biography of Richard Love," in *Song of the Loon*, by Richard Amory (Vancouver: Arsenal Pulp Press, 2005), 216.
7. Richard Amory, untitled interview with *Vector* (June 1970), reprinted in *Song of the Loon*, 223 (hereafter cited as *Vector* interview).
8. Though Amory's statement is often mentioned, it is not always clear whether critics even believe his claim. How, for example, should one take Mark D. Jordan's question and answer? "But why implicate Montemayor and his continuator, Gil Polo, Renaissance founders of the Spanish pastoral? Because Amory too is playing with and at a pornographic neobaroque." Jordan, *Recruiting Young Love: How Christians Talk about Homosexuality* (Chicago: University of Chicago Press, 2011), 111.
9. See Eve Kosofsky Sedgwick, *Touching Feeling: Affect, Pedagogy, Performativity* (Durham, NC: Duke University Press, 2003).
10. James Levin, *The Gay Novel: The Male Homosexual Image in America* (New York: Irvington, 1983), 252. Among the more recent examples are Byrne R. S. Fone, *A Road to Stonewall: Male Homosexuality and Homophobia in English and American Literature, 1750–1969* (New York: Twayne, 1995), 274 ("homosexual pornography"); Gregory Wood, *A History of Gay Literature: The Male Tradition* (New Haven: Yale University Press, 1998), 161 ("soft pornographic romance"); and Jordan, *Recruiting Young Love*, 111 (see note 8).
11. Hugo Rennert, "The Spanish Pastoral Romances," *PMLA* 7 (1892): 10–11.
12. Michael Bronski, "Introduction," in *Song of the Loon* (2005 ed.), 10.
13. John Cull, "Androgyny in the Spanish Pastoral Novels," *Hispanic Review* 57 (1989): 317.
14. Amory, *Vector* interview, 223.
15. Amory, *Song of the Loon: A Gay Pastoral in Five Books and an Interlude* (San Diego: Greenleaf Classics, 1966).
16. Amory, *Vector* interview, 225–26.
17. Jorge Montemayor, *La Diana*, ed. Juan Montero (Barcelona: Critica, 1996), 170. Unless otherwise noted, all translations from the Spanish are my own. The Spanish reads:

"Quien entra mire bien cómo ha vivido / y el don de castidad si le ha guardado / y la que quiere bien o le ha querido / mire si a causa de otro se ha mudado / y si la fe primera no ha perdido / y aquel primero amor ha conservado / entrar puede en el templo de Diana."

18. Ibid., 171.
19. Amory, *Vector* interview, 223.
20. Amory, *Song of the Loon* (1966), 33–34.
21. Fredrick A. de Armas, "Caves of Fame and Wisdom in the Spanish Pastoral Novels," *Studies in Philology* 82 (1985): 332.
22. Ibid; Montero, ed., *La Diana.*
23. RoseAnna Muller, ed., *La Diana,* by Jorge Montemayor (New York: Mellen, 1989), 28.
24. An unpublished memoir by Amory, in the possession of Richard Fullmer, mentions his own experiments with hallucinogenic drugs, very much a part of the culture at the time.
25. Montero, ed., *La Diana,* 168. The Spanish reads "evoca la idea de felicidad y aparece desde el primer momento como sabia que se encarga de remediar los males que causa el amor."
26. Ibid., 165. The Spanish reads "El recinto solo es accesible a quienes superan una prueba que mide la castidad y fidelidad amorosas."
27. Montero, ed., *La Diana,* 165, 170.
28. De Armas, "Caves of Fame and Wisdom," 332.
29. Amory, *Song of the Loon* (1966), 95.
30. Ibid., 114.
31. The castle does appear in Gil Polo's novel, but it is not the axis of the narrative. De Armas writes: "At first glance, it appears that Gil Polo has not effected any changes on the wisdom abode. Felicia still resides in a palace, although this structure appears at the end, rather than in the center of the novel. Yet, turning to book three, we do encounter a central episode that corresponds to the temple-axis at the center of Montemayor's pastoral." De Armas, "Caves of Fame and Wisdom," 345.
32. Ibid., 358, 340.
33. Ibid., 352.
34. Amory, *Song of the Loon* (1966), 132.
35. Rennert, "The Spanish Pastoral Romances," 11.
36. Muller, ed., *La Diana,* 15.

# "A Life *Entirely without Fear*"

## HINDUS, HOMOS, AND GAY PULP IN CHRISTOPHER ISHERWOOD'S *A MEETING BY THE RIVER*

Jaime Harker

Early in Christopher Isherwood's 1967 novel, *A Meeting by the River*, Patrick, on his way to India to persuade his brother Oliver not to become a monk, receives a special gift from his lover, Tom, in Los Angeles:

> That coverless and obviously much thumbed-through paperback novel you suddenly pulled out of your pocket and gave me at the airport—*wow* (as you would say)!! You know, you might at least have warned me what it was about! I suppose I should have guessed, from your wicked grin. Anyhow, I didn't. After we'd taken off, I opened it in all innocence at the first chapter and almost immediately found myself in that sizzling love scene between the character called Lance and that younger boy. Did you think that a hard-boiled publisher couldn't be shocked? I began blushing, yes actually! And then I suspected that my neighbor was reading it too, out of the corner of his eye. So I put the book away for private consumption later—behind a locked door![1]

The appearance of a dirty book in a novel that has been understood as Isherwood's most religious is surprising. Two years before, Isherwood's biography of the founder of his branch of Hinduism, *Ramakrishna and His Disciples*, publicly proclaimed his religious identity just as interest in Eastern religions was peaking. Though Hinduism marks all of Isherwood's American novels, *A Meeting by the River* was his most Hindu fictional experiment, incorporating setting (India), terminology, and rituals. The novel's "much thumbed-through paperback," however, connects Isherwood's Hinduism to his deep investment in Cold War queer print culture. There was a new iteration of queer pulp by the mid-1960s, one that Isherwood followed with interest: gay pulp published by straight erotica firms and marketed as both sex- and gay-positive. Gay pulp, though seemingly out of place, is essential to the plot and the structure of *A Meeting by the River.*

Isherwood had long been interested in erotic literature. Private obscene documents circulated in his English circle for years, including pornographic poems by W. H. Auden. Isherwood's novel *The Last of Mr. Norris* (1935) features a Swiss-family-Robinson idyll of young boys that one character, Baron Pregnitz, reads obsessively, much to the narrator's delight; Arthur Norris's carefully protected collection of masochistic masterpieces includes one written by himself. A dirty book figures in the "Mr. Lancaster" section of the final version of *Down There on a Visit* (1962); an early draft of the same novel includes an "artiste" who manages a pornography reading room:

> Peter's eyes got used to the gloom as he walked along the desks, glancing at the books and their titles. There were *David Copperfield Confidential, Moby's Dick, Inside Madame Bovary.* By the time he reached *Wuthering Heights and How He Got Up There,* Peter knew pretty much what to expect. Like the other volumes, it was a mimeographed typescript. He switched on his lamp and opened it at random: "You ready for it, Cathy honey?" "You bet your life I'm ready for it, Heathcliff sugar." "I'm going to give it to you, Cathy." "Okay, Heathcliff, you go ahead and give it to me. Let's see you give it to me. Just you quit your bragging and give it me right now—or else I'll get to start thinking you don't have it, Big Boy, maybe not any more than Edgar Linton does." "I'll show you if I have it, Cathy. I'll show you right this minute. Lookit, Cathy, lookit, lookit, lookit!" (Here a reader had scribbled on the margin of the page: "Dialogue most unconvincing and psychology poor. The author obviously knows *nothing* about the English upper middle class.")[2]

Isherwood's comic send-up of battered and dog-eared typescripts, existing parasitically on high culture, clearly sets up dirty books as slumming. Their mock-literary titles, invoking Dickens, Melville, Flaubert, and Bronte, and the literary criticism at the end of the hilariously bad sex scene become the basis for Isherwood's campy tone, even as the details suggest direct knowledge.

Typescripts such as these had been bubbling under the surface of mainstream publishing for quite a while. Roger Austen, in *Playing the Game*, details an extensive manuscript, dated 1925, that collected gay erotic short stories that were in circulation between the world wars. Simon Sheppard includes two post–World War II examples in his 2007 anthology *Homosex*. Philip Clark, in an earlier essay about Guild Press, discusses at greater length than he does in his essay in this volume the phenomenon of gay samizdat: "manuscripts passed from hand-to-hand, from gay man to gay man, copied and distributed at high prices in the days when possession of such stories was illegal." He found examples in the Guild Press files at Cornell University.[3]

Isherwood wrote his own samizdat story in 1959: "Afterwards." In it, the story's narrator, recently bereft of his partner, becomes involved with a couple. He has an affair with one partner, moves away for a year, and then, in the end, discovers that he is really in love with the other member of the triangle. The narrative includes a number of the elements that would later figure prominently in gay pulp: explicit sex scenes, social commentary that protests the subordinate social status of homosexuals, and a happy ending. Isherwood wondered whether "Afterwards" was "sheer pornographic sentimentalism," but concluded that it had "some emotion." In any event, he chose to preserve it in his archive.[4] It is striking to see how many of the features of "Afterwards"—the explicit descriptions of sex, the happy ending, the emphasis, in the end, on romance—recur in 1960s gay pulp.

The new gay pulps, circulating in paperback rather than typescripts, were both explicit about sex and positive about gay identity. Michael Bronski concludes that they "almost always presented gay sex as horny, happy, and healthy. The 'shadows' had disappeared, and gay sex was now as bright and as clear as day."[5] The year 1966, as Isherwood was hard at work on his Indian novel, was a banner one for this new publishing venture. Victor J. Banis's novel *The Man from C.A.M.P.* was satiric, hilarious, and irreverent. Richard Amory's *Song of the Loon,* a self-described "pastoral," depicted a mythic Indian tribe that places man love at the center of its culture. Each chapter includes an initiation in the "way of the loon," with a new sex partner. The pious, pedantic tone marks this novel as the new bible of gay life, and it became the best-selling gay pulp of the 1960s. The number of new titles now grew exponentially.

These novels often abound in explicit sex scenes—usually one or more per chapter—but they also, like "Afterwards," feature romance. Indeed, Banis argues that pulp novelists' greatest contribution was love and commitment for gay characters: "The choice to pursue a life together was not for the most part available to the characters in those earlier gay novels. . . . It was the gay paperback writers of the 1960s who first (and not without considerable risk) truly bridged that gap between frustrated love and the possibility of a long-term commitment. No longer did the characters in the novels of these writers have to be separated by the end of the book through tragedy or cure. 'Happy ever after' became a possibility they could choose."[6] "Pornographic sentimentality" was essential to gay pulp; not just explicit images of sex, but surrounding cultural narratives that authorize that sex, are essential. The two Adams no longer needed to be cast out of the Garden. *Song of the Loon*'s dreamlike setting, on the frontier and up the river, is the prototype for this. In gay pulp, sex does not bring the fall; sex is what makes paradise.

Isherwood complained bitterly to his agent about the pulp press Lancer Books being given the right to reprint *A Single Man* and *A Meeting by the River,* a transaction that placed his 1960s fiction firmly within the new phenomenon of adult bookstores. But Isherwood's investment in a public literary reputation did not always match his private obsessions and enthusiasms. Though none of the groundbreaking 1966 pulps were in his library, his diaries show him reading gay pulps avidly, if not always approvingly. While visiting San Francisco in 1967, he records: "We spent a lot of the morning in two queer bookshops, the Adonis and Rolland's, where we bought *Sex Life of a Cop; Go Down, Aaron; Teleny; Like Father, Like Son; A Fool's Advice; The Beefcake Boys.* Buying such books is a sort of political gesture which is infinitely more satisfactory than actually reading them."[7] He became friends with Samuel Steward in the early 1970s. Steward wrote gay pulp under the pseudonym Phil Andros, and Isherwood not only read the Phil Andros novels but praised them.[8]

Isherwood did preserve one gay pulp in his library: Larry Townsend's 1971 *The Sexual Adventures of Sherlock Holmes* (by "J. Watson").[9] Isherwood's longstanding love for Sherlock Holmes may explain why this book made the cut. The novel is like *The Man from C.A.M.P.* in its queering of popular culture. In this version, however, Watson is just out of the army and making ends meet by turning tricks in the local pub. A friendly pimp sets him up with Holmes, who takes him to his flat and beds him. The presence of this novel in Isherwood's permanent library, along with his references to other pulps in his diaries, letters, and novels, authorize a more thorough investigation of how the cultural phenomenon of gay pulp manifests itself in *A Meeting by the River.*

Before turning to the novel, however, there is one other curious link it provides to gay pulps that may be worth recording. In 1968 Isherwood and Don Bachardy collaborated on a dramatization of the novel. This stage version of *A Meeting by the River* was not produced until 1972, when the Mark Taper Forum in Los Angeles gave it a week's run with a cast that included Laurence Luckinbill, Sam Waterston, and a young actor named Gordon Hoban; the three united later the same year for a single performance in New York City. According to one of Isherwood's biographers, Peter Parker, Isherwood "developed a crush" on Hoban. That in itself is not remarkable, but what is interesting is that Hoban went on to write a series of pulp novels himself, between 1976 and 1984, under the pseudonym Tom Hardy (some of which he later reprinted under his birth name, before his untimely death due to complications from AIDS in 1993).[10]

The novel *A Meeting by the River* is structured as a series of journal entries written by Oliver and letters written by Patrick to his brother, his mother, his wife, and his lover, Tom. Oliver's impending ordination as a Hindu monk drives the plot of this novel, but Patrick's relationship with Tom provides a counterpoint. This cursory overview, however, does not indicate just how thoroughly pulp infuses the book's structure and plot. Patrick has made a fortune pushing back the proprieties at his stuffy publishing firm; his first success was the memoir of "Anita Hayden . . . one of the leading musical comedy and film stars."[11]

Patrick's description of the affair shows his own investment in the lucrative pulp of the era, despite his employment by a reputable firm: "Her memoirs were pretty hot stuff . . . and I, as a very junior partner, had to use all my arts of persuasion to get Uncle Fred and dear old G.B.V. to touch them with a barge-pole. G.B.V. . . . asked me if I wanted to bring disgrace on a firm whose list had been adorned by the names of some of the noblest (and least-read) Edwardians. However, persuasion won the day, the memoirs were published and they made us such a shamefully large sum of money that the matter was never mentioned again. But that was only the first of my various ventures into vulgarity" (22).

Patrick has taken "vulgarity" to another level in his latest venture—overseeing a movie version of one of his novels. His publishers condemn the move publicly, but then "each has come to me behind the other's back and asked if he might make a small investment in the film out of his own pocket! Which will show you to what an extent I've already corrupted them. I sometimes feel slightly satanic" (23). In other words, Patrick is an avid disseminator of trash, an enabler of the very trend in publishing that led to that coverless, well-thumbed gay pulp.

His campy delight in "vulgarity," his pleasure in satanic corruption, and his interest in sex with men should have made gay pulp a welcome revelation. And yet, he is shocked that such things are being read openly. As he writes to Tom: "I know you weren't recommending it to me for its literary value and so your feelings won't be hurt when I say that it's probably the greatest trash I ever read in my life—and I'm speaking as a professional reader of trash, remember!—but that doesn't make it any the less exciting. Admittedly I haven't had much experience of this sort of literature. I realize that it's being mass-produced nowadays, especially in your own enlightened country. Funny to think that, when I was your age, even, this book couldn't have been published openly and sold on the counter!" (66).

Patrick's self-identification as "a professional reader of trash" is self-deprecating, but he still insists, as Isherwood did, that he can distinguish between the "literary" and "trash." His impressed observation that "when I was your age, even, this book couldn't have been published openly and sold on the counter" allows Isherwood to let his readers know about the new phenomenon of gay pulp and highlights the generational conflict between Patrick and Tom. Tom represents the new, liberated consumer of gay pulp: bold, proud, and out enough to kiss his married lover at the airport in public. Tom even uses pulp as a sort of how-to manual. Patrick discovers that one of the most dramatic moments of his affair with Tom has been a reenactment of a torrid pulp love scene:

> You certainly must have intended me to get the stunning surprise I did get when I reached that chapter where they go to Tunnel Cove—otherwise you'd have prepared me for it in advance. Of course, I know that hundreds of tourists must have walked through that tunnel and out on to the reef, so it really isn't strange that some writer should have hit on the idea of setting a scene there in a book. But that particular kind of scene and those particular characters! Tom, I've got to know this, *did you deliberately make us re-enact it*? It would be just like you, yes, I can believe it of you, it's exactly the sort of wonderful sweet idiotic crazy thing you *would* do. . . . I love the romantic silliness of your doing it, but at the same time I can't help feeling, to put it mildly, embarrassed! (83–84)

Isherwood is winking at his gay readers in the know by suggesting how textual this emerging gay identity is. Authentic passion may just be a construction from new, mass-produced texts.

Tom does more than reenact specific sexual acts, however. He also uses the gay pulps as a guide to finding love. Patrick becomes the romantic pulp hero incarnate for Tom:

> While I was reading the novel I suddenly remembered something—actually it was on the same night we got back from that trip, we were having dinner, and you told me that there was a character in a book you'd read that you used to think about a lot and hope one day you'd meet someone like him. The way you told me made it clear you meant that now you *had* met someone, and it was me. . . . But when I asked you about the book itself you smiled and got all mysterious. Now I realize that obviously the character was Lance in this novel. With all due respect to him, I must say I hope you consider

> me an improvement—because the way he talks is a bit overripe for my taste, and I don't greatly care to inherit the author's description of him as "faunlike"! (67)

Tom uses gay pulp as a model for his own romantic future and projects those fantasies onto Patrick, finally calling him at the monastery in India to declare his undying love.

It turns out that Patrick is not an improvement on Lance. Tom's mistake is simply this: Patrick is a character from a gay pulp, but he is the villain, not the romantic lead. Patrick was also based, at least partly, on Dell publisher Frank Taylor, the successful paperback editor who also branched into film and was, incidentally, a bisexual who chased beautiful boys but waxed rhapsodic about hearth and home.[12] One might suspect Isherwood of equating Patrick's literary and moral corruption, and the logic of the text supports this conclusion. Patrick is false, constructing multiple versions of himself for mother, wife, brother, and lover, and the reader discovers his elaborate lies to be both self-serving and unnecessary.

Consider Patrick's attempted corruption of his brother. He first tries to lead Oliver back to the flesh by a display of his own naked body:

> I walked into the room and found him stark naked. . . . He proceeded to do a lot of pushups, forty at least, and then about a dozen jumps, raising his arms and landing with his feet apart, then jumping to bring them together again. He did these jumps very deliberately, facing me and grinning at me, with his teeth looking whiter than ever in his flushed brown face. And I couldn't help being aware of his rather big penis slapping against his bare thigh as he jumped. Patrick always had a beautiful body and it is still in perfect shape, he must exercise all the time. You can tell that he's been lying in the sun completely nude. (70)

Oliver is reminded of "some corny scene in an old Russian novel, where the woman tempts the young monk" (71). But Isherwood's readers may well be reminded of key scenes from gay pulps, where naked seductions, with a "rather big penis," are common. Even the implied incest—Oliver later reveals, "When I was going through my Freudian phase, I used to wonder if I wasn't actually in love with him, romantically and even physically" (115)—has its counterpart in queer pulp.

Patrick reenacts his own gay pulp scene. Later, he appropriates the language of pulps. Patrick's ostensible confession to Oliver about his love affair with Tom turns into another opportunity for corruption and seduction. Oliver records:

> If I was shocked, it wasn't by Patrick's story but by the way he told it. When he started off, his language was very restrained, in fact it was sometimes almost comically formal. . . . But soon his tone changed and he began talking very frankly and using four-letter words with a sort of aggressive relish. For instance, he told me how Tom and he had driven to some deserted cove up the coast to the north for a weekend, and how they'd been on a rock right above the sea and Tom had grabbed hold of him and they had torn off each other's clothes. I suppose it was really a relatively ordinary scene of lust, but Patrick made it sound strangely horrible, uncanny and bestial, like two animals devouring each other alive. He described exactly what they did to each other, and I noticed once again how fetishistic the words can be that we use for sexual acts. It was as if the mere uttering of them was nearly as exciting to Patrick as the act itself. (143–44)

When Patrick decides to come clean, as it were, telling Oliver, "I need to know that you know this about me" (143), he struggles with the right language. In the middle of his discussion, he shifts from formal to salacious, borrowing language directly from his "much thumbed-through" gay pulp. With four-letter, fetishistic words, Patrick transforms this potentially life-changing experience into a titillating tale that, like the novel itself, gave him "a personal thrill, a sexual kick" (145). A major purpose of gay pulp novels is to make the words as exciting as the act and to invite the reader to join in. Indeed, Oliver believes that Patrick is trying to entice him. Isherwood suggests something about the political and cultural effect of these novels in the way in which they provided a model of coming out that was provocative, challenging, and performative.

Yet Patrick is not simply a villain and provocateur; he is also an embodiment of camp (a term that Isherwood made popular in his 1954 novel *The World in the Evening*).[13] He is superficial and facetious with everyone in his letters. His letter to his brother about his wife is a good case in point:

> She claimed that the news didn't surprise her in the least. Either she

> knows you a lot better than I do—from a different angle, *bien entendu*—or else she was showing off her feminine intuition! She sends you her love and says she hopes you'll return to England in due course and instruct her in The Way. She also asks if there's a Hindu order of nuns into which she may aspire to be received, because she wants to renounce the world as soon as the children have grown up. I accused her of simply wanting to renounce *me,* but this she denied hotly! (27)

Patrick's facetious tone here (exclamation points, capitalization) marks him as a camp character. Patrick is irreverent, gently mocking, flattering, and self-deprecating. He makes Oliver slightly ridiculous, solely through his facetious tone. His letters to his mother—"Certainly my prayers are no good to anyone, but my loving thoughts are with you as ever" (101)—show a gentler irony, while his letters to his wife are much more cutting: "I'm well aware that I'm making myself sound bitchy, not to say malicious" (107). Despite the constructions of multiple personas, the camp tone is consistent.

In his letters to Tom, Patrick confides that camp is meant to protect his "true" self, which includes the self that loves men. This comes into conflict with the emerging ethos Tom represent, one that would, in the 1970s, reject camp as self-hating: "I know how you hate any sort of pretence and concealment, and I admire you for that. But we must never forget, when we go against the majority, that we're forced to be like guerrillas, our chief weapon is cunning. We can't ever attack openly. That's just exactly what the enemy wants us to do, so he can destroy us. If we're bold and rash, we're simply putting a weapon into his hands. Defiance is a luxury we can't afford" (88).

The gay man as secret agent trope emerges; embodied by the deceptive Patrick, it becomes a suspect strategy, devious and ultimately false.[14] Patrick's elaboration on his technique emphasizes this: "We have to be cunning. There's nothing dishonourable in that, it can even be a lot of fun. We'll play a game against them, Tom, and we'll outfox them and laugh at them while we're doing it. Do you know, I have a feeling that playing this game is going to be what binds us together more than anything else? It'll be you and me against the world! And although we're its enemies, we'll make this idiot of a world accept us and admire us, perhaps reward us, even—that'll be our triumph and private joke!" (88). This notion of deception as a mad camp aligns Patrick with a pre-Stonewall gay ethos. Patrick briefly rejects this game of outfoxing when he imagines a life with Tom and a more positive and open gay identity, which emerges simultaneously, from his exposure to gay pulp and to the monastery. The forces that would lead to gay liberation and reject the dissembling of the "private joke" are bubbling in this novel, even if they do not win the day.

Conversely, Isherwood uses the structure and values of gay pulp to introduce his more serious pedagogical aims for Hinduism. For Isherwood, both Hinduism and homosexuality were minority consciousnesses. The two brothers must come out as cultural others, representing both Hinduism and homosexuality. *A Meeting by the River* provides encoded messages about gay pulp, but it is much more explicit in its primer about Hinduism. In fact, the novel spends considerable time defining Hindu terms: *Swami, sannyas, gerua, Mahanta, darshan.* It also defines key Hindu concepts, through Oliver's journal, through letters back home, and through dialogue between the two brothers.

Patrick's letter to his wife gives a good example of the novel's pedagogical strategy: "The Hindus believe that all one's work should be done symbolically, as though it was some kind of a religious ritual which has no practical usefulness, only intrinsic spiritual significance as an offering to the Supreme Being or whatnot—in other words, what's important is one's attitude to the performance of the action itself, not to its results—success and failure are regarded as equally irrelevant. (Forgive this clumsy exposition of what's probably kindergarten stuff to you; I only include it because it's part of the story.)" (107). Those asides justify definitions and theological explanations that Isherwood deemed essential to his story, but they also provide a roadmap of sorts for those interested in Hinduism. Readers learn how to greet an Indian holy man properly, what the colors of the robes mean, how key religious rituals happen and what they mean.

Victor Marsh argues that Isherwood's Hinduism was thoroughly enmeshed in his queer self-identification.[15] That enmeshment was, as Katherine Bucknell suggests, uniquely tied up in camp, in his appreciation of its rites, in its framing of guru/disciple relationships, even in its understanding of all human endeavor as ultimately trivial and meaningless. "In a sense," Bucknell argues, "*maya* itself is camp—it is the 'as if' world in quotes."[16] In his diary, Isherwood attributed his understanding of Hinduism to "having been around Swami so much *and* understanding camp."[17] Similarly, Patrick's campy persona prepares him to understand and embrace Hinduism, and sets up Isherwood's explicit pairing of camp and Hinduism.

Hindus and homos are linked in still other structural ways. Hinduism provides a model for symbolic paternal and fraternal bonds that Isherwood parallels and queers in the relationship between Patrick and Tom. This was a long-standing rhetorical gesture of Isherwood's; Tom McFarland notes that Isherwood described his relationship with the Swami Prabhavananda and with Don Bachardy in almost precisely the same terms: an absolute devotion untouched by jealousy or expectations. Isherwood had long been interested in younger men; Auden's letter to Isherwood in the 1940s, as they commiserated about their younger lovers, is revealing: "As you say, we Father-Shadows can only stand aside and pray."[18] But Hinduism transfigures that promiscuous coupling of fathers and sons from wolves and punks to gurus and disciples.

In his diary during the late 1960s, he described his relationship with Bachardy in just this way: "How *can* love be profane if it really is love? In my own case, hasn't my relation with Don now become my true means of enlightenment?"[19] In a later entry, he mused that "a householder's life is not simply that he is not a monk but that he loves a human being rather than God. So he must learn to love God through that human being."[20] Later, Isherwood clarified this idea in a longer passage:

> I realize more than ever that this is IT. Not just an individual, or just a relationship, but THE WAY. The way through to everything else. . . . Vivekananda writes, "Religion is the practice of oneness with the infinite, the principle that dwells in the hearts of all beings, through the feeling of love." If you are tuned in on personal love, then you are on the same wavelength as infinite love. There may be terrific interruptions from the static of egotism and possessiveness, but at least you *are* on the right wavelength and that's a tremendous achievement in itself.[21]

Isherwood's insistence that a personal and sexual relationship is a potential means to the divine elevates gay relationships to the status of religious ritual.

In some of Isherwood's own writing about Hinduism, he insists on the spirituality of sex, even sex that was not monogamous. Isherwood embraced devotion that must be devoid of possession or jealousy: "The love of God described by [the mythic sage] Narada is a love in which there can be no jealousy, no struggle of egos, no desire for material advantage or exclusive possession, no dread of desertion; a love which is incapable of unhappiness."[22] Isherwood's claim that one learns divine love through physical and emotional love pushes the boundaries of conventional morality. He imagined a transcendence that constructed homosexuality not as sinful deviance but as natural, multiple encounters with the Absolute. So he insisted in an interview with Carolyn Heilbrun:

> Why shouldn't you be completely promiscuous? If you could only appreciate the sacredness of one-night stands—and realize that these are all God's creatures, you know, they're all my brothers or sisters. . . . I don't see, theoretically, why there shouldn't be the most powerful sort of love, like St. Francis's, applied to one-night stands, where you really love a different person each night. But that's very advanced. . . . Really, to have that feeling, that you are overwhelmed with empathy and with love, not to mention lust, for a person that you just meet for a few hours, that's surely a *very* advanced state to be in. I can imagine that it'd be very near a kind of enlightenment.[23]

Isherwood's reframing of one-night stands, not as narcissism or exploitation but as a means to enlightenment, is one of the most radical aspects of his camp Hinduism. It is also a version of camp Hinduism that remained carefully veiled in his official statements on his faith.

But perhaps Isherwood's gestures toward queer fraternal bonds are radical enough in *A Meeting by the River*. Oliver establishes a Platonic cross-racial relationship, and Patrick forms a sexual Anglo-American relationship. When Oliver became a believer, he set up house with his Swami:

> It seemed odd to me at first, being in this relationship to an older man—partly, I suppose, because Father died when we were both so young, partly because I'd never lived with only one other person before, but always in institutions and communities, or by myself. The Swami took it quite for granted, however. And soon he began referring to me as his "disciple" . . . a disciple in the literal Hindu monastic

> sense, a novice monk who serves his guru and is trained by him like a son, and who will become a swami himself in due course. (20)

The father/son relationship is the model for the guru/disciple bond, one that can never be broken by the guru. Oliver's Swami tells him this explicitly: "Don't you know the Guru can never run away from his disciple, not even if he wants to, not in this life, not in any other!' When he said this, I was kneeling beside his bed straightening the bedclothes, and he put his hand on my head, and patted it. He didn't do this very often. I always felt it was a special kind of blessing" (52–53). Oliver's homosocial bond is celibate but intimate, and it violates a number of cultural taboos about relationships between men.

Patrick describes his relationship with Tom in strikingly similar terms, as an idyllic fraternal bond:

> I've told you how I've always been very much attached to my brother Oliver. . . . Tommy, since I had that dream, I'm certain that *you* could be my brother—the kind of brother I now know I've been searching for all these years, without ever quite daring to admit to myself what it was that I wanted. I suppose I was frightened off by the taboos which surround the idea of brotherhood in the family sense—oh yes, they encourage you to love your brother, but only as far as the limits they've set—beyond that, it's a deadly sin and a horror. What I want is a life beyond their taboos, in which two men learn to trust each other so completely that there's no fear and they experience and share everything together in the flesh and in the spirit. I don't believe such closeness is possible between a man and a woman—deep down they are natural enemies—and how many men ever find it together? Only a very few even glimpse the possibility of it, and only a very few out of that dare to try to find it. We are going to dare, aren't we? We must, Tom, or we shall never forgive ourselves. (131–32)

Patrick's articulation of a brotherly relationship as a model for gay partnership is close to Isherwood's own. It toys with incest taboos (remember Patrick's naked performance for Oliver), but more importantly, it insists that gay relationships are family relationships; as Elizabeth Freeman argues, "In queer life such gendered and even generational crossings, at least, are eminently possible."[24] Patrick's dream of a homosocial utopia parallels Oliver's own relationship with his Swami.

Indeed, utopian dreaming becomes prophetic vision for both Oliver and Patrick. In *A Meeting by the River*, the visions are not individual but partnered, revealing a homosocial ideal between men. Patrick's comes first and prompts his proposal to Tom:

> This was much more than a dream, it was so intense it was a sort of vision. I mean, there was a burning pleasure and then an utter fulfillment with you, nearly as good as that shattering moment we had together at Tunnel Cove. But the whole experience went far beyond just sex, it was actually a glimpse of a life which you and I were living together! That's why I call it a vision. Tom, I'm certain this wasn't an ordinary dream-fantasy built up out of memories of the past. Explain it any way you want, *I know* I was experiencing something which hasn't happened yet and perhaps never will happened, but which *could*. . . . I *can* tell you one thing—this life I got a glimpse of was of such a closeness as I'd never even imagined could exist between two human beings, because it was a life *entirely without fear*. (130–31)

Patrick sees a life in which gay relationships are—as they were for Isherwood—a means to spiritual enlightenment. The insistence, twice, that this is not simply a sex dream but a vision gives it an import and sympathy that even Patrick's unreliable narration cannot undermine.

Oliver has his own homosocial domestic vision the night before his ordination, when he was struggling with the decision to become a monk:

> Presumably it was a few moments before waking that I saw Swami. Yes, I can say I did literally see him, although this wasn't a vision in the waking state. But seeing him was only a part of the experience of his presence, which was intensely vivid, far more so than an ordinary dream. Also, unlike a dream, it didn't altogether end when I woke up. . . . We were domestically together as we used to be in the old ways. . . . I knew that Swami was "dead," and I knew that nevertheless he was now with me—*and that he is with me always, wherever I am*. . . . Now we are never separated. I woke up actually *knowing* that. (172–73)

Oliver discovers through his vision that he has found the perfect father—one who will never desert him, even after death. His is also a life entirely without fear, with a partnership that transcends death.

For both Hindus and homosexuals, however, making the word flesh is treacherous. Oliver doubts the reality of his relationship with the guru and almost leaves the monastery. Patrick does reject his vision, dumping Tom and returning to his wife and the double life of camp. Even Isherwood's quest for a "home self" was sometimes cagey and contradictory. He refers to gay pulp, but he does not commit its indiscretion; we do not hear the four-letter, fetishistic words. Patrick is a character who lends himself to a number of conventional interpretations; Isherwood cannot quite bring himself to embrace Patrick as a lovable antihero, in the way he could Mr. Norris (of *Mr. Norris Changes Trains*), Sally Bowles (of *Goodbye to Berlin*), or Paul (of *Down There on a Visit*). By framing his positive descriptions of homosexuality through a deceptive, callous adulterer, Isherwood undoes many of the embedded "happy, horny, and healthy" images derived from the pulps. It is too easy, by the end of the novel, to dismiss "a life lived entirely without fear." Isherwood was not quite ready, in 1967, to claim that the relationship between Patrick and Tom could be as spiritually productive as the relationship between Oliver and his guru.

Nor was Isherwood ever entirely comfortable talking about his faith. Marsh argues convincingly that Isherwood remained an ardent devotee, and found in Hinduism a solution to the spiritual dilemma queer men face. But he did so privately; publicly, he struggled to articulate this notion, even when he wrote his spiritual autobiography, *My Guru and His Disciple*, over fifteen years later (after his very public celebration as a gay writer had commenced). He wrote no fewer than eight versions of his afterword, and one discarded paragraph suggests his difficulty: "Having written it, my first reaction is a sort of defiant embarrassment. I realize how embarrassing, not to say gooey, this material will seem to many, perhaps most, of the people who read it. But then I become defiant and think, well, if it *isn't* embarrassing, that means it has no quality of shock. And if it's not shocking, then it can't really be any good, because nothing—no kind of so-called persuasion—could be as shocking as this material ought to be, if it really gets through to the reader in prime condition."[25] "Defiant embarrassment" is a useful term to describe Isherwood's relationship to faith in his public persona. But this is also the term he uses in his memoir *Christopher and His Kind* (1976) to describe his public relationship to his homosexuality. Coming out as both a Hindu and a homo was an ongoing struggle for Isherwood.

In the end, though, Isherwood redeems all the struggles of his characters—and perhaps his own. At the end of Oliver's vision, the Swami and Oliver speak about Patrick: "I'm to try to remember always, from this moment on, that Patrick is in Swami's care and in Swami's presence—even though he himself may be utterly unaware of it now and for some time to come. . . . No wonder Swami seemed amused! If you look at this objectively, it's a pretty comic situation. Poor old Paddy—he's in a state of grace! And he's going to discover it the hard way. He doesn't dream what he's in for, but he'll find out before long" (141–43). Isherwood's notion of grace, as he explained in his lecture "Divine Grace," was not about forgiveness or redemption but about enlightenment, which could come in any number of ways. But the result of that discernment was to go beyond conventional notions of morality: "My master told me that when I see, when I am in that mood, I see God playing in so many forms, God as a saint, God as a sinner, God in the wicked, God in the diabolical. That God playing, as it were, with different masks."[26] God can even be found in a campy, bisexual seducer. Not many novels offer gay characters a state of grace, even one so vaguely threatening and ironic. Hindus and homos find a détente of sorts in *A Meeting by the River*, a state of grace that redeems both in their oppositional identities.

At the end of the novel, Oliver takes his vows and becomes a monk, and Patrick bows down before him to take the dust from his feet. The final line unites homos and Hindus in a ritual of perfect acceptance and love: "And everybody was smiling and murmuring, as much as to say how charming it was of Patrick to play this scene according to our local Hindu rules, and how very right and proper it was that we two brothers should love each other."

# NOTES

A different version of this essay appears in my book *Middlebrow Queer: Christopher Isherwood in America* (Minneapolis: University of Minnesota Press, 2013). Excerpted with permission. An earlier, shorter version was delivered in 2010 at the annual meeting of the American Studies Association, as part of the panel "Rereading Queer Pulp: Commodities, Sexualities, and Social Change," sponsored by the Society for the History of Authorship, Reading, and Publishing.

1. Christopher Isherwood, *A Meeting by the River* (1967; Middlesex, England: Penguin Books, 1970), 38.
2. Isherwood, draft of *Down There on a Visit,* CI 3097 (carbon copy of CI 1056), Papers of Christopher Isherwood, 1864–1997, Manuscripts Department, Huntington Library, San Merino, CA (hereafter cited as Isherwood Papers).
3. Austin writes: "The sort of fiction that was neither published nor publishable is typified by a curious typewritten manuscript, 'Boys, Men, and Love,' by 'J. P. Starr,' dated 1925, and donated by Manuel boyFrank to the One, Inc. library in Los Angeles. . . . This 600-page work included some semi-erotic short stories in the form of personal narratives." Roger Austin, *Playing the Game: The Homosexual Novel in America* (Indianapolis: Bobbs-Merrill, 1977), 47. Simon Sheppard includes two mimeographed stories dating from 1945 and 1950 in his anthology *Homosex: Sixty Years of Gay Erotica* (New York: Carroll & Graf, 2007), 1–16. Philip Clark discusses samizdat in "The First King of Pornography: H. Lynn Womack and Washington D.C.'s Guild Press," in *The Golden Age of Gay Fiction,* ed. Drewey Wayne Gunn (Albion, NY: MLR Press, 2009), 93. See also the essays by Clark and Whitney Strub elsewhere in this volume.
4. Isherwood, *Diaries, Volume 1: 1939–1960,* ed. Katherine Bucknell (New York: HarperCollins, 1996), 822; Isherwood, "Afterwards," unpublished manuscript, July 9–July 31 1959, CI 1015, Isherwood Papers
5. Michael Bronski, ed., *Pulp Friction: Uncovering the Golden Age of Gay Male Pulps* (New York: St. Martin's Griffin, 2003), 199.
6. Victor J. Banis, "The Gay Publishing Revolution," in Gunn, *Golden Age of Gay Fiction,* 117.
7. Isherwood, *Diaries, Volume 2: 1960–1969,* ed. Katherine Bucknell (London: Chatto & Windus, 2010), 485. The books that he names are Oscar Peck, *Sex Life of a Cop* (Fresno, CA: Saber Books, 1967); Chris Davidson, *Go Down, Aaron* (San Diego: Greenleaf Classics, 1967); Oscar Wilde (attributed), *Teleny* (North Hollywood, CA: Brandon House, 1967); Dennis Drew, *Like Father, Like Son* (San Diego: Publisher's Export Co., 1967); Carl Corley, *A Fool's Advice* (San Diego: Publisher's Export Co., 1967); and Aaron Thomas, *The Beefcake Boys* (San Diego: Greenleaf Classics, 1967).
8. Justin Spring, *Secret Historian: The Life and Times of Samuel Steward, Professor, Tattoo Artist, and Sexual Renegade* (New York: Farrar, Straus & Giroux, 2010), 362. For more on Phil Andros see Ann Marie Schott's essay elsewhere in this volume.
9. J. Watson [Larry Townsend], *The Sexual Adventures of Sherlock Holmes* (New York: Olympia Press, 1971).
10. Peter Parker, *Isherwood: A Life Revealed* (New York: Random House, 2004), 669, 686. I thank Drewey Wayne Gunn for pointing out the connection between Hoban and Hardy.
11. Isherwood, *A Meeting by the River,* 22. Further page references will be cited parenthetically in the text.
12. Isherwood, *Lost Years: A Memoir, 1945–1951,* ed. Katherine Bucknell (New York: Harper Collins, 2001), 169.
13. Isherwood, *The World in the Evening* (1954; Minneapolis: University of Minnesota Press, 1999), 110–11.
14. The "secret agent trope" was a common gesture of gay identity before Stonewall. In an environment when simply being gay was viewed as treasonous, and faced with oppressive laws and social disapproval, many gay men spoke in code and

imagined themselves, ironically or otherwise, as members of a secret society innately opposed to mainstream American values. For more on this topic, see Jaime Harker, *Middlebrow Queer: Christopher Isherwood in America* (Minneapolis: University of Minnesota Press, 2013), chap. 6.

15. Victor Marsh, *Mr. Isherwood Changes Trains: Christopher Isherwood and the Search for the "Home Self"* (Melbourne: Clouds of Magellan, 2010), 15, 87, 143. For more on Isherwood's relationship to Hinduism, see A. R. H. Copley, *A Spiritual Bloomsbury: Hinduism and Homosexuality in the Lives and Writings of Edward Carpenter, E. M. Forster, and Christopher Isherwood* (Lanham, MD: Lexington Books, 2006), 183–272; and Jeffrey Paine, *Father India: How Encounters with an Ancient Culture Transformed the Modern West* (New York: HarperCollins, 1998), 193–226.
16. Katherine Bucknell, "Introduction," *Diaries, Volume 2*, xxviii.
17. Isherwood, *Diaries, Volume 2*, 232.
18. Tom McFarland, "'Always Dance': Sex and Salvation in Isherwood's Vedantism," in *The Isherwood Century: Essays on the Life and Work of Christopher Isherwood*, ed. James J. Berg and Chris Freeman (Madison: University of Wisconsin Press, 2000), 243; W. H. Auden to Isherwood, June 23, 1943, CI 2992, Isherwood Papers.
19. Isherwood, *Diaries, Volume 2*, 465.
20. Ibid., 486.
21. Ibid., 511.
22. Isherwood, *The Wishing Tree: Christopher Isherwood on Mystical Religion*, ed. Robert Adjemian (New York: Harper & Row, 1987), 75–76.
23. Carolyn G. Heilbrun, "Christopher Isherwood: An Interview" (1976), in *Conversations with Christopher Isherwood*, ed. James J. Berg and Chris Freeman (Jackson: University Press of Mississippi, 2001), 143.
24. Elizabeth Freeman, "Queer Belongings: Kinship Theory and Queer Theory," in *A Companion to Lesbian, Gay, Bisexual, Transgender, and Queer Studies*, ed. George E. Haggerty and Molly McGarry (New York: Blackwell, 2007), 295–314, quotation on 310.
25. Isherwood, draft of afterword to *My Guru and His Disciple*, CI 1114, Isherwood Papers.
26. Isherwood, "Divine Grace," CI 1038, Isherwood Papers.

# Transcendent Submission

## RESISTANCE TO OPPRESSION IN JAY GREENE'S *BEHIND THESE WALLS*

Nicholas Alexander Hayes

Brooks Peters, in his blog devoted to gay pulp books, describes buying the novel *Pretty Boy* by Jay Greene when he was a youth. Brooks reveals the titillation and arousal associated with encountering his first pulp novel. In addition to homoerotic content, Peters recognized that "Jay Greene had a perverse genius for contrasting fantasies of gay utopia with the hypocrisy of civilized society." Many pulp authors embraced the fact that " 'happily ever after' became a possibility they could choose" even if the "prospect was perhaps romantically unrealistic," as Victor Banis puts it in his essay "The Gay Publishing Revolution."[1] Greene's pessimistic vision resists the cultural acceptance and eventual expectation of such endings that developed throughout the late 1960s and 1970s. His first novel (if one can go by the series numbers Midwood Press assigned its books), *Behind These Walls*, typifies the way the author contrasts individual desires and social restrictions. It prepares the reader for the world Greene explored in eighteen novels published with Midwood between 1968 and 1972, with two more to appear in 1976.[2] Perhaps it is his acute social critique that, more than anything else, accounts for the high regard that so many gay pulp aficionados feel for Greene's body of work. Although he is not widely known, his readers recognize him as one of the true masters of the genre.

Fellow pulp author Roland Graeme sums up Greene's oeuvre: "His body of work is unique for its style, his ability to tell a story, and above all for his predominately dark, pessimistic vision."[3] Peters corroborates Graeme's assessment: "It is a dark, vicious world out there, according to Jay Greene. . . . And one risked utter ruin and rejection by surrendering to one's secret yearnings." To reveal this vision, Greene places his characters in physically and emotionally destructive environments. Still, despite the seeming impossibility of enduring happiness, the author assures his readers, "A moment [of pleasure] can be forever."[4] This vision of the world is already fully articulated in *Behind These Walls*. There we watch this dark dynamic play out within the physical features of the Seneca County Reformatory for Boys (the novel's main setting), whose agents control young men and their delinquent activities even as the inmates of the reformatory temporarily resist that control through acts of pleasure and submission to their lovers. In the creation of this fictional world, Greene was working his way toward much the same understanding of the prison world as a microcosm for society that Michel Foucault would articulate in *Surveiller et punir* (1975), translated into English as *Discipline and Punish* (1977). A more literal translation of the French title would be "Watch and Punish," emphasizing the relationship between observation and control, a social aspect that Greene elaborates on in his narratives.

The protagonists of Greene's novels contend with the limitations of their physical environments and the emotional oppression they impose, even though their resistance is inherently a lost cause. The futility of resistance highlights Greene's nonacceptance of the two nascent utopias of contemporaneous gay pulp: the one in which love overcomes all impediments and the one of perpetual sensual immersion. His rejection functions as an extended commentary on the structural circumscriptions of discourse and society. For Greene, these restrictions are most clearly represented by reformatories and boarding schools, settings he frequently returns to.[5] In a chapter titled "Docile Bodies," Foucault elaborates on the shift from the concept of the heroic body to the moldable body in a variety of socially endorsed institutions, including monasteries, barracks, factories, schools, and other institutions of discipline.[6] Greene's protagonists struggle against agents who inherited the concept of discipline: teachers, guards, institutional functionaries. Foucault further notes that architectural design and use of space and time help these agents discipline the body so that it might become useful.

Greene's protagonists demonstrate that despite the author's rejection of gay utopias, he is neither a defeatist toward nor an apostate of the forces of gay liberation. Central to the role of the main characters in a Greene novel is a position in which they defy the forces of discipline and refuse docility. Foucault observes, "A body is docile that may be subjected, used, transformed, and improved" (136). While certainly Greene's boys are subjected and used, they only transform based on acceptance of their individuality. This acceptance, even if short lived, provides a position from which they can resist the agents of multifarious disciplinary institutions. Foucault summarizes the central force of a disciplinary institution after enumerating its numerous functions: "In short, it *normalizes*" (183). The crisis points in many of Greene's novels indicate moments of contentment being provided in the struggle against normalization and the physical locations and social pressures that inculcate it.

Greene, in his novel *The Cadets*, describes the way structural restrictions shape social interactions: "Everything was programmed, cut-and-dried. Nothing could happen spontaneously. Life had to be lived according to rules set down by some giant machine which had long ago taken over the responsibility of thinking for people, of governing their actions, of planning their very lives."[7] The antagonistic settings of his novels reveal how the direct disciplining that occurs in such environments is emblematic of larger societal disciplining of identities, especially sexual identities, through various technologies of power. In *Behind These Walls*, Greene engages in a discussion of these technologies even as he recounts the erotic adventures of juvenile delinquents: "The state legislature was of the opinion that a sound program of rehabilitation through job training would prepare the boys at Seneca for 'useful and productive lives' once they left the reformatory. Consequently, when the compound was built, the original intention was for it to be more like a vocational trade school than a juvenile workhouse."[8] Greene indicates that it is important for the reader to understand that the main setting of the novel is built upon the legacy of incarceration as it developed in the eighteenth century and was manifested in the American penal system. This heritage is even represented in the fact that *reformatory* has at its etymological roots the impetus to reform, to form again, to remold.

The legislature's plan, which originally included educational spaces, vocational programs, and highly trained staff, represented a belief in the ability to improve an individual through discipline. Greene then notes, "After the first few years of operation under this system, however, the legislature found that maintenance of the program was costing far more than they were willing to allot in the state's yearly budget and follow-up reports on boys who had left showed astonishingly poor results" (47). The legislature brings in a new regime at the reformatory, halving the budget at the cost of the higher educational aims and social reform. Greene indicates that the technologies of power devolve into an acephalic state, and means of control are maintained out of inertia. The mechanics of these systems interfere with gay utopic visions. The reformatory still attempts to render the inmates "useful and productive," yet the new use and productivity expected from the boys is rooted in cultivating and exploiting delinquency rather than reforming and reintroducing the inmates to society.

In such oppressive discursive environments, pleasure alone cannot provide a permanent exit since it is implicated in a struggle against the larger inequities of society. Foucault elaborates on the conditions that prevent pleasure from being a means of escape: "In discipline, punishment is only one element of a double system: gratification-punishment" (180). Inherently, pleasure carries with it the essence of gratification, which locks it into the dialectic of discipline. Oppressive environments shape pleasure (even in its frequently illicit forms); inmates who become lovers are often cellmates, students who passionately embrace are often dorm mates. Greene presents a precarious promise in the failed acts of resistance through sex: a better life is possible, but not for those who are trapped in injurious social institutions.

The reformatory that is the setting of *Behind These Walls* provides a physical environment that allows Greene to comment on restrictions and resistance. The protagonist, Skip Harding, introduces a poignant conflict because his actions are informed by an inchoate understanding of how racial and class bias reinforce the larger system of restrictions and the application of power. Throughout the book, Skip struggles to form and preserve an emotional connection with his abused African American roommate, Leroy. The restrictive space and Skip's burgeoning view of identity and sexuality both shape and hinder the romantic discourse between the two young men. Skip witnesses similar pressures in the developing relationship between another inmate, Paul, and Paul's roommate, Rick. Representatives of the reformatory's official power structure, the guard MacGloughlin (Mac) and the cafeteria supervisor Grizzy, destroy the possibility for these emotionally supportive relationships to endure. The harmful functions of these representatives are further aided by the architecture of the reformatory and the social inequities of other inmates (in particular the effeminate Charles.)

More so than in most cases, the novel's cover clues readers in to the structural elements of the world they are about to enter. Pulp novels, of course, whether dealing with gay, lesbian, or straight subjects, did not sell based on reviews but by their covers, which in general offered salacious images designed to incite a potential reader's prurient interest, often with no regard for the actual contents of the book. But the designers at Midwood seem to have actually been aware of the content of *Behind These Walls*, and the uncredited artist opted for sexual subtlety and honestly tried to suggest the pathos that charges the novel and some of the apparatuses that Greene used to structure his narrative.[9] The photographic image is claustrophobic. A man in a denim shirt stands with crossed arms. He glares down at a shirtless man, who reclines on his side, fingers nonchalantly held to his lips, glancing up at the standing figure as if in desire. The standing figure dominates the half-naked, seemingly vulnerable figure. Although their attire and positions hint at a gay theme, there is none of the campy or blatant homoeroticism found in so many pulps. The lack of these elements reinforces the book's refusal to incorporate themes of joyous and unencumbered love or sexual release. A single naked bulb dangles halfway down the cover, just to the left of the standing man. The light radiates across the cover, opening the space to the tension of the figures. A stucco wall fills the background. The room lacks an exit. There is no suggestion of deeper space; everything is reduced to the shallowness of surface. The cover's depiction of an interpersonal relationship determined by space and lighting is emblematic of the subjects and elements of setting that influence the narrative.

The image does not read exclusively as an image of incarceration, but the front cover text establishes the setting: "The compelling story of young boys in prison." Inside the book Greene issues a disclaimer and establishes the literal insignificance and symbolic significance of the setting: "The Seneca County Reformatory for Boys is, of course, a product of my imagination. It bears no actual resemblance to any such institution to my knowledge and should not be thought of as anything more than a metaphor for the prison in which we all live—are all inmates confined for crimes against each other—whether we admit these offenses or not" (5). Although the disclaimer speaks metaphorically, Greene's imagined milieu for the young men and their restrictions and resistance prefigures Foucault's analysis of actual places of incarceration in *Discipline and Punish*. In particular, the depiction of the delinquency that led to his characters' incarceration resonates with Foucault's argument that "the establishment of a delinquency that constitutes something like an enclosed illegality has in fact a number of advantages" (279). The agents of control who are embodied in the novel by Mac and Grizzy manage the inmates' delinquency by limiting, controlling, and utilizing illegality. Greene illustrates how the penal system in *Behind These Walls* reduces agency to delinquency before reappropriating its now perverted energies into the apparatus of physical and emotional control. The damage inflicted on these boys represents a tool that can make their delinquency useful for the reformatory. Yet Greene reminds the reader that institutional systems of abuse and control can be temporarily resisted through selfless submission to another's pleasure.

The reformatory's original mandate to turn convicted youths into "useful and productive members of society" is accentuated by the orderly and efficient design of its grounds.[10] The staff deliberately make use of the architecture to limit both normative and illicit activities of the inmates. Foucault notes that "the infinitely scrupulous concern with surveillance is expressed in the architecture by innumerable petty mechanisms" (173). Control, often pinioned to surveillance, of the inmates is essential for the staff, and they use any aspect of the reformatory—sleeping arrangements, bathroom protocols, work stations—to exert it. On the surface, the imposed limitations are meant to prevent antisocial behavior and hinder illegality by providing staff with continuous access to the inmates so they can observe and intervene in the boys' activities. True to Greene's pessimistic vision, the staff use this access to cultivate and utilize the boys' delinquency for their own benefit. One physical component of the reformatory that illustrates the way the architecture and rules work in tandem to provide access to the inmates is the doors. Although the doors have no locks, the boys are conditioned not to leave their rooms at night except to go to the bathroom by themselves. The proscription is so ingrained in the inmates that they will not break it even when it comes to evading or preventing violence. Of course, the non-normative behaviors the staff cultivate in, cajole from, and force on the boys are mostly compulsory homosexual acts.

Grizzy's use of his kitchen typifies the way the reformatory's space is used to control the inmates. When Skip is brought to the kitchen for his work assignment, Grizzy tells Skip that he can make the boy's life easier if he submits to the older man's sexual advances. An acceptance of Grizzy's overtures would provide evidence that Skip has internalized the social apparatus. Skip, however, resists the cook's advances despite the threat of retaliation. In order to force the boy into compliance, Grizzy sends Skip to the sweat box, a cruelly designed washing station where the boys are locked in and forced to endure the relentless steam and filth produced by cleaning the cafeteria's dishes. As Skip's sense of self is eroded by the exhausting work, the space and its function fracture his will: "By the time [Skip] heard a rattle outside the door, he was ready to submit to whatever it was the simple-minded cook wanted. Nothing, he told himself, would be as horrible as this" (109). In the context of the Seneca County Reformatory, as Foucault writes of institutions of discipline, "the individual body becomes an element that may be placed, moved, articulated on others. Its bravery or its strength are no longer the principal variables that define it; but the place it occupies, the interval it covers, the regularity, the good order according to which it operates its movements" (164). In Greene's environment, the regulation of the body takes a destructive turn. Although he does illustrate a disciplining of the body through restrictions, this process wears down the boys' inherently noble virtues: their brave resistance, their loving strength. For Greene the bodies and psyches of his young men are still more worthy of desire when they possess "strength and bravery" as their moral core. Throughout the narrative, he depicts how something essentially human and compassionate is lost through the development of discipline and use of physicality by authority figures.

The lighting in the dormitories illustrates another way the architecture of the reformatory is used to manipulate the actions of the boys. A master switch controls all the lights except for those in the halls. In contrast to the mutable lighting of the dorm rooms, the row of naked bulbs in the hall burns continuously, casting eerie light underneath the boys' doors (69). The hall lighting serves as a reminder of the lack of control the boys have; the constant light acts as a demarcation between the semiprivate space in which the boys have a modicum of free action and the public space in which they lack any control. Foucault observes, "Visibility is a trap" (200). The inmates are certainly more vulnerable to institutionalized violence since they are always potentially viewed. The guards can also deprive the boys of the use of semiprivate spaces because they control the light in the dorm rooms. The loss of freedom includes both the physical limitations of moving in darkness and the institutional regulation of going to sleep at lights out. Thus the control of lighting exemplifies the subjugation of the inmates to their guards. In one of the dormitories, the guard Mac has asserted near-total control of his charges. In large part, Mac's power is displayed by his control of the master light switch and its ability to limit the use of the boys' living space.

Despite its oppressive function, the architectural space does not entirely act to crush inmates; it provides objects of desire for the boys, thus revealing another way in which discipline engages with a gratification-punishment system. The space determines which inmates will have consensual sex and share the pleasures that allow them to resist the prohibitive pressures of the reformatory. Sleeping arrangements preordain the two main love stories that thread their way through the book. These romances represent forms of opposition to the staff's methods of control since they provide relationships in which the inmates can act on their own volition. But the master switch that controls the lighting limits the activities of the boys when they are in their private space and affects the speed and quality of their encounters. When the lights go off, the boys are supposed to go to sleep. Even when they fight this imperative, their action is limited. The noises of sex are not always muffled; the noises of violence are easily discerned. The sounds that accompany these actions add an element of menace to frequently tense situations because it allows the guards knowledge of illicit behavior, which in turn becomes an opportunity for the staff to interject violence to align the boys to the reformatory's official and unofficial behavioral imperatives.

One example of how Greene demonstrates this use of institutional space occurs on Skip's first night at the reformatory (73–81). In what he assumes to be the privacy of his room, Skip watches his African American roommate, Leroy, undress. At first, Skip thinks that he should avert his gaze; he wants to respect the space Leroy occupies. But Skip cannot escape that he, too, occupies the space, and he realizes that they must find a way to coexist in their assigned space. He longs for Leroy's body, but this is no romance premised on equality and love. Nor is it the interracial titillation found in many pulps of the period. The inescapable fact remains that their romance (just like that of their neighbors Paul and Rick) is premised on the accessibility to one particular body provided by their assignment to the same room. Despite the aleatory nature of their desires, once they negotiate their access to pleasure they are able to create a meaningful engagement. The relationships between inmates that Greene describes resonates with Foucault's observations that institutions of correction produce delinquency and provide a space in which delinquents form mutually beneficial social bonds.[11]

The initial violence between inmates eventually transforms into sexual pleasure that allows the incarcerated young men to defy the physically exhausting and emotionally deadening activities the reformatory's structure elicits.[12] This violence also serves as a way for inmates to negotiate sexual access. Skip and Leroy's story dominates the narrative and provides the clearest example of the dynamics at play in such negotiations. On Skip's first night at the reformatory, Leroy assumes that his new roommate has asserted desire for him in their shared space. He is often gazed upon as an object and sets up a zone of hostility to prevent forced degradation. Leroy covets the dominant position in the room since it is the only space where he cannot be objectified, racially or sexually. To this end, he messes up Skip's bunk to show dominance. The boys negotiate the tension over the space through fighting. But before the fight begins in earnest, the lights are shut off, signaling that the reformatory's functionaries retain the ultimate control of the space. In the middle of the fight, Skip thinks, "*Why? Why do we have to fight? Why can't we . . . love?*" (81). Both boys seem to share this idea concurrently. It provokes an intensification of the fighting as they attempt to extinguish their desires through conflict. Rolling on top of each other, they are almost at the point of transforming hostility into eroticism. Finding an erotic understanding becomes a way to co-occupy this space. For an instant violence seems futile, and an erotic expenditure would seem to become an acceptable form of discourse for the roommates.

To highlight the inevitable triumph of institutional restrictions, Greene does not permit this attempt at pleasurable and meaningful intercourse to play out. Mac enters the room before either Skip or Leroy can act on their emotional connection. The guard's actions foreshadow the eventual dissolution of all joyous unions in *Behind These Walls*. The inherent hostility is akin to Foucault's assertion about the perception of homosexuality that "people can tolerate the pleasure, but they can't accept the happiness."[13] Mac escorts Leroy to the dormitory bathroom and rapes him. The two homosexual acts are paired with violence, yet the institutional forces act only to suppress the one that could result in happiness. But Greene also permits the reader to see that this violation serves as a reminder that although the boys were in contention over access to the space, true control of the space is only granted to the functionaries of the reformatory. The rape scene shows that at an institutional level consensual sexual activity has more barriers and restrictions than sexual violence and exploitation. To this end, Greene allows Skip to bond with Leroy only after Leroy has been sexually brutalized. This sequence of events is in keeping with the novel's general thwarting of actions that are simply joyous or mutually beneficial. The location of Leroy's rape seems like a cruel reminder of this point. At night, the inmates are only allowed to leave their rooms to walk to the communal bathroom, and only one boy at a time may go. This restriction has been put in place to limit fraternizing and other problematic behaviors that might lead to consensual homosexual activities. The bathroom retains its alternate potential as a location for sex, despite the reformatory's regulation, yet the lack of an accepted or acknowledged prohibition of rape allows the room's potential to further service the institutional elements of control instead of the individual drives to pleasure and resistance.

Not only architectural features, but inmates themselves are used to reinforce the reformatory's control. Mac leverages willing agents of delinquency against young men who resist institutional restrictions. Foucault contends that "delinquency, with the secret agents that it procures, but also with the generalized policing that it authorizes, constitutes a means of perpetual surveillance of the population" (281). Mac's main sexual interest, Charles, reveals the ways in which the reformatory mirrors the Foucauldian thought by pressuring an illegal body into service of the system of oppression. As an effeminate homosexual, Charles (also referred to as Petunia) possesses a delinquent body that is particularly vulnerable to institutionalized abuses. To preserve his existence, Charles serves the staff by manipulating other boys into undermining their own forms of resistance. His plotting, like Mac's violence, serves the reformatory's implicit objective of controlling inmates. He plots against all of the young lovers (Skip and Leroy, Paul and Rick), undermining their attempts at resistance through emotional connection and sexual pleasure. Charles uses his body and gossip as a seductive and corrosive force against those who continue to resist the social constraints of imprisonment. Perhaps because their purposes are aligned, Mac takes a genuine gratification in being with Charles. Their relationship does not hold love, but there is an analogous characteristic in it: Mac dominates the willing Petunia, who in turn subtly manipulates Mac. Their social functions are interlocked and self-enforcing. The way their relationship functions is best illustrated in the scheme to exploit Skip toward the end of the novel. Charles tells Mac that Paul was servicing Skip in the kitchen—a lie that Grizzy has told to excite Charles. The fey boy uses this gossip to sway the guard into forcing Skip to join their sexual exploits (145). And once the object of their oppression, Skip, has been positioned, he undergoes brutalization that surpasses even the rape to which Leroy is subjected.

In contrast to Mac's aptness at handling willing inmates, Grizzy is not always successful at controlling the boys and their delinquency. His occasional failures are exemplified in his seduction of the inmate Paul. Afterward the cook is unable to continue manipulating the boy or use him to control other boys, for Paul rejects the cook's further advances. The seduction is only possible in the first place because Paul has not yet been able to negotiate a sexually equitable relationship with his roommate, Rick. During the act, Grizzy conflates the boy with a serviceman whom he once craved. After the boy is quick to ejaculate, Grizzy says, " 'The Bull' was that way, too . . . the first time. Maybe that's a good name for you: 'Baby Bull!' You like that, boy? Wanna be my 'Baby Bull?' " (60–61). This scene can be illuminated by Foucault's argument that "in a disciplinary regime . . . individualization is 'descending': as power becomes more anonymous and more functional, those on whom it is exercised tend to be more strongly individualized; it is exercised by surveillance rather than ceremonies, by observation rather than commemorative accounts, by comparative measures" (193). Grizzy's overlay of one man on the other deprives Paul of his name. The cook marks his motivating objective of desire as anonymous (without a name or without a specific name), or at least synonymous (having the same name), by calling Paul "Baby Bull." Paul certainly is not the authority figure in this scene, but neither is Grizzy. The cook's nostalgic desires frame him, more so than Paul, as a possessor of punishable desires—indicated by his discharge from the navy. The revelation that the reformatory's functionaries can fail the institutional imperative to totally control the inmates is one way that Greene illustrates the social complexity in a setting that could easily render characters as caricatures of victimizers and victims. With the exception of this incidental success with Paul, Grizzy is better able to make his charges pliant through the use of the sweat box. This narrative element reinforces the linkage between architecture and the staff's ability to use force.

The reformatory staff (even those members who are not directly culpable in sexual exploitation) tacitly tolerate the use of violence because it reinforces the mandate to shape and control the inmates and their value. In one scene, the reformatory's director shows explicit trust in Mac's judgment on the fate of Leroy (whom Mac has just raped). The molestations undermine resistance to institutional objectives by devaluing the erotic energies of the boys. These energies threaten the integrity of the reformatory because they temporarily liberate the inmates from the physical pressures of the architecture and the staff through sexual pleasure and emotional connection. In this context, Grizzy is able to show how he effectively serves the institution. The methods of forcing the boys into sex follows a pattern of use outlined in *Discipline and Punish:* "To begin with, there was the scale of the control: it was a question not of treating the body, en masse, 'wholesale,' as if it were an indissociable unity, but of working it 'retail,' individually; of exercising upon it a subtle coercion, of obtaining holds upon it at the level of the mechanism itself—movements, gestures, attitudes, rapidity: an infinitesimal power over the active body" (136–37). Although sexual abuse happens throughout the institution, it is specifically manifested as violence against a single body at a time. The individual nature of the abuse emphasizes its isolating power. The methods of control target individuals in order to render them more malleable to the reformatory's pressures. Further, when the cook convinces an inmate to submit to his sexual advances in exchange for not having to wash dishes, he effectively forces the boy to devalue his sexual impulse, potentially damaging the boy's ability to use it to form emotional connections and to resist the dehumanizing influence of the reformatory. Skip only refuses the older man's offer because he is in the process of forming a bond with Leroy. But after the cook forces him into the sweat box for several hours, Skip is ready to express his willingness to trade real emotional connection for less grueling work. Grizzy's engagement in such commerce serves to illustrate that the delinquency of the boys is socially useful through their conversion into commodities.

Commodification of the boys represents one of methods the staff of the Seneca County Reformatory has to access the usefulness of the inmates' delinquency. It also represents a force that boys attempt to resist. The boys are aware of their exchangeable status, which further complicates their attempt to use sexuality as a tool for resistance (and critiques the sexual liberation ethos even as it is happening). This knowledge gives their struggle an added poignancy. For instance, Skip acknowledges he slept with men for rides and food when he traveled before his incarceration. The economic exchange superseded the pleasure the boy could obtain from these encounters. Even his arrest is precipitated by his status as a commodity. Police discover him and an older man who has agreed to pay the boy $10 for sexual services outside a bus station (13–18). The authorities focus judicial attention on Skip because his age and lower economic status prevent him from possessing a viable agency. In contrast, the authorities find no need to punish the middle-aged, middle-class family man who has solicited Skip because the man's status signals he is an agent of the same normative power structure as the police. Foucault concludes that the penal system differentiates between certain groups: "Penality would then appear to be a way of handling illegalities, of laying down the limits of tolerance, of giving free rein to some, of putting pressure on others, of excluding a particular section, of making another useful, of neutralizing certain individuals, and of profiting from others" (272). The institutional forces consciously seek to mark the boys as objects. After his conviction and assignment to service in the reformatory's kitchen, Skip consciously rebuffs Grizzy not because the older man seeks to use him or disgusts him—Skip has slept with worse on the road. He resists his status as commodity and the control the institution tries to exert because he has a connection with Leroy. Skip's status and fight against it, I think, resembles nothing so much as Georges Bataille's description of an Aztec sacrificial victim: "Being a thing, he cannot truly be withdrawn from the real order, which binds him, unless destruction rids him of his 'thinghood,' eliminating his usefulness once and for all."[14] Skip's defiance indicates his inevitable destruction by the pressures at the reformatory, when the stark violence that defeats his resistance shatters the young inmate's psyche, sending him into a rigid, catatonic state as the novel ends.

Resistance culminates with the realization that selfless submission to a lover can temporarily alleviate the forces of institutional oppression for the boys who populate Greene's novels. In this spirit, Skip struggles to explain the nature of their oppression to Leroy on their first night together. Although miscommunication dominates Skip's first attempt at unmasking the discourse, his basic sympathies and sensitivities eventually convert Leroy to acts of selflessness. After Leroy's rape, Skip enacts Greene's thesis that willful submission to someone else who is oppressed strengthens resolve against all oppression. He first exposes himself emotionally to his roommate by revealing that he hustled for money and food. Skip argues that their actions have been limited and controlled by people with power, but Leroy does not quite believe Skip's position that oppression occurs regardless of race. Skip still wants to demonstrate love to Leroy because he believes it will allow them to resist the institutional forces that control them, and he convinces Leroy to let him perform nonreciprocal oral sex. Through this act Skip demonstrates his selflessness, and although Leroy's sexual gratification does not immediately enlighten him, it is the catalyst for a transformation away from hypersensitive reaction to selfless interaction. Paul faces a similar surrender. When his roommate and lover, Rick, forces him into anal intercourse, Paul escapes into the fantasy of selfless surrender to preserve his identity and his love for Rick. Paul recalls "the old saying" that if one is raped one should lie back and enjoy it. He accepts the assault and realizes that it is not in fact a punishment—it is another expression of selfless subservience, another form of resistance to the bleakness of their lives in the reformatory. In another of Greene's novels, one of his characters puts it this way: "To be loved you must be hurt."[15] This formula encapsulates the way loving relationships begin and end in Greene's vision of the world. Still, the loving, willing submission to another between the initial and final thresholds provides tempered joy and resistance to the various methods of institutional control.

Selflessness is the most essential grace in Greene's work, but it is a precarious quality. Skip's willingness to please Leroy without thinking of his own pleasure represents the crucial element for resistance available to the oppressed in Greene's world. Leo Bersani, in *Homos,* describes similar interactions: "Masochistic jouissance is hardly a political corrective to the sadistic use of power, although the self-shattering I believe to be inherent in that jouissance, although it is the result of surrender to the master, also makes the subject unfindable as an object of discipline."[16] Even though the surrender that lovers in Greene's books undergo is no more masochistic than that of any star-crossed lovers, their particular surrender does allow for a fight against complete objectification. Yet the element of genuine resistance wavers in Leroy's psyche, and he reverts to viewing himself and Skip as objects of discipline. The day after their first sexual encounter, Skip's unexplained sullenness troubles Leroy. He incorrectly interprets his roommate's lower level of social engagement as evidence that another white man used him. Upset, Leroy takes comfort in reminiscing about a Puerto Rican man who would fellate and then pay him. His acceptance of his role as a commodity causes him further frustration, since Skip did not even pay him. Without faith in Skip's form of struggle and without monetary compensation, Leroy has no proof of the value of his experience with his fellow inmate. Unable to immediately integrate the new potential valence of sexual activity, Leroy returns to a base conception of sex informed by the implementation of force at the institution. He grudgingly becomes obedient to the organizing concepts of the reformatory (even though he fights the staff's attempts at direct physical control of him).

Leroy's return to acceptance of the prevailing conceptual order is not surprising since, as Foucault comments on the Panopticon (the place of potentially perpetual surveillance), "This architectural apparatus should be a machine for creating and sustaining a power relation independent of the person who exercises it; in short, that the inmates should be caught up in a power situation of which they are themselves the bearers" (201). Essentially, the apparatus of power is psychologically internalized, and this apparatus manifests in Leroy as a debased understanding of sex. Leroy overcomes his conceptual obedience in the final scenes of the novel. Frustrated after a day in which he had to clean the scene of his own rape, he assumes that Skip has exploited him. He, therefore, decides to reciprocate the assumed objectification by forcing his roommate to become obedient and please him. They fight verbally. Greene describes the tensest moment of the argument: "The Negro boy glowered at him in the dark, his eyes flashing the full fire of hatred. 'Stinking white trash,' he spat. 'And *you* the one who give me the lecture about *using* people'" (135). Skip reveals that he is exhausted from his labor in the sweat box and that he could have avoided such labor by giving in to Grizzy's advances. In frustration Skip counters Leroy's claim: "Last night I thought I found something that *meant* something—something that made me want to give up the kind of life I had before—something that was so precious to me I didn't want to foul it by going through the physical motions of it with someone who made me sick to my stomach" (137). Leroy relents in his demands and orally services Skip. In this moment, Leroy discovers that his lover was correct and that willing submission is a way to resist oppression. He experiences the pleasure of giving pleasure. He understands that far from debasing himself, like Charles does, he has truly become someone's sublime equal.

What Skip teaches Leroy is that submission to a lover is the lost anodyne for the world's suffering. Like many of Greene's protagonists, he is willfully blind to the extreme violence to which love opens him in favor of its more immediate and orgasmic benefits. Throughout Greene's body of work, many secondary characters, like Charles, mitigate institutionally condoned violence by becoming obedient to the violence of their oppressors. Obedience to an institution and submission to a lover are strange poles in Greene's universe. Obedience, whether compulsory or voluntary, ends in psychic corruption. Through it, characters preserve their existence, but they lose their virtue; like Charles, they become cruel and treacherous. In contrast, submission to a lover permits resistance to these influences. Pleasure is clearly transcendent when Leroy offers his body to Skip. In describing the blowjob, Greene tells the reader: "It seemed like forever. It seemed like only a moment. But when the end came, Skip cried out so sharply he feared everyone in the dormitory would hear" (138). Skip's pleasure exists outside of time and becomes rapturous. It is in the transcendent moments institutional forces are temporarily subverted because the inmates are able to act and feel beyond the influence of cruel guards and horny cooks.

Despite such resplendent pleasures, the architecture of the reformatory and the control it offers the staff overcome any countermeasures. At the moment Leroy realizes his love for Skip, Mac barges into their room. The guard's intrusion again emphasizes that no space or act can preserve resistance. Mac takes Skip to the guard's room—the only room that has a lock. He forces Skip to submit to oral sex by Charles. Then he anally rapes the boy. Leroy crashes into the room and beats Mac to death. Battered and flawed, Leroy and Skip have seemingly scored a victory over the reformatory. But Leroy's action augurs the ultimate victory of institutional control, since if he attempts to stay with his lover he will be sent to the penitentiary. Leroy decides to flee the reformatory but promises to find Skip after his eventual release. Amid disaster, Greene captures a moment of pure devotion—the two are selfless in love. True to the author's dark vision, this moment cannot last, and Charles shoots Leroy with Mac's gun before escape is possible. The resistance by these particular inmates to the institutional apparatus is undone. Nevertheless, the possibility of resistance through selflessness remains, no matter how temporary struggle might be.

*Behind These Walls*, like most of Greene's novels, presents oppression and violence inflicted by a seemingly invincible institution. These settings and their inevitable victory over their youthful victims lend credence to Brooks Peters's and Roland Graeme's assessments of Greene's corpus as dark and pessimistic. His rejection of the utopias imagined by members of the gay community during the initial phases of liberation should not be read as a condemnation of homosexual relationships. His insistence that selfless devotion to a lover's pleasure stands in stark contrast to devastation imposed by institutional pressures. Greene refuses to give his readers the false comfort of utopia, literally "no-place." Rather, he imagines ways for gay men to live and have pleasure in a world hostile to them.

Resistance is valuable not because it is successful but because it can exist. The precarious spaces that resistance creates allow identities to emerge that express a higher ethos. Greene's narratives do not prevent his readers or his characters from imagining healthy, horny, happy futures. The novels suggest that projecting these dreams into a world that does not support them leaves individuals vulnerable to the social machinery of oppression. Greene insists that selfless resistance to normative pressures is by itself virtuous. In addition to this social dynamic, Greene links into another concept to which Foucault would later give voice: "The delinquent is also to be distinguished from the offender in that he is not only the author of his acts (the author responsible in terms of certain criteria of free, conscious will), but is linked to his offence by a whole bundle of complex threads (instincts, drives, tendencies, character)" (252–53). Greene shows this by his choice of characters who are not merely rough trade, a staple of earlier pulp novels, but who are instead pulled into their behaviors by complex social forces and their personal volition. The characters must learn something essential about their drives and themselves before they can engage in transcendent acts of submission. These lessons remain useful decades after the publication of his novels. One need only read about the rash of suicides by gay teens prompted by institutionally tolerated bullying after the turn of the last millennium to recognize that the acceptance of homosexuality is far from universal, and the utopias promised gay men are still beyond reach for many.

## NOTES

1. Brooks Peters, "Page Boys: Camp Art of Gay Pulps," *An Open Book,* Dec. 13, 2011, http://brookspeters.blogspot.com/2011/12/muscle-boys.html; Victor J. Banis, "The Gay Publishing Revolution," in *The Golden Age of Gay Fiction,* ed. Drewey Wayne Gunn (Albion, NY: MLR Press, 2009), 117.
2. See Tom Norman, *American Gay Erotic Paperbacks: A Bibliography* (Burbank, CA: privately printed, 1994), 54–55; and Ian Young, *The Male Homosexual in Literature: A Bibliography,* 2nd ed. (Metuchen, NJ: Scarecrow Press, 1982), 87.
3. Graeme adds in parentheses, "not my personal cup of tea, but God knows I can still relate to it." Roland Graeme, e-mail to Drewey Wayne Gunn, Feb. 16, 2011; I thank Wayne Gunn for passing portions of this e-mail along to me.
4. Peters, "Blood, Sex & Tears: The Tortured Souls of Jay Greene's *Behind These Walls,*" *An Open Book,* Dec. 10, 2011, http://brookspeters.blogspot.com/2011/12/blood-sex-tears.html; Jay Greene, *Bitter Wine* (New York: Midwood, 1969), 174.
5. Some of Greene's novels published by Midwood that include such settings are *Tony's Room* (1968), *The Cadets* (1969), *The Godson* (1970), and *The Colonel's Boy* (1972). Other restrictive spaces, including a nineteenth-century merchant vessel in *Pretty Boy* (1968), a high school in *Rough Trade* (1969), and a mansion in *Cruising* (1970), represent similar uses of architecture for social control.

6. Michel Foucault, *Discipline and Punish: The Birth of the Prison*, trans. Alan Sheridan (1977; New York: Vintage, 1995), 135. Subsequent page references cited parenthetically in the text refer to this edition. In 1975, the year the French edition appeared, Foucault said in an interview: "Prison is not unique. It is positioned within the disciplined society, the society of generalized surveillance in which we live." His interviewer, Roger Pol-Droit, adds, " 'What is so astonishing,' Foucault asks, 'about the fact that our prisons resemble our factories, schools, military bases, and hospitals-all of which in turn resemble prisons?' " Roger Pol-Droit, "Michel Foucault, on the Role of Prisons," *New York Times*, Aug. 5, 1975 (originally published in *Le Monde*).
7. Jay Greene, *The Cadets* (New York: Midwood, 1969), 80.
8. Jay Greene, *Behind These Walls* (New York: Midwood, 1968), 47. Subsequent page references cited parenthetically in the text refer to this edition.
9. The front cover can be seen at www.librarything.com/work/11891981.
10. Greene describes the reformatory as "situated in the upper part of the state, in a region of gently rolling hills and prosperous farmland. In keeping with the tranquility of the surroundings, it was designed as a compound of low, two-story buildings, rather than a massive brick and steel prison. A main building—housing the dining hall and kitchen, infirmary, the laundry, various work shops where the boys were supposedly taught trades which would prepare them to take up 'useful' lives when the left the reformatory, and the administration offices—occupied the central position in the compound, with the dormitories built in a square around it" (28).
11. As Foucault writes, "The prison cannot fail to produce delinquents" (266). Greene's critique is parallel to much of Foucault's on the issues of the bonds delinquents form. Foucault observes, "The prison makes possible, even encourages, the organization of a milieu of delinquents, loyal to one another, hierarchized, ready to aid and abet any future criminal act." (267). Greene would certainly agree that loyalty in prisons aids and abets criminal sexuality. The delinquent characters who do create hierarchized relationships are usually those who are most aligned or useful to the system of corrections. There is a significant difference, however: Greene indicates that his protagonists strive for nonhierarchized relationships.
12. These activities include officially required work, such as kitchen duty, and unofficial obligations like sexually pleasing the staff.
13. Michel Foucault, "The Gay Science," trans. Nicolae Morar and Daniel W. Smith, *Critical Inquiry* 37, no. 3 (Spring 2011): 392.
14. Georges Bataille, *The Accursed Share*, vol. 1, trans. Robert Hurley (1989; New York: Zone Books, 2007), 60.
15. Greene, *Bitter Wine*, 169.
16. Leo Bersani, *Homos* (Cambridge: Harvard University Press, 1995), 99.

# The Heroic Quest

## DIRK VANDEN'S *ALL* TRILOGY

Drewey Wayne Gunn

David Nimmons, in *The Soul beneath the Skin,* his thought-provoking study of post-Stonewall gay men, ties the quest for self-actualization to Joseph Campbell's dictum "Follow your bliss." Nimmons expands on the idea: "We are in a different dance with bliss [from that of our heterosexual counterparts] from the first moment we step into gay communal life. It begins with coming out, our definitional rite of passage. Born alone, every one of us must first face his fears, vote for bliss, and follow his heart to find his soulmates. This process, wholly personal yet deeply communal, requires us each to honor a private truth in order to join a public community." This acknowledgment, he stresses, becomes "the first step in our archetypal hero's journey, our initiation into a new kind of manhood. It is an act of bliss seeking, collectively and individually."[1] This coming-out process has become such a staple of gay writing that some critics claim it is now overused. It would be irresponsible, however, to ignore this defining stage in our lives.

Though examples of coming out occur in fiction published both before and after World War II, the first considerable body of such stories dates from the gay pulp explosion in the mid- through late 1960s. Current reportage would lead me to believe that younger and younger people are now coming out and thus beginning their quests at an early age. That was not true of my generation, the generation that provided the characters in these early pulps. The entry on "Out" in *Completely Queer: The Gay and Lesbian Encyclopedia* reflects what I remember: "Into the 1960s—and even later for some people—lesbians and gay men tended to value discretion in themselves and others." It then adds something I do not remember: "The term 'out,' in fact, originally referred only to a person's first sexual experience with a member of his or her own sex." The entry concludes by saying that "it was more common in the days before Stonewall to speak of a veteran gay man or lesbian 'bringing' a neophyte out, rather than a person 'coming out' of his or her own volition."[2] But by the late 1960s, pulp fiction shows clearly that "coming out" on one's own was the normal meaning of the term.

The pulps, in recording this shift in paradigms, heralded the advent of a new age. In the larger perspective, the Stonewall Inn riots are as much a logical culmination of earlier tendencies in gay culture as they are a harbinger of events to come. The 1960s pulp heroes who embark on the quest for an authentic gay identity are often in their late twenties to mid-forties. By and large, they lack any sort of guideposts to point their way and have to depend on luck as much as pluck. But for the first time a truly substantial number are embarking on the archetypal search for Self, the heroic quest that Campbell called the monomyth. Just at the moment the definition of "out" was changing, Dirk Vanden launched his *All* trilogy, each novel about the quest of a different man. All three heroes search for a new, more authentic life by coming out on their own terms. With great self-awareness, they face the symbolic road ahead: "It's like a—what did they call it, those knights that went looking for something? You know, King Arthur and all? A quest!"[3] It is their heroic quests that I want to examine.

Before I begin, perhaps it would not be amiss to indicate why the stories Vanden and similar authors had to tell had such an impact on readers by recounting a bit of my own search for bliss. Though the heroes of these novels largely lacked guides for their quests, such novels themselves became guides for people like me. Two score and two days after the Stonewall Inn riots, I turned thirty. Not that I then knew anything of the riots. It was not until Gay Pride marches became a regular feature that I first heard about Stonewall. The important thing at the moment was my age, not its date. In the parlance of the times, I had become "the enemy." That did not bother me. I was more concerned with Nick Carraway's realization: "Before me stretched the portentous, menacing road of a new decade." Having attended a church-affiliated university as an undergraduate, I also understood the symbolic spiritual significance of becoming thirty. What was my mission, my quest?

I knew I was gay. Accepting that fact had never been a problem. But I did not have the faintest idea what to do with the fact. I certainly wasn't ready to proclaim it to the world. I had always been the bookish type, but no helpful guidebooks on how to be gay existed. Appropriating the voice of the main character in Vanden's *All or Nothing* I could say, "I made an effort to read as much as I could about homosexuality . . . But I finally decided that the men who had written those books didn't know what they were talking about."[4] Charles Silverstein and Edmund White's *The Joy of Gay Sex* appeared too late to be of any help. The gay fiction I encountered by such writers as Tennessee Williams, Gore Vidal, James Baldwin, and John Rechy was no more help in teaching me how to live; in fact, it mostly frightened me. In retrospect, I see that I learned more from Nathaniel Hawthorne and Graham Greene, mostly for how to fly below the radar—which meant, unfortunately, also flying below anyone's gaydar. There was little chance anyone would out me sexually.

A brief visit to San Francisco in 1966 had left me floundering. I attended a showing of Andy Warhol's *My Hustler*. I had never been in a room with so many good-looking young men, all obviously gay, many already dressed in the uniform that later, in the 1970s, came to be called the clone look.[5] The testosterone-filled air rendered me so nervous that I left the cinema before the film was over. On the same visit I found my first pornographic magazines in an adult bookstore. "I remembered the terror and excitement I'd felt as the door closed behind me and I'd looked around, seeing my fantasies explode into life on the wall in huge pictures," one of Vanden's protagonists recalls of his similar visit to a San Francisco adult bookstore.[6] In what I later discovered was a classic move for men of my generation, I picked out the gay magazine I wanted and sandwiched it between two straight magazines. The attempt at subterfuge of course made no sense, as was driven home when the clerk said, "Oh, these two [the gay one and a straight one] are on sale." Only then did it dawn upon me that he didn't give a flip about the contents of the magazines or about my sexuality; he was interested only in the contents of my wallet.

Then, in 1969, on the paperback bookracks of the local convenience store in the small ranching town where I taught, I began discovering the gay pulp novels that Greenleaf Classics, Olympia Press, and similar paperback presses were publishing. The first book I bought remains etched on my memory: *Fruit of the Loon* by "Ricardo Armory." I had never read anything like it. It was the first evidence I received that gays could actually be homosexual and happy. In short order, I discovered the novel it was parodying, *Song of the Loon* by Richard Amory, as well as *2069* by Larry Townsend (and two years later his *Sexual Adventures of Sherlock Holmes* by "J. Watson"), *The Gay Haunt* by Victor Jay (Victor J. Banis), and others that I no longer remember by name. Always I checked out other customers in the store and the identity of the clerk before I bought one, my heart pounding. Whether I used them as a masturbatory aid, I no longer remember. Probably. But it was the feeling that these books were about me that kept me returning to the racks.

They became my guidebooks, much more helpful to my education than all the sex manuals being turned out during the decade (the worst being David Reuben's travesty, *Everything You Always Wanted to Know about Sex*). These pulps, however, did not provide one crucial bit of information: what to do if one were stuck in a small Texas town. So I followed their advice and took the archetypal journey to the city, a gay pilgrim's progress. I fled not to San Francisco, as so many of the pulp heroes did, but all the way to Copenhagen, on a Fulbright teaching grant. There I finally felt safe to put into practice what until then had remained theory. Without the liberating influence of gay pulps, I feel certain it would have been years before I had gathered up nerve to do anything. Their cultural and psychological importance for gay men of my generation cannot be overstated.

One writer I did not encounter on those paperback racks at the time was Dirk Vanden, the pseudonym adopted by Richard Fullmer. He published seven novels between 1969 and 1971. His first four were published by Greenleaf Classics in its oversized format, which did not fit into the regular racks. The *All* trilogy would fit, but I simply missed them. Vanden is one of the few pulp names, along with those of his friends Richard Amory (Richard Love), Larry Townsend, and Phil Andros (Samuel Steward), to be dropped with some frequency in literary histories, primarily in Vanden's case because of his (somewhat erroneous) association with the leather and S/M scenes.[7] I am not sure what my reaction would have been had I discovered his works at the time. Several of his novels are more violent than I would have preferred, though they all work toward the positive resolution I so badly needed. They are populated by the same crowd that I had fled in that San Francisco movie house, but by then my own attire was imitating that same audience's. Certainly, when I first read the *All* trilogy in 2010, it brought back many memories, besides the trip to the adult bookstore, of similar moments I had experienced. And I recognized many of these characters from my own encounters.

The *All* trilogy was widely and enthusiastically reviewed. Ralph Collins, in a review of *I Want It All* for *The Voice*, commented, "Vanden writes beautifully, and his stories are always extremely readable." Reviewing *All or Nothing*, Michael Perkins, in *Screw* magazine, labeled him a "novelist who has decided to write about gay life realistically and even propagandistically," while Victor DeStefano wrote enthusiastically in *California Scene*, "Of its genre, it has to be the best book ever written." Peter Hadley argued in the newspaper *GAY* that, based on the first two books, the author "is more than just a sex book writer. His characters go through some very erotic scenes, but their coming out, their growing awareness of their homosexuality and its positive meaning is much more important to the book than the erotica. He makes some very important positive points about homosexuality, and that is a good thing." John Francis Hunter (John Paul Hudson), in his review of *All Is Well* for *GAY*, wrote that in "talking about what writers like Vanden are saying from the present peculiar gay viewpoint and how well they say it vis a vis each other . . . his is the best of the lot yet. Since he writes about the middle-class closet of today and one man's escape from it with the aid of the youth *Weltansicht* and drugs as catalysts, it seems to me that *All Is Well* is presently the *Zeitgeist* novel of early '70s gaydom." Amory wrote for *Vector*, "This is a thick, prosy work, introspective, thoughtful, sometimes much too essayistic, but always ingenious, probing, suspenseful." And Marc Williams, in his review of *All Is Well* for the *Mattachine Society Magazine*, echoed DeStefano's assessment of the previous novel in the series: "This has got to be the best gay book on the scene today."[8]

The trilogy bears obvious comparison to Amory's *Loon* trilogy. Each of the three novels similarly tells an independent story, but one that connects up with the others, with the various characters all coming together in the final volume.[9] In his memoirs, Vanden credits his discovery of *Song of the Loon* for giving him the courage to try publishing again after earlier disappointments.[10] The two men became and remained friends until Amory's premature death. In both trilogies, the major characters are on quests of various sorts. Both authors record examples of the psychic damages caused by organized religion. Both believe in the reality of visionary experiences. Both lustily celebrate the joys of sex, and neither believes in monogamy. And both extol masculinity as a virtue. Whereas Amory's quests take place in pastoral settings of the nineteenth century, however, Vanden's are very much in the contemporary West and grapple with very realistic present-day problems.

*I Want It All* was published by Frenchy's Gay Line in 1969. The story of twenty-seven-year-old-ranch hand Warren Miller, its first-person narrator announces in the opening pages that he has a didactic purpose in recounting what has happened to him. He wants to help his readers better understand themselves, accept themselves, and stop listening to "bullshit" in the hopes that "we can find out what it really means to *love* somebody."[11] His personal quest begins as a result of his stepping in to stop Bill Thorne from castrating Brad Nelson but then joining in twelve men's collective rape of the stranger. Bill has taken Brad out into a dark alley behind a bar in a small ranching town near Greeley, Colorado, after he agreed to a blowjob from the "queer." During the ensuing frenzy, both Warren and Bill recognize that Warren and Brad are mirror images of each other. In seeing himself in

Brad, Warren acknowledges that he is homosexual. He decides that for his own safety, as well as his growing sense of disgust for the crowd he has been hanging out with, he must leave the place. He departs across the deserts of Utah and Nevada for San Francisco in pursuit of Brad.

On his way he has two encounters with self-loathing homosexuals; he meets several more in San Francisco. He concludes that one is born with one's sexual nature, but social restrictions corrupt and distort homosexuals' basic humanity. For a while Warren hustles for a living. Then he stumbles into a position as a barman. He finally reconnects with Brad at the baths, and they set up housekeeping together. Strains develop in their relationship. Disgruntled with their life, Warren picks up a policeman, who appears to threaten him with death, but it turns out to be a sadistic prank. As a result he emerges from his funk, and he and Brad accept the same lesson that Amory teaches in *Song of the Loon:* monogamy is not a necessary component of commitment; love and sex are not identical. Once they sort this out, they recommit to an open, free-wheeling relationship. Their new beginning allows the novel to end in joint laughter.

The second volume, *All or Nothing,* was first published by Frenchy's Gay Line in 1970. A revised and expanded version was published in the Other Traveller series by Olympia Press in 1971; it is this version that I read. *All or Nothing* begins at the same point as *I Want It All* does, but this time we see the rape scene from the viewpoint of thirty-two-year-old bartender Bill Thorne. One of two sons of a bishop in the Mormon Church in Idaho, he (like Warren) has tried to adhere to the image society held up for him to emulate; he has served in the military and been married, even (unlike Warren) having a son. But well before the madness in the alley, he has sensed, as have his fellow townsfolk, that he does not conform to their norm. Andy Morrison, an enlisted man who had been a participant in the rape scene, in a strange transformation of his own introduces Bill to a bisexual hippie couple. Fueled by potent marijuana, the three men and the woman let fall all sexual barriers and therein force Bill to confront his true nature.

As a result, Andy challenges Bill: "Be free. Don't let anyone fuck with your mind."[12] Bill likewise departs across the western deserts, though for

Los Angeles, in search of Brad Nelson in order to apologize, but hoping to find Warren Miller to admit his love for the man. In Los Angeles he finds that Brad has left, destination unknown. He encounters a man named Neil, who takes him under his wing. As a result of the intense emotions unleashed by his participation in a full-fledged orgy, induced again by marijuana, Bill feels the need to think and decides to resume his physical journey in search of greater self-knowledge. After a series of turns, he ends up in San Francisco just before the New Year. Yet another marijuana-inspired orgy, during which Bill is fisted for the first time, culminates in the arrival of Brad and Warren. They put him through a symbolic atonement process, and Bill joins them in their home.

*All Is Well* was published in the Other Traveller series in 1971, shortly before the press reissued *All or Nothing*. It switches scenes completely, telling the story of Bill's brother, thirty-five-year-old Robert Thorne. He is the owner of a small advertising agency in Salt Lake City. He has a wife, to whom he refuses to give a divorce, and three children, two of whom she freely admits were actually sired by his business partner. Robert has already been introduced in the previous novel as Bobby; we know that he forced himself sexually on Bill when they were teenagers, but then his Mormon upbringing crashed down upon him. This novel covers three crucial days in his life. It too begins with a gay sexual awakening, begun on his return from a conference in San Francisco, but one spread out between two strangers (lawyer John Adams and an unnamed man) and in stages, culminating with recovered memories of his rape of his brother. New in this novel is the protagonist's concern about his son, Chuck, who he fears is gay. As a result of his accidentally dropping mescaline, he shares an intense visionary experience with Chuck. As he comes down, his son urges him to cut loose from all the false social bonds that hold him prisoner.

Robert's readiness to heed the challenge is spurred on by a series of threatening letters that he has been mysteriously receiving. All addressed to "Robber," they have planted the idea that Chuck is gay. (He is, but by the time Robert is sure of the fact, it no longer seems important.) He agrees to give his wife the divorce she wants. But before he can move further, he has to confront the fact that his psyche has fragmented, that he is an example of a split personality. He is the one who has, unknowingly to him, been writing the letters. If he is to find the wholeness he so desperately desires, he must get "Rob," the name he gives to the dark, threatening letter-writer, and Robert to communicate. He decides that he must find his brother, who—a call to his Idaho home reveals—is in San Francisco. He departs alone across the desert. Rob emerges during the trip and insists that his true name is Bobby. His divided psyche leads Robert to contemplate, but then reject, suicide. Encountering his brother again sexually, he regains a sense of completeness and renames himself Bob. The novel ends with Bob's letter to his son anticipating their being reunited for a moment (when he returns to Salt Lake City to sign the papers) and recording that he now lives with Bill, Warren, and Brad.

In 1995 the author revised *I Want It All.* Then, in 2011, he brought out *All Together: The All Trilogy,* a revision of all three novels, the second one now titled *All the Way.*[13] The covers of all the volumes throughout the trilogy's career reproduce drawings by the author. I have leafed through the collection, as well as the movie script he developed from the first novel (available only on his website), but so far have refrained from reading them. They appear at a glance to be better written books, but they are products of the author's maturity, no longer examples of gay pulp. I am also intrigued by the difference in the physical act of reading: just holding the large-sized and thick one-volume trade paperback in my hands is not the same as holding the now forty-year-old small paperbacks, redolent of memories of my own earlier years.

The protagonists of all three novels are on the heroic quest as defined by Joseph Campbell in *The Hero with a Thousand Faces,* Robert in the most complex (and perhaps most satisfactory) way. Campbell outlines this quest in these general terms. The hero leaves his ordinary environment and arrives at "the threshold of adventure." Here he faces his first test. If he passes, "then the hero journeys through a world of unfamiliar yet strangely intimate forces, some of which severely threaten him (tests), some of which give magical aid (helpers). When he arrives at the nadir of the mythological round, he undergoes a supreme ordeal and gains his reward." The inherent nature of that reward is "an expansion of consciousness and therewith of being (illumination, transfiguration, freedom). The final work is the return." The hero takes back the insights that he has gained to reconstruct his world.[14]

All three stories begin with a protagonist disgruntled with his lot, floundering in the situation in which he finds himself, wanting change. Warren sums up, "I was drunk, and lonely, and pissed-off at everything—especially myself," knowing that "something was happening out there in the world where I ought to be." Bill recognizes, "Something was wrong with me. Something terrible." Robert laments, "I felt as though my entire body, including my brain, was trussed up with invisible cords. And that terrible feeling that something disastrous was coming closer and closer and closer." Reflecting on his failed marriage, the twin daughters who are not his, and his uncertain relationship with his son, he sums up, "It seemed I'd been in some kind of emotional deep-freeze for five numb, endless years." A brief glimpse of other possibilities leaves him with "a terrible empty feeling deep in my body."[15]

Mark Thompson, in his spiritual autobiography *Gay Body: A Journey through Shadow to Self,* makes some observations pertinent to these men's condition. Thompson writes, "Somewhere inside every gay man there's a wounded boy who stopped growing. Who simply gave up and shut down." As a result one enters a "twilight zone" he labels "the Gay Shadow." Thompson continues, "The shadow contains the inferior parts of ourself we wish to deny, the shameful and neglected aspects of personality. Every person has a shadow, for it is an integral part of one's psyche." Then he makes a point that is so relevant to the condition Vanden's heroes are wrestling with: "But when left unclaimed, it becomes a dangerous thing: the repression, primitiveness, and hostility it contains invariably seeps out to contaminate others and our own being."[16]

A chance sexual encounter with an openly gay stranger leads to violence in the first two novels and serves as a momentary respite in the hero's self-destruction in the third. But the sex somehow helps focus each one's individual inchoate feelings. For Warren and Bill, the stranger is Brad Nelson, whom they rape. Of him, Warren says, "All I could think of was getting inside him! Into him completely!" He feels Brad "knew some sort of secret he could tell me—a secret that would let me know who I was and what the whole stupid mess was about." As Bill takes Brad, he feels, "My body was like something empty, like a vacuum, but filling, filling slowly." For Robert, the stranger is John Adams, whose words "You really don't know who I am, do you?" he interprets on a symbolic level rather than the literal one intended.[17]

In recording their reactions to the encounters, all three use the imagery of the threshold. Warren says, "Tonight some doors had been opened for both Bill and me, but Bill was slamming his closed again. . . . As for my own doors, I wasn't at all sure they could ever be closed—even if I wanted them to be." Speaking literally, Bill says, "For a moment I leaned on the closed door, staring at the spot where I'd stood when the queer first propositioned me. I slid the bolt closed on the door. Then I went into the toilet stall and threw up." Later he says, "It was as though I stood before a door, a door which, when opened completely, would expose mysteries and secrets undreamed of. And the door was ajar. . . . I felt, for a moment, an overwhelming sadness because I hadn't been able to open that door into truth. But I knew it was there. Some other time I could open it." Robert can no more than his brother take the decisive step across the threshold just yet; even less than Bill can he admit that he is the one holding back, taking refuge in the passive voice: "It seemed that a door of some sort had been opened, just slightly, and beyond that door had been something I'd wanted all my life, something warm, sincere—something beautiful—and then the door had been slammed in my face."[18]

A stranger heralds the call to adventure; a person close to each issues the actual directive to begin the quest. The evening that Brad is so brutally raped, Bill speaks telepathically to Warren: "Get your ass outa town, Warren Miller, and don't bring it back or we'll do worse to you!" During Bill's incredible high with Andy Morrison and the hippie couple, Andy and Bill have an exchange that works on both a literal (Bill is in the shower) and a symbolic level:

> "Come on, man," he said softly. "Time to come out."
> "I don't know how," I told him confidentially.

As they come down from their high, Andy "looked at me seriously. 'You're good people. But man, this town is ruining you. You know that?' " There then follows this exchange:

> "What about you, Bill?" he asked.
> "I'm leaving." I looked at him. "Today."
> "That soon, huh? . . ."
> "I'd be crazy to stay."
> "You're right about that."

Andy now explicitly spells out the significance of Bill's decision by comparing the journey he is about to take to the quest of the Knights of the Round Table in search of the Holy Grail. The religious motif is picked up again at the decisive moment launching Robert's search. On Easter Sunday, the time of rebirth, resurrection, Robert has a mescaline-induced series of visions. As he is coming down, wrestling with his new insights, his son asks him, "Dad . . . when are you going to get to hell out of here?"[19] All three men experience dreams that seem to offer keys from their deep unconscious to their futures.

The three men heed their calls. Each leaves Colorado or Utah to head to California: Warren in search of Brad, Bill in search of Warren (though he ostensibly is looking for Brad, in order to apologize), Robert in search of Bill. The first part of their journeys takes them through a common archetypal waste land made up of "rocky brown rolling hills—grey cedars and scorched grass"—"dark unfathomable shapes on the sides of the freeway [that] became grey blurs whizzing past." Then (we are in Robert's mind here): "At one point I looked back and saw the stark, empty black hills and desert stretching behind me—like my life; and just after one o'clock, I passed over the summit and started down into the lush green valleys of California. It seemed to me to be beautifully symbolic: I was leaving a dead vacant past, moving into something fresh and new—a rebirth, a coming alive after a long-long empty winter." At his threshold Bill says, "I wondered how different my life would become once I got there? One thing was certain, it would never be the same again." After arriving in Los Angeles and meeting up with another man, he echoes Robert: "I'd just awakened from a long hibernation, a winter's sleep, filled with ugly, unhappy dreams, into this new place."[20] Problems are not solved, however, simply by relocation. The symbolic passage represents desire rather than fulfillment.

Warren has little difficulty accepting that he is gay. When he realizes that he "could get turned-on by the sight of another man's naked body," he muses, "I didn't suddenly panic and try to kill the guy—I didn't get all hung-up on guilt and try to kill myself—I didn't decide I'd been 'born queer' and had to make the best of it—and I sure as hell didn't decide that now I had to call myself 'Mary'! When it happened . . . I decided to find out as much as I could about this 'new me' I'd discovered." For the Thorne brothers, it is more difficult. Their Mormon upbringing blighted their teenage sexual encounter and thwarted their acceptance of their sexuality. Bill has already left the church, but only now is he getting up the courage to question its teachings. After an intense moment with Andy, he feels awe: "Here I'd done something that, all my adult life, I'd believed was almost as bad as murdering someone. . . . I'd made love to another man; *and I'd enjoyed doing all of it!*" Robert continues to let Mormon strictures dictate his public actions, to the verge of destroying his family and himself. The repression of his desires has fragmented his psyche. He has to become whole again in order to admit, "I'm a queer. I'm a cocksucking homosexual and probably have been my entire life, only I just didn't have the good sense to know it." This admission will come only far along in his quest.[21]

As they take to the road, all three men face a series of tests. Warren meets a hitchhiker who is the one to initiate sex, but then needs to be mistreated in order to climax: "Like a Jekyll and Hyde character, something ugly had come into him." Next, Warren initiates oral sex with a "straight" rodeo competitor who, after climaxing, attacks him. Warren retaliates, using the cowboy's own blood as lubrication to rape him anally. After this failure, Warren resumes his journey, "nothing but empty dark highway ahead of me."[22] Later tests face him in San Francisco. He discovers that a wide range of gay types exists and that he cannot identify with everyone on that gamut, especially those who are queeny, bitchy, campy. In quite a different way, soon after his arrival in California, Bill likewise fails his first test. When asked if he is gay, he "automatically" denies it. He later muses that "always before I'd been afraid that admitting such feelings would destroy my manhood.

Always before the males willing to [have sex with other males] had been less than men, soft, effeminate, giddy girl/boys—queers—fags."[23]

In his review of *All Is Well,* John Francis Hunter criticized this aspect of the novel: "The fault I bother mentioning in this little gem of a work is that in its rampaging celebration of maleness it approaches male chauvinism, offering little counsel or comfort to the effete, the androgynous or the poorly-hung."[24] Hunter's criticism is accurate, but it ignores the tensions under which those of us who were reared in oppressive communities lived. It was not easy for us to reconcile the constant injunction to "be a man," not to act like "a girl," with the evident homosexuals we knew: effeminate men who got the knowing wink behind their backs (and who may not, of course, even have been gay). Martin Levine, in *Gay Macho,* argues that "gay men enacted a hypermasculine sexuality as a way to challenge their stigmatization as failed men, as 'sissies.' " Looking at precisely the period Vanden is describing, he writes, "At first, some gay men took on the look of hip masculinity favored in the counterculture. . . . But by the early 1970s, gay men embraced other marginalized, but far more masculine definitions of masculinity. They expressed their new sense of self by wearing the attire of the working class. . . . Traditional masculine themes were heartily embraced—in part as a new kind of camp (as in . . . The Village People), . . . and in part as a vigorous assertion of a newfound, and passionately embraced successful masculinity."[25] Physical changes of costume and hair not only led to greater social and political visibility but became symbolic of spiritual transformations.

Rejection of the outward effeminate does not mean rejection of the *anima,* to use Jung's term, as much as it entails sorting out her positive and negative aspects. A hippie woman is an instrumental part of the quarternity that launches Bill's coming out (replete with symbolism and nomenclature that suggest Mary's union with the Holy Trinity). Later Bill spends Christmas with a "semi-hippie couple" in Oregon. Warren, Brad, and Bill come together to form "The Family." As Bill describes it to Bob, it is a group of kindred spirits who care for each other, who nurture each other, and who seek a higher spirituality outside the strictures of organized religion. The Jungian analyst John Beebe believes that "the man who takes his homosexuality seriously enough to work on finding a relationship with a male partner and making it prosper also develops a relationship to the anima within and . . . finds 'her' of inestimable value in strengthening his ability to contain the tensions of the partnership while sustaining contact with himself." Beebe holds that development of the anima then "deepens and secures his inner relation to his homosexuality as well as his lived relationships in the outer world with other homosexual men."[26] Unlike the two men that Warren encounters on the road, such men are willing to share their softer side with each other; they eschew all role-playing in sex. Michael Perkins, in his review, wrote that *All or Nothing* shows "that the gay world is somehow tenderer and more feeling than the straight world."[27] Stripping naked asserts masculinity; it also exposes vulnerability. "To love somebody—and be loved—is the most . . . the *only* important thing in life! Everything else takes its meaning from that."[28]

The novels are very much a part of their time; this was the era of Timothy Leary (mentioned by name in *All Is Well*). For each of the men, drugs provide insight into the spiritual cosmos. They ease the protagonists' acceptance of their sexuality. They link minds in a transcendent way. They prepare the men, in the hippie jargon of the time, to tune in to the beauties of nature. Chuck takes his father to a restaurant called Mother Earth; it is presided over by a larger-than-life poster of Yoko Ono. As Hunter noted in his review, contemporary music also plays a big role in promoting Robert's transformation into Bob. Unidentified lyrics drop frequently into the text; the Beatles are their major source, but one especially significant (and repeated) phrase comes from the rock opera *Jesus Christ Superstar.*

Images of doubling, twins, reflections, mirrors, and Narcissus repeatedly occur across the three novels. At several significant points, all three men find themselves looking in mirrors, seeing their reversed reflection. Mirrors threaten Robert, seduce him; but at a crucial moment a mirror will save him. J. E. Cirlot's entry for "mirror" in his *Dictionary of Symbols* presents a kaleidoscope of possible interpretations. A mirror, he writes, can be "a symbol of the imagination—or of consciousness"; it can also be seen as "the instrument of self-contemplation as well as the reflection of the universe," and thus its symbolism is linked with "water as a reflector and with the Narcissus myth: the cosmos appears as a huge Narcissus regarding his own reflections in the human consciousness." Cirlot connects the mirror to moon symbolism and thus to the feminine, the anima, and he notes that a mirror can also take "the mythic form of a door through which the soul may free itself." Hand mirrors are "emblems of truth" and "aids to conjugal happiness as well as a protection against diabolical influences." And perhaps most significantly, the mirror "stands for twins (thesis and antithesis)." Mark Thompson writes, "Gay men are led to the center of their souls—to a true Self—by the Double, who appears in our lives as if he is a gift from the gods."[29]

As soon as Warren sees Brad, he recognizes that "it was like . . . like looking down at *myself!* . . . [H]e could have been . . . my twin . . . my brother . . . *Me!*" In this Narcissus-like reflection Warren momentarily perceives the beauty of his truer self and thus receives a glimpse of Self.[30] Describing the same scene, Bill uses almost identical language, but then, for him, it becomes even more complicated: "For a split second, it wasn't Warren Miller and some look-alike queer in an alley, but myself and my brother: I was kneeling with Bob bending over me, and above us the dark mass of an old tree." During his visionary experience with the hippies, Bill finds himself looking at himself: "I had split in two," flesh and spirit. When Warren feels free to reject monogamy, in an echo of Plato's *Symposium,* he finds "that feeling came back—the feeling of being two parts of the same thing—one person." Robert says that he and Bill as children were "more like twins than just brothers."[31] Their incestuous relationship can be taken, following Jung's lead, to symbolize "the longing for union with the essence of one's own self, or, in other words, for individuation."[32] Joseph L. Henderson, following the lead of Paul Radin, accepts the theme of Twins as the final stage in the evolution of the hero myth. Twins represent ego and alter-ego, which can be reconciled to complete the Self.[33]

It is one thing to accept one's homosexuality; it is another to build a gay identity. Warren is taken under wing by a shaman figure, Ash, upon his arrival in San Francisco. He is instructed in the language, the symbols, the conduct, and the safe zones for gays. Soon after his arrival in Los Angeles, Bill laments, "I felt naked in more ways than one—new in a strange city, not knowing where to find help if I needed it." But even at the time of his declaration, he is in the hands of his first guide to the new world he is entering. With Neil he understands for the first time that sex with another man can be good ("I felt good, and that's all there was to it. His body felt good against mine. Having sex with him had felt good. Even drinking his cum had been good!"). Neil takes him to gay bars and introduces him to gay friends. One of them, Judd Carter, conducts Bill through the next stages of his initiation. Lacking traditional rituals to mark our rites of passage, we have to invent our own. W. B. Yeats observes, "But Love has pitched his mansion in / The place of excrement; / For nothing can be sole or whole / That has not been rent." Mark Thompson says of the anus, "When properly opened, it becomes a portal through which the spirit of homo-masculinity can impregnate one's soul." Fisting becomes a ritualistic act to take Bill to the next level of his development. First he learns to give; later he becomes the receiver. Warren and Brad reappear. First performing a healing ritual of atonement, they baptize Bill with urine. And then Warren penetrates him: "I saw myself split in two—like Warren and Brad—twins. . . . My body dissolved."[34]

Symbolic death is the portal to the transformation of the Self, the supreme liberation from all that hinders the development of the self, the rite of passage that permits the emergence of the new. Robert early recognizes the signification of this stage: "I'd been trying to tell myself that my life *had* to change, that, in effect, I had to 'die'!" At one point, Bill feels that he is surrounded by figures from his past, "taunting me. It was like being dead, stretched out in my coffin." Warren undergoes the ritualistic encounter with death in comical, one might say "satyric," terms. Having reached a rough spot in his relationship with Brad, he picks up a policeman and takes him home. There the officer proceeds to tie him up and then threatens to kill him with his gun while taking him sexually. Brad arrives in the nick of time to save Warren from the phallic weapon (Warren "shoots" as the cop's "finger [tightens] on the trigger"), only to find that the gun was loaded with blanks. The incident provides the two lovers with the impetus to redefine their commitment: the moment "turned out to be just the beginning."[35]

The Thorne brothers especially have to work hard to free themselves of the false strictures that their homophobic upbringing has created, which blight true self-actualization. The Jungian-oriented psychotherapist Robert H. Hopcke observes that "behind the fear of the same-sex other is a devastating fear of the self." Homophobia manifests itself in "a fear of taking pleasure in one's own body; a lack of intimacy with other men and women, and a concomitant lack of validation and community; or, as a more extreme example, a near-paranoid sense of competition with and persecution by the very people who might be expected to mirror oneself and one's soul—those who are like ourselves." He sums up, "If homophobia is indeed a fear of the self, then it is almost certainly a fear of the Self, particularly the Self in its ambivalence."[36] Bill laments how his family and his community locked him inside himself with all "the memorized scriptures from my childhood, all the *Thou shalts* and *Thou shalt nots*." Far along in his search for authenticity, he acknowledges, "I'd spent entirely too much of my life letting the whores and the cowboys, the Bishops and the 'Authorities' tell me how to live my life. . . . [I]t was time I started taking control myself."[37]

For Robert, the church's heterosexist doctrines at first seem insurmountable. He will not divorce the wife he has probably never loved and with whom he no longer has sex. He cannot permit himself or his son to engage in sex with men; therefore, he cannot handle the guilt he feels for having coerced his own brother into fellatio. He punishes himself—more deeply than he realizes. Robert first begins pulling out of the psychological morass into which he has sunk when his son catches him naked in his bedroom, hallucinating on mescaline. He suddenly has an epiphany: "Why had I ever felt that my body was shameful or terrible? God made man in his own image! *His Own Image!* [That] meant that *I, me,* Robert Randolph Thorne, had been created in the image of God. . . . What possible *right* did I have to be ashamed of my body? That would mean that I was ashamed of God!" For the first time he judges his own father—"Good old holier-than-anyone, wife-hating, children-hating, God-loving Dad"—and realizes what a curse he has been living under his entire life.[38] Now he can strive to avoid the same homophobic mistakes with his own son.

At this point, however, Robert still does not realize just how gravely his father's patriarchal creed has cursed him. It takes the greater part of his journey before he snaps to the truth that he, himself, has written the threatening letters. Under the pressure of guilt, his personality has fragmented. Robert/Robber, Rob, and Bobby are different aspects of his personality, and Rob endangers them all. One could analyze what has happened to Robert in Jungian terms as a nonintegrated persona, shadow, and ego. Or in Freudian terms as a case in which the superego has overpowered the ego to such an unhealthy extent that the id is retaliating. After Bobby forced himself sexually on Bill, he refused any more to answer to that nickname. He became Robert, accepting the tenets and creeds of his patriarchal upbringing to direct his every step. Robert became the Robber (the person to whom all the threatening letters are addressed) who stopped Bobby's development short and removed all joy from his life, creating the "wounded boy." Rob's anger is so great that he tries to lure Robert/Robber to kill himself. The tormented man is saved when Rob does not recognize his own image in a mirror and is frightened enough that Robert regains control. The narrow escape forces him to acknowledge that, as his first step, "I had to start learning to live with both Robber and Rob, learn to cope with them as parts of my personality, not as two evil spirits who took control of my body." This new, integrated personality he calls "Bob." His first act is to seek out his brother at the bar where he has been told Bill goes, the Phoenix: "the name sounded very apropos of all that had been happening to me. . . . The last three days had been like a passage through Purgatory, a cleansing, a baptism-by-fire; but this was the real beginning."[39]

Vanden rarely plays with words or names. Those he gives to the baths and the bars that his characters frequent, however, often do have symbolic significance. Warren and Brad both take jobs as bartender at the Cosmos. Without recognizing him, Bob first reunites with his brother at "the Temple . . . known as the Ganymede Baths"—"Ganymede, in whose name shines joy (*ganusthai*) and intelligence (*medea*)," Vittorio Lingiardi tells us in his study *Men in Love*.[40] Of their sexual encounter, Bob says, there was "no guilt, no shame, no need to withdraw into myself! . . . I wasn't hearing voices in my head any more! No chattering, no scolding, no arguing. Something had happened to Robert and Bobby."[41] Lingiardi's observations about the "sacred precincts of Sodom" may be apropos. He postulates that "cruising-space can constitute a real and also virtual world, both impersonal and intimate, where the 'strangeness' of the stranger contains the imprint of one's own suspended self. . . . When a gay man goes cruising, his identity may be suspended in a state of *transitional sexuality*, a point between the anguish caused by a fear of a loss of self and the quest to find a container which would enable the consolidation of self."[42] Bob exults, "I was filled with him! . . . My body dissolved then and there!" A filled hole becomes a means to fulfill wholeness. It is then that Bob heads for the Phoenix. The first image that he notices is a "golden design" that "looked like an *A* and an *O* fused together," Alpha and Omega.[43] Farther into the bar he sees a giant mural of Cosmic Man looming over mountaintops, with all their symbolic signification. On this site he and Bill name each other.

The Quester becomes, in Campbell's terms, the Master of Two Worlds. He balances inner serenity and outer necessity. Robert, ready to be consumed into Bob, says that at last "I had found myself. . . . I felt like I'd passed some kind of mysterious test—and had just graduated with honors!" Campbell postulates that the Hero now completes the circle by returning home to take back his newfound knowledge as a boon. Such a return obviously makes no sense for our heroes. Neither Colorado nor Utah is likely to accept the gifts they have to offer. Bob will fly back briefly to sign the papers dissolving both his marriage and his partnership in the business, but that is it. Instead, their return functions on a symbolic level. As Bob walks across the Phoenix, he feels, "It was like *coming home*—back to a forgotten beginning—returning from a thousand-year pilgrimage into strange and unwelcoming lands." Bill acknowledges, "I knew I would have to settle somewhere and see if I could start putting into practice the things I had learned." But he also reminds us that a quest is never finished. Individuation is a continuing process, not a one-time accomplishment. The Self is a goal, not an achievement. In the epilogue to the novel, Bill says, "There is no real ending to any story; something keeps it going; you finish one sequence and go on to the next; the last chapter of one book becomes the first in the sequel, and so on and so on, and the world spins, and very very slowly mankind inches closer and closer toward realization of what it is."[44]

Vanden clearly wanted his trilogy to function as liberation literature. In the prologue to *I Want It All,* Warren says that "if just one guy picks up this book, and reading about what happened to me when I found out about myself . . . if it helps just that one guy to understand himself better, if it helps him live with himself and the rest of the world, then it really doesn't matter how many snobs and prudes and puritans get upset by it, does it?" He goes on to attack "laws and morals . . . based on The Bible . . . written in a time when everybody *knew* the earth was flat," then extends his attack to preachers and psychiatrists.[45] In the author's note to *All Is Well,* Vanden speaks in his own voice to say, "There are very few books which advance the idea that being gay isn't as wretched and sinful as we've all been taught to believe it is." He continues, "There is a tremendously exciting reformation going on, all over the world, and I feel that gay people are going to wake up and find themselves in the vanguard of that reformation. But in order to 'wake up' we must first understand ourselves."[46]

I looked to see if the author retained these comments when he revised the novels. The author's note to *All Is Well* has disappeared, but the narrator's prologue to *I Want It All,* though stylistically revised, remains intact. Both the 1995 edition of *I Want It All* and the collected edition of 2011 have the same historical note at the beginning. Vanden reminds us that, when that first volume was published, "Nixon was president, Reagan was governor. . . . We were still illegal—it wasn't until 1976 that California decided consensual homosexuality wasn't a punishable crime. It would be 10 years before anyone had even *heard* of AIDS. Amazingly, those were the days of our innocence. . . . 'Stonewall' had yet to happen. Harvey Milk was yet to be elected. The 'sexual revolution' had just barely begun."[47] It is easy to forget how heady it was to be gay in the 1970s, when having sex in itself could be construed as a political act and, as John Rechy proclaimed in *The Sexual Outlaw,* "The promiscuous homosexual [was] a social revolutionary."[48] Rereading the *All* trilogy brought me pleasant memories of that optimistic period in our history and of my own, much tamer quest, at the exact same time as these protagonists', to get out of the closet and successfully find my own soulmate. The trilogy can now function not only as a literary achievement but also as a historical document—an important one to aid our understanding of the journey to the gains we presently enjoy.

# NOTES

1. David Nimmons, *The Soul beneath the Skin: The Unseen Hearts and Habits of Gay Men* (New York: St. Martin's, 2002), 155.
2. Steve Hogan and Lee Hudson, *Completely Queer: The Gay and Lesbian Encyclopedia* (New York: Henry Holt, 1998), 424.
3. Dirk Vanden, *All or Nothing* (New York: The Other Traveller [Olympia Press], 1971), 100.
4. Ibid., 161.
5. Martin Levine writes: "The clone was, in many ways, the manliest of men. He had a gym-defined body. . . . He wore blue-collar garb—flannel shirts over muscle T-shirts, Levi 501s over work boots, bomber jackets over hooded sweatshirts. He kept his hair short and had a thick mustache or closely cropped beard. There was nothing New Age or hippie about this reformed gay liberationist. And the clone lived the fast life. He 'partied hard,' taking recreational drugs, . . . having hot sex with strangers." Martin P. Levine, *Gay Macho: The Life and Death of the Homosexual Clone*, ed. Michael S. Kimmel (New York: New York University Press, 1998), 7–8. See also Shaun Cole, *"Don We Now Our Gay Apparel": Gay Men's Dress in the Twentieth Century* (Oxford: Berg, 2000), 71–118.
6. Vanden, *All Is Well* (New York: The Other Traveller [Olympia Press], 1971), 159.
7. Michael Perkins, *The Secret Record: Modern Erotic Literature* (1976; New York: Masquerade Books, 1992), 225–26; James Levin, *The Gay Novel: The Male Homosexual Image in America* (New York: Irvington, 1983), 297; Edmund Miller, "Erotica and Pornography," in *The Gay and Lesbian Literary Heritage: A Reader's Companion to the Writers and Their Works, from Antiquity to the Present*, ed. Claude J. Summers (New York: Henry Holt, 1995), 262; Robert Nashak, "Sadomasochistic Literature," ibid., 623. Simon Sheppard included an excerpt from *I Want It All* in *Homosex: Sixty Years of Gay Erotica* (New York: Carroll & Graf, 2007), 53–68.
8. Ralph Collins, blurb (c. 1970) on back cover of *All of Me* (see note 13); Michael Perkins, blurb (c. 1970) on back covers of *All or Nothing* and *All Is Well;* Victor DeStefano, blurb (Feb. 1971) on back cover of *All or Nothing;* Peter Hadley, blurb (c. 1970) on back cover of *All Is Well;* John Francis Hunter, "The New Erotica: *All Is Well!,*" *GAY,* Dec. 6, 1971; Richard Amory, "Vanden's Best Book," *Vector,* March 1972; Marc Williams, "My View," *Mattachine Society Magazine,* Christmas 1971.
9. Neil DeWitte provides a summary of all three *Loon* volumes, as well as the parody, in "The Gay Western: Trailblazing Heroes Stake Their Claim," in *The Golden Age of Gay Fiction*, ed. Drewey Wayne Gunn (Albion, NY: MLR Press, 2009), 224–26, 234.
10. *It Was Too Soon Before: The Unlikely Life, Untimely Death, and Unexpected Rebirth of Gay Pioneer Dirk Vanden* (Maple Shade, NJ: Lethe Press, 2012), 112. See also his 2011 interview with me, "Dirk Vanden: Pioneer of Gay Literature," www.lambdaliterary.org/features/08/10/dirk-vanden-pioneer-of-gay-literature/.
11. Vanden, *I Want It All* (San Rafael, CA: Frenchy's Gay Line, 1969), 7.
12. Vanden, *All or Nothing*, 99.
13. Vanden, *I Want It All* (Sacramento, CA: Brass Ring Books, 1995); *All Together: The All Trilogy* (n.p.: loveyoudivine Alterotica, 2011); *I Want It All: A "Mental Movie"* (2011), www.dirkvanden.net/iwantitall_mentalmovie.pdf. *All Together* won a Lambda Literary

Award for best gay erotica. The three novels are also available as individual e-books. Despite its title, *All of Me (Can You Take All of Me?)* (Pittsburgh: RoseDog, 2010) is not a continuation of the trilogy—though in a strange way it does provide a kind of commentary on it. There are three main characters who function as one character at three stages in his life, in much the same way as in Edward Albee's *Three Tall Women.*

14. Joseph Campbell, *The Hero with a Thousand Faces* (New York: Pantheon, 1949), 245–46.
15. Warren: Vanden, *I Want It All,* 9 (compare *All or Nothing,* 9, where he says much the same thing); Bill: *All or Nothing,* 51; Robert: *All Is Well,* 17, 19, 24.
16. Mark Thompson, *Gay Body: A Journey through Shadow to Self* (New York: St. Martin's, 1997), 8–9.
17. Vanden, *I Want It All,* 16, 29; *All or Nothing,* 27; *All Is Well,* 24, 95.
18. Vanden, *I Want It All,* 22; *All or Nothing,* 30, 86; *All Is Well,* 26.
19. Vanden, *I Want It All,* 22; *All or Nothing,* 74, 98–99; *All Is Well,* 122.
20. Vanden, *I Want It All,* 42; *All Is Well,* 154, 174; *All or Nothing,* 105, 122.
21. Vanden, *I Want It All,* 5–6; *All or Nothing,* 97; *All Is Well,* 188.
22. Vanden, *I Want It All,* 56, 73.
23. Vanden, *All or Nothing,* 113, 119.
24. Hunter, "The New Erotica."
25. Levine, *Gay Macho,* 5, 28–29. Like many of us at the time, I cringed when I saw the bitchy queens in the film version of *The Boys in the Band* (1970). I now enjoy the film, but I was intrigued to learn from the documentary *The Making of the Boys* (2010) that Edward Albee—eleven years older than I—felt the original stage version was a mistake. Mark Thompson, in *Gay Body,* recalls that he left the movie "feeling deflated by its morbid portrayals" (75).
26. John Beebe, "Toward an Image of Male Partnership," in *Same-Sex Love and the Path to Wholeness,* ed. Robert H. Hopcke, Karin Loftus Carrington, and Scott Wirth (Boston: Shambhala, 1993), 153. Robert H. Hopcke's work *Jung, Jungians, and Homosexuality* (1991; Eugene, OR: Rèsource, 2002), offers provocative insight into the gay individuation process, particularly chapters 6–8, which discuss the archetypal feminine, the archetypal masculine, and the Androgyne.
27. Perkins, blurb on back cover of *All or Nothing.*
28. Vanden, *I Want It All,* 190. The Jungian analyst Robert Bosnak makes some observations that are germane to our heroes' discoveries in his essay "Individuation, Taboo, and Same-Sex Love," in Hopcke et al., *Same-Sex Love,* 264–72.
29. J. E. Cirlot, *A Dictionary of Symbols,* 2nd ed., trans. Jack Sage (New York: Philosophical Library, 1971), 211–12; Thompson, *Gay Body,* 72.
30. Vanden, *I Want It All,* 12. Lyn Cowan observes that "in that eternal moment of gazing into one's reflection . . . , one may perceive one's beauty as one's true self, and one's truth as a beautiful self." For her, it is the path to romantic love. See her essay, "Homo/Aesthetics, or Romancing the Self," in Hopcke et al., *Same-Sex Love,* 132.
31. Vanden, *All or Nothing,* 20, 85; *I Want It All,* 220; *All Is Well,* 71. At one point, when Warren must introduce himself—much as Maurice did to Scudder in E. M. Forster's novel—he says his name is Brad (*I Want It All,* 63).
32. Quoted in Cirlot, *A Dictionary of Symbols,* 157.
33. Joseph L. Henderson, "Ancient Myths and Modern Man," in *Man and His Symbols,* by Carl G. Jung et al. (Garden City, NY: Doubleday, 1964), 113–14, 124, 130. See

also Howard Teich's essay "Homovision: The Solar/Lunar Twin-Ego," in Hopcke et al., *Same-Sex Love,* 136–50.

34. Vanden, *All or Nothing,* 115, 123 (can any reader today experience the electric shock such sentences gave readers at the time?), 181–82. Thompson, *Gay Body,* 214. The lines from Yeats are in "Crazy Jane Talks with the Bishop."
35. Vanden, *All Is Well,* 155; *All or Nothing,* 158; *I Want It All,* 213, 223. See Thompson, *Gay Body,* 201, for several pertinent observations about this stage of the process.
36. Robert H. Hopcke, "Homophobia and Analytical Psychology," in Hopcke et al., *Same-Sex Love,* 80–81. The whole essay (68–87) is worth reading.
37. Vanden, *All or Nothing,* 87, 162.
38. Vanden, *All Is Well,* 106–7, 108.
39. Vanden, *All Is Well,* 186, 190–91.
40. Vanden, *All Is Well,* 197. Vittorio Lingiardi, *Men in Love: Male Homosexualities from Ganymede to Batman,* trans. Robert H. Hopcke and Paul A. Schwartz (Chicago: Open Court, 2002), 25. The symbol of Ganymede may show up indirectly in *All or Nothing:* Bill goes to a bar, the Eyrie, where he encounters Judd Carter, who guides him into another important stage in his quest. One may also note that, since Ganymede is traditionally depicted as nude when he is carried aloft by the eagle, the pair form the emblem of the winged serpent, the transcendent Phallus. (In a footnote Lingiardi says, "The name 'Ganymede' may also come from 'shining genitals'" [189].) The Phallus is the subject of a mural in the bar Bill has just left, the Colosseum. Similar symbolic paintings appear in all three novels. Much more could be said about them, as well as about the protagonists' dreams and visions.
41. Vanden, *All Is Well,* 205.
42. Lingiardi, *Men in Love,* 115, 121.
43. Vanden, *All Is Well,* 204, 211.
44. Vanden, *All Is Well,* 205, 208, 212; *All or Nothing,* 163, 183.
45. Vanden, *I Want It All,* 6–7.
46. Vanden, *All Is Well,* [vii]. The title *All Is Well* is probably an ironic reference to the Mormon hymn, "Come, Come Ye Saints," in which the refrain "All is well! All is well!" appears four times. Not only the hymn's title but lines within the song take on special meaning when read in conjunction with the novel; for example: "Though hard to you this *journey* may appear, / *Grace* shall be as your day," and "We'll find *the place* which God for us prepared, / Far away, *in the West*" (italics added). I thank Jaime Harker for bringing the hymn to my attention. She further notes that it "was written when the Mormons were crossing the plains; they were kicked out of [various states] for their strange religious beliefs and whispers about polygamy. So it was a kind of defiant anthem of an oppositional identity; they were seeking a refuge away from mainstream society, a utopia in which they were free to believe and act as they chose. Going to the West for Mormons meant Utah, and it's a very clever rewriting of this theme by Vanden to use San Francisco as the new Zion." E-mail, Dec. 31, 2011.
47. Vanden, *I Want It All* (1995), 5; *All Together,* [ix].
48. John Rechy, *The Sexual Outlaw: A Documentary* (1977; New York: Grove Press, 1984), 28. Beginning in *Fag Rag* in 1971, Charley Shively published a series of articles under the title "Cocksucking as an Act of Revolution." See Rodger Streitmatter, *Unspeakable: The Rise of the Gay and Lesbian Press in America* (Boston: Faber & Faber, 1995), 194–95.

# An End to the Way

## PULP BECOMES CLASSIC DOWN-UNDER

Jeremy Fisher

In Australia, all of which lies south of the Equator, the summer break is between November and February and covers Christmas and New Year. These holidays and the warm weather combine to slow life down. Nothing much happens in Australia in January. Everyone is in a holiday mood. The country parties.

In the summer of 1974, when I was nineteen years old, my lover and I went on a vacation. I was on break from university, and my lover had taken leave from his job as a psychiatric nurse. We'd decided we would travel north from our home in Sydney, in the state of New South Wales, to Queensland, one of two Australian states named after Victoria, whose successors still take their place as Australia's constitutional monarch. Victoria's prurient influence looms large in Australia; she was still queen (for another 22 days) when Australia became a nation on January 1, 1901.

Since we had the usual family commitments for Christmas, my lover and I proposed to set out for Queensland after New Year's Day. I hadn't been there since I was a young boy, when my family lived in a tropical town just south of the state border. My lover had never been that far north.

He had grown up in Wollongong, an industrial city eighty miles south of Sydney. (Sydney, in turn, is about 640 miles south of Brisbane, which is the capital of and the biggest city in Queensland.)

Being the age we were, we didn't plan our trip in much detail. We simply bought second-class train seats for Brisbane and traveled north overnight. The train, then and now, takes about seventeen hours to make its way from Sydney's Central to Brisbane's Roma Street station. We had to sit up all the way, since we were in second class. Traveling that way wasn't much fun, we decided as we rested in our dingy Brisbane hotel after our arrival.

We spent a day or two in hot, muggy, and rather dull Brisbane; then, again without much thought or reasoning, we booked a train farther north to Cairns. We again booked second-class seats because we saw that the train left Roma Street at 10:00 a.m. and arrived in Cairns at 2:30 p.m. We were so green we didn't realize that the 2:30 p.m. was actually two days after the train left Brisbane, as the distance between Brisbane and Cairns is almost twice that from Sydney. But as we looked once more at our timetable, this became clear to us about half an hour after we left Brisbane. We didn't want to spend two nights sitting up, so we grabbed our bags and alighted from the train at the next stop.

Australia in January 1974 was still a country searching for its own identity. Just thirteen months before, it had emerged from twenty-three years of conservative government. The new Labor government, under prime minister Gough Whitlam, had set itself an ambitious reformist agenda. Within days of its election it had reversed earlier policies committing troops to the war in Vietnam and had recognized the government of China. It also had an impressive package of social policies to enact. The rights of women to equal pay and recognition under the law were quickly implemented. The new government did not do much, though, with regard to the decriminalization of homosexuality. The Australian Labor Party included a significant number of Catholic parliamentarians whose church opposed decriminalization. In any case, the national government could do little on this matter; its powers with regard to such laws extended only to the Australian Capital Territory—a small buffer of land surrounding the national capital, Canberra, in New South Wales—and the enormous but sparsely populated Northern

Territory. Legislation relating to the criminalization of homosexuality for the rest of Australia was in the hands of the governments of the six states of Australia. One of these, South Australia, had pioneered homosexual law reform in 1972 (and in 1895, South Australia had also been the first political territory anywhere in the world to allow women both to vote and stand for election).

In New South Wales, where I lived, homosexuality remained illegal until 1984, but the city's gay scene had been outrageous though somewhat discreet from the 1960s. I'd been enjoying it since I'd moved to Sydney at the beginning of 1973 from the country town where I had completed my secondary schooling. One of the aspects of that town I remember best was the bookshop established by a former English teacher at the high school. Mr. Barnwell was a left-winger, and a relatively open-minded one. His shop carried titles such as *The A–Z of Love* (translated from the Danish), D. J. West's *Homosexuality* in the Penguin edition, Mary Renault's Greek-themed historical novels, Kyle Onstott's *Mandingo* and other books by Onstott and Lance Horner, as well as paperback editions of Jean Genet's works. I'd bought copies of all of these and read them in my bed at night before falling asleep into lascivious dreams.

Queensland, the state where we had come to vacation, was an aberration even in Australia. Since 1968 it had been run by a conservative peanut farmer, Johannes Bjelke-Petersen, who would remain in power for almost twenty years. He encouraged his police officers to use the strong arm of the law, which they did with relish. One of their most infamous abuses of force was the violent reaction to demonstrators protesting the presence of the all-white, apartheid-supporting South African Springbok rugby team that played in Brisbane in 1971. So that the game could go on without protest, Bjelke-Petersen declared a state of emergency, which meant that the police had completely unfettered use of force.

His police officers kept files on dissidents as well, though this was not unique to Queensland; the same was also true in New South Wales. In recent years, I have been able to access a copy of the file the Special Branch of the New South Wales Police maintained on me after I had been thrown out of Robert Menzies College at Macquarie University in Sydney in May 1973 for the crime of being openly homosexual. The file shows I was followed, and some of the activities I was involved in were referred to the federal Australian Security Intelligence Organisation, the equivalent of the CIA. I have also requested a copy of my ASIO file, but have been informed that it has been destroyed because, at some stage in the last forty years, I was deemed to be no threat to national security.

The New South Wales Police also attacked gay demonstrators in July 1978, laying into them with truncheons and boots, and injuring fifty-three. This incident is commemorated today in the annual Sydney Gay and Lesbian Mardi Gras, an event that attracts over 500,000 people each year, many of them from other countries. Back in 1974, however, the Queensland police and the figures who governed them were more fearsome still. In New South Wales civil liberties were paid some respect; in Queensland they did not exist. Meetings of more than three people were prohibited. Bjelke-Petersen's government was particularly homophobic, forging links with right-wing Christian fundamentalists and demonizing what was deemed aberrant sexual behavior.[1]

This was the place where my lover and I had stepped down from the train. We found ourselves in the conservative rural town of Gympie, about one hundred miles north of Brisbane. We immediately asked about a train back to Brisbane. The laconic station master advised us in a slow drawl that "the next train to Brisbane, well, that'll be tomorra," so we sought out a place to stay for the night. We found a shabby hotel on the main street—two stories, bars on the ground floor and accommodations above. The hotel had a verandah that extended over the footpath to provide shade for pedestrians and, on the upper level, a space for guests to take the air. The concept of a gay couple was so foreign in Gympie at that time that it was no problem for us to book a room together, albeit one with single beds. The room had no television. There was a separate lounge where guests could gather to watch a black-and-white screen. This didn't appeal at all, so I walked out into Mary Street in search of some reading matter.

I found a news agency a few doors away. As in most such shops, newspapers were stacked near the counter at the front while the rest of the place was filled with rows of magazine shelves. There were also some tables loaded with what were described on a hand-lettered poster as "bargain paperbacks." I sifted through these and almost immediately found one that featured a naked male torso on the cover as well as the words "A novel about hidden sex between men—penetrating—honest—telling it like it is." The word "penetrating" was repeated on the back cover: "A penetrating and honest examination of a life barely imagined by those who do not live it."

This was enough penetrating for me; I knew this was a book I had to have. The book was called *No End to the Way* and the author's name on the cover was Neville Jackson.[2] I slid it under a magazine and purchased both.

While it made no impression on me at the time, what was odd about *No End to the Way* was the fact that it was an American paperback. At that time, British publishers generally held the rights to the Australian market, and American books of any sort were quite uncommon. Pulp titles were even more rare. In the 1960s and 1970s, American publishers began to make inroads into the Australian market. At the same time, Australian booksellers were rebelling against the Traditional Market Agreement, which had been made between American and British publishers after World War II and divided the English-speaking world between the United States and its possessions (and sometimes Canada) and the British Commonwealth.

What the agreement meant was that, when a book was published in New York and rights were sold to a British publisher, that publisher almost always gained British Commonwealth rights, which included the right to sell the book in Australia. Thus Australians were unable to purchase the book until it was available in a British edition, which might be years after its first American publication. The same worked in reverse—Australians couldn't import an American edition of a book that was available in a British edition—so it is likely that *No End to the Way* came to Gympie as part of a shipment of remaindered American books.

Booksellers, eager for stock cheaper than was supplied by the British publishers, bought these in bulk in the United States and brought them in for sale. Technically the practice was illegal, but it still continues to this day. Unfortunately, my purchase of the book as a remaindered edition suggests that it met with little success in the US market, where it was first published as a paperback by Macfadden-Bartell in 1969, and a forthcoming biography bears this out. The author was paid an advance of US $1,000, and Macfadden-Bartell printed 100,000 copies but sold only 29,000 in two and a half years.[3]

Macfadden-Bartell had been founded by Bernarr Macfadden in New York in the early twentieth century, and in 1961 his company merged with the media interests of the Bartell family. Macfadden, an outspoken advocate of body-building and various health regimes, had pioneered the magazine *Physical Culture*, as well as *True Story, True Detective*, and *True Romances*, in the first three decades of the twentieth century. In the 1960s the company was a sizable player in trade publishing and mass market paperbacks. It published the mass market edition of Jess Stearns's homophobic *The Sixth Man*, as well as a number of books by 1964 Republican Presidential candidate Barry Goldwater and Donald Webster Cory's *The Lesbian in America* in 1965.[4] The Macfadden-Bartell edition of *No End to the Way* was bought from the original English publisher, Barrie & Rockliff, and perhaps not given much editorial scrutiny (the spelling remains British, so it may have been printed from the same plates as the UK edition). The US edition received little attention, unlike the British editions.

Though credited to Neville Jackson, *No End to the Way* was written by the prolific Australian author G. M. (Gerry) Glaskin, who spent the 1950s and 1960s living in Singapore, then in Amsterdam. It was first published in London in 1965, then in a new paperback edition by Corgi Books in 1967. This paperback edition was reprinted, and Corgi brought out a further edition in 1985. Glaskin wrote about the 1985 edition in a letter to the Australian Society of Authors in 1985: "Just out of interest, this is a special 're-issue' after three editions in 1967, 67, 68 from the original Barrie & Rockliff 1965 hardcover edition. Some books do manage to live 20 years."[5]

Despite the sensationalism of its cover blurbs, *No End to the Way* offers a positive account of homosexual life, and the ending, while distinctly downbeat, is brighter than those in most gay novels of the period. Indeed, Glaskin's "happy" conclusion to his book presented major problems for his publisher in 1965, since at the time the Home Office in Britain required that stories about homosexuals lead to a tragic end, usually death. While in later years Glaskin claimed his publisher forced a pseudonym on him to protect his name, correspondence between the parties reveals the pseudonym was Glaskin's idea all along.[6] Ironically, the book would prove to be his most successful.

Because of the severe censorship operating in Australia at the time, *No End to the Way* was banned from importation into Australia on its publication in the United Kingdom in 1965. Thanks to its origins in Victorian morals and ethics, for much of the twentieth century Australia was subject to one of the most rigorous censorship regimes in the English-speaking world (only South Africa was more stringent). Government regulation remained rigid even in the face of absurdity. For instance, J. D. Salinger's *Catcher in the Rye* (1951) was banned for import in 1957, though it had been freely available and was even in the Parliamentary Library. Various other libraries also had copies of the book, donated by the US ambassador. The resulting flap forced the Customs Minister to overturn the ban and initiate a review of his department's censorship mechanisms. This led to a reduction in the list of banned books from around 16,000 to 178.[7] It was not until 1969, however, that the possession of most banned books was made legal. Until that time, all works that made reference to male homosexuality were routinely banned, even academic and scientific texts.[8] (Even D. J. West's rather dry account of homosexuality, which I'd bought in the bookshop of the town where I grew up, had been banned for a period. I bought the book more because it had once been banned than because of its content. It wasn't a title I read at night.)

Though the lurid covers of both the Corgi and Macfadden-Bartell paperbacks screamed pulp, surprisingly the Australian censors regarded *No End to the Way* as a work of a different order. They accepted it as serious literature, as a 1965 report from A. Hope Hewitt, the first woman member of the Censorship Board and a lecturer in literary studies at the Australian National University in Canberra, reveals. At that time, Gore Vidal's *The City and the Pillar,* which had first been banned in 1947, was being reconsidered by the board. Hewitt compared Vidal's novel to *No End to the Way,* noting that if, in 1965, the time had come to release books on homosexuality, these two "would be good, serious fictional studies with which to start."[9] The Censorship Board unbanned *No End to the Way* in 1966 on appeal, and *The City and the Pillar* was also made available to Australians at the same time.

Since the time I first purchased *No End to the Way* hoping it would be a titillating read, I've come to know a great deal about it and its author. Because I had bought an American edition, at first I was unaware the author was Australian. That such a book could be written by an Australian was incomprehensible to me. At that time, I had never encountered any Australian books that offered even limited homosexual perspectives, though, as I have since discovered, there were some floating about.

Kenneth (Seaforth) Mackenzie's *The Young Desire It*, dating from 1937, features a teacher sexually interested in a schoolboy. It has been described as "an intensely introspective account of a boy's experience of love, both homosexual and heterosexual," so introspective in fact that a reader could be forgiven for considering the book trying. Nevertheless, the prominent Australian gay historian Garry Wotherspoon calls it "truly a book before its time," and adds that "its sympathetic portrayal of homosexuality is remarkable even today."[10]

But to interpret the highly coded text, some knowledge of an otherwise unmentioned and unknown parallel world was required, as was true of other books that had some interface with the Australian homosexual world. Wotherspoon has also shown that Christina Stead's *Seven Poor Men of Sydney* (1934) and Kylie Tennant's *Tell Morning This* (1967) offer evidence of knowledge of camp subcultures, with varying degrees of coding.[11] Tennant's novel includes this scene:

> "You saw those young men? Nonnie asked. "They thought we were trying to get the Archibald Fountain [a bronze work in Sydney's Hyde Park featuring naked warriors in a Greek style] removed. So extraordinary!"
>
> "Homosexuals," Dr Cranitz said blandly.
>
> "But why should they worry about the fountain? I admit it's a beautiful thing, and I wouldn't want to see it moved myself . . ."
>
> "It is their meeting-place"
>
> "Surely not! How do you know?"
>
> "My dear lady." Dr Cranitz said resignedly, "it is so, I assure you."[12]

How did Dr. Cranitz know, indeed!

In Stead's *Seven Poor Men of Sydney*, Michael Baguenault half-crazedly roams over the Eastern Suburbs area of Sydney toward what is known as the Gap, a space in the headlands over the Pacific notorious for suicides, where he is to throw himself into the sea: "A young fellow standing near a street lamp came into its light, while approaching Michael modestly. His small hands were manicured, his fine wrists and delicate neck were blackish as with coaldust, but his hairless face, with oval cheeks, was pink and powdered. His eyes, large and timid, looked appealingly at Michael. Michael brushed rudely past him. The boy retreated to the fence once more to wait. Michael heard steps, the boy coming after him, he thought, and he looked back—only a tram conductor going home from the depot."[13]

The two paragraphs that follow describe an old man with a "long, sensuous, finely modelled mouth," who is followed by a "tough," who has a "bad face, repulsive concentrated eyes and thick jaw." When Michael looks "uneasily" back, "the young man and old man had gone down the hill and around the corner." These are interesting last visions before his suicide. Given that elsewhere Michael, who was an effeminate child, confesses his love for his half-sister Catherine because that is like loving himself, and that his closest relationship is with the crippled Kol Blount, who later expresses great love for him, modern readers could be forgiven for questioning Michael's sexuality. Perhaps Stead considered Michael a closeted homosexual, but if so it is too closely coded to be clear.

Wotherspoon also mentions Jon Rose's semi-autobiographical novel *At the Cross* (1961), narrated by seventeen-year-old Jon. This book comes close to having an overt homosexual narrator and scenes of gay sex. But while Jon's heterosexual dalliances are documented, there are other lovers where the story simply stops. Two examples: "Watching them [Cliff and Dennis] I became more and more sad at leaving this flat. I liked it and it liked me, but I had to go and stretch my own wings. I went back into the bedroom. Dennis was sitting in a little heap on the pillow, Cliff stood looking at an invisible spot in his underpants. I gave them a half-hearted smile, looked at the light switch, and said 'Can I sleep on the outside?' " And, "I suddenly felt drunk and very sad in a strange way. At that second I saw a low fence and sat down on it. As I was sitting, a half familiar voice said 'You all right?' I looked up, saying yes, but I couldn't really see properly. The voice said 'I live just here. Would you like some coffee?' " The book inspired Alex Harding's musical comedy *Only Heaven Knows*, which was first performed by the Griffin Theatre Company at the Stables Theatre in Sydney in 1988.[14]

Wotherspoon mentions a few other novels—Colin MacInnes's *June in Her Spring* (1951), Elisabeth Lambert's *The Sleeping House Party* (1951), and Stuart Lauder's *Winger's Landfall* (1962)—that reveal some aspects of homosexual life, but only the last has an overtly homosexual narrator or narrative.[15] The anonymous review of Lambert's book in the Australian literary journal *Southerly*, though, slyly notes, "Miss Lambert's airy English perhaps achieves its best effects in the portrayal of certain city types, with their peculiar idiom, whom she has observed."[16]

*Winger's Landfall* concerns Harry Shears's attempt to discover what happened to his half-brother Danny, who fell overboard from the passenger ship *Cyclamen*. He was in unrequited love with Danny: "Of course I loved him, he admitted bitterly. What choice did I have? That's how I'm made. But at least he never knew. I was always too careful for that."[17] While this is ostensibly a British novel, there is a close identification with Australia and some acute observations of Sydney, Melbourne, and Fremantle. Danny's mother had lived with Harry's father for a while in London before moving out to Australia to escape domestic violence, taking the children with her.

Harry is a winger, the nickname for an onboard steward. He joins the ship in Sydney, having knocked out the man he is replacing on a street at night, and he shares a peak (cabin) with other wingers. The novel includes a number of other gay characters. "Marilyn" is a sixteen-year-old flirt. There's an alcoholic queer winger who tends meals drunk. Another character, Diamond Lil, claims to be the queen in charge of the ship, having displaced Patience Strong. Patience picks Harry as gay: " 'Camp as a row of tents, that one!' said Patience emphatically. 'They can't fool Auntie!' Tensely Harry walked on into the saloon, conscious of the tightrope stretching before him."[18]

And on leave in Melbourne: "There was a young Greek soda-jerker, a curly-headed Olympian gone a-begging. Harry straddled a bar stool and talked to him over a milk-shake while the kids in the corner were getting acquainted. Fortunately no more talent entered the bar, so Harry didn't have to go through the motions of a pick-up. 'You like it here?' Harry asked the

Greek. The youth pouted, olive smooth, mobile-featured; and, in their glances, while they talked about the climate, they spoke, as it were, an older and more civilized tongue." Later, Harry asks young Prince: " 'You want to?' Harry murmured against his ear. 'Be my boy? You know?' 'Yeah, if you like . . .' Prince gulped. 'I don't mind.' "[19]

The two conduct a relationship as Harry investigates the mysterious Bernard and his hold over a group of bellboys, a group to which he discovers Danny once belonged. When the ship docks in at Colombo in Ceylon, he follows them and finds that Bernard is part of a Buddhist-Christian religious order, though this involves the boys bathing naked in a swimming pool. Back on board ship, Bernard reveals that Danny spoke in voices about "his brother." Harry spurns Prince, "compelling himself to ignore the disgusting knife-twisting pain in his chest, and the impulse to rush back to the washroom while there was still time."[20] The book ends curiously, with Harry having bashed unconscious and possibly killed Bernard and the police arresting him on Prince's information. He goes into an epileptic shock, the same as Danny suffered, which it transpires made him jump overboard. The book thus has the appropriate tragic ending for an English gay novel of that time.

Indeed, that a tragic ending was expected makes *No End to the Way* all the more remarkable, since both main protagonists survive, although not necessarily happily. The book was also far too overt to have been considered by any Australian publisher, even those with pulp fiction lines. There were quite a number of such publishers operating in Australia in the 1950s and 1960s. Even so, pulp did not develop fully in Australia since, as a small English-speaking market, it has never had enough buyers to sustain a market for homegrown pulp. There were some moves to popular forms early in the twentieth century, but while the New South Wales Bookstall Company published popular titles with lively covers by authors such Norman Lindsay, Vance Palmer, and "Steele Rudd" from the 1880s to 1946, by the end of World War II the company reverted to being simply a retailer and distributor of books and magazines. It was during this same period, however, that Australian pulp began to flourish. A dollar crisis in 1940 forced the Australian government to impose restrictions, and these led to all US publications being refused entry to Australia, not just those whose publishing rights were restricted.[21]

Companies such as Invincible Press, Currawong, Cleveland, and Horwitz (first as Transport Publishing and then under a number of imprints) leaped into the gap created, publishing pulp by both Australian and foreign writers. The Australian writers these publishers worked with included well-known names such as Jon Cleary and Frank Clune. Horwitz also published A. G. Yates (better known by one of his pseudonyms, Carter Brown), J. E. McDonnell, and Gordon Clive Bleeck (who wrote under various pseudonyms). These writers were given a heavy workload. Bleeck's schedule for Horwitz might be two westerns, a science fiction title, and a 24,000-word "space opera" a month.[22]

Perhaps the most significant of the Australian pulp publishers was Horwitz, which only very recently disappeared as a publishing entity when the Horwitz family liquidated their last remaining interest in adult magazines. Cleveland Publishing still produces westerns in Sydney, the city where most Australian pulp publishers were located. In the mid-1950s, Cleveland was producing eighteen westerns a month; Horwitz produced twenty-four titles a month. As part of this output, Horwitz published four novels—all 130 pages exactly, as were all of their pulp editions—by the distinguished Australian poet Bruce Beaver (1928–2004). These books were *The Hot Summer* (1963), *Hot Sands* (1964), *The Hot Spring* (1965), and *The Hot Men* (1965), and they are much more populist—and possibly popular—than any of Beaver's poetry. Beaver was just one of many otherwise respectable Australian writers who succumbed to the quick, if not lucrative, financial lure of pulp.

Horwitz also produced a series of books for adults, with titles such as *Wife Swap Orgy* (1974), *Society Stud* (1973), and *Orgy* (1972). Because of Australia's strict censorship laws, pulp did not develop the sensationalist, high-pitched edge that it gained in the United States until its dying days in the 1970s, even though, as the cultural historian Noel Sanders writes, "The word for the pulp paperback industry in Sydney in the early 60s is, without a doubt, 'sleazy.' "[23]

Horwitz was also responsible for the pulp crime novels of Carter Brown, the most well-known pseudonym of A. G. Yates. It successfully resold these to NAL/Signet in the United States. It also published the Australian artist and author Norman Lindsay's naughty *The Cautious Amorist* in 1962, which had been banned from importation into Australia since May 1933, when it was first released in the United States.

Though Horwitz and its fellow pulp publishers were producing books in the romance, crime, mystery, western, and military genres, there was almost no homosexual content in the output of Australian pulp publishers. This reflected the conservative moral outlook of the time as well as the small size of the Australian market. Horwitz's Scripts Publications imprint, however, offered at least one title with a gay theme. The book was published in 1974, the same year I found *No End to the Way* in Gympie, and it was imaginatively titled *The Gay Way.*[24] It is written by Mark Harris, one of the many pseudonyms used by Carl Ruhen, who wrote numerous titles for Horwitz, including *The Violent Ones* (1966), *The Naked Vampires* (1971), *The Naked Voyeur* (1971), *Lesbian Love-Slave* (1972), and *Porno Girls* (1974). More recently, Ruhen has written novelizations for popular Australian televisions series and movies, including *The Road Warrior* (*Mad Max 2*), the film that introduced Mel Gibson to North American audiences in 1981.

The cover of *The Gay Way* features a photograph of a young man with longish hair, head to the side, eyes closed, shirt raised up to the neck to expose chest and nipples. A woman behind the man is raising his shirt. The cover text announces, "Men craved his body . . . A woman needed his passion . . . His choice was her or . . . *The Gay Way.*" The story concerns nineteen-year-old Danny, who, as the back-cover description says, "had gone to bed with men before many times, but in a rather fizzy, party sort of way." He has a girlfriend, Erica, who, though she is not a virgin, is holding out giving herself to him because she wants some commitment from him. Danny takes her to a gay party, where she finds herself neglected by him. When she says she wants to go home, he offers to drive her, but she says she'll take a taxi. She doesn't leave, but goes outside and sits in the garden. When she comes back in later, she finds Danny kissing Gerald. She then leaves. Danny goes home with Gerald and has sex, but takes Erica to the beach next day. He tells her all, as well as that Gerald has invited him to dinner that day. She persuades him to take her to Gerald's, where she confronts Gerald and triumphantly leaves with her man. There are indications that Danny will test Erica, but she's to be a "tower of strength" to help him overcome his attraction to men, of which he says, "It wasn't serious. It never was."[25] There is some sympathy for Gerald as well, despite the boy-gets-girl conclusion.

Another Mark Harris novel, *Society Stud* (1973), concerns a tough, macho man, Talbot. One night when Talbot is drunk, he is taken in by the friendly Kirby, who performs oral sex on him as he falls asleep. In another chapter Kirby admits this, offers Talbot breakfast, and tries to do it again. Talbot kicks him away. He feels "grubby." There is little sympathy in this story for Kirby, who later is severely bashed by two rough types he invites home.

It would not be until the early 1970s, after Stonewall and the emergence of gay liberation in Australia, that there would be magazines and tabloid newspapers with a clear gay focus in an Australian context.[26] Stories came later. I was responsible for one of the first, "Fragments," published in 1975.[27] Magazines such as *Campaign* and *Gay Changes* were also publishing short stories and other fiction. The first collection of homosexual stories and poems, *Edge City on Two Different Plans* (1983), which features several works of mine, was published by a collective that had set up a magazine, *Inversions*, in 1980.[28] A number of emerging gay Australian writers were first published there, including Garry Dunne and Dave Sargent. The group later published the magazine *Cargo* and books under the Blackwattle Press imprint. Today, they publish under the online imprint gay e-books. Mel Keegan's work began to be published in 1990. Both Christos Tsiolkas's *Loaded* (filmed as *Head On*) and Graeme Aitken's *Fifty Ways of Saying Fabulous* appeared in 1995.[29] The output of Australian gay work since then has been slow, but steady. No specifically gay imprint has been able to survive in print form, because of the small size of the Australian market. Publication of gay works is reliant on the whims and market focus of more mainstream publishers, even when those publishers are still small.

All of that history, though, was still to occur when I first encountered *No End to the Way*. When I began reading it, I didn't even realize it would be part of that history. It was only after some pages, twenty in fact, that it became clear the book was set in Australia. Cor, the handsome Dutchman Ray Wharton has just picked up in a bar, is walking with Ray to Ray's car. Cor tells Ray he was studying architecture in the Netherlands before he came out to Australia. With that revelation, I was prepared for more clues. It gradually became clear that the book was not set in Sydney, which seemed the most obvious setting since on the first page there is a reference to the harbor, a Swedish freighter, and its second officer: "a wild thing in the cot; about the best slice you can remember in years." Rather, much of the action in the book takes place in Glaskin's hometown of Perth, Western Australia, as does much of his writing. The sustained second-person narrative voice Glaskin uses throughout makes this novel continue to stand out more than forty years after its first publication. This difficult technical device gives it both an intimacy with the reader—for the "you" is "me"—and a narrative distance I did not first appreciate. In terms of the point of view, the reader is continually seeing through the eyes of the narrator: "Impossible to think that he was the first one to seduce you, when you were just eighteen, almost as many years ago. The first one after Uncle Kev, that is."[30] That leads to other understandings outside the "ego" of the reader. But Glaskin successfully manipulates the second voice so that the reader identifies, and distances, but ultimately must accept a gay narrative point of view. By avoiding the first person, Glaskin allows, in fact almost forces, his readers to place themselves in Ray Wharton's place ("you get another letter") and even understand "Uncle Kev" (the sixteen-year-old uncle who has sex with his much younger nephew, Ray, a relationship that lasts for some years until Uncle Kev is killed on his motorbike at twenty-one).

Even though he was a prolific author, to my shame I had never heard of Gerry Glaskin in 1974. In 1951, the manuscript that would become his novel *A World of Our Own* (1955) was commended by the judges of the Commonwealth Jubilee Literary Competition, but while that and subsequent works sold well in Europe, he never achieved a major public profile in Australia. He was around forty years old when he wrote *No End to the Way*, roughly the age of his second-person narrator, Ray Wharton. While Glaskin had sex with men, in the early 1960s he wasn't openly homosexual, nor is Ray. Glaskin's lover for many years (beginning in 1968) has told me that for some time the couple lived in two adjoining flats, rather than together, to avoid being considered queer, though they shared an apartment in later years.[31] Glaskin even told his publishers that he intended his book "as a deterrent rather than an encouragement of that kind of life, which I feel that the conventional melodramatic and mostly untrue endings of suicides, etc., never accomplish."[32] When he wrote this, he was living with Edgar Vos, who would become a prominent Dutch couturier, in Pieter Corneliszoon Hoofstraat, Amsterdam, though not in an open relationship.

*No End to the Way* is the story of a man who lives in the shadows. Ray Wharton knows full well what he is, but he is unable to show this in his work or other overt parts of his life. His love life must remain secret. Glaskin sets this world up with his first description of the gay bar where Ray will meet Cor: "If the cops come in to scour round, it always looks respectable enough. And the rest of it's a very respectable pub, one of the city's best. Just a bit old and in need of a face-lift. Country people use it a lot, in the residential part." The pub is "the kind of pub the gays always seem to pick out and make their own, the world over" (an early Australian use of "gays"). Ray has gone there for "the ones that *aren't* obvious . . . that most everybody wants; what's called 'rough trade' or, if it's not so rough, just 'trade.' Casual adventurers. Or week-end dabblers. Sometimes only once a month, once a year. And bisexuals. There's no end to the variety of types in the games."[33]

The reference to bisexuals in important; Cor turns out to be married and a bisexual. This leads to the conclusion of the book: "But about six months later you get another short letter, just to say that he's marrying again, to an Australian girl this time, yes a real girl, but one who understands, he says. Her father owns a string of chain stores; he's taking her up to the north of Queensland, to manage one of them. If there's one thing he can't face, he says, it's loneliness; just the mere prospect of it frightens him to death. And he can't see anything but loneliness ahead of you in the *gay* life, not these days. So he wishes you luck, and again sends his love."[34]

For me, in 1974, this revelation that Ray Wharton would continue in the "*gay* life" (the italics are in the original), while Cor departs for nervous bisexuality, was an inspiration and evidence that there was honor and respect in the love I had been blessed with (this may well have been because it had been only six months before that I had tried to commit suicide after being expelled from Macquarie University). Glaskin keeps his narrator proudly, determinedly gay. There's none of the falsity that underlies *The Gay Way.* I needed that assurance in 1974, and it is still relevant today.

Cor, the blond "god" Ray falls for, didn't complete the architectural study he began in the Netherlands, not that it matters in Australia. " 'I'd still have to do it all again. Europe's architecture just won't *do* for Australia,' he adds. And it's not just sarcasm, but more a kind of light amusement. 'Like medicine and law, and several other things,' he goes on, and the whole silly point of it rubs you raw, you almost hate the country, the way it wantonly makes so much waste of its new migrants and, much more personally, treats people like yourself as some kind of criminal."[35]

The book says a great deal about Australia in the 1960s, especially life in the west and Perth, a city which is so remote from almost everywhere else. "His guest from the east is fattish, fortyish, with red hair going bald, freckles. Bruce tells you he's the chairman of some government tribunal, just visiting the state for a few days before going back again."[36]

Read today, *No End to the Way* is still as strong a text as when I read it in 1974. Even so, there are some difficulties that distance brings to the fore. There is a concentration on social status that seems at odds with the other liberated views of the narrator. For example, Ray wonders what a schoolteacher and a shop assistant (Roy and Andy) are likely to have in common and is briefly disappointed when he finds out that Cor is a bar steward in a club, since it doesn't align with his own job as an advertising agent. Nevertheless, it was the first book I read of which I could say "this book speaks in my voice," and the fact that it was Australian as well has made me regard it ever since as a precious jewel.

The historian Graham Willett argues that *No End to the Way* is the strongest literary representation of the fear that homosexuals experienced in the 1950s. He writes:

> The characters, who are, in Ray's pithy phrase, perfectly well adjusted to their maladjustment, are nonetheless subjected to the relentless pressure of a society that neither understands nor approves of their

> kind. All of this is reflected in a debilitating day-to-day fear: of the disapproval of family and friends; of being beaten up by the men they meet in bars; of blackmail; of police entrapment; of arrest, exposure, and disgrace. It is reflected too, in intolerable constraints on daily activities: in only being able to kiss good night if the street was dark enough; only being able to hold hands in cinemas and in the car if their touching was out of the line of sight; in searching for a flat where the windows were not open to on-lookers who might see them forget themselves for a moment and kiss.[37]

Glaskin's novel today has evolved into a work of major significance in Australian literature since my first encounter with it as a piece of discarded, and at one time banned, American pulp. In his landmark book *A Guide to Gay and Lesbian Writing in Australia,* Michael Hurley writes that it is "the first Australian novel narrated from an openly male homosexual point of view."[38] It is the pioneer, leading the way for many other stories, both serious and slight, that tell of my country, my world.

## NOTES

1. See Shirleene Robinson, "Homophobia as Party Politics: The Construction of the 'Homosexual Deviant' in Joh Bjelke-Petersen's Queensland," *Queensland Review* 17, no. 1 (2010): 29–45.
2. Neville Jackson (G. M. Glaskin), *No End to the Way* (New York: Macfadden-Bartell, 1969).
3. John Burbidge, *Dare Me! The Life and Work of G. M. Glaskin* (Melbourne: Monash University Press, forthcoming), chap. 9.
4. Jess Stearns, *The Sixth Man: A Startling Investigation of the Spread of Homosexuality in America* (New York: Macfadden-Bartell, 1961).
5. G. M. Glaskin to Bill Larkins, editor of *Australian Author* (Australian Society of Authors), Jan. 30, 1985, in author's possession.
6. John M. Bunting to Humphrey Hare, Barrie & Rockliff, May 2, 1962; Bunting to G. M. Glaskin, Feb. 1, 1963; Glaskin to Bunting, Nov. 18, 1963; all in Barrie & Rockliff collection, Random House Archive and Library, Rushden, UK.
7. Stuart Glover, "Case Study: Literature and the State," in *Paper Empires: A History of the Book in Australia, 1946–2005,* ed. C. Munro and R. Sheahan-Bright (St. Lucia: University of Queensland Press, 2006), 165–73; Marita Bullock and Nicole Moore, "Banned in Australia: Introducing Australia's Bibliography of Banned Books," www.austlit.edu.au/specialistDatasets/Banned/bullockMoore.

8. Nicole Moore, "Secrets of the Censors: Obscenity in the Archives," paper presented at the National Archives of Australia, Canberra, May 2, 2005, www.naa.gov.au/about-us/research-grants/margaret-george-award/award-recipients/moore-paper-2004-old.aspx.
9. Quoted ibid.
10. Kenneth (Seaforth) Mackenzie, *The Young Desire It* (London: Jonathan Cape, 1937); W. H. Wilde, Joy Hooton and Barry Andrews, *Oxford Companion to Australian Literature* (Melbourne: Oxford University Press, 1985), 446; Garry Wotherspoon, *"City of the Plain": History of a Gay Sub-culture* (Sydney: Hale & Iremonger, 1991), 29.
11. Garry Wotherspoon, "A 'Glimpse through an Interstice Caught': Fictional Portrayals of Male Homosexual Life in Twentieth-Century Sydney," *PMLA* 122, no. 1 (2007): 344–47.
12. Kylie Tennant, *Tell Morning This* (Sydney: Angus & Robertson, 1967), 266–67.
13. Christina Stead, *Seven Poor Men of Sydney* (London: Peter Davies, 1934), 277.
14. Jon Rose, *At the Cross* (London: Andre Deutsch, 1961), 30, 43; Michael Hurley, *A Guide to Gay and Lesbian Writing in Australia* (Sydney: Allen & Unwin, 1996), 195.
15. Stuart Lauder, *Winger's Landfall* (London: Eyre & Spottiswode, 1962).
16. Anonymous, "The Lure of Crime," *Southerly* 12, no. 3 (1951): 176.
17. Lauder, *Winger's Landfall*, 86.
18. Ibid., 51.
19. Ibid., 75, 126.
20. Ibid., 241.
21. See the online exhibit *Sensational Tales: Australian Popular Publishing 1850s–1990s*, at the website of the Special Collections division of Baillieu Library, University of Melbourne, www.lib.unimelb.edu.au/collections/special/exhibitions/pulp/. The original exhibit, curated by Ian Morrison, was on display at the Baillieu Library from January to May 2000.
22. Toni Johnson-Woods, "The Mysterious Case of Carter Brown, or, Who Really Killed the Australian Author," *Australian Literary Studies* 21, no. 4 (2004): 74–88.
23. Noel Sanders, *The Thallium Enthusiasms and Other Australian Outrages* (Sydney: Local Consumption Press, 1995), 118
24. Mark Harris (Carl Ruhen), *The Gay Way* (Sydney: Scripts Publications, 1974).
25. Ibid., 98.
26. A landmark event in the history of gay liberation in Australia was the Australian publication of Dennis Altman's *Homosexual: Oppression and Liberation* in 1971 (despite his being Australian, it was first published in the United States, in 1970). While Dennis studied and taught in the United States, he was a lecturer at the University of Sydney and a prominent member of Sydney Gay Liberation in 1973, when I first met him.
27. Jeremy Fisher, "Fragments," *GLP: A Journal of Sexual Politics*, Jan.–Feb. 1975: 62–67.
28. Gary Dunne, Dave Sargent, Louise Wakeling, and Margaret Bradstock, eds., *Edge City on Two Different Plans* (Leichhardt: Sydney Gay Writers Collective, 1983).
29. Christos Tsiolkas, *Loaded* (Sydney: Vintage, 1995); Graeme Aitken, *Fifty Ways of Saying Fabulous* (Sydney: Vintage, 1995).
30. Jackson, *No End to the Way*, 12.
31. Leo Van de Pas, conversation with author, 2004.

32. Glaskin to Bunting, Nov. 18, 1963, Barrie & Rockliff collection, Random House Archive and Library.
33. Ibid., 11.
34. Ibid., 191.
35. Ibid., 20.
36. Ibid., 44.
37. Graham Willet, "The Darkest Decade: Homophobia in 1950s Australia," *Australian Historical Studies*, 28, no. 109 (Oct. 1997): 120–32.
38. Hurley, A Guide to Gay and Lesbian Writing, 190.

# Appendix
# A Sampling of 1960s Gay Pulp Authors

**Asterisk denotes that an essay discussing this author appears in the present collection.*

*RICHARD AMORY (Richard Love, 1927–1981). ABD, University of California–Berkeley; Spanish teacher. Seven pulps (Greenleaf, Olympia, Freeway, 1966–1974), including *Loon* trilogy, other westerns, and a mystery. See Cesar Love, "Biography of Richard Love," in *Song of the Loon,* by Richard Amory (Vancouver: Arsenal Pulp, 2005), 215–17.

TERYL ANDREWS (Thom Racina, b. 1946). MFA, Goodman School of Drama; television soap writer (five-time Emmy nominee). Five pulps (101, Greenleaf, Taurus, 1968–1970), beginning with *Rough Trade, Italian Style.* Literary hoax as Grant Tracy Saxon (Warner, 1975): *The Happy Hustler.*

*PHIL ANDROS (Samuel M. Steward, 1909–1993). PhD, Ohio State University; English teacher; tattoo artist. Seven pulps (Brian, Guild, Eros, Le Salon, Greenleaf, 1969–1975), beginning with *$tud* and including a series of erotic police stories. Memoir by Steward: *Chapters from an Autobiography* (San Francisco: Grey Fox, 1981). See Jim Kepner, "Steward," in *Gay & Lesbian Literature,* ed. Sharon Malinowski (Detroit: St. James, 1994), 360–62; Hubert Kennedy, *The Ideal Gay Man* (New York: Harrington Park, 1999), 42–44; Justin Spring, *Secret Historian* (New York: Farrar, Straus & Giroux, 2010); *Contemporary Authors.*

JAMES BARR (James Barr Fugaté, 1922–1995). Attended unknown university; US Navy veteran; activist; author of *Quatrefoil* (1950). One pulp (Paperback Library, 1966): *The Occasional Man.* Papers at Wichita State University. See Hubert Kennedy, *The Ideal Gay Man,* 36–39, and *A Touch of Royalty* (San Francisco: Peremptory,

2002); James T. Sears, *Behind the Mask of the Mattachine* (New York: Harrington Park, 2006).

*VICTOR J. BANIS (b. 1937). Over fifty pulps under his own name and various pseudonyms (Brandon, Greenleaf, Olympia, Barclay, Medco, 1966–1970), including the first nine volumes of the *C.A.M.P.* series, other mysteries, supernatural stories, and historical and contemporary romances. Memoir: *Spine Intact, Some Creases*, ed. Fabio Cleto (Genoa, Italy: ECIG, 2004); rev. ed. (Rockville, MD: Borgo, 2007). See *Contemporary Authors*.

SHANE V. BAXTER (Victor Norwood, 1920–1983). US Marines veteran; adventure writer. One pulp (Greenleaf, 1969): *The Sultry Stud*. See *Contemporary Authors*.

*CARL BRANCH. See James H. Ramp.

JAMES COLTON/COULTON (Joseph Hansen, 1923–2004). Activist; mystery writer (Shamus Lifetime Achievement Award, 1992); teacher. Ten pulps (National Library, Greenleaf, Brandon, Olympia, 1966–1971), beginning with *Lost on Twilight Road* and including other psychological studies and two murder mysteries. See James W. Jones, "Joseph Hansen," in *Contemporary Gay American Novelists*, ed. Emmanuel S. Nelson (Westport, CT: Greenwood, 1993), 189–96; Jim Kepner, "Hansen," in Malinowski, *Gay & Lesbian Literature*, 177–80; Ted-Larry Pebworth, "Hansen," in *The Gay and Lesbian Literary Heritage*, ed. Claude J. Summers (New York: Holt,1995), 357–58; C. Todd White, *Pre-Gay L.A.* (Urbana: University of Illinois, 2009); Josh Lanyon, "The Play of Shadows and Light," in *The Golden Age of Gay Fiction*, ed. Drewey Wayne Gunn (Albion, NY: MLR, 2009), 153–66; *Contemporary Authors*.

JOHN CORIOLAN (William Corington III, b. 1915). Stage producer; teacher. Three pulps (Award, Olympia, Renaissance, 1968–1975), beginning with *A Sand Fortress*.

CARL V. CORLEY (b. 1921). Civil servant; artist. Twenty-one pulps (Publisher's Export Co., Award, Greenleaf, 1966–1971), including *Gay Trilogy*, many with covers by the author. Fictionalized autobiography, published anonymously: *The Different and the Damned* (San Diego: Publisher's Export Co., 1968). Papers at Duke University. See John Howard, *Men Like That* (Chicago: University of Chicago, 1999), 193–220.

*DICK DALE. Nine pulps (Greenleaf, 1967–1968), beginning with *Gay on the Range*.

*GUY DANDRIDGE. Six pulps (Guild, 1967–1971), beginning with *Jerry and Jim*.

ANGELO D'ARCANGELO (Josef Bush, b. 1933?). Author of *Homosexual Handbook* (Olympia, 1968), famous for outing J. Edgar Hoover. One pulp (Olympia, 1969): *Sooky*. See Jack Nichols, "Angelo d'Arcangelo: The World's First Outer," *Gay Today*, Feb. 16, 1998.

CHRIS DAVIDSON (Christian Davies). Fifteen pulps (Greenleaf, 1967–1969), including *Caves of Iron* and *Go Down, Aaron* (both 1967).

DOUGLAS DEAN (Douglas Dean Goodman, 1920–2006). Attended University of Washington; stage and film actor, director, drama critic, and playwright. Twelve pulps (Greenleaf, 1969–1972), beginning with *Madder Music, Stronger Wine*. Autobiography: *Maria, Marlene, & Me* (San Francisco: Shadbolt, 1993). Papers at University of Minnesota.

SAMUEL L. DODSON. See Marcus Miller.

CARL DRIVER (Philip H. Lee). Eleven pulps (Publisher's Export Co., Cameo, Barclay, Pendulum, Le Salon, Greenleaf, 1967–1972), beginning with *Gay Cruise*.

JACK EVANS (Jan Ewing, b. 1946). BA, Oberlin College; US Navy veteran; graphic artist. Nineteen pulps (Monkey, Guild, 1969–1975), beginning with *Home Is Where the Hard Is*. Memoir: "Biker's Boy Redux," in Gunn, *Golden Age of Gay Fiction*, 97–102.

FELIX LANCE FALKON (George H. Scithers, 1929–2010). BS, U.S. Military Academy; MS, Stanford University; military engineer; science fiction writer, editor (four Hugo Awards); artist (as Graewolf). Four pulps (Greenleaf, 1969–1971), all erotic science fiction. Drawings included in *A Historic Collection of Gay Art*, ed. Falkon (San Diego: Greenleaf Classics, 1972); rev. ed., *Gay Art*, ed. Falkon and Thomas Waugh (Vancouver: Arsenal Pulp, 2006), 120–27. See John Clute, "Scithers," in *The Encyclopedia of Science Fiction*, ed. Clute and Peter Nichols (New York: St. Martin's, 1995), 1079; *Contemporary Authors*.

KARL FLINDERS (Milton Saul). Nine pulps (Olympia, 1969–1972), including five-volume *Twelve Inches* series.

*ALEXANDER GOODMAN (George Haimsohn, 1926–2003). BA, University of California–Berkeley; musical comedy writer (*Dames at Sea*, 1966); photographer (as Plato). Nine pulps (Guild, 1964–1969), beginning with *The Soft Spot*. Photographs included in *Uncovered*, ed. Reed Massengill (New York: Universe, 2009), 84–99.

*JAY GREENE. Twenty pulps (Midwood, 1968–1976), beginning with *Behind These Walls*.

DAVID GRIFFIN (Robin Maugham, 1916–1981). Attended Cambridge University; barrister. One pulp (Paperback Library, 1967): *The Wrong People*. Papers at the University of Texas–Austin. See Jim Kepner, "Maugham," in Malinowski, *Gay & Lesbian Literature*, 252–53; *Contemporary Authors*.

E. V. GRIFFITH (1927–2003). Poet, editor of poetry magazines, editor of anthology *In Homage to Priapus* (Greenleaf, 1970). Papers at Stanford University.

LANCE HORNER (Kenric Lancaster Horner, 1902–1973). BA, Boston University; advertising designer; antiques dealer. Ten paperback originals (1960–1971), including *Rogue Roman* (Pyramid, 1969). See Michael Bronski, "Kyle Onstott & Lance Horner, *Child of the Sun*," in *The Lost Library*, ed. Tom Cardamone (n.p.: Haiduk, 2010), 145–50; obituary, *Contemporary Authors*.

PETER TUESDAY HUGHES (1940?–2005?). Travel agent. Thirty-four pulps (Greenleaf, Surry/Surree, 1968–1978), including gothic romances, mysteries, science fiction, supernatural stories, historical and contemporary romances, and political fiction.

ALLAN JAMES. Six pulps (101, Greenleaf, Eros, 1968–1970), beginning with *Summer of the Studs*.

HADRIAN KEENE. Two pulps (Award, 1969): *Seventh Summer* and *Noon and Night*.

*BRUCE KING (Avery Willard, né Avery Willard Parsons Jr., 1921–1999). Photographer, filmmaker, newspaper publisher (*Gay Scene*, 1969–1992), writer. Four pulps (101, Taurus, 1967–1969), beginning with *Summer Awakening*. Subject of film documentary *In Search of Avery Willard*, directed by Cary Kehayan (2012). Photography archives: New York Public Library; Kroch Library, Cornell University.

DALLAS KOVAR. Five pulps (Greenleaf, Midwood, 1968–1972), all Westerns, including a trilogy. See Neil DeWitte, "The Gay Western," in Gunn, *Golden Age of Gay Fiction*, 228–30.

WILLIAM J. LAMBERT III (b. 1942). BBA, Washington State University; US Army veteran. Ninety-six pulps under his own name and various pseudonyms (Greenleaf, Bee-Line, Le Salon, Trojan, Hamilton, Surry/Surree, Arena, 1969–1982), including first gay werewolf tale. Autobiography and bibliography as William Maltese: *Draqualian Silk*, ed. Robert Reginald (Rockville, MD: Borgo, 2010).

LANCE LESTER (George Davies). Walt Disney Studios illustrator. Eleven pulps (Greenleaf, Hardboy, 1967–1975), including *Cruising Horny Corners* and *Gay Vista*. One pulp as Ricardo Armory (Greenleaf, 1968): *Fruit of the Loon*, a parody. Twenty-three pulps as Clay Caldwell (Surry/Surree, 1972–1983). Seven pulps as Thumper Johnson (Surry/Surree, 1975–1985), mostly sports stories.

TOM LOCKWOOD. Probably attended Duke University or University of North Carolina; author of *Destination Nowhere* (Castle, 1966). Two pulps (Greenleaf, Award, 1966): *Sons of a Beach* and *The Ugly Club*.

JULIAN MARK (Vincent Lardo, b. 1937). Mystery writer; entertainment editor (*The*

*Advocate*). Eight pulps (Greenleaf, Ram, 1967–1975), beginning with *Little Boy Lavender.*

MARCUS MILLER. Sixteen pulps (Greenleaf, 1967–1970), many, if not all, written by Samuel L. Dodson (b. 1926). Other Dodson pseudonyms include Sam Dodd (Greenleaf, 1968): *Donnie and Clyde.* He often collaborated with Victor J. Banis. See Banis, *Spine Intact, Some Creases.*

JAMES H. RAMP (1898–1968). Four paperback originals (Farfare, 1966–1967), including *The Love Smeller* and *Wild Strawberry Patch.* One pulp as Ross Hossannah (Star, 1965): *Gay Vet.* Possibly two pulp story collections as Carl Branch (Greenleaf, 1968), including *All Shades of Gay.* See *Gay Bookworm* (Quatrefoil Library), Nov. 1989; Hubert Kennedy, *The Ideal Gay Man*, 41–42; "James Ramp," *Queerest Library Ever* (LGBT Resources blog, San Francisco Public Library), Nov. 30, 2011, www.queerestlibraryever.blogspot.com/2011_11_01_archive.html.

*LOU RAND (Lou Rand Hogan, 1910–1976). Chef. One pulp (Saber, 1961): *The Gay Detective,* with the first gay American private investigator.

PETER RANDOLPH. Three pulps (Guild, Greenleaf, 1967–1969), beginning with *Sextet.* Guild also published a collection of his drawings, *Art Portfolio Number Two* (1966).

K. B. RAUL. Two pulps (Paperback Library, 1964, 1968): *Naked to the Night* and *A Hidden Hunger.*

LARRY TOWNSEND (Michael L. Townsend, 1930–2008). BA, University of California–Los Angeles; counselor and industrial psychologist; S/M master; associated with various magazines, including *Drummer.* Sixteen pulps (Greenleaf, Olympia, 1969–1972), mostly dealing with the leather world. See *Contemporary Authors.*

*DIRK VANDEN (Richard Fullmer, b. 1933). BFA, University of Utah; stage director; artist. Winner of a Lambda Literary Award, 2012. Seven pulps (Greenleaf, Eros, Olympia, 1969–1971), including *All* trilogy, with covers by the author. Memoir: *It Was Too Soon Before* (Maple Shade, NJ: Lethe, 2012).

## OTHER WRITERS

Rocky Heck of San Francisco's Bolerium Books has provided other names that may interest readers and scholars: Kim Allyson (John M. Kimbro, b. 1929), Tony Barron, Matt Bradley (Peter T. Scott), Tony Calvano (Thomas P. Ramirez), Floyd Carter, Ed Culver, Arnold Dixon, Mark Dunn, Len Harrington, John Maggie, Gene North (Neils

Grant Jr.), James J. Proferes (1922–1995), Aaron Thomas, and Carlson Wade (1928–1993). Michael Bronski, in *Pulp Friction* (New York: St. Martin's Griffin, 2003), adds Jack Love and Jeff X. Not all these writers are gay; Ramirez, for example, is straight.

The great flowering of pulp novels did not end until the demise of Blueboy Library (Surree) in 1978. Some writers of note from the 1970s include Bruce Benderson (b. 1946), Billy Farout (William Barber, 1946–1994), Roland Graeme/Michael Scott (Brad Alan Deamer, b. 1952), Tom Hardy (Gordon Hoban, 1941–1993), John Ironstone/Martin Moore/F. W. Love (Frederick LaCava, b. 1945), and Marco Vassi (1937–1989).

# Notes on Contributors

BETH M. BOULOUKOS received a PhD from Cornell University in Hispanic studies. Her work focuses on how early modern Spanish themes are developed in twentieth-century narrative and film. She is an acquisitions editor in Latin American and Iberian studies, gender and queer studies, and education at SUNY Press. She has taught at Fairfield University and is currently an affiliated member of the Languages, Literatures and Cultures Department at the University at Albany–SUNY.

PHILIP CLARK coedited *Persistent Voices: Poetry by Writers Lost to AIDS* (2010). His essays have appeared in such collections as *The Lost Library: Gay Fiction Rediscovered; The Golden Age of Gay Fiction; 50 Gay and Lesbian Books Everybody Must Read;* and *The Oxford Companion to the Photograph.* He is currently editing the selected poems of Donald Britton and researching the life of Guild Press publisher H. Lynn Womack.

JEREMY FISHER is a senior lecturer in writing at the University of New England in New South Wales, Australia. He is the author of *Perfect Timing* (1993; translated into Vietnamese, 2008), *Music from Another Country* (2009), and *How to Tell Your Father to Drop Dead . . . and Other Stories* (2013). He has had a long career in Australian publishing as an editor, indexer, and publisher and was executive director of the Australian Society of Authors prior to his academic appointment. He was an early member of gay liberation in Australia.

JAMES J. GIFFORD is a professor emeritus of humanities at Mohawk Valley Community College. He is the author of *Dayneford's Library: American Homosexual Writing, 1900–1913* (1995) and the editor of *Imre* by Edward Prime-Stevenson (2003) and *Glances Backward: An Anthology of American Homosexual Writing,*

*1830–1920* (2007). He and Philip Clark are currently preparing a scholarly edition of Prime-Stevenson's *The Intersexes*.

DREWEY WAYNE GUNN is a professor emeritus of English at Texas A&M University–Kingsville. He is the author of *Mexico in American and British Letters: A Bibliography* (1974), *American and British Writers in Mexico, 1556–1973* (1974; translated into Spanish, 1977), *Tennessee Williams: A Bibliography* (1980; rev. ed., 1991), *The Gay Male Sleuth in Print and Film: A History and Annotated Bibliography* (2005; rev. ed., 2013); the cotranslator with Jacques Murat of *Arthur Rimbaud/Paul Verlaine: A Lover's Cock and Other Gay Poems* (1979); the coauthor with William Maltese of *Ardennian Boy* (2007); and the editor of *The Golden Age of Gay Literature* (2009).

JAIME HARKER is an associate professor of English at the University of Mississippi. She is the author of *America the Middlebrow: Women's Novels, Progressivism, and Middlebrow Authorship between the Wars* (2007) and *Middlebrow Queer: Christopher Isherwood in America* (2013), and the coeditor of *The Oprah Affect: Critical Essays on Oprah's Book Club* (2008). She has published articles on nineteenth-century women writers, Japanese translation, composition, and twentieth-century book history

NICHOLAS ALEXANDER HAYES is an instructor at DePaul University–The School for New Learning. He is the author of the book *NIV: 39 & 27* (2009). He received an MFA in writing from The School of the Art Institute of Chicago and has taught courses in queer literature at Columbia College in Chicago and gender representations at DePaul University.

RANDALL IVEY teaches English at the University of South Carolina–Union. His creative and critical works, including two story collections and a book for children, have been published in the United States and in England.

REED MASSENGILL is a writer and photographer whose work spans the genres of biography (*The Art of George Quaintance*, 2010; *Portrait of a Racist*, 1994), corporate history (*Becoming American Express*, 2000), and photography (*Brian: A Nine-Year Photographic Diary*, 2000; *Massengill Men*, 1997; *Massengill*, 1996). As a collector, curator, and editor, he has produced *Uncovered: Rare Vintage Male Nudes* (2009), *Self-Exposure: The Male Nude Self-Portrait* (2005), *The Male Ideal: Lon of New York and the Masculine Physique* (2004), *Champion* (2003), and *Roy Blakey's '70s Male Nudes* (2001).

ANN MARIE SCHOTT holds an MA in English from the University of Mississippi and has taught literature and composition. Her research interests include postmodernism, violence, gender, and sexuality, especially regarding men and masculinity in twentieth-century American literature.

WHITNEY STRUB is an assistant professor of history at Rutgers University–Newark, where he also teaches American studies and LGBT studies. He is the author of *Perversion for Profit: The Politics of Pornography and the Rise of the New Right* (2011) and has contributed articles to *Journal of Social History, Journal of the History of Sexuality, American Quarterly, Journal of Women's History,* and *Radical History Review.* He is currently completing a book on the 1957 *Roth v. United States* obscenity case.

PAMELA ROBERTSON WOJCIK is a professor in the department of Film, Television, and Theater and director of the Gender Studies Program at the University of Notre Dame. She has published widely on performance, camp, film music, genre, and stardom, and is the author of *Guilty Pleasures: Feminist Camp from Mae West to Madonna* (1996) and *The Apartment Plot: Urban Living in American Film and Popular Culture, 1945 to 1975* (2010).

# Index